THE MATERIAL CULTURE
OF DEATH
IN MEDIEVAL JAPAN

THE MATERIAL CULTURE
OF DEATH
IN MEDIEVAL JAPAN

Karen M. Gerhart

University of Hawai'i Press
Honolulu

© 2009 University of Hawai'i Press
All rights reserved
Printed in the United States of America
14 13 12 11 10 09   6 5 4 3 2 1

Library of Congress Cataloging-in-Publication Data
Gerhart, Karen M.
 The material culture of death in medieval Japan / Karen M. Gerhart.
   p.   cm.
 Includes bibliographical references and index.
 ISBN 978-0-8248-3261-2 (hard cover : alk. paper)
 1. Funeral rites and ceremonies, Buddhist—Japan—History—To 1500. I. Title.
 BQ5020.G47 2009
 294.3'4388095209024—dc22
                                        2009009200

University of Hawai'i Press books are printed on acid-free
paper and meet the guidelines for permanence and durability
of the Council on Library Resources.

Designed by University of Hawai'i Press production staff

Printed by Sheridan Books

CONTENTS

List of Illustrations vii

Acknowledgments ix

Note to the Reader xi

Introduction 1

The Rituals of Death

1. Death in the Fourteenth Century 15
2. Funerals in the Fifteenth Century 50

The Material Culture of Death

3. Objects of Separation and Containment 83
4. Ritual Implements for Funerals and Memorials 113
5. Portraits of the Deceased 147

Notes 179

List of Japanese Words 219

Bibliography 231

Index 249

Plates follow page 100

ILLUSTRATIONS

Figures
1.1 *Thirteen Buddhas* 23
1.2 Death talisman (*monoimi fuda*) 27
1.3 Five-tiered stupa (*gorintō*) and pagoda-like stupa (*hōkyōintō*) 31
1.4 Wooden grave markers (*sotoba*) 32
2.1 Physical arrangement for Prince Yoshihito's seventh seven-day service 61
2.2 Order of ritual implements in Yoshimitsu's funeral procession 73
2.3 Order of ritual implements at Yoshimitsu's cremation site 74
3.1 Ryōnin's coffin 87
3.2 Shinran's coffin 88
3.3 Hōnen's coffin 89
3.4 Hōnen on his deathbed 90
3.5 Moving screens (*gyōshō/hoshō*) 95
3.6 Movement of corpse at cremation site 100
3.7 *Kuginuki, gorintō, sotōba, zushi* 108
3.8 Enclosure at Shinran's grave 109
3.9 Enclosure at Nichiren's grave 110
4.1 Dragon heads (*ryūzu sao, tatsugashira*) 120
4.2 Banners of five colors (*goshiki ban*) 122
4.3 Hōnen's first memorial service 131
4.4 Set of Buddhist ritual implements 132
4.5 Hōnen's second memorial service 134
4.6 Hōnen's third memorial service 135
4.7 Hōnen's fourth memorial service 136
4.8 Hōnen's fifth memorial service 137
4.9 Hōnen's sixth memorial service 138

4.10 Ritual implements on Gokurakuji's altar   140
4.11 Priest striking the chime for Ryōnin's death   142
4.12 Death of a nun, with scrolls of Amida Triad, *myōgō*, and teacher's portrait   144
4.13 Special Nenbutsu ceremony   145
5.1 Portrait sculpture of Enchin (Okotsu Daishi)   151
5.2 Portrait of Ashikaga Yoshimitsu   160
5.3 *Shin-ei* of Priest Hōnen   167
5.4 Portrait of Hōnen (*ashibiki no miei*)   168

Plates

Plates follow p. 100.
1 Ten kings of hell and scenes of punishment
2 Memorial tablet (*ihai*)
3 Nichiren's cremation
4 Hōnen's cremation
5 Shinran's cremation
6 Nichiren's funeral procession—torch, lotus flower, banners, dragon-head banner hooks
7 Nichiren's funeral procession—censers, musical instruments, flower vase, candle holder, scrolls, sutra tables
8 Nichiren's funeral procession—offering trays and vessels, memorial tablet, shoes, cloth cord
9 Nichiren's funeral procession—palanquin, canopy, helmet, sword, riderless horse
10 Nichiren's funeral procession—Kamakura warriors
11 Hōnen's seventh memorial service

ACKNOWLEDGMENTS

As a first attempt to reexamine the way we look at, talk about, and write about ritual objects, my study is indebted to many people who helped make this book possible. For the financial support that created time for research and writing, I am grateful to the University of Pittsburgh Faculty of Arts and Sciences for awarding me a Type I Summer Grant, to the Japan Council and the Mitsubishi Endowment at the University of Pittsburgh for supporting two research trips to Japan, and to my colleagues in the Department of the History of Art and Architecture for granting me course release time. Publication of this volume was assisted by generous subvention grants from the Japan Council and Asian Studies and from the Mary and John Edwards Publication Fund at the University of Pittsburgh.

I would especially like to thank Katheryn Linduff and Anne Weis for reading and commenting on several chapters. I was also fortunate to have the opportunity to team-teach courses with Kathy Linduff and Evelyn Rawski that significantly broadened and stimulated my thinking about death rituals in East Asia. I am also indebted to the graduate students in my seminars for many fruitful discussions that helped shape my ideas about death rituals and portraits.

Other colleagues also offered much appreciated advice and encouragement. I want to express deep gratitude to Gene Phillips and Yonekura Michio for discussing their ideas with me and for generously sharing their resources. Gene offered thoughtful observations on, and corrections to, the entire text and has been an unfailing supporter. I also had fruitful conversations with James Dobbins, Patricia Fister, Greg Levine, and Chari Pradel about my research on death rituals. Pat Fister also assisted me in locating hard-to-find sources through the library at the Nichibunken in Kyoto. My skills in reading *kanbun* were greatly enhanced by two summer workshops coordinated by Joan Piggot. Kurushima Noriko and Endō Motoo from the Historiographical Institute at Tokyo University were unstintingly helpful throughout my struggles with the texts, and Kako Hatakeyama worked with me in Pittsburgh to recheck critical passages. Needless to say, any faults that remain in the text are my responsibility.

I remain forever indebted to my editor at University of Hawai'i Press, Patricia Crosby, for having faith in the project; to Naomi Richards, who edited the manuscript with uncanny skill and great patience; to my friend Sarah Blick for reading countless versions of the manuscript with good cheer; and to Scott for his unfailing support throughout.

NOTE TO THE READER

Japanese names are given in Japanese order—surname followed by given name, as in Ashikaga Yoshimochi. Sometimes the name of an individual's retirement cloister (usually ending with –*in*) appears in place of the family name. Monks' names also generally have two parts; although neither is a family name, the first part is often used alone, as in Kisen for Kisen Shūshō.

On first appearance, the titles of narrative handscrolls are given in Japanese with English translations following in parentheses, as in *Shinran shōnin e-den* (Illustrated biography of priest Shinran). Thereafter, because these titles have many alternative translations, to avoid confusion they are referred to by their Japanese titles alone.

Temple names usually include the suffixes *ji* or *dera* (temple). A large temple complex might well contain subtemples; their names include *-in* or *-an* with a hyphen, as here. No hyphen is used for the name of an independent temple ending in *in* (such as Tōjiin). The names of individual temple halls are designated *dō*, as in Konjikidō.

There are several methods for indicating a year in the premodern Japanese lunar calendar. To simplify, I use the standard format year, month, day. So, for example, the sixth day of the second month occurring in the Western year 1345 is given as 1345.2.6. In endnote citations of texts I have included the calendrical era (*nengō*) as it appears in the text; thus Jōwa 1.2.6 is the first year, second month, sixth day of the Northern Court's calendrical era Jōwa.

In medieval records, notations of time designated by means of the twelve branches (*jūnishi*) are imprecise. For these, I have given approximations, with the Japanese notation in parentheses: "about 8 p.m." or "between 7 and 9 p.m." for *inu no koku*.

I have approximated Western measures for Japanese ("about 3 feet tall" for 3 *shaku*, 3 *sun*) to give readers some sense of the sizes of various objects; likewise for distances ("about 120 yards" for 36 *jō*). But because systems of measuring economic value were extremely complicated before the Tokugawa period, and rates of exchange and corresponding weights of coins fluctuated greatly, I have used the Japanese terms as they appear in the written records, such as 3 *kan* 600 *mon*, and have not attempted conversion to present monetary units. *Kan* and *kanmon* appear interchangeably in the texts; *chōmoku* (bird's eye) is another term, this one descriptive, for the Chinese-style copper coins with central holes in them that were used in the Muromachi period. One *kan* or *kanmon* equaled a string of 1,000 *mon*; one *hiki* referred to 10 such coins. Coins of that shape had originally been imported from China during the Kamakura period.

INTRODUCTION

Death is an event of cataclysmic separation. The deceased, once appropriately disposed of, cannot be seen, touched, conversed with. So we use rituals and ritual objects to help bridge the gulf, suture the wound to the collective body of family and of community, and overcome a sense of powerlessness in the face of death. This study looks at the way these special objects functioned in Japanese death rituals of the early medieval period. The first half examines case studies, culled from written records, that illustrate how elite members of Japanese society negotiated the boundary between the living and the dead through their funerals and memorial services. The second half deals with various types of funerary structures, painted and sculpted images, and other ritual articles that served in such negotiations, and analyzes their crucial roles in the performance of mortuary rituals.

Ritual Studies

"Ritual" is a charged concept, and one that has been well explored by anthropologists, religious historians, and scholars in other disciplines. Much has been written about death rituals, but this is the first study in any language to analyze the critical role of material objects in the practice of medieval Japanese death rituals.

In the West, in the late nineteenth and early twentieth centuries, ritual became an area of special interest to scholars in the newly developing field of anthropology.[1] In the mid-1970s a fully interdisciplinary discussion of ritual emerged and the field of ritual studies was born, engaging scholars from a wide range of disciplines, including religious studies, anthropology, theology, history, performance studies, literature, and the visual arts. Among these later scholars, S. J. Tambiah, Catherine Bell, and others have noted that words not only describe rituals but are part of the performance itself.[2] Likewise, I argue that ritual objects are not simply visual appendages to the ritual sequence but are part of the structure and performance. My way of interpreting the objects that accompany the rituals of death in this study is similar to Jessica Rawson's characterization of the ritual function of Shang and Zhou bronzes in China: ". . . all rituals communicate through physical structures and objects. Indeed, the whole impact of a ritual must depend on a close fit between the objects, physical structures and location of the ritual and the ritual procedures that are used."[3] Physical objects, then, are crucial components of the actions performed. As the real focus of my study is not the rituals themselves so much as the relationship between the rituals and physical objects, I use the word "ritual" in its broadest and most obvious sense, as a series of prescribed actions that form part of a religious ceremony. I also employ the terms "ritual" and "ceremony" more or less interchangeably throughout. Certainly, much more could be done to elucidate the construction and meaning of the rituals themselves, but I leave this to other scholars.

Material Culture

Scholarship on the material things that people use in their daily lives is relatively recent, much of it written in the twentieth century. Broadly defined as "all data directly relating to visible or tangible things such as tools, clothing, or shelter which a person or persons have made,"[4] material culture is an approach relevant for most disciplines in the humanities, but one of special interest to scholars in anthropology, archaeology, and art history, because artifacts are essential source material in these disciplines. Although objects play important roles in forms of religious activity, historians of religion have tended, in general, to privilege religious texts over images and artifacts.[5] Scholars in Japan became interested in material culture in the 1970s as a way to better engage in the debate between Marxist and non-Marxist economic historians.[6] Their publications ultimately helped to make material culture and the lifestyles of common people acceptable subjects of academic study in history and related disciplines.[7]

Scholarship on the material culture of death in any period of Japan's history is negligible. But the topic of death per se in premodern Japan has been well researched, and many such studies include details about the built structures and ritual objects that accompany the dead. Although these publications straddle the line between ritual studies and studies of material culture, none has focused on the interaction between material culture and the rituals of death. Among the most comprehensive studies on death are Haga Noboru's *Sōgi no rekishi* (1970) and Gorai Shigeru's *Sō to kuyō* (1992). Both trace Japanese funeral practices exhaustively, from ancient through modern times. Gorai's book, in particular, is a massive compendium of terms and practices that includes much useful information on the historical context of Japanese funerary structures and ritual objects. More recently, the historian Katsuda Itaru published two important books on the topic of medieval death. In both *Shishatachi no chūsei* (2003) and *Nihon chūsei no haka to sōsō* (2006), Katsuda focuses on death in the medieval period as it evolved from earlier precedents. All three authors rely heavily on historical sources to support their interpretations, but Gorai also includes photographs of modern-day death rituals and related structures and objects, whereas Katsuda reproduces sections of medieval handscrolls to illustrate objects in his discussions. Itō Yuishin's chapter "*Moromoriki* ni miru chūsei sōsōsai bukkyō" in *Sōsō bosei kenkyū shūsei: haka no rekishi* (1989) and Suitō Makoto's "Morosuke no sōsō girei to chūsei no sōsai bukkyō" in *Chūsei no sōsō, bosei* (1991) were immensely helpful in interpreting medieval Buddhism in the context of the Nakahara funerals discussed in Chapter 1. My research is deeply indebted to the pioneering work of these Japanese scholars, and in particular to Katsuda, whose combination of text and visual material greatly influenced the shape of my project. None of the Japanese studies, however, focuses specifically on how the ritual objects functioned during the funerary and mortuary rituals.

Art History

Many of the objects discussed in my study, like clothing, coffins, enclosures, and grave markers, are not of a caliber to interest art historians. Conversely, other objects that accompanied medieval funerals have been and are studied by art historians but not considered within their ritual context. Once essential to the performance of death rituals, such objects as painted portraits, folding screens, sutra scrolls, and Buddhist implements are today generally classified as "art" and are valued primarily for their aesthetic excellences. That these objects now reside in museums or in the museumlike context of temple treasuries has further isolated them, causing them to lose much of the original numinous quality of their symbolism and function, and making it difficult to see them as other than objects made for pleasure and display. Indeed, one of the deplorable effects of the modern museum is to encourage the decontextualization of art works and to divest them of their centuries-old, multilayered meanings. True, their original owners also valued the preciousness of their materials and the quality of their craftsmanship, but primary to these owners was the particular function performed by the objects within the context of the ritual.

Art historians have tended to neglect the study of Buddhist ritual implements. This avoidance seems to be particularly true of Japan, where exhibition catalogs of temple collections, usually written by historians of religion and of art, introduce only a few ritual implements in contrast to the great preponderance of the temple's Buddhist paintings and sculptures. For example, the 2001 exhibition catalog of treasures from Daigoji includes fewer than twenty entries on Buddhist implements (*hōgū*) and limits information about them to comments on their general role in the ritual adornment of the temple and a brief mention of ceremonies for which they were used; the remaining ninety or so entries treat paintings, calligraphies, and sculptures.[8] This is not to say that Buddhist institutions were poor in ritual implements—quite the contrary. It is likely that ritual implements seldom appear in exhibitions and are little written about because they are intimately known by the Japanese public, which requires no detailed explanation of their function.

In the West the objects themselves and how they functioned in Buddhist rituals have only recently emerged as topics of interest among art historians. Indeed, until recently the important questions—by whom, when, where, and why certain implements were used—were not asked. The 1996 catalog for the exhibition at the Katonah Museum of Art, curated by Anne Nishimura Morse and Samuel Crowell Morse, focused broadly on Buddhist ritual objects and their roles in the ornamentation of ritual space. In their introduction to the catalog the authors state that elite Japanese patrons of Buddhism were inordinately fascinated with the "visual splendor of the material adornments," and they advance the idea that the "most important rituals were often closely tied to aesthetic experience."[9] In a separate essay in the catalog, Kawada and Morse categorize ritual objects as "articles of ornamentation (*shōgongū*)" and refer to them as "Buddhist decorative arts."[10]

The year 1998 saw a significant shift in the current evaluation of ritual implements with the publication of the catalog *Buddhist Treasures from Nara* accompanying an exhibition that brought many important Buddhist works from the Nara National Museum in Japan to the Cleveland Museum of Art.[11] In the foreword Michael Cunningham, curator of the exhibition, asserted that the objects exhibited should not be considered "art" in the traditional sense, that, "as much as we wish to consider the extraordinary objects in this exhibition as 'works of art,' in fact, they were neither created nor conscientiously safeguarded as such." Rather, he said, the articles in the exhibition are "vehicles toward gaining spiritual insight and awakening."[12] The catalog is also noteworthy because Cunningham carefully analyzes a significant number of the exhibited ritual utensils and lays stress on their ritual functions.

The trend of historians of both art and religion studying the objects and images of religious practice as integral elements of that practice continues to gather momentum. In 2000 several essays published in a special edition of the *Japanese Journal of Religious Studies* discussed the significance of mortuary objects, and in 2001 Robert and Elizabeth Sharf published an edited volume of essays, *Living Images: Japanese Buddhist Icons in Context*, devoted to treating

Buddhist icons as integral elements in Buddhist practice.[13] Neither publication, however, provided (or intended to provide) a sustained analysis of the role of material culture in medieval mortuary rituals.

The work of these and other scholars has been critical in bringing the function of images and objects in Buddhist rituals to the attention of the scholarly community and the public.[14] I particularize their approach by questioning whether the ritual implements that accompany Japanese Buddhist funerals and memorial services fall under the rubric of art at all. Certainly, most are plentiful, durable, and produced by workshops—traits that effectively remove them from most definitions of "art." Furthermore, nearly all were designed to perform specific functions and not primarily for aesthetic appreciation, which further suggests that they are perhaps better classified as religious objects.

This study overlaps ritual studies, material culture, and art history but is not contained completely within any one of these areas. I am interested in the rituals for the context they provide to the objects, and in the objects for how they functioned within the rituals. The terms "art" and "artwork," in particular, are insufficient for this study, and I avoid using them throughout.

The types of objects explored in this study fall roughly into two categories: objects specific to death rituals and funerals, and implements used in mortuary events but also in other Buddhist contexts. The former were made and used for a single funeral and generally included objects in close proximity to the body, such as coffins, clothing, carriages, enclosures, grave markers, gates, and folding screens, whereas the latter comprised altar tables, bronze flower vases and censers, cloth banners, canopies, musical instruments, and sutra scrolls, all used and reused in a variety of Buddhist ceremonies. Objects of certain types, such as portraits and memorial tablets, might fit either category.

This study will examine how all these objects were used, and how such a diversity of articles reflected the religious practices of early medieval Japan. It will employ a combination of sources, including documents explaining how such articles were used and in which rituals, contemporary illustrations, and surviving objects. Taken together, such sources reveal how rituals and ritual objects not only helped to comfort the living and give sustenance to the dead, but also guided and cemented societal norms of class and gender.

Methodology: Manuals, Records, and Illustrations

I have attempted to view the material culture of death through the lens of contemporary medieval chronicles and illustrations. This involves a close reading and interpretation of funeral manuals, diaries, and other records, coupled with a careful examination of medieval illustrated handscrolls, which offer details of how implements were used in mortuary rites.

Historical Texts

Early in Japan's history, official edicts issued by the emperor established the guidelines for the proper performance of death rituals. Even the earliest proclamations make it clear that rules governing rituals were meant to reinforce the contemporary social order. For example, the mid-seventh-century *Hakusōrei* (Orders for simple burials), issued by Emperor Kōtoku (r. 645–654) as part of the Taika Reforms of 646, exhorted the people to refrain from ostentatious burials with admonitions and prohibitions such as burial mounds should be kept low; inner and outer coffins should not be decorated or lacquered; the shroud should be made to last only until the bones decayed; no metal grave goods of any type should be placed in the tomb, rather, grave goods, from figures to chariots, should be made of clay; no pearls or jewels should be placed in the mouth of the deceased, nor should jade armor be used.[15] Kōtoku clearly intended to control the cost of and the visual impact made by tomb mounds, coffins, and grave goods in Japan.[16] Numerous burial codes, all similarly restrictive, were issued by the court in the following centuries and can be found in special sections of the Yōrō (718) and Engi codes (927–967).[17]

Of more immediate interest for this study are a number of later funeral manuals, all written by elite members of Japanese society, who also sought to proclaim and reinforce the existing social order. The most relevant are *Kichiji shidai* (Order of auspicious affairs; late 12th c.),[18] *Kichiji ryakki* (An outline of auspicious affairs; date and author unknown),[19] *Sōhōmitsu* (Esoteric funeral practices; early medieval period),[20] and *Daizōkyō* (Great collection of sutras).[21]

Shukaku Hosshinō (1150–1202), the second son of Emperor Go-Shirakawa and the sixth-generation *monzeki* of the Shingon-sect temple Ninnaji, is thought to be the author of *Kichiji shidai*.[22] Little is known about the second text, *Kichiji ryakki*, but it seems to be a compilation of rituals based on *Kichiji shidai* and perhaps other, now lost, texts. Both show the influence of Shingon Buddhism on the proper steps to be taken after the death of a royal. As such, both texts were likely intended to update imperial funeral practices in the late Heian period and to emphasize the importance of Esoteric practices at a time when their dominance was being challenged.

Other texts recount the procedures for the funerals of monastics. *Sōhōmitsu* is an early medieval record of unknown authorship that revised earlier Shingon funeral procedures. The section on standard ceremonies for transferring merit (*ekō*) in *Daizōkyō* is useful in understanding the Chinese Buddhist monastic codes relating to funeral and memorial services that were adopted in Japan. I have incorporated information from these manuals to help explain and support my text and illustrations.

Another important source of information about elite Japanese funerals are the daily records kept by high-ranking Buddhist priests and members of the court. The Muromachi-period diaries that I examined are written in a linguistic style called *wayō kanbun* or "Japanese-style Chinese." The texts look like Chinese, but contain specifically Japanese vocabulary and honorifics, making them difficult to decipher. *Moromoriki* (Record of Moromori), a lengthy chronicle written by the courtier Nakahara Moromori during the era of the Northern and Southern Courts (1336–1392), supplies unusually detailed coverage of the mortuary events following the deaths of his father and mother. The author gives remarkably complete information about the rituals held during the forty-nine days after death and about the cycle of memorial services that took place in following months and years. My analysis of *Moromoriki* is intended to illustrate the sequence of rituals associated with the death of a high-ranking member of society in the mid-fourteenth century. This text also provides a wealth of information about practices not common in later, more traditional Buddhist funerals.

Filling in the lacunae are a number of fifteenth-century records such as *Jishōindono ryōan sōbo* (Complete record of national mourning for Lord Jishōin), *Kennaiki* (or *Kendaiki*; Record of Kenshōin Naifu Madenokōji Tokifusa), *Kanmon gyoki* (Record of things seen and heard), and *Inryōken nichiroku* (Daily record of the Inryōken, a cloister within Rokuon'in). These texts provide surprisingly vivid details about the lying-in-state period that immediately followed a death as well as the funeral service proper. Here we find crucial accounts of the placement of the ritual objects and their spatial relationship to the corpse and to the participants in the newer, Zen-influenced, funerals. *Jishōindono ryōan sōbo*, for example, includes a diagram that locates each participant and each ritual implement in the funeral procession for Ashikaga Yoshimitsu (d. 1408.5.6) and at his cremation site. *Kennaiki*, written by the Muromachi-period courtier Tokifusa, of the Fujiwara Kajūji line, and covering the nearly thirty years from Ōei 21 (1414) to Kōshō 1 (1441), gives a thorough description of the funeral of the fourth Muromachi shogun, Ashikaga Yoshimochi, who died on 1428.1.18. Written by an imperial prince, Fushiminomiya Sadafusa, *Kanmon gyoki* covers an almost identical time period, from Ōei 23 (1416) to Bunnan 5 (1448).[23] Beginning on 1416.11.20, Sadafusa chronicles the death ceremonies held for his father, the imperial prince Yoshihito (1361–1416), who would posthumously become the grandfather of the future emperor Go-Hanazono. *Inryōken nichiroku* was written by two Zen Buddhist priests, Kikei Shinzui and Kisen Shūshō; Kikei wrote the entries from 1435.6.1 to 1441.7.6, and from 1458.1.10 to 1466.9.5; and Kisen those from 1484.8.18 to 1493.9.23. Beginning on 1463.8.8, Kikei relates the death rituals conducted for Hino Shigeko, member of an important court family and wife of the sixth Ashikaga Shogun, Yoshinori (1394–1441; r. 1429–1441).[24]

These documents give exhaustive information on medieval mortuary rituals and are extraordinarily rich sources for the objects and structures used in the rituals, providing detailed accounts of their positioning and function. The accounts span the fourteenth and fifteenth centuries, allowing me to examine a continuous century of Japanese medieval death practices: Nakahara Morosuke and his wife Kenshin died in 1345, Ashikaga Yoshimitsu in 1408, Prince Yoshihito in 1416, Ashikaga Yoshimochi in 1428, and Hino Shigeko in 1463. These texts have the further advantage of illustrating funerals of all social levels within the educated elite, and of both men and women. They include a male court bureaucrat (Morosuke) and his wife (Kenshin), an imperial prince (Yoshihito), two shoguns (Yoshimitsu and Yoshimochi), and a female member (Shigeko) of an elite court family connected through marriage to the Ashikaga family of shoguns. The examples represent individuals from different religious backgrounds, whose funerals include a surprisingly eclectic array of rituals loosely associated with *onmyōdō* (yin-yang practices), Shingon and Tendai Buddhism, the Ji school of Pure Land Buddhism, and Zen Buddhism. The sheer diversity of the examples makes it difficult to perceive and track changes over time in funerary customs within a specific societal level, so that goal remains beyond the scope of this study. Furthermore, although the examples make clear that Zen funerary practices intersected and impacted the rituals of death across a broad spectrum of classes and for both sexes in the fourteenth and fifteenth centuries, a systematic study of the extent and effects of Zen practices are for religious historians to sort out.

Historical Images and Monuments

Notwithstanding the wealth of information about mortuary rituals that texts provide, they seldom describe what the often sumptuous ritual objects looked like and how they were arranged. For a "picture" of the types of material objects utilized in the rituals, I looked to images of funerals and memorial services found in illustrated medieval handscrolls and to surviving examples of mortuary art and architecture. The most useful illustrated scrolls include *Hōnen shōnin e-den* (Illustrated biography of priest Hōnen; 14th c.), *Zenshin shōnin Shinran den-e* (Good and true illustrated biography of priest Shinran; late 13th c.), and *Nichiren shōnin chūgasan* (Annotated illustrations of priest Nichiren; early 16th c.). All these depict the lives of monks dedicated to Pure Land Buddhism, although Nichiren's link was tenuous; he abandoned his early studies of Pure Land teachings in favor of devotion to the *Lotus Sutra*. Regardless of sectarian affiliation, however, the existing handscrolls illustrate funeral processions and cremation scenes that, by the fifteenth century, had become typical of Buddhist funerals. I am aware that the texts and illustrations I have relied on do not stem from a single Buddhist tradition, but problems related to sectarian differences are not at issue here. I did not find any illustrated biographies of Zen priests from my chosen period, probably because such scrolls were not customarily made in the Gozan temples. It is important that, nonetheless, all of the documents, visual and textual, display to some degree the influence of Zen Buddhism on the rituals of death.

I am mindful that the objects discussed in Section 2 are not those specifically employed for the funerals described in Section 1. Many implements designed for funeral use, such as coffins, carriages, grave enclosures, and so forth, were made of ephemeral materials, not intended to survive. Other ritual objects belonged to Buddhist temples, not individuals, and were used and reused for countless funerals and other rituals, making it less important to talk about the particular objects than to consider the *types* of implements.

This integrative use of text and image enables me to present a comparatively full range of mortuary objects and structures used by a representative group of Japanese elites in the period 1345–1463. I have limited the scope of this project to members of the imperial family and court, high-ranking military families, and Buddhist priests, because these are the individuals for whom the most ample documentation remains. Scholars have asserted that Buddhism was transformed from an elite to a popular religion during the Kamakura period (1185–1333) and that Buddhist funeral practices thereafter began to appear at least occasionally among the general populace;[25] but only members of elite groups kept records, composed diaries, and commissioned illustrated handscrolls. As a result, it is their funerary customs that remain to some degree accessible to us. In contrast, the customs of other nonelite groups in medieval Japan have been little studied because textual evidence is scarce.[26] Although some medieval popular stories include descriptions of funerals, it was priests or courtiers, not commoners, who wrote most of them, and we have little understanding of their intent or their audience.[27] Thus, the study of these nonelite groups requires a different type of data and is outside the scope of this project.[28]

The majority of my textual evidence focuses on laypersons' funerals, which were not traditionally depicted in illustrated scrolls. Therefore I have utilized images of the funerals of important priests like Hōnen, Shinran, and Nichiren who, as the founders of sects of Buddhism in Japan, were sufficiently important to have their lives and deaths memorialized in narrative scroll paintings. But in medieval Japan the boundaries between elite laypersons and clergy were rather fluid: most lay Buddhist followers took the tonsure at some point in their lives; for some the ritual was even performed after death. Thus, it is not surprising that the funerals for elite laypersons were similar to those for illustrious Buddhist priests, allowing the depictions of the priests' funerals to fill the lacunae quite credibly.

The Organization of the Book

Part 1 of the book, "The Rituals of Death" (Chaps. 1, 2), introduces the death rituals typically performed for elite lay individuals in the fourteenth and fifteenth centuries and establishes a vocabulary for the ritual objects that accompanied them. Chapter 1, "Death in the Fourteenth Century," provides a detailed description of the funerals of and subsequent memorial services for two members (a man and a woman) of a family of court officials in the mid-fourteenth century. Also discussed are prefuneral rites, such as the ceremony of taking the tonsure (*shukke no gi*) and the ceremony of putting on the mourning clothes (*chakufuku no gi*), and postfuneral rites, such as the gravestone offering ceremony (*sekitō kuyō*), along with directives about the numbers and types of alms (*fuse*) presented to the priests who conducted the services, the types of images that were offered, and the sutras and incantations performed. Alms and offerings are part of the material culture, but are also characteristic of the economic forces involved in the development of complex funerary rites. Additional examples would broaden the scope of our understanding of this century, but few contemporary records for the Nanbokuchō period (1336–1392) discuss funeral arrangements in detail.

Chapter 2, "Funerals in the Fifteenth Century," discusses the rituals performed at fifteenth-century funerals, including the closing of the coffin lid (*sagan*), moving the coffin out of the residence (*igan*) and to the cremation site (*kigan*), and the final offerings of tea (*tencha*) and hot water (*tentō*) to the deceased. This chapter includes details and diagrams illustrating the organization of the funeral procession and the arrangement of the ritual objects in the temple and at the cremation site; it also deals with the positioning of the corpse and of those in attendance. The detailed specificity of these ritual performances reflects how important it was to maintain the balance between the needs of the living and of the dead, and underscores the care that was taken by the family, priests, and society to honor these demands. These first two chapters are crucial, for without them the objects discussed in the following chapters have no context.

Significant changes in the practice of death rituals can be seen reflected in the documents that survive from these two centuries. Although new funerary customs modeled on ancient Chinese Confucian ancestor rites were transmitted to Japan along with Zen Buddhism in the twelfth century, it is unclear how well integrated these innovations were by the fourteenth century, even among elite circles. With the new customs came new rituals, such as displaying portraits of the deceased during the funeral, and new ritual implements, such as wooden ancestral tablets, both of which originally served in Confucian ancestor rites but became intertwined with Chinese Buddhist mortuary rituals and were brought to Japan as components of Zen funerary practice.[29] Yet these objects receive little attention in the texts on fourteenth-century funerals. My research suggests that fourteenth-century funerals for court personages show greater variation and less structure than those of the Ashikaga shoguns in the fifteenth century, which epitomize Zen-style funerals based on the Chinese monastic model. The two centuries present a pivotal period in the development of Japanese funerary rituals, characterized by transition in the fourteenth century and codification of the new Chinese-inspired rites within elite funerary practice in the fifteenth century.

Part 2, "The Material Culture of Death" (Chaps. 3–5), addresses the types of objects treated in texts and visualized in contemporary illustrated handscrolls and in extant objects. The texts investigated in the first section refer to a number of ritual objects in their descriptions of funerals and memorial services but seldom describe those objects in detail. Perhaps, for contemporaneous readers, the objects required no description. For us, they do. We want to know how large the coffins were and how they were made, which ritual implements were used for the memorial services, and how and where they were arranged. We are interested in who commissioned the portraits of the deceased, when they were displayed and where, and who saw them. These questions are the focus of this section, and the objects are amply illustrated.

The three chapters show the critical importance accorded the visual components and aspects of death rituals. Ritual structures marked the boundaries between the living and the dead and guided the eyes of the mourners to their proper objects, restricting and revealing certain sights as necessary. Specialists handled the ritual implements in a prescribed manner of interaction; the objects did not function simply as passive recipients of veneration. Images were arranged in a strict order and mourners were encouraged to approach them in a certain manner. Colors, smells, sounds, and sights were all coordinated in the funeral and its aftermath in order to mend the tear in the social fabric caused by death.

Chapter 3, "Objects of Separation and Containment," therefore surveys a range of built structures that were used to enclose and contain the body after death and to separate the dead from the living. In Japan, as in most cultures, this process began on the deathbed. The structures include golden folding screens (*kin byōbu*) that surrounded the body from the moment of death until cremation or burial, coffins and carriages that contained and transported the body to its final resting place, silk-wrapped wooden fences that surrounded the cremation site, and special constructions to entomb the corpse. The addition of each container or enclosure provided another layer of protection for the living and represented a further stage in the process of separating the living from the dead.

Chapter 4, "Ritual Implements for Funerals and Memorials," examines the primary ritual implements and their uses. Traditional Buddhist implements (*hōgu*) were used to adorn (*shōgon*) and thereby sanctify Buddhist sanctuaries, and a number were also carried in the funeral processions and used for the memorial services that followed. These included banners (*ban*), canopies (*tengai*), long-handled censers (*egōro*), musical instruments—cymbals (*basshi*), gongs (*shōko*) and metal bowls (*kinsu*)—offering utensils and vessels (*mitsu gusoku*, *rokki*), sutra scrolls and wooden sutra tables (*kyōzukue*). These objects helped to visually "frame" the ritual space, and their relocation during critical junctures helped to mark the passage of time.[30]

Chapter 5, "Portraits of the Deceased," addresses the types of and uses for portraits at funerals and memorial services. Although scholars are aware that portraits of the deceased were of central importance in Japanese death rituals throughout the premodern era, existing studies tend to view portraits primarily as sources of historical and social information. My study analyzes the terminology for mortuary portraits and raises questions that have not been satisfactorily explored, such as when and where the portraits were displayed, who commissioned them and when, and what types of rites were performed before them.

Physical objects combined with particular rituals helped the living negotiate the boundary between death and life. When death occurred, mourners sought and found solace in the symbolism of the object, and often in its specific connection to the deceased. Some objects were even imbued with special properties that were believed to facilitate communication with the departed or to improve the deceased's situation in the afterlife. By analyzing these objects through texts, images, and the surviving objects themselves, we gain a sense of how they were perceived and used, and why they were treasured, thereby restoring them (as much as possible) to their original contexts. This volume raises many questions that extend beyond the scope of the project, but it is my hope that scholars from a wide range of disciplines will use it as a springboard to expand upon current knowledge of death rituals and the function of ritual implements in their performance.

THE RITUALS OF DEATH

DEATH IN THE FOURTEENTH CENTURY   1

Many societies in far-flung parts of the ancient world developed surprisingly similar ideas about death and how best to deal with it. For example, archaeological evidence from ancient Etruria (ca. 500 BCE), which included tomb goods such as vessels for cooking, toilet articles, and armor, suggests that the Etruscans believed in a life beyond the grave that closely resembled their lives on earth. Likewise, writings by the Chinese Confucian scholar Xunzi (ca. 310–215 BCE) record that the living made preparations for the deceased as if the latter were still alive, and elite burials contained similarly useful objects for the deceased to use in the afterworld. Thus, dealing with death—ascertaining that death has occurred, disposing of the body, preventing the dead from harming the living, finding a new position for the soul in the afterworld, and, finally, healing the rupture created in the family and community—poses universal problems for the living. Complex rituals, aptly called "strategies for the afterlife," were developed in all societies as an important way for the living to deal with the unknowns associated with death.

Ritual structures have been the subject of research by countless scholars, but Arnold van Gennep's (1873–1957) insights into the internal organization of ritual systems are particularly relevant to understanding Buddhist death rituals. His analysis suggests that rituals facilitate the passage of the individual from one state to another while moving through life to death. Van Gennep argued for a tripartite structure of death rituals, consisting of a beginning (preliminal), a middle (liminal), and an end (postliminal).[1] The first stage extends from the moment of death until the funeral. It separates the deceased from the living relatives and is marked by rites of purification and symbolic references to the deceased's loss of the old identity. At this stage, preliminal rites are performed for the deceased, such as washing the body, shaving or cutting the hair, changing the clothing, and segregating the dead from the living (in some cultures the dying are segregated). In the second transitional stage, the corpse is relegated to a place that is symbolically outside the traditional order, such as a grave, and liminal rites are performed to reflect permanent separation through burial or cremation of the body. Often at this time the bereaved are also isolated for a period of mourning, adopting different modes of dress, abstaining from certain foods, and refraining from work. The final stage consists of acts of incorporation in which the deceased is welcomed into their new state and integrated into the community of ancestors. These postliminal rites, such as giving the deceased a new name or the mourners partaking of a communal meal, are designed both to install the dead in the afterlife and to restore the mourners to temporal society.

Rituals associated with death among the elite in medieval Japan followed this pattern. They can be divided into three distinct segments that dealt with the preparation for death and the act of dying, the funeral and burial or cremation, and the mourning rites—forty-nine days of deep mourning that included offerings to facilitate the transfer of merit to the deceased, followed by regular memorial services and additional offerings extending through at least the third year. The practice of intricate ceremonies makes it clear that proper ritual behavior was believed necessary to the karmic balance of the soul as it passed through the critical forty-nine-day period after death. It was believed that during this time the soul would be reborn in a Buddhist paradise such as the Pure Land, or in another form.[2] The rituals, if done properly, enabled the living, by the quantity and quality of their offerings, to affect the judgment passed in the courts of the afterworld on their relative's soul.

Buddhism has a long history of participation in Asian funerals. In Japan, monks affiliated with Tendai, Shingon, and Pure Land Buddhism have performed funerals for themselves and members of the imperial family since at least the seventh century. Although each group favored a distinct set of rituals and sutras,[3] their funerals often included an eclectic mix of religious traditions.[4] The rites for Zen Buddhist funerals were introduced into Japan in the late eleventh or early twelfth century and were based on rituals detailed in the Chinese monastic codes of the eleventh century.[5] These codes were in turn constructed within the cultural context of long-standing Chinese traditions, which included ancient Confucian canonical texts and Daoist beliefs; the result was a peculiar set of beliefs that amalgamated filial devotion and ancestor worship with the ritual practices of Buddhism.[6] In particular, the funeral rites for Chan abbots contained important elements of Confucian mourning and memorial practices, most specifically the prominent display of mortuary tablets and portraits of the deceased.[7] Chan funerary rituals also contained substantial elements from Esoteric Buddhist teachings, and Pure Land funeral rites in Tang China influenced those developed by other schools.[8] It is no wonder, then, that Chinese Chan Buddhist beliefs about death were complex and ambiguous, as the funerary practices that had developed around death in China were often at odds with Buddhist beliefs about the nature of impermanence and of multiple reincarnations.[9] Perhaps in part to facilitate conversions to Buddhism, such fundamentally contradictory attitudes toward death were accepted into religious practice, and Chan teachings were modified over time by taking into account the popular beliefs.[10] Alan Cole argues that the sophisticated rituals for the funerals of abbots in China were intended to display the abbot as a "powerful Buddhist saint figure," who even in death retained power and authority through his position in the monastic lineage and his existence in the monastery's ritual life.[11] When Chan funerary rituals reached Japan, members of the court and the military elite chose to model their funerals after ceremonies for Chan abbots rather than those for ordinary monks, probably because they believed their high rank in society was best represented by the elevated display of their own images—painted, carried in procession to the cremation site, and then preserved for posterity—and because they hoped to maintain their secular power in the persons of their descendants.

At a typical funeral for a Zen abbot in Japan, nine special rites were performed for the deceased in the following order.[12] First, the body was carefully bathed and dressed and then placed in the coffin (*nyūgan*). It was then transferred (*igan*) from the room where the priest had died to the Lecture Hall, and three rites were performed while the body lay in state in the hall: the coffin lid was closed (*sagan*), the deceased's portrait was hung above the altar (*kashin*), and a wake in the form of a priest's consultation with the deceased was held (*tairyō shōsan*). The coffin was then moved to the cremation grounds (*kigan*), where libations of tea (*tencha*) and hot water (*tentō*) were offered. The final rite was the lighting of the funeral pyre (*ako, hinko*). Presumably all of these symbolic actions were performed for the elite layperson in Japan, although the sources I consulted contained no mention of individual consultation with the deceased in the lay rites.

Religious historians suggest that the Zen style rather quickly became the model for funerals in Japan, even for those performed by most other Buddhist sects.[13] The situation was in fact more complex. The records I examined show that the funerals of many elite lay individuals, particularly those in the fourteenth century, did not strictly follow the directives of traditional Zen funerals, but combined vestiges of earlier funerary traditions with the newer elements, resulting in a decidedly eclectic approach to funerary ritual. The case studies in this section reveal a number of death practices not associated either with earlier Buddhist funerals or with the new Zen style of funerals.

A notion of what these funerals comprised may be gleaned from the many accounts of the deaths of family members and close friends chronicled in the daily records of courtiers and priests. Yet no one individual provided sufficient detail to permit a comprehensive reconstruction of a given funerary rite. The lack of precise or complete information may proceed from the universal human aversion to dealing with death, or perhaps from more specific associations between death and pollution in Japan. But the records were primarily intended to instruct future generations on the proper performance of the rituals. Much attention was given to the names of the individuals who participated in the funerals, because participants of high rank exalted the prestige of the deceased and his family. The authors of these records did not have us in mind. They wrote about what interested them and about what their descendants should know.

In some accounts relevant sections are simply missing. For whatever reason, I found no single source that gave a complete accounting of the process from the time of death through the lengthy period of the memorial services. Therefore I have had to examine a number of medieval diaries and records from a broad span of time and illustrative of the practices at various levels of elite society. The result is of necessity a pastiche of ritual death practices covering approximately a hundred-and-twenty-year period, 1345–1463. This first chapter documents the performance of death rituals for one man and one woman of the court in about the middle of the fourteenth century, focusing particularly on how various ritual objects were utilized during the ceremonies.

A number of descriptions of the funerals of Zen monks exist,[14] but relatively few sources offer particulars on lay funerals in the fourteenth century. Among them, *Moromoriki*,[15] a lengthy chronicle written by the courtier Nakahara Moromori during the era of the Northern and Southern Courts (1336–1392), provides unparalleled detail about the mortuary practices of that time. The diary covers the events that followed the death of the author's father, Morosuke, on the sixth day of the second month of 1345, and of his mother, Kenshin, six months later, on the twenty-third day of the eighth month. The author supplies information on the specific rituals held during the forty-nine days after Morosuke's death and on the memorial services that continued many years after. *Moromoriki*, however, is *not* forthcoming about the initial lying-in-state period, nor does its author say much about the actual funerals themselves. My translation and analysis of the relevant sections of *Moromoriki*, therefore, are intended to give the reader a comprehensive understanding of the flow of the various rituals associated with death in the fourteenth century, as well as some insight into a wide range of other practices related to medieval lay funerals.

Nakahara Morosuke (?–1345)

We begin with an account of the death of Senior Secretary Nakahara Morosuke[16] who expired about ten o'clock in the morning on the sixth day of the second month of 1345 (hereafter dates are abbreviated by year, month, day, so 1345.2.6).[17] A large section of text immediately prior to his death is unfortunately missing in *Moromoriki*, and the entry for the following day is only partial. This lacuna makes it difficult to grasp fully the structure of the funeral itself, but another source helps fill some of the gaps in this text. *Entairyaku* relates that a few days before his death, Morosuke sent his eldest son, Moroshige, to the residence of Tōin Kinkata, Minister of the Right (*sadaijin*), to request an imperial sanction to allow his father to take the tonsure.[18] In the medieval period, Buddhist believers cut off their hair or shaved their heads and took Buddhist vows when they became gravely ill, either as a way to gain merit and prolong their lives or to aid them in reaching salvation after their deaths. Presumably this act also gave lay individuals the right to monastic funerals. Taking Buddhist vows when death was imminent seems to have been a practice that started with the imperial house in the late ninth century and spread to the court.[19] By the medieval period most courtiers, when death seemed imminent, made such requests as a matter of course, but Morosuke died before his could be officially tendered. In fact, Moroshige had just arrived at the gate of the minister's residence with the request when he was informed of his father's death.[20] Though posthumous ordinations were not uncommon at that time, we do not know if this was done for Morosuke.

Kōei 4 (1345) 2.9:[21] Hearth-fire God; *Nichibutsu* and Seven Buddha Images Drawn

Three days after Morosuke died, his body was transported to Ryōzen, a family burial ground in the Higashiyama foothills, located between Yasaka Shrine and Kiyomizudera (both in Kyoto).[22] The text does not state clearly whether Morosuke was buried or cremated, but because he was taken directly to the cemetery, we may infer that he probably received a burial. Although Nakahara Morosuke and his wife Kenshin (died six months later) were both buried, all four of the individuals studied in Chapter 2 were cremated. Buddhist doctrine did not mandate the burning of the body, but the practice was associated with and performed in emulation of the cremation of the Buddha.[23]

On the same day, after the cortege carrying the corpse set out, we are told that the hearth-fire god (*kamadogami*)[24] was "cut on the left side of the west face" (*nishi men no hidarikata kore o kiru*) and sent along the same road the funeral procession had taken to Ryōzen in Higashiyama.[25]

Little else is said in the text about this interesting practice. Mention of a hearth-fire god first appears in the early eighth-century *Nihongi*, where its "cutting" and connection to funerals is hinted at in the early myths. According to *Nihongi*, the fire god, Kagutsuchi, caused Izanami's death because he burned her as she gave birth to him. Later, Izanagi cut Kagutsuchi into a number of pieces in retaliation for her death.[26] The early records therefore connect the hearth-fire god with death and explain why it needed to be destroyed. Ancient records contain no mention of images of the hearth-fire deity, but archaeological evidence reveals that clay cooking stoves called *kamado* were discovered in horizontal stone chamber tombs dating to the Kofun period (ca. 300–550), suggesting that cooking stoves were used for the preparation of (or to symbolize preparation of) food offerings that took place at the ancient tomb mounds. This solidifies a link between the hearth-fire god, the clay stoves that housed it, and early death rituals.[27]

It is unclear when anthropomorphic images associated with the god of the hearth fire appeared, but at some point a pair of deities formed of clay or wood, known as Okitsuhime no mikoto (female) and Okitsuhiko no kami (male), were enshrined in the kitchen of the imperial palace and received offerings from the person(s) in charge of preparing food.[28] This practice then spread to members of the court and later to commoners, who enshrined the images in their kitchens to protect their hearth fires.[29] Although most sources do not connect these kitchen gods with death, the offerings made to them by the food preparers suggest a link to the food offerings and cooking stoves found at early grave sites. In *Moromoriki* the ritual of breaking and discarding the *kamadogami* seems to be related to the story of a similar action in the *Nihongi*, suggesting that in the mid-fourteenth century the hearth-fire god still retained strong associations with death.[30] What remains unknown, however, is what form the hearth-fire god discussed in *Moromoriki* took.

Although the *kamadogami* was not recorded for earlier Nakahara funerals, the description in *Moromoriki* of destroying the hearth-fire god was not an isolated example of the practice. Indeed, taking the female hearth-fire deity to the mountains and discarding it when the head female member of the house died is a custom documented in earlier court writings. *Heihanki* (also *Hyōhanki*), a mid-twelfth-century diary by the courtier Taira no Nobunori, for example, tells us that on the day of the funeral for Fujiwara no Tadamichi's wife, Sōshi, 1155.9.16, the *kamadogami* was supposed to be sent to the mountains. Since the person in charge forgot to perform this important act, the ritual was conducted after her funeral, on 9.21. This and other examples of performing the *kamadogami* ritual upon the death of important women members of the family can be found in early records,[31] but this practice was seldom recorded in conjunction with the funerals of men.[32] Therefore either the destruction of the hearth-fire god for Morosuke's funeral was truly unusual, or it was generally not recorded for men. That the *kamadogami* in these early sources were distinguished as either male or female suggests they were a gendered pair, as with the later male and female kitchen gods, Okitsuhime no mikoto (female) and Okitsuhiko no kami (male).

What "cutting" the hearth-fire god actually entailed is also a mystery. Suitō proposed that cutting meant breaking into pieces, which assumes that it was a clay oven or some other type of image made of clay.[33] If the image was made of wood, however, cutting would precisely describe one method of destroying it. It is also possible that the verb "to cut" was used symbolically in the text, to replicate its use in the *Nihongi* story, where the fire god Kagutsuchi was cut into pieces. In all, the "cutting of the hearth-fire god" in *Moromoriki* seems to have a multiplicity of meanings, but it likely derived from the association of fire with food offerings prepared at death and referred to cutting, breaking, or destroying the source of the fire in order to destroy or retaliate against the source of the death, thereby eradicating the impurities associated with death.[34] That the *kamadogami* was sent to Ryōzen immediately after the corpse may also suggest that fire was taken from the hearth at the residence to light the cremation fire. We have no indication, however, that Morosuke was cremated, and the practice of moving the hearth-fire god is documented in cases where we know the person was buried.

It is clear from the above discussion that not all of the ritual actions surrounding funerals in medieval Japan were connected to Buddhist practice. Protecting the living from the pollution caused by death was a serious concern even in pre-Buddhist Japan, where contact with the corpse was carefully avoided because of its decay and also because it was feared that harmful spirits might attach themselves to it. Tanaka Hisao explained that originally it was believed that these spirits could cause harm or even death to the living, but later such spirits seem to have been conflated with the soul of the deceased, and the deceased's spirit itself came to be viewed as potentially dangerous.[35] Thus, rituals such as "cutting the hearth-fire god" continued to be included in some funerals for added protection, but Buddhism predominated in mortuary contexts because it offered comprehensive solace, providing the dead with relief from suffering and the living with a host of useful methods for dealing with the dangers of pollution associated with both the corpse and the spirit. In short, Buddhist cremation took care of the decaying corpse in a purifying and timely manner, and the memorial services pacified the soul of the dead.

On the same day that the corpse and the hearth-fire god were transported to the grave site, a Buddhist image maker named Ryōchi came to the Nakahara residence and drew images of the *nichibutsu* and seven Buddha images (*shichitai gobutsu*). The cost was a thousand copper coins (1 *kanmon*) for creating the *nichibutsu* and three thousand (3 *kanmon*) for the other seven images.[36] Thus we know that these were painted images, but are told nothing more about their appearance. The pictures were made to be used during the forty-nine-day mourning period of Buddhist rituals that followed the funeral—seven seven-day periods beginning with the day of death, during which mourners visited the grave, heard Buddhist sermons (seppō), read and dedicated sutras[37] and images, and made offerings and performed offering services (kuyō) for the repose of the deceased's soul. Termed tsuizen, these were actions taken by the living to help the deceased achieve in death what he or she had failed to achieve in life.

On the next day (2.10), a Yin-Yang Master (onmyōji; also onyōji) was summoned to the Nakahara house to perform certain divinations that would decide the schedule for Morosuke's memorial services,[38] including the proper dates, the days when the grave could be visited, and the date when the gravestone would be erected.[39] The role of the Yin-Yang Master in scheduling funerals and memorials remained important throughout the fourteenth century, but it was marginalized in the funerals of the later Ashikaga shoguns (see Chap. 2).

Kōei 4 (1345) 2.12: Daily Buddha Offering Ceremony

On 2.12 the first Daily Buddha Offering Ceremony (nichibutsu kuyō) was performed in the Fourth Chamber of the Nakahara residence, and continued to be conducted there daily throughout the forty-nine-day mourning period.

I was unable to find mention of this term (nichibutsu kuyō) in other sources, but surmise that it entailed hanging a painted Buddhist icon and making offerings. We know the nichibutsu was a single painting, probably mounted as a hanging scroll, because the painter Ryōchi received a separate sum of money for its production (see 2.9 above). The Japanese characters for this term literally mean "daily buddha(s)," but we are given no further details. The nichibutsu may have been a single scroll that depicted all the buddhas and bodhisattvas used throughout the mourning period—either ten (jūbutsu) in total (seven for the forty-nine-day period, plus one each for the one-hundredth day, the first year, and the third year after death), or thirteen (jūsan butsu), which included three additional images representing the seventh, thirteenth, and thirty-third years after death.[40] Most sources suggest that the practice of invoking the Thirteen Buddhas (and bodhisattvas) for memorial services had evolved in Japan by the fourteenth century, but was not popularized until the following century (Figure 1.1).[41]

Moromoriki makes it clear that the practice of invoking seven buddhas or bodhisattvas and displaying their individual images was in place by the mid-fourteenth century, but it is not certain that the nichibutsu image was the Ten or Thirteen Buddhas.

Because the convention of invoking the Ten or Thirteen Buddhas is thought to have developed from an early Chinese belief in the Ten Kings (jūō) of the Underworld, who came to be regarded as avatars of the Ten Buddhas, it is also possible that the nichibutsu mentioned in the text was a painting of the Ten Kings of Hell (Plate 1). Such paintings displayed the judgments and, if

Figure 1.1. *Thirteen Buddhas.* Artist and date unknown. Hanging scroll.
Source: Private collection. Photo by T. Masuzaki.

decreed, torments that the soul underwent during the forty-nine-day period; they also often depicted the original buddha form of each king as well. Apocryphal texts associated with belief in the Ten Kings required the descendants to perform special rituals and make frequent offerings during the forty-nine days after death to enable the deceased to avoid immense suffering and be reborn in a heavenly realm.[42] Little has been written about when and where such images were used in Japan, but we know that in China the Ten Kings were strongly associated with death and the mourning period.[43] Thus, it is possible that such paintings were displayed during offering services as sharp reminders to the living to perform the proper rituals for the deceased.[44] In sum, whether the *nichibutsu* was an image of the Ten or Thirteen Buddhas or an image of the Ten Kings, its purpose and result were the same. Offerings could activate the buddhas to protect the deceased and the living during this perilous time or could influence the kings favorably in their judgment of the deceased, making either image appropriate as a spur to aid the deceased.

The entry for 2.17 provides information about the cost of the memorial services. The priest in charge of the ceremonies (*dōshi*), Kūichibō,[45] received a donation (*fuse*)[46] of one string of a thousand copper coins (1 *kan*) for performing the Daily Buddha Offering Ceremony each day of the first week, and the priests invited to perform the Buddhist services (*hōe*) for the deceased each received five hundred copper coins (500 *mon*)[47] on each seventh day throughout the mourning period.

The Daily Buddha Offering Ceremony for Morosuke took place every day of the first week; other rituals were generally performed at one-week intervals on each of the seven important seventh days. For Morosuke, these weekly rituals typically included a performance of the *nijūgozanmai*, a Buddhist sermon (*seppō*), hanging the appropriate image, reading (and sometimes copying) the *Lotus Sutra*, a banquet or repast (*ōban*) for the mourners, and donations to the priests to increase merit for the deceased. The *nijūgozanmai* in this text refers to a group recitation of Amida's name that was intended to generate merit for the deceased. In *Moromoriki*, it was always performed on the evening preceding each seventh-day service. The offerings made on Morosuke's behalf at these ceremonies included items of the deceased's clothing, candles, special writing paper (*danshi*),[48] rolls of white cloth, straw sandals, copies of sutras, Buddhist paintings, and money.[49] Cash donations were also given to the participating priests. Although the money given to the priests in effect served as payment for services, it was also thought to positively affect the status of the deceased. Incense, prayers, and "burnt offerings" (*goma*) were placed before the Buddhist images, and family members repeatedly made written requests (*fujumon*) for additional sutras to be read on the deceased's behalf (for which extra payment was made). That many different kinds of objects accompanied the elaborate ceremonies and were presented as offerings underscores their importance in proper ritual behavior. It also suggests that funerals provided a healthy source of income for Buddhist temples by the mid-fourteenth century. The living clearly believed that the quantity and quality of these objects could positively affect the judgment on their relative's soul as it passed through the crucial forty-nine-day period on its way to rebirth.

The seven seventh-day ceremonies were important because it was believed that the soul was examined on the first day of each of the seven weeks after death by one of the Ten Kings of Hell at an intermediate site, the "dark realm" (*meikai* or *meifu*), which is similar to the Christian idea of Purgatory.[50] Beginning in the Kamakura period, three additional kings were called upon, on the one-hundredth day and on the first- and third-year anniversaries. In Japan, each king was considered a secondary manifestation of a primary buddha (*honji butsu*), who embodied the promise of salvation. That is why the seven Buddhist images commissioned on 2.9 were needed—on each of the seventh days the image of the buddha that correlated with the judgment king for that day would be hung. Offerings of incense and sutra recitations would be made to the appropriate buddha on behalf of the deceased, in the hope that merit generated by the offerings would positively influence the king's judgment. The first seven days after death and the forty-ninth day after death were generally considered the most important markers, because if a person was not reborn by the first memorial, it was thought that he had escaped the cycle of rebirth completely and been transported to a Buddhist paradise; if he had not been so fortunate, he would be reborn in one of the six "paths" of existence (*rokudō*)—the realm of celestials (*tenjindō*), the realm of titans or warriors (*ashuradō*), the human world (*ningendō*), the state of animals (*chikushōdō*), the limbo of hungry ghosts (*gakidō*), and the various hells (*jigokudō*)—by the forty-ninth day after death. As the living could not be certain where their departed stood in this process, they conducted numerous rituals and made copious offerings during the first week to help him escape the cycle of rebirth, and again on the forty-ninth day to enhance the likelihood of his rebirth in the best possible of the six "paths." Thus, Buddhist mortuary rites provided the living with a way to help the dead (and by extension, themselves) obtain salvation, without needing to possess any particular religious wisdom.[51]

To this end, on the seventh day after Morosuke's death (*shonanoka*), 2.12, the image of Fudō Myōō was hung, as this image was the manifestation of the king Shinkō, who presided over that period. For the second seventh-day memorial (*futananoka*) it was Yakushi (2.19); the Shaka image was hung for the third (*minanoka*, 2.26); Kannon for the fourth (*yonanoka*, 3.4); Jizō for the fifth (*itsunanoka*, 3.11); Fugen Bosatsu for the sixth (*munanoka*, 3.18); and Amida Buddha for the seventh seventh-day memorial (*shichinanoka*, 3.25). The order in which Buddhist images were displayed for Morosuke's memorials differs from the more traditional pattern of Fudō, Shaka, Monju, Fugen, Jizō, Miroku, Yakushi Nyorai, suggesting either that the order was not yet fixed in the fourteenth century or that it varied according to sectarian preferences.[52] It becomes readily apparent that an enormous number of images of buddhas and bodhisattvas must have been commissioned for countless memorial ceremonies throughout the premodern era, leading us to conclude that a great majority of the Buddhist images that remain today may have been originally made for death ceremonies of one sort or another.

Kōei (1345) 2.12: Visits to the Grave and Death Talismans

In theory, Moromori and his older brother Moroshige visited their father's grave (*haka mairi*) at Ryōzen in the Higashiyama foothills on every seventh day, accompanied by priests who chanted special sutras and incantations (J. *darani*) designed to assist their father in attaining a better rebirth. But the Yin-Yang Master's calculations determined that on the first seventh day (2.12) neither should travel to the grave site because it was an inauspicious day (*suinichi*)[53] for their mother, Gozen Onkata, who was not permitted to go on that day either. That immediate family of the deceased could not approach his grave at this time reemphasizes the seriousness with which the Japanese regarded death as pollution; death pollution was especially powerful around graveyards, and particularly affected those who had been in closest contact with the corpse. Therefore, on this first seventh-day memorial, only the priests, accompanied by other extended family members, went to the grave and recited the *Bonmō no jūjū*, *Hōkyōin darani*, *Kōmyō shingon*, *Amida kyō*, and the *Nenbutsu*.

All of these recitations had special meaning for the deceased. The *Bonmō no jūjū* was a recitation of the ten major precepts for bodhisattvas, enumerated at this time to remind all present what was required. The *Hōkyōin darani* was a powerful incantation believed to enable one's ancestors who might be undergoing torments in hell to be instantly reborn in Amida's paradise; the *Kōmyō shingon* was a mantra that could empower sand, which was then sprinkled on the body of the deceased to remove all evil karma and enable the soul's deliverance; both the Amida Sutra and the *Nenbutsu* are basic canons of Pure Land Buddhism, which describe the glories of Amida's paradise and whose recitation provides the means to get there. Although *Moromoriki* cites additional sutras used for memorial services, these five were recited most often during Morosuke's forty-nine-day mourning period. In general, texts thought to provide strong "magic" were desirable, regardless of their sectarian origins.

Also on 2.12, a special talisman against death pollution (*monoimi fuda*) was stood up inside the small gate (not the main gate) of the Nakahara residence. The talisman, made of Japanese cedar, was almost three feet tall (3 *shaku*). A priest wrote the Sanskrit seed syllable (J. *shuji*)⁵⁴ for Dainichi Buddha on the upper center part of the board, to its right the *kanji* for "Dainichi Sanskrit letter," and beneath the seed syllable the Japanese word *monoimi*, a term associated with ritual seclusion or abstinence and used to avoid the dangers of unusual and frightening phenomena, of which death was one (Figure 1.2).

The talisman was designed to protect those who entered the gate, but also those who lived within (Morosuke had died at home, so death pollution was a serious problem for those inside the residence).⁵⁵ The talisman was removed every evening and, according to *Moromoriki*, precedent determined that it should only be used through the second seventh-day memorial on 2.19. Presumably, the danger would have diminished by then.

Kōei 4 (1345) 2.19: Ceremony for Taking the Tonsure and Ceremony for Changing Clothes

On the second seventh day of mourning (2.19), the deceased's wife, Gozen Onkata, took the tonsure and became a Buddhist nun in the "leaving-the-house ceremony" (*shukke no gi*). It was customary for upper-class women in the medieval period to cut their hair and renounce the world after the death of their spouses, although earlier this choice was rarely expected or practiced.⁵⁶

Moroshige and Moromori, wearing white robes (*hitatare*), began the day with a visit to their father's grave, their first visit, since the Yin-Yang Master had advised against their going on 2.12. Later they attended their mother's special hair-cutting ceremony, which was held in the Fourth Chamber, where Morosuke had died. Two female attendants helped their mother wash her hands in a metal

Figure 1.2. Death talisman (*monoimi fuda*).
Source: Nakahara Moromori, *Shiryō sanshū: Moromoriki*, 11 vols. (Tokyo: Gunsho Ruijū Kanseikai, 1968), after image in vol. 2, p. 274.

bowl. A lacquered wooden comb and two paper cords for tying up hair (*motoyui/ motoi*) were placed on top of ten sheets of special paper, and a large tray (*hirobuta*) was prepared. Following an earlier tradition, dating to the Shōwa era (1312– 1317), Gozen Onkata first turned to the northwest in the direction of the family's clan deity at Hirano Shrine, then north toward the emperor, then southeast toward her mother and father (either toward their residence or the site of their graves). In so doing, she announced her decision to enter seclusion to the clan deity, the emperor, and her parents. Then she faced east, and the attendants divided her hair into two parts. While this was being done, the priest went out and placed one silk robe, a special large Buddhist surplice, and an everyday surplice in the large tray.[57] He set the tray before Gozen, then picked up the razor and shaved her head, starting on the left side. The priest left the room while the nun donned her new garments. After receiving the five precepts (*gokai*) and the Buddhist name (*hōmyō*) Kenshin, she withdrew behind bamboo blinds. A thin robe with pale green lining, a white ancient-style skirt (*mo*), and a measure of white cloth were presented to the officiating priest as donations.

For women to renounce the world after the death of a spouse was not typical in the mid-Heian period; it became much more common in the medieval period. There were three different types of tonsure—full, partial, and cropped hair[58]—but the tonsure described in *Moromoriki* does not exactly fit any of the three. Full tonsures were commonly associated with death, however, and indeed the text says that Kenshin's head was "shaved," suggesting a full tonsure. On the other hand, she received only five of the ten Buddhist precepts and continued to live at home until she died, conditions more typically associated with the partial tonsure of a novice who remained in the world. As explained in the text, the nature of Kenshin's tonsure is ambiguous.

On this and every seventh-day memorial, a repast was served in the Drawing Room (*tsune no godei*) of the residence,[59] attended by both priests and courtiers. The Buddhist sermon was then performed in the south side of the Fourth Chamber, where Morosuke had died. Enshōbō, the head priest (*chōrō*) of Chōhakuji,[60] officiated, and Kūichibō and Ryōshinbō,[61] who served as the *komorisō*, attended him. *Komorisō* were priests who went into seclusion, usually remaining in a room and chanting sutras on behalf of the deceased for the duration of the mourning period. In *Moromoriki*, the priests did not remain strictly secluded but participated in all of the death rituals held for Morosuke, including visiting his grave.[62] On this second seventh-day memorial for the deceased, the image of Yakushi was hung and Kūichibō and Ryōshinbō gave a ritually shortened reading (*tendoku*) of the *Lotus Sutra*.[63] The *Bonmō no jūjū* and *Kōmyō shingon* were also performed. Following the ceremony, priests and courtiers bathed, presumably for purification.

About eight o'clock in the evening of 2.19, the ceremony of changing clothes (*chakufuku no gi*) was held. The two weeks prior from the day of Morosuke's death had been taken up with the funeral and with getting the ritual schedule settled. The ceremony on 2.19 marked the family's entry into the official period of mourning, when they exchanged their black court robes for white mourning robes and abstained from eating certain foods and from going out to work. Moromori, his elder brother Moroshige, their elder sister Nakahara Goryō, and their mother Kenshin (now a nun) participated. The ceremony was performed first for Moroshige as the eldest son. In the eastern corridor[64] of the Sōkyoku of the residence,[65] Moroshige stood ready, wearing a black-dyed silk upper garment (*kariginu*).[66] He stepped up on the veranda wearing shoes and sat facing northwest on a thin round mat under the southern eaves of the building. He stood while the mourning robe (*sofuku*)[67] was presented. Moroshige again sat facing the northwest, and a black lacquer tray, bearing three types of vegetables and a soup, was placed in front of him.[68] After the chopsticks were stood up, a Buddhist invocation (*nenjū*) was recited. *Moromoriki* is the only diary among those I read that mentioned this interesting positioning of the chopsticks. In both China and Japan sticking chopsticks upright into a bowl of rice is something done only as an offering to the dead.[69] As the text says that Moroshige was offered only soup and vegetables, it is unclear where the chopsticks were placed. After Moroshige ate one mouthful, his tray was taken away. Next, his black upper garment and hat were removed, and he was assisted into a white jacket (*hitatare*), the color for mourning garments in medieval Japan.

Next, Moromori performed the same ritual in the western corridor of the Sōkyoku; he also faced northwest. His actions were identical, except that Moromori sat under the northern eaves of the building. Their mother, Kenshin, then sat in the northern corridor of the Shinden. She wore a black-dyed short robe with half sleeves (*koginu*) tied with a plain black silk sash and a Buddhist surplice; she also sat facing the northwest. Kenshin, having already taken the tonsure, did not change into mourning clothes.[70] The sister, Goryō, sat near her mother. Facing northwest, she put on a black-dyed plain silk robe (*heiken*) tied with a special sash and a Chinese-style short jacket (*karaginu*) of hemp fabric dyed black. In accordance with custom, the two women, unlike the men, were not offered any food, and Goryō, although not a nun, did not wear white mourning robes.

A catalog that lists the clothing and accouterments for this ceremony was appended to the back of the original text for 2.19 in *Moromoriki*. That list essentially reiterates the information given above but includes further details, such as quantity, color, and, in some cases, the cost of the items. The following is my translation of selected sections (words in parentheses are as they appear in the text):[71]

(1) Two robes (*shōzoku*) dyed black (*fushikane*) for Moromori and Moroshige; two large hanging curtains (*katabira*) dyed light blue

(2) Two plain silk (*heiken*) court caps (*eboshi*)
(3) Two light-blue cypress fans (*hiōgi*); cypress fans with painted flowers but no gold or silver leaf were used
(4) Two pairs of shoes (*kutsu*) with strips of black-dyed paper affixed to their bottoms (or insides?)
(5) Two black-dyed plain silk sashes (*obi*) for Moroshige and Moromori; large-opening pants (*ōguchi hakama*)
(6) Two black lacquer boxes (*hikiire*)
(7) Two trays (*tsuigasane*); also two white mourning robes (*sofuku*) and two black-dyed sashes
(8) A short-sleeved hemp-cloth robe (*koginu*), approximately 3 *shaku* in length and dyed black, and a surplice (*kesa*) also dyed black
> The above [8] was for the nun (Kenshin), following precedents set by Higodono's mother (also a nun) in the Kenchō era (1249.3.1–1256.10.5)
(9) A plain silk sash and a special sash for formal wear (*kake obi*), both dyed black
(10) A short Chinese-style hemp jacket with sleeves (*karaginu*) dyed black
> The above [9 and 10] were for my sister Goryō.

In addition to simply documenting the numbers and types of the clothing and accouterments, the list was likely intended as a helpful record for future generations.

This second seventh-day memorial was clearly a momentous one, marked by several notable events like the hair-cutting ritual and the mourning-clothes ceremony. Many of the most important rituals, sutra recitations, and offerings had now been completed, and it was believed that by this time both the living and the deceased had passed beyond the most dangerous period. To an extent, life in the Nakahara household returned to a more normal pattern after this memorial. The Daily Buddha Offering Services continued to be held and special sutras were read on behalf of the deceased, but the doors of the Imperial Palace Archives Office (Fudono; also Kyōshoden) were reopened, suggesting a return to regular activities at the court. The Archives Office had been closed since Morosuke's death, because this was where he had worked. A new senior secretary, Nakahara Morokō, was appointed by this date, although the ceremony for his official assumption of the position (*shosan no gi*) had not yet been held, because the family was still in mourning.

The third and fourth seventh-day memorials were held on 2.26 and 3.4 respectively. Both were typical memorials that included visits to the grave, sermons and banquets, and offering services. The images of Shaka (2.26) and Kannon (3.4) were brought out and displayed in the Fourth Chamber as sutras were read. After the ceremony the family made special written requests for sutras to be read by the priests, and donations were given.

Kōei 4 (1345) 3.6: Stone Pagoda and Grave Enclosure

On Morosuke's one-month death anniversary (3.6),[72] a stone pagoda (*sekitō*) measuring about 3 feet tall (3 *shaku*, 3 *sun*) was erected as a marker at his grave and a grave enclosure (*kuginuki*) was constructed around it.[73] The use of stone to mark Morosuke's grave suggests a kind of permanence, signifying the durability of the Nakahara lineage, as many earlier graves and even contemporary graves for persons of a lesser status went unidentified or marked by more ephemeral wooden grave markers. More important, the act of ordering and making this mortuary sculpture produced merit for the donor and the artisan, which could then be transferred to the deceased. We are told that this particular day was chosen for placing the grave marker because it was deemed auspicious by the Yin-Yang Master and because it marked Morosuke's one-month death anniversary. Other contemporary records confirm that the appropriate time to erect the stone marker was approximately one month after death.

Early in the morning on 3.6, Moroshige proceeded to the grave in a carriage with the two *komorisō*, Kūichibō and Ryōshinbō. Moromori did not attend this important ceremony, because for him it was a day for ritual abstention. It apparently took many hours to prepare the grave properly under Kūichibō's watchful eye, suggesting that one of the responsibilities of the *komorisō* was preparing the

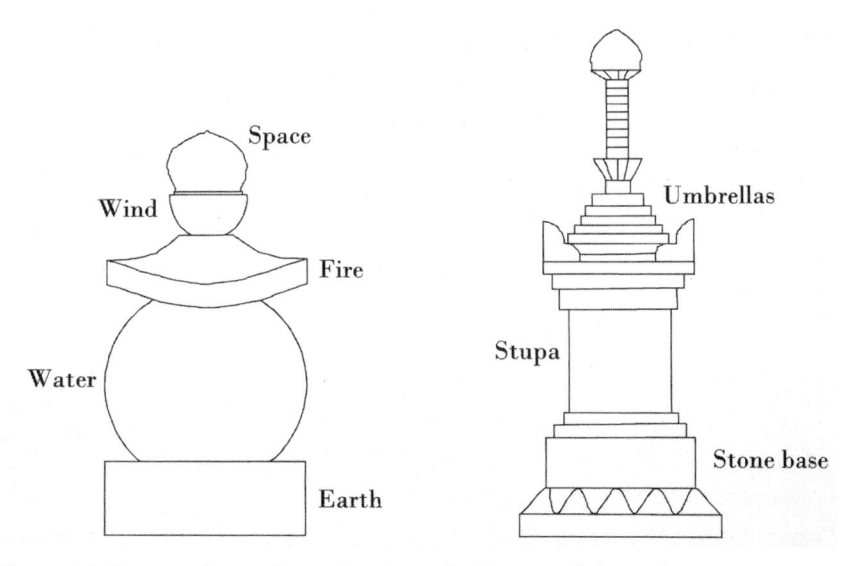

Figure 1.3. Five-tiered stupa (*gorintō*) and pagoda-like stupa (*hōkyōintō*).
Source: Drawing by Adriana Maguina-Ugarte.

Figure 1.4. Wooden grave markers (*sotoba*).
Source: *Tōji to Kōbō daishi shinkō: Tōji mieidō, chikai to inori no fūkei*, ed. and comp. Tōji (Kyōōgokokuji) Hōmotsukan (Tokyo: Benridō, 2001), after image on p. 102.

grave mound and arranging for the monument.[74] The grave was said to be particularly excellent, but the text does not describe the marker other than to refer to it as a stone pagoda or tower; nor are we told whether the enclosure was made of wood or stone. It is likely, however, that the grave monument was either a five-tiered stone stupa (*gorintō*)[75] or another pagoda-like stupa (*hōkyōintō*),[76] because both types were popular in the fourteenth century.

Sanskrit letters had been carved into the stone marker and were also written on the corner and middle pillars of the enclosure. During the ceremony the five Buddhist colors (blue, yellow, red, white, and black) were painted on the upper parts of the pillars of the enclosure. Before the stone was put in place, the *Hōkyōin darani* and *Kōmyō shingon* were chanted to prepare the site. After the marker was erected, the *Hōkyōin darani*, *Bonmo no jūjū*, and *Kōmyō shingon* were recited, followed by the *Amida Sutra* and the *Nenbutsu*. The text mentions that the precedents called for wine and rice to be prepared at Ryōzen, but there was not sufficient time, so the mourners returned to the residence for a repast in the Drawing Room. On 3.20, 3 *kan* 600 *mon* were conveyed to Kūichibō to pay for the stone marker and the enclosure.

From the first seventh-day memorial through the fourth, a time of approximately four weeks when no stone marker was yet in place, we are told that sections of four sutras—one per week—were placed on the grave to mark and protect the site. The sutras[77] were copied onto wooden slats or tablets called *sotoba* and then placed at the four corners of the grave, with each tablet representing one of the four seventh-day memorials. The first tablet was placed in the northeast corner facing south, and on each successive seventh day, moving clockwise, another tablet was positioned at another corner of the mound. The tablets thus served as temporary markers, as well as a form of offerings, until the official grave marker could be erected on 3.6.[78]

Kōei 4 (1345) 3.11: Gravestone Offering Ceremony and Written Pledges for Donations

The order of the fifth seventh-day memorial on 3.11 was changed slightly to accommodate a special gravestone offering ceremony (*sekitō kuyō*), which was conducted in front of the new monument. Throughout the day, members of the family copied first lines of the *Lotus Sutra* (*tonsha*) (probably on *sotoba*) to accrue merit for Morosuke in the afterlife. A literal translation of *tonsha* is "quick copy." In accruing merit by the copying of a sutra, a *tonsha* served as an effective surrogate for the whole (usually very long) text. The usual repast was served at the residence and a Buddhist service was held in the Fourth Chamber. For this memorial the Jizō image was displayed. After the service, the male members of the family and the male guests proceeded to the grave where the copies of the *Lotus Sutra* were offered on Morosuke's behalf.

Kuichibō performed the offering ceremony, sitting on a round mat in front of Morosuke's grave. The text says that in the past this ceremony was generally held in a hall, suggesting that a grave hall (*byōdō*) was usually constructed near a grave site. There being no hall yet on 3.11, the *komorisō* recited the *Bonmō no jūjū* and *Kōmyō shingon* directly in front of the stone monument. Next a group of nuns performed a special *Nenbutsu* (*ichiji nenbutsu*). At some point in the ceremony Moroshige placed the sutras that the family had copied earlier that day, along with copies of the *Jōdo sanbukyō*[79] and a *Nenbutsu* donated by Nakahara Yūa,[80] in the northeast section of the grave. Here, too, it is unclear whether the copied sutras were placed inside the enclosure (possibly in a metal box), or whether they were inscribed by the family on *sotoba* and placed around the grave.

Moromori also sent two folded letters (*tatebumi*)[81] pledging donations (*fuse chūmon*) to Kūichibō on this day. One enumerated the donations (*fuse*) and the other specified amounts for additional gifts (*kabuse*) intended to further increase merit for Morosuke. Enshōbō, the priest who conducted the service, received 300 *chōmoku*, a measure of white cloth, and ten sheafs of paper. The two *komorisō*, Kūichibō and Ryōshinbō, each received 100 *hiki* and ten bundles of plain paper.[82] Donations offered by the family on this day (3.11) are enumerated below (Table 1).

Table 1. Donations on 1345.3.11

Zenni Onkata (mother)	10 sheafs of *danshi*
Nyōbō Onkata	10 sheafs of *danshi*
Hime Goryō Onkata (sister)	10 sheafs of *danshi*
Moromori	10 pairs of sandals (*Tennōji zōri*)
Kūshō (deceased's younger brother)	10 sheafs of *danshi*
Nakahara Moroyumi	10 sheafs of plain paper (*zōshi*)
Nakahara Yūa	1 armrest (*yorikakari*)
Nakahara Zengaku	10 sheafs of *danshi*

With the exception of the sandals and the armrest, the donations consisted of different types of paper, writing paper (*danshi*) being the most common offering.

Kenshin did not visit her husband's grave until the following day (3.12), and Goryō was not permitted to approach her father's grave until 3.18. These prescriptions regarding visits were handed down by the Yin-Yang Master, based on special divinations. When the two women finally did go to Morosuke's grave, they traveled very early in the morning in palanquins (*koshi*) rather than in carriages (*kuruma*) like the men. Thus, throughout the forty-nine day period of mourning the mourners at the grave were almost exclusively men, with the exception of a group of nuns who performed *Nenbutsu* recitations at the grave. When the deceased's wife and daughter visited the grave, they either went early, before the graveside service, or stayed inside their palanquins at the site; sometimes they visited on days other than the official memorial days. They were kept apart from the male mourners probably because women were believed to be naturally polluted by their menstruations, and this pollution might be magnified to a dangerous degree when brought into contact with the impurity of the corpse.

Kōei 4 (1345) 3.12: *Hokke* Mandala Offering Ceremony

Although 3.12 was not one of the regular seventh-day memorials, the Yin-Yang Master's divinations had designated it as a day of particular good fortune (*kijitsu*). On this day, a Hokke (Lotus) mandala, believed to be efficacious in preventing calamities and increasing merit, was offered on Morosuke's behalf. The text does not describe the mandala, but extant examples suggest that it included Buddhist figures drawn within the petals of a lotus flower, similar to a Womb World mandala.[83] A simple meal was prepared for the priests and courtiers, who received it in the Drawing Room of the Nakahara residence. This was followed by the offering ceremony for the Hokke mandala (*Hokke mandara kuyō*). A treasured copy (*kohon*) of the *Lotus Sutra* was dedicated in the Fourth Chamber, where Morosuke had died. Priest Enshōbō presided over the dedication, assisted by Kūichibō and Ryōshinbō, who read the first lines from the *Lotus Sutra* being offered. Then the three priests together chanted lines from the *Juryō-bon*[84] and the *Kōmyō shingon*. On this day no requests were made for sutras, nor were any donations given to the priests for their chanting, probably because this was not a regularly scheduled memorial day. Similarly, there was no ritual bath after the ceremony and no official visits to the grave. According to the text, this procedure was in keeping with precedents set in the Enkyō (1308–1311) and Shōwa (1312–1317) eras. Earlier that morning Kenshin made a private visit, her first, to the grave, although her daughter, Goryō, could not accompany her because she had been ordered to practice ritual abstention.

The sixth seventh-day (3.18) memorial followed the pattern of the other five, but is notable because Goryō was permitted to visit her father's grave for the first time. Because the forty-nine days of deep mourning would end soon, on 3.23 the family requested that the Yin-Yang Master decide upon the next schedule of mourning events, which included placing horizontal beams inside and outside the gate of their residence, applying a chisel to the wooden flooring,[85] permitting the immediate family members to return to work, and holding the first monthly memorial.[86]

Kōei 4 (1345) 3.25: Sutra Requests and Dedications

The final seventh-day mourning ceremony for Morosuke took place on 3.25. Amid a light morning rain, Moroshige, Moromori, the two *komorisō*, two nuns, and a number of other family members and retainers traveled to the grave for the ceremony. The priests shook their staffs (*shakujō*) while chanting the *Hokyōin darani*, *Bonmō no jūjū*, and *Kōmyō shingon*. The nuns then performed the *Nenbutsu*. We are told that Goryō also visited the grave on this day, but remained in her palanquin; Kenshin is not mentioned. After everyone returned home, a repast was served to the seated courtiers and priests in the Drawing Room. Enshōbō performed the Buddhist service in the Fourth Chamber in front of a hanging scroll of Amida. The offerings for this memorial included "quick copies" (*tonsha*) of the *Lotus Sutra* written by members of the family. Additionally Kūichibō and Ryōshinbō read lines from an ancient copy of the sutra.

Then the three priests together recited the *Bonmō no jūjū* and *Kōmyō shingon* on behalf of the deceased. Next, two letters pledging donations and one folded paper (*origami*)[87] were presented to Kūichibō; the donations and supplementary gifts were taken to him later. On this day, twelve letters requesting sutra readings (*fujumon*) were sent to the priest; each included gifts of money (*zukyōmono*) of 30 *mon* each as payment. These were presented to the priest along with an "allowance" (*rokumotsu*) of 300 *mon*. One *kanmon* was donated for the final ritual fire ceremony (*goma kechigan*) that was to be performed on Morosuke's behalf, and 500 *mon* for his final Buddhist service (*reiji* [*sahō*] *kechigan*), which would be held at dusk. One *kanmon* was offered to beggers (*saka hinin*), one to prisoners, and donations of 200 *mon* each were given to the temples of Rokkakudō, Yūzūdō, and Ungoji.[88]

The giving of donations to prisoners and beggars was part of the general framework of charity supported by Buddhist temples in medieval Japan. Over time, however, if donations were not willingly proffered, the *hinin* (literally, "nonhumans")[89] began to demand them. Many *hinin* lived near the base of Kyoto's many hills (*saka*) and thus came to be called *saka hinin*. They sometimes transported corpses for the wealthy and claimed to be able to "purify" death pollution, further cementing their connection to the process of death in medieval Japan.[90]

After all was finished, the two *komorisō* withdrew from the room, followed by the two nuns. The carved Buddha image and other ritual implements that had been brought to the Fourth Chamber for the services were all returned to their original places in the Jibutsudō, the small chapel within the residential quarters. Thus the service for the final day of mourning ended successfully. On the following day (3.26) Moromori was permitted to eat fish for the first time since his father had died, and he could now return to work.

As at every seventh-day memorial, letters requesting sutra recitations were submitted to the priest Kūichibō. Moroshige, Moromori, Aki Nyūdō[91] (Engen), Shōgeki (Moroyumi), Hyōbu Daibu Nyūdō (Ryōen), Motokuni, Iekuni, Kunikane, Kenshin, Nyōbō Onkata, Hime Goryō, and the nun (*bikuni*) Keibutsu[92] wrote the requests at this memorial. Using essentially the same phrases, each letter states that the author was presenting donations to the priests on behalf of the deceased so that the deceased's spirit (*seirei*) might be delivered from the cycles of birth and death (*shutsuri shōji*) and live in Amida's Pure Land (*gokuraku*).

A few of the letters, however, include information about additional offerings that are of particular interest. In addition to the more common sutras mentioned above, one relative offered a donation for a priest's recitations of the thirty-third fascicle of the *Shuryōgongyō*, another for 30,000 repetitions of the *Kōmyō shingon*, a third offered a donation for readings of the forty-eighth fascicle of the *Amida kyō*, and one offered a painted image of an Amida Triad.[93] The deceased's wife, Kenshin, dedicated a copy of a painting of a *raigō sanzon*, an image of Amida, Kannon, and Seishi welcoming an aspirant into the Pure Land, and also a portrait of the deceased (*miei*); both were to be used for later memorials. The daughter, Goryō, offered a donation for invocations of Amida's name (*Amida nyorai myōgō*)[94] to be chanted one million times. Eleven individuals made additional donations as "meritorious acts" to increase merit for the deceased (*tsuizen kabuse*). Their donations included multiple sheaves of writing paper (*danshi*), twenty candles (*rōsoku*), one round straw mat (*mushiro*), ten pairs of straw sandals (*Tennōji zōri*), and one tea bowl (*chawan*).

Kōei 4 (1345) 3.30: Monthly Memorials

The Buddhist service for Morosuke's first monthly death memorial (*gakki*) was held on 3.30.[95] A light meal was first served to the priests and participants in the Drawing Room of the Nakahara residence. Then everyone moved to the Jibutsudō, where a wooden statue of Amida and an ancient copy of the *Lotus Sutra* were kept. Kūichibō and Ryōshinbō read lines from the *Lotus Sutra*. Kūichibō was in charge of the service and received one role of *kuzu*,[96] a bundle of seaweed, and one round straw mat for his services; Ryōshinbō also received a round mat. After the service the two priests visited Morosuke's grave unaccompanied by the family members; all was according to precedent. On this day offerings were presented both for the Buddha (*bukku*) and for Morosuke's spirit (*reiku*). We are told that the offerings for the spirit were prepared at the residence and taken to the grave by the priests because this was the way it had been done during the Shōwa era (1312–1317), but we are not given any information about the type of offerings. Throughout *Moromoriki* we are told that certain actions follow precedents set during earlier eras, particularly the Shōwa (1312–1317) and Enkyō (1308–1311) periods, suggesting that the family was using the funerals of recently deceased relatives as models for the rituals.

The format for this monthly memorial was clearly modeled after the seven sevens, but was simpler and shorter. Generally, only two priests presided, with Kūichibō officiating. But on the rare occasions when three priests attended, Enshōbō officiated (5.6). The text does not explain how the chief priest for each service was chosen, but probably the highest-ranking priest in attendance took charge of the service. The most common types of donations given to the attending priests for their performances at the monthly memorials were rolls of white cloth, various types of paper, and fans. Another important change was in the venue for the monthly memorials, which moved from the Fourth Chamber of the Nakahara residence to the small chapel, the Jibutsudō, located within the residential compound.

Even more interesting, the object of the offerings changed, suggesting that a crucial adjustment had taken place in the way the deceased was viewed. During the forty-nine-day period the deceased was addressed as he had been when *alive*, and the *extended* Nakahara family presented offerings on his behalf. After this period, however, Morosuke's *spirit* was recognized as the recipient of offerings prepared by the *nuclear family*. These changes seem to indicate that Morosuke was beginning to be viewed as a family ancestral spirit. Nonetheless, official Buddhist rites presided over by priests were still continued, as is attested by the hundred-day memorial and the annual memorial services described below.

The Japanese concept of the spirit is complicated. The ontological status of the dead, where they resided after death, the nature of their power, and even the efficacy of the rituals conducted for them are ambiguous. The goal of a Buddhist funeral and the offerings made during the subsequent forty-nine days was to enable the deceased to enter a Buddhist paradise or to attain a good rebirth. But Buddhism also provided rituals for the spirit well after that crucial period, usually until the thirty-third year after death. This practice probably developed in response to an ancient and prevailing notion that the spirits of the dead remained polluted (and in need of purification) and also dangerous (and in need of appeasement) for several decades before they could fully become family ancestral spirits. Such enduring pre-Buddhist ideas about the spirit, coupled with the reality of continuing financial benefit to temples performing the memorial ceremonies, undoubtedly encouraged the continued performance of Buddhist rituals long after there was any persuasive doctrinal need to do so.[97]

Kōei 4 (1345) 5.17: One Hundred-day Memorial

On the one-hundredth day after Morosuke died, a special memorial service was to be conducted.[98] Because this day (5.17) had been deemed inauspicious, the Yin-Yang Master ordered special sutra readings earlier in the week instead. The structure of this special memorial was similar to the final memorial (seventh seventh-day) of the forty-nine day period, with the *nijūgozanmai* performed the previous night (5.16) and a banquet for the participants held in the Drawing Room. Priests Kūichibō and Ryōshinbō chanted sections of the *Lotus Sutra* in unison, followed by recitations of the *Bonmō no jūjū* and the *Kōmyō shingon*. After the ceremony, Moromori presented two folded letters and the donations for the day to Kūichibō.

Moromori lists five items that were offered on his father's behalf that day: (1) a painting of Kongō Dainichi Nyorai; (2) a copy of the eleventh fascicle of the *Lotus Sutra*, part of which had been written by Morosuke before he died and was then completed by Moroshige, who also mounted it and added string and a title; (3) 1 *kan*, 500 *mon*, offered in place of copies of one part of the eleventh fascicle of the *Lotus Sutra*; (4) wooden grave tablets (*sotoba*), on which phrases from the *Lotus Sutra* were written by several mourners; and (5) a group recitation of Amida's name to generate merit for the deceased (*nijūgozanmai*) and the special *Nenbutsu* (*betsuji nenbutsu*) that had been performed the previous evening.

After the ceremony, the priests and mourners went to the grave hall, Ryōzenden, at the cemetery, and the *Bonmō no jūjū*, *Hōkyōin darani*, and *Kōmyō shingon* were performed followed by a *Nenbutsu* (*ichiji nenbutsu*). Thus, we learn that by the one-hundredth day, a hall had been built at the grave. The structure may have been as simple as four pillars and a roof, or something more substantial with walls. This memorial was bound to generate merit for the deceased, we are told, because not one thing was out of order. In other words, because the rituals were performed properly, it was believed that the merit produced by the actions and offerings would successfully transfer to Morosuke.

Jōwa 2 (1346) 2.6: First-year Memorial

Whereas the Buddhist service for the one-hundredth-day memorial took place in a room of the Nakahara residence, the first-year memorial (*ikkai ki*) was held in the Buddhist chapel at the residence, the Jibutsudō.[99] On 2.5, the day before the service, the small chapel was made splendid.[100] Two wooden statues were placed on the altar to serve as the main images—an Amida Nyorai and a Nyoirin Kannon, which was taken out of its container (suggesting it was a hidden Buddha, or *hibutsu*). A portrait (*eizō*) of the deceased, probably the same one Morosuke's wife, Kenshin, had dedicated at his forty-ninth-day memorial, was hung near the two Buddhist icons.

This is significant, because it was the first time that a portrait of Morosuke was displayed. Yet for the funerals of the Ashikaga shoguns just fifty years later, the portrait appeared much earlier, usually at the funeral, when it was hung in front of the corpse. The Nakahara seem to have been following an earlier tradition, popular with the court for centuries, of commissioning the portrait for later memorial services but not for the funeral itself. That Morosuke was (probably) buried rather than cremated, that many ancient customs, like destroying the *kamadogami*, were important features of his funeral, and that such an eclectic mix of sutras was recited throughout, suggests that his funeral did not closely conform to the typical format for Zen-style funerals.

On the day of the one-year memorial, the family began by visiting Morosuke's grave in the morning. Priests and family alike copied the *Lotus Sutra* (*Hoke kyō*, 8th fascicle), the *Heart Sutra* (*Hannya shingyō*) and the *Amida Sutra* (*Amida kyō*) throughout the day. The *komorisō* Kūichibō and Ryōshinbō arrived for the repast held for the participants in the Fourth Chamber. When the meal was finished, Enshōbō conducted the sermon in the Jibutsudō and read lines from a copy of the *Lotus Sutra* written by Morosuke before his death. The three priests together then chanted the *Bonmō no jūju* and *Kōmyō shingon*, while the men of the Nakahara family listened from the "southern resting place" and the women from the "northern resting place."[101] The reason the men and women were segregated in rooms located in different directions is likely related to Chinese yin-yang theory, in which yin is associated with the north, female, darkness, and passivity, and yang with the south, male, light and warmth, and activity. This is yet another example of the prominence of ancient traditions in Morosuke's mortuary rites.

After the ceremony the priests and mourners proceeded to the grave hall at Ryōzen. Moroshige and Moromori made the journey in a carriage, wearing plain black silk robes and carrying undecorated fans made of cypress wood. The proper rituals were performed at the hall, and the *Bonmō no jūjū*, *Hōkyōin darani*, and *Kōmyō shingon* were chanted. But, following an earlier precedent, the *Nenbutsu* was not recited on this day. The priest who tended the graves (*hakamori hōshi*) was presented with a gift of money. Then Moroshige's attendant placed phrases from the *Lotus Sutra* and the *Zuigu darani*[102] inside the grave enclosure (presumably these were written on wooden grave tablets). The text also notes that the family did not go out of mourning on this day. Although generally the immediate family would cease wearing mourning clothes after the first-year memorial, the Nakahara could not do so because Kenshin had died six months after her husband. Therefore, Moroshige and Moromori had to remain in official mourning until after their mother's one-year memorial ceremony in the eighth month.

Jōwa 3 (1347) 2.5: Third-year Memorial

The third-year memorial (*sankai ki*), held two years after Morosuke's death, was one of the last important death memorials conducted by the priests for the family.[103] On the evening before the fifth day of the second month of 1347 (this memorial was moved up one day by the Yin-Yang Master for various reasons), the Jibutsudō at the Nakahara residence was made splendid once again by installing the images for the ceremony. First the two wooden sculptures of Amida and Nyoirin Kannon were enshrined. Then a new painting of an Amida Triad with portraits (*eizō*) of both parents, Morosuke and Kenshin (also now deceased), was installed near the two statues. The painter (*eshi*) Sōen Hōgen had prepared the paintings at a cost of 300 *hiki*.[104] The morning was spent copying the *Lotus Sutra* (8th fascicle) and phrases from the *Heart Sutra* and the *Amida Sutra*. Four priests attended this ceremony, one more than usual, emphasizing its importance in the ritual sequence. The repast was served in the south side of the Fourth Chamber of the residence, attended by the four priests, the deceased's two sons, and three other guests. Everyone then moved to the Jibutsudō for the service, officiated by Priest Enshōbō. Sections of the *Lotus Sutra* were read, followed by sections of the *Bonmō no jūjū* and *Kōmyō shingon*. Once again, during the recitations, the men sat in the "southern resting place" and the women in the "northern resting place." Letters requesting sutras were given directly to Ryōshinbō at this time, and the donations were sent to him the following day.[105] The participants visited the grave, where the priests again chanted the *Bonmō no juju*, *Hōkyōin darani*, and *Kōmyō shingon* and the nuns performed the *Nenbutsu*. Although no memorial services were held on the following day (2.6), a number of priests chanted sutras throughout the day to commemorate the actual death date.[106]

Nakahara Kenshin (1289–1345)

Kōei 4 (1345) 8.23: Death and Burial

As mentioned earlier, Moromori's mother, Gozen Onkata, died in this same year on 8.23 at about six o'clock in the evening at the age of fifty-seven.[107] After taking Buddhist vows on 2.19, she was known by her Buddhist name, Kenshin. She became ill shortly after taking those vows, and various medical treatments were unavailing. Keibutsubō[108] and Kōichibō, who attended her deathbed as her religious guides (*chishiki*), chanted the *Nenbutsu* with her forty-two times, and then she closed her eyes.[109] Kenshin's death only six months after her husband's was difficult for the family, who once again had to face the loss of a loved one, the division-of-possessions ceremony (*sōzoku no gi*),[110] and yet another period of mourning. Shinshōbō Rōken, the esteemed priest (*chōrō*) of Kenshin's temple, the Jizōdō, decided that the funeral and schedule of memorials should follow ritual precedents set at the time of her paternal grandmother's death in the Bunei period (1264–1275) and her mother-in-law's death in the Karyaku period (1326–1329). Although the basic ritual structure designed for Kenshin was the same as that for Morosuke, some notable differences are apparent.

One important difference is that Kenshin's funeral and the actions that preceded it are better documented, because the text is intact. On the night of 8.23, between nine and eleven p.m., we are told that her body was carried out of the Nakahara residence in secret on a palanquin and taken to the Jizōdō, a subtemple of Hōjiji at Shijō Bōmon.[111] Moving the corpse in secret and at night was another practice continued from the Heian period. It was devised to limit the number of people who came in contact with the pollution associated with the corpse and also to hinder wandering spirits from attaching themselves to the body. The text suggests that the sect affiliation of Kenshin's temple was Ikkō, which means they were Pure Land, but the term could refer either to the Ikkō-ha, a subsect of the Ji sect, or to the Ikkō-shū, another name for the Shin or True Pure Land sect. Itō Yuishin argues that the priests of the Jizōdō belonged to the former for two reasons: (1) the Ji sect, founded by Ippen, were believers in Jizō, and many Ji sect temples, including the one discussed here, enshrined images of this bodhisattva; and (2) the Ji sect was particularly vigorous at this time in the early decades of the fourteenth century.[112]

After priests performed the proper rituals (not described in the text), the body was immediately carried to the hall at Ryōzen that same night and buried (*dosō*) in accordance with the precedents they were following. This may mean that Kenshin was buried near the hall or even inside it, perhaps under the altar, a fairly common practice for imperial women in the Heian period.[113] The hearth-fire god (*kamadogami*) was also carried to Ryōzen on this day, as it had been for

Morosuke, and the priests again performed the proper rituals when it arrived. The nuns (*komorini*) then went into seclusion. From this we know that it was customary for nuns to seclude themselves when a woman died.

On 8.26 Moromori went to the Jizōdō to present money for sutras to be read and to make offerings to the Amida Triad and to the sacred images (*katashiro*) of his father, his mother, Kenshin, and his deceased sister, Gakumyō. Generally, *katashiro*, "alternate or proxy forms or shapes," are paper images of humans used by the Yin-Yang Master for purification ceremonies involving ablutions or for exorcisms that transport misfortune from the body to the proxy, which is then disposed of, usually by throwing it into a river. The "proxy forms" here, however, were likely portraits of Moromori's deceased relatives. Thus, it appears that the family had anticipated Kenshin's demise, probably because she was ill for so long, and had had a portrait prepared for use when needed. Morosuke's portrait, on the other hand, was not mentioned until his final memorial (on the forty-ninth day) when Kenshin had it dedicated, suggesting that his death was probably unexpected and the portrait had to be commissioned after he died.

The chronology of events tells us that Kenshin was taken to the Jizōdō only hours after she died on the evening of 8.23, and that her body was then transported to the cemetery where she was buried either later that night or very early the next morning. We are not told how the corpse was treated, who participated, or where the encoffining took place. The burial was extremely quick, no doubt in part because of the warm weather at that time of year. Because Kenshin had been ill for so many months, it is also likely that the relatives had given some previous thought to her funeral. In addition, Kenshin herself may have made certain preparations, although none are mentioned.

Kōei 4 (1345) 8.27: Problems in Scheduling the Memorials

On 8.27 the Yin-Yang Master appeared at the gate of the Nakahara residence to discuss the schedule of mourning for Kenshin.[114] His recommendations to the family were complicated by several problems. The first was that Kenshin's death had occurred while the family was still in mourning for her husband. If the dates of Kenshin's memorials followed convention, one of her seven seventh days would fall on her husband's monthly memorial. We are not told why this would be a problem, but the Yin-Yang Master was concerned enough to suggest certain changes to her memorial schedule. Another problem was that Priest Rōken of the Jizōdō, even before the Yin-Yang Master was consulted, had made some of his own decisions about the funeral and the mourning rituals to follow, so that they would comply with earlier precedents. Thus, in some matters the diviner was circumvented and perhaps even contravened. Third, the seventh day after Kenshin's death was 8.29, which happened to be the day of an important seventh-year memorial service for Emperor Go-Daigo (d. 1339.8.16) at Tenryūji.[115] Also, 8.29 fell on an inauspicious day for her eldest son, making changes in the ritual schedule even more imperative.

Because of these problems and conflicts, the Yin-Yang Master attempted to alter the regular schedule of memorials for Kenshin. He divined that there was no need for the ceremony for changing clothes, probably because the family was still in mourning for Morosuke, and that only a short memorial service should be held on 8.29, with a grander Buddhist ceremony delayed until 9.3. Visits to the grave were also delayed until 9.3, the date of the first full memorial ceremony (which was really her second seventh-day memorial). These recommendations were problematic for the family, who questioned him in depth about them. The change of date of the first memorial would cause distress throughout the forty-nine-day period because it would alter all subsequent memorials, and it meant that two ceremonies had to be planned for each—a minor remembrance on the proper original day and the official ceremony on the day recommended by the diviner. Nonetheless, assured that no harm would befall Kenshin as a result of the delay of the first service and the other changes, the family ultimately agreed to follow the diviner's altered schedule.

Therefore, on 8.29 the Ikkō priests held a small ceremony at the Jizōdō, but sutras and mourning talisman cards were omitted on this day. One or two priests went to the grave unaccompanied by the family, commanded to do so by the head of the Jizōdō (and in opposition to the Yin-Yang Master's recommendation). Offerings were made at the temple to the image of Fudō. As there is no indication that new images were made for Kenshin's memorials, it is likely that because Kenshin and her husband's deaths were so close together the same painted images were used throughout Kenshin's offering ceremonies.

The second seventh-day memorial was held on 9.3, the date prescribed by the Yin-Yang Master, who had moved the date back from 9.6. The mourning talisman was properly set up at the great gate of the Nakahara residence before Rōken, the head priest of the Jizōdō, accompanied by an acolyte, arrived around noon. The clergy and family partook of a meal and attended the sermon. The invited priests read from the *Lotus Sutra* and that sutra was copied onto grave tablets; offerings were made to the Yakushi Nyorai image on this day. The head priest received donations of 100 *hiki*,[116] and family members gave additional gifts of various types of paper. The donations for the first memorial were also collected on this day. After the sermon, the priests chanted the [*Hōkyōin*] *darani*, *Kōmyō shingon*, *Nenbutsu*, and the *Lotus Sutra*. Moromori and his sister Goryō visited the grave privately, but Moroshige, the eldest son, was suffering from a fever and could not go. In fact, Moroshige was ill throughout most of the forty-nine days of mourning for Kenshin and was absent from the funeral and unable to attend many of the memorials.

On 9.6, the correct day for Kenshin's second memorial, Morosuke's monthly memorial (*gakki*) was held as scheduled. Kenshin's third seventh-day memorial was held on 9.13, her fourth on 9.20, fifth on 9.27, sixth on 10.5, and the final memorial on 10.10 (moved back two days from 10.12). Whenever one of Kenshin's memorials was moved to a different date so as not to conflict with one of her husband's, either Moromori or Moroshige took it upon himself to make offerings to her spirit (*goryō*) at the Jizōdō, with more complete Buddhist services held at the residence on the alternative days designated by the Yin-Yang Master. As discussed earlier, no mention was made of offerings to Morosuke's spirit until after the forty-nine days of deep mourning for him. Thus, private offerings by family members without the participation of Buddhist priests seem to have been viewed as veneration of an ancestor, whereas offerings made under Buddhist priestly auspices were specifically intended to generate merit on behalf of the deceased.

The major difference between the memorials held for Morosuke and those for Kenshin is that Kenshin's were simpler and shorter. Morosuke's memorials occurred more regularly and continued for a longer period of time—fifty-four monthly memorials are recorded for him in *Moromoriki*, but only forty-three for Kenshin. This may indicate that the memorial schedule for male heads of families commanded more time and more resources than that for their wives.

Jōwa 1 (1345) 11.28: A Gravestone for Kenshin

There were other significant differences as well. A comparison of Kenshin's and Morosuke's gravestones is instructive.[117] On 11.11 the family first discussed the matter of Kenshin's gravestone with Priest Rōken of the Jizōdō. On the following day the Yin-Yang Master was sent a request to decide on a schedule for erecting the stone. On 11.16 a sum of money (3 *kan*, 500 *mon*) was sent to the Jizōdō to pay for the stone and grave enclosure.

Kenshin's gravestone was put in place less than two weeks later, on 11.28 of 1345.[118] Moroshige visited his mother's grave together with Moromori, the head priest of the Jizōdō, and one of his acolytes to erect the gravestone. The text is clear that the Ikkō priests were responsible for Kenshin's stone and its proper placement. The stone was exactly 3 *shaku* tall (about 3 feet), slightly shorter than Morosuke's stone at 3 *shaku* and 3 *sun*. An enclosure was erected around the grave. Sanskrit letters had been written on both Morosuke's gravestone and his enclosure, but no mention is made of writing on Kenshin's. The most notable difference between the two gravestones, however, is the timing of their placement. Morosuke's gravestone was erected one month after he died; Kenshin's was not put in place until just before her one-hundredth-day memorial (11.30). This may represent traditional timing for men and women, but it is more likely that the time for erecting gravestones was not yet codified in the mid-fourteenth century. Itō Yuishin concurs that this was likely the case, but also believes that for legitimate heirs of the lineage it was standard to erect the gravestone before the fifth seventh-day memorial (thirty-five days after death) and to hold the offering ceremony for the grave tablets during that fifth memorial.[119] Thus, the difference in timing may have resulted from Kenshin's social position—she did not belong to the Nakahara lineage—as well as her gender.

Jōwa 1 (1345) 11.30: Kenshin's One Hundredth-day Memorial

The structure of Kenshin's ceremony was similar to Morosuke's one-hundredth-day memorial, but the payments of money and gifts made on her behalf differed significantly in quantity and quality from Morosuke's. I have compared the offerings below in Table 2.

The results show that Morosuke's memorial was more costly—over three times more expensive—and was attended by a greater number of mourners (and thus more contributors).[120] The amount of money given to the priest in

Table 2. Donations on Kenshin's and Morosuke's 100th-day Memorials

Donations (*fuse*)	Kenshin	Morosuke
Chief priest	300 *hiki*	1,000 *hiki*
	wakame—1 bundle	cotton—3 *ryō*
	silk cloth and *kesa*	cloth of paulownia flowers—1 roll
		white linen/hemp cloth—10 quires
		wakame—1 bundle
Invited priests	3 *ren*	300 *chōmoku* each
	wakame—1 bundle	
Invited nuns	3 *ren*	
Additional donations (*kabuse*)		
	danshi—10 quires	*danshi*—10 quires
	white cloth—1 *tan*	white cloth—1 *tan*
	chōmoku 100 *hiki*	*danshi*—10 quires
	zōshi—10 quires	*danshi*—10 quires
	zōshi—10 quires	*mushiro*—1
		chōmoku 100 *hiki*
		danshi—10 quires
		danshi—10 quires
		danshi—10 quires
		danshi—10 quires

charge of Morosuke's memorial service was considerably greater than the amount given to the priest of the Jizōdō and, in general, the gifts presented at Morosuke's memorial were of higher quality (i.e., *danshi* is a high-quality paper compared with the more common *zōshi*). Furthermore, apart from her two sons, women initiated all the offerings at Kenshin's memorial. For Morosuke, all contributors were men, except for his wife, his daughter, and the wife of his eldest son, Moroshige. Rituals on behalf of deceased family members and donations for the performances of these rituals must have placed heavy burdens on the family's time, and if the payments made to ritual specialists throughout the lifetime of an individual were tallied, the total would be staggering.[121]

Comparing the Mortuary Rites for Morosuke and Kenshin

From the two preceding accounts we see how differently the deaths of a husband and wife were approached. In general, fewer sutras were recited at Kenshin's memorial services, and they were of a different type from those chanted for Morosuke. Most notably, her rites were short of Esoteric sutras and incantations, such as the *Bonmō no jūjū*, *Hōkyōin darani*, and *Kōmyō shingon*, which were regularly recited at Morosuke's memorial services and also during visits to his grave. No sutras are even mentioned in the text for Kenshin until her second seventh day on 9.3 (which was also her first official memorial) when, we are told, the *Lotus Sutra* was copied onto grave tablets and the [*Hōkyōin*] *darani*, *Kōmyō shingon*, and *Lotus Sutra* were chanted during the service. Throughout the forty-nine-day period, the *Lotus Sutra* was most often the sutra copied onto grave tablets for Kenshin,[122] but this, the second memorial, appears to be the only time that recitations of the [*Hōkyōin*] *darani* and *Kōmyō shingon* were included in her Buddhist services. On 9.20, Kenshin's fourth-week memorial, only the *Lotus Sutra* was recited at the service. Moromori on his own, however, recited six hundred repetitions of the *Kōmyō shingon* on this occasion to help his mother attain deliverance from transmigration (*tokudatsu*) and to transfer merit (*ekō*) to her.[123] For Kenshin's forty-ninth-day memorial service on 10.10, phrases of the *Myōhō renge kyō* were copied onto *sotoba* and Moroshige offered a written request for additional copies of the *Myōhō renge kyō*,[124] *Kaiketsu no nikyō*,[125] *Hannya shingyō*,[126] and *Amida kyō*[127] to be made on his mother's behalf.[128] Thus, the sutras recited at Kenshin's memorials were those commonly associated with Pure Land sects; only male members of the family offered a wider variety of sutras for their mother.[129] The types of sutras recited at the service and the grave for Kenshin are quite different from the more eclectic mix presented for Morosuke.

This observation also points up other interesting variations between the funerals and memorial rituals held for Morosuke and those for Kenshin. Both husband and wife were interred at Ryōzen, because this was the Nakahara family cemetery. Ryōzen, located in Kyoto's eastern hills near Kiyomizu temple, had been a well-known burial site since at least the Heian period. It was one of the three largest cemeteries in the Kyoto area, along with Toribeno, also in the eastern hills, and Funaoka Nishino, northwest of the city. At the time of Morosuke's death, a Tendai temple overseen by Ryōzen Hōin Chōkan was located near the Ryōzen cemetary.[130] But Higuchidera managed the Nakahara graves.[131] Thus, it appears that when a man of the Nakahara family died, the head priest of Higuchidera, at this time Kūichibō, arranged the funeral and attended to the placement of the gravestone. But when a woman died, Rōken, the head priest of the Jizōdō, along with the Rokujō nuns (probably Rokujō Jishū, a form of Pure Land founded by Ippen) had great influence over the funeral and memorial rituals that followed.

In general, Buddhist priests had much more authority over the events of Kenshin's funeral than over Morosuke's. The Ikkō priests forestalled or successfully opposed some of the Yin-Yang Master's scheduling recommendations in arranging Kenshin's funeral and memorials, and they took complete charge of her grave marker, which they erected two days before the one-hundredth day memorial on 11.30. For Morosuke's rituals, the Yin-Yang Master set the dates and Kūichibō oversaw the details. In the fifteenth-century examples discussed in the next chapter, it is clear that the Yin-Yang Master became further marginalized, as temple priests actively managed more of the scheduling.

The formidable influence of the Yin-Yang Master and of rituals peculiar to *onmyōdō* in the funerals of the Nakahara may be attributed in part to their hereditary government position. As Senior Secretary (fourth rank), Nakahara Morosuke and his sons worked in the Archives Office of the Imperial Palace. They had little political clout but considerable knowledge of the *onmyōdō* texts that were housed in the archives, and they were often asked to assist other courtiers in looking up precedents for ritual practices in these texts.[132] Thus their familiarity with yin-yang practices had a significant impact on the way they conducted their funeral rituals. For example, it was the Yin-Yang Master, not the Buddhist priest, who divined the schedule for the placement of Morosuke's memorial stone (1345.3.6), dictated when the mother and daughter could first visit Morosuke's grave (3.12 and 3.18), and decided when the courtiers could approach Kenshin's grave (9.3). The Yin-Yang Master also divined the schedule for erecting her gravestone and for her monthly memorials, although the family questioned and the Ji sect priests overturned some of his recommendations. The influence of the Yin-Yang Master in the lives of the Nakahara was not limited to funerals and memorials. Throughout *Moromoriki*, yin-yang experts were consulted to determine the timing of the family's most important decisions and events, including repairs to the residence, funerals and marriages, and performance of various astrological rituals.

There is another point of contrast in the mortuary activities for Morosuke and Kenshin: although they were buried at the same cemetery,[133] their spirits were venerated at separate sites. When and why this tradition began is an interesting topic for further research, but the practice of venerating male and female spirits at separate sites did not apply only to Morosuke and Kenshin in the mid-fourteenth century. It appears to have been practiced for at least several generations in the Nakahara family, because throughout *Moromoriki* we find that the majority of monthly memorials (*gakki*) and later memorials (*onki*)[134] for male ancestors took place at Higuchidera and for females at the Jizōdō. Death memorials conducted in the Jibutsudō of the residence were for immediate relatives, parents, and siblings, whereas those at Higuchidera were for earlier generations of ancestors.[135] Thus, ancestors known personally by the living were literally kept "close to home"; only as names and faces faded from memory were ancestors' memorials moved to family-connected temples outside the residence.

Moromoriki provides abundant information about the memorial services held for two members of a family of court officials in the mid-fourteenth century, but because the text is not forthcoming about how the corpse was treated or, more important for this study, about the funeral itself or the role played by objects in it, it is necessary to seek this information in other sources. A number of extant sources fully document the funerals of Zen priests in the fourteenth century, but few do the same for lay individuals.[136] Additional examples for other social groups such as the military elite would be helpful in documenting how lay funerals changed from the fourteenth to the fifteenth century. In particular, we should like to know how closely other lay funerals in the fourteenth century were modeled on funerals for Zen abbots and whether they included the nine special rites for the deceased, including the display of the portrait at the funeral. Unfortunately, few records exist from the Nanbokuchō period. The first Ashikaga shogun, Takauji (1305–1358) died in Enbun 3.4.30, and an account of his funeral, for example, would supplement the information in *Moromoriki*. But little is known about Takauji's funeral, other than that a Zen funeral was held at Shinnyoji on 1358.5.2, and that the seven memorial services followed at Tōjiji at regular intervals.[137] The only mention of any image at Takauji's funeral states that, on the day of his final memorial service (6.17) a standing image of Jizō Bosatsu was displayed.[138] One year after he died, a portrait of Takauji was dedicated. But this portrait and others were commissioned for later memorial services; there is no indication that any portrait was displayed at the funeral or during the forty-nine-day period of mourning.[139]

One source, *Taiheiki*, suggests that the funeral for Takauji included a number of important characteristics that made it comparable to later Zen-style funerals, and therefore very different from the funerals for the Nakahara. *Taiheiki* notes that priests performed the special rituals for closing the coffin lid (*sagan*), moving the corpse to the cremation site (*kigan*), offering tea (*tencha*) and water (*tentō*) to the corpse, and lighting the cremation fire (*ako*)—none of which were recorded for either Morosuke or Kenshin.[140] Mention of these rituals suggests that Takauji's funeral contained many of the major components associated with the Zen-style funerals performed for later Ashikaga shoguns, but the source is somewhat suspect because it is not contemporary with Takauji's death, although the narrative covers the appropriate time period from 1318 to 1367. Because *Taiheiki* is a prose narrative, written at various stages by many people, it is difficult to know if such rituals were actually performed for Takauji or whether they were added to the story at a later date because they became important for the funerals of succeeding Ashikaga shoguns.[141] Therefore the next chapter will attempt to answer some of the questions that remain about the structure of the later rituals and the use of objects in funerals from the fifteenth century.

FUNERALS IN THE FIFTEENTH CENTURY 2

By the first half of the fifteenth century, changes had been made to the basic structure of the funeral that resulted in the codification of key rituals, or at least parts of them. The most extensive evidence of that systematization can be seen in the descriptions of the lying-in-state period of the corpse and of the cremation. Nonetheless, although the four funerals discussed in this chapter contain new components borrowed from Chinese Chan Buddhist funeral traditions, we still find ample evidence of a powerful residual tradition of earlier Japanese funerary practices.

Surprisingly vivid details about the process of the lying-in-state period and the subsequent funeral services can be found in four fifteenth-century records—*Jishōindono ryōan sōbo* (Complete record of national mourning for Jishōin), *Kanmon gyoki* (Record of things seen and heard), *Kennaiki* (Record of Kenshōin Naifu Madenokōji Tokifusa), and *Inryōken nichiroku* (Daily record of the Inryōken [a cloister within Rokuon'in]).

The four texts examined relate important mortuary practices immediately after the deaths of each of four influential figures in the fifteenth century—Ashikaga Yoshimitsu (d. 1408), the imperial prince Yoshihito (d. 1416), Ashikaga Yoshimochi (d. 1428), and Hino Shigeko (d. 1463)—including information about the treatment, movement, and placement of the body between the time of death and the time of cremation, and particulars about the objects used during the rituals and the construction of the cremation sites. All of these funerals except the last took place in the first half of the fifteenth century, and Shigeko's not much later, and their similarities far exceed their differences. The surviving accounts offer far more mortuary detail than we have for the mid-fourteenth-century funerals of Nakahara Morosuke and Kenshin (Chap. 1).

The four case studies are intended to familiarize the reader with the general organization of fifteenth-century funerals and with the essential rituals that accompanied the deaths of important individuals. These case studies also serve to introduce the most important ritual implements used in the new style of funerals. Although chronologically the funeral of Ashikaga Yoshimitsu (d. 1408.5.6) is the earliest of the four examined in this chapter, I have chosen to place it last, because two pivotal diagrams of his funeral illustrate precisely and effectively how the various objects and implements discussed in the previous sections were arranged.

Prince Yoshihito (1361–1416)

The funeral of Prince Yoshihito, a son of Emperor Sukō (1334–1398) of the Northern Dynasty and an heir to the throne, was held on 1416.11.24.[1] Yoshihito's second son, Prince (*shinnō*) Fushiminomiya Sadafusa, both participated in the funeral proceedings and recorded them in his diary, *Kanmon gyoki*.[2] William Bodiford described Yoshihito's funeral as "an excellent example of a Zen funeral for an affluent patron,"[3] but in fact *Kanmon gyoki* describes many practices associated with ancient imperial funerals.

Ōei 23 (1416) 11.20: Incantations and Folding Screens

On 1416.11.20,[4] the text tells us, Prince Yoshihito was near death. He had been ill for nearly a year, during which time priests had tried innumerable Buddhist incantations (*kaji*) to heal him. Now, however, he was unable to swallow food or water, and as Buddhist nuns (*bikuni*)[5] chanted sutras, he closed his eyes and died.[6] Those who had attended him wept at his passing, and the senior monk (*chōrō*) of Daikōmyōji made incense offerings on his behalf. Daikōmyōji served as a major mortuary temple (*bodaiji*) for the Northern line of the imperial family in the fourteenth century. In 1336, when Emperor Go-Fushimi died, his empress, Kōgimonin (Fujiwara Neishi), took the tonsure and became a nun. In 1339 she had Daikōmyōji built near the Fushimi Palace in Go-Fushimi's memory.[7] The first three emperors of the Northern Dynasty, Kōgon, Kōmyō, and Yoshihito's father, Sukō, were interred at the temple's burial grounds, and this Zen temple played an important role in Prince Yoshihito's funeral.

Planning began immediately for Yoshihito's funeral and cremation (*dabi*),[8] which was to be held four days later, on 11.24. The monks of Daikōmyōji, in consultation with various court officials and priests of other important temples, decided the schedule of events for the funeral. Yoshihito was to be cremated, following the precedent of his father and a long tradition of imperial cremations going back to that of Empress Jitō in the early eighth century. Yoshihito's funeral was to be less elaborate than his father's, presumably because he died a prince, not an emperor. It was made known that his wife intended to take the tonsure.

The special Buddhist healing incantations used when Yoshihito seriously ill were not new in the fifteenth century. Described as an esoteric healing technique, *kaji* had been brought to Japan in the ninth century by Priest Kūkai (773–835) and used for healing illnesses, along with traditional Chinese medicine.[9] Evidence abounds that members of the court used Buddhist incantations as aids to ward off illness and death in eleventh- and twelfth-century tales such as *Genji monogatari* and *Eiga monogatari*, but the term is even older, appearing in ancient Buddhist texts such as the Garland Sutra (*Kegon kyō*). *Kaji* (Skt. *adhisthāna*) are defined as special prayers that allow the Buddha's power to be transferred to sentient beings in order to protect them.[10] Early attempts to cope with death in Japan included protection of the living *and* the deceased—in other words, protecting the living from pollution by the corpse and keeping the unburied or uncremated corpse safe from rampaging angry spirits that might wish to harm it.[11] Buddhism became popular with the early court in part because it offered powerful protective phrases against these spirits and against death's pollution of the living; Buddhism also provided clerics who were willing to come in contact with the dead. The latter represented a significant refinement over the ancient practice of simply abandoning the ill and infirm in fields, along rivers and roadways, and in public gateways as a way of keeping the pollution associated with death far from the living.[12]

The spells and invocations performed by Buddhist priests, often self-ordained wandering ascetic monks called *hijiri*, at the Heian court (794–1185) were primarily designed to drive away malevolent spirits attempting to invade the ill or moribund body. Thus, it is clear that such spirits were believed to contribute to death. Probably before Buddhism, and certainly along with it, rituals were developed or adopted to deal with them. In ancient Japan, in order to invigorate and keep the individual's own spirit in the body (and thereby prevent spirits from inhabiting it), soul-shaking (*tamafuri*) or soul-quieting (*tamashizume*) rituals were performed on the dying.[13] When a person actually stopped breathing, however, it was reasoned that the spirit had become separated from the body and could not find its way back. In such instances, it was first necessary to ascertain if it would return. Most often people simply waited and prayed for several hours or overnight to see if the spirit would reappear, after which attempts might be made to recall it to the body through a special soul-summoning ritual, called *tamayobi* or *shōkon*.[14] This ritual consisted of a relative carrying a robe that belonged to the deceased up onto the roof of the building that housed the corpse, facing north, and calling the deceased's name three times while waving the robe.[15] The ritual, which originated in China, appears to have been practiced regularly in ancient Japan, but only sporadically by the imperial family and members of the court in the eleventh century.[16] Although the ritual itself is seldom mentioned thereafter, countless written accounts describe weeping courtiers crying out to the deceased to return, unable to comprehend that the person had gone.[17] The grief so openly expressed in these early texts suggests the influence of Chinese Confucian customs, in which emotional expressions of loss and long mourning periods were considered proper filial behavior.

It appears, then, that people customarily continued to feel strongly that the spirit left the body at death and to hope fervently for its return. As Buddhism became more established, a specifically Buddhist rite for calling back the soul was also practiced in Japan, with most examples dating from the twelfth century or later.[18] Most likely, this Buddhist rite appropriated the earlier role of *tamayobi*, which does not appear in medieval sources. Most medieval descriptions of death, however, describe a considerably more restrained set of practices than those found in earlier texts. Thus, the new Zen Buddhist rituals seem to have replaced some of the earlier Confucian-based practices surrounding death in Japan and resulted in the effective channeling of people's raw emotions into different ritual forms.

In the evening of 11.20, after determining Yoshihito's death, the priests of Daikōmyōji shaved his head (*rakuhatsu*), bathed his body (*mokuyoku*) and dressed it in new robes, and moved it to a raised straw mat. Folding screens (*byōbu*) were set up around the corpse in the Daily Life Palace (*tsune gosho*) of the Fushimi Palace,[19] while monks chanted the *Kōmyō shingon* mantra.[20] It is likely, although not explicitly noted in *Kanmon gyoki*, that the priests also performed a ritual called *dosha kaji*, where sand invested with this mantra was sprinkled on the body, to remove evil karma and enable Yoshihito to attain Paradise. *Kichiji shidai*, a late eleventh-century manual written to regulate imperial funerals, stipulated that the special sand should be sprinkled over a paper or raw silk shroud (*hikiōi*) in the area of the head, chest, and feet.[21]

The actions of the Daikōmyōji priests were fairly standard. Shaving the head, bathing the body, dressing it in clean robes, and setting up folding screens around the dead or dying individual can be documented in Japan from at least the early eleventh century.[22] As it was believed that malignant spirits could travel only in straight lines, angled folding screens protected the body from such presences seeking to inhabit it now that its own spirit had fled. Shaving the head and giving Buddhist precepts effectively accorded a layperson the same rights as a monk to a Buddhist funeral. Yoshihito's ordination is not mentioned in *Kanmon gyoki* for this date, but it may have taken place before his death.[23] During the Heian period close attendants of the deceased usually assumed responsibility for bathing the corpse, which entailed wiping the face, hands, and feet with a leaf of *shikimi* "Japanese star anise"[24] dipped in water while calling the deceased's name twice.[25] By the medieval period, however, it was more commonly Buddhist priests who performed the task of bathing the body. Clearly, the substitution of priests for family members and household attendants in the funeral preparations was directly related to the sophistication and complexity of the newly introduced Zen-style rituals and to the development of strategies to manage pollution. It was no longer feasible for elite families to attempt to perform all of the new rituals correctly themselves, and over time they became dependent on Buddhist priests for almost every act connected with a death.

Generally, folding screens or cloth curtains hanging from stands (*kichō*) used in conjunction with death were reversed, placed with the decorated sides facing away from the deceased. When Fujiwara Kishi died (1025), for example, we are told that the corpse was laid out with her head to the north and that the curtain stands and screens in the room were reversed.[26] *Kanmon gyoki* does not stipulate whether the screens were reversed, so we cannot say with certainty that this was done for Prince Yoshihito. Reversing the screens might be interpreted in several ways. The reversed screens certainly emphasized that the situation was not a "normal" one, and thereby served as a visual marker that the state of death was different from that of life. Screens also served as perceptible boundaries between the living and the dead, keeping death contained and separated from the living outside.

Ōei 23 (1416) 11.21: Calling for the Will and Recitations for Divine Protection

On 11.21 a number of people arrived at the Fushimi residence south of Kyoto to plan the cremation.[27] Yoshihito's will or last testament (*okibumi*) was now requested and consulted. His testament dictated every aspect of the funeral—the head of Kongōin (a subtemple of Tenryūji) would light the cremation fire, the head of Hatsukadō would recite sutras and *darani*, the senior monk of Daikōmyōji would perform the ceremony for the cremated remains (*kotsu butsuji*), the forty-ninth-day memorial services (*chūin no gi*) would be held at that temple, and so forth. The will also stipulated that ten monks should go into seclusion as *komorisō*. Haste was urged in all proceedings because it was near the end of the year, when preparations for the New Year got under way. The temple priests decided that Yoshihito's cremation would take place three days later, on 11.24. Yoshihito's wife and other women of the court took the tonsure immediately (on 11.21) and later that evening a group of nuns (*bikuni*) arrived to chant sutras.

Yoshihito's wife's tonsure was probably a ceremony performed for the sake of form. In contrast to Morosuke's wife, no mention was made of Yoshihito's wife receiving any precepts. This suggests that her tonsure was not a full renunciation. It also took place very soon, also in contrast to Morusuke's wife, who did not cut her hair until the second seventh day of mourning (two weeks after he died). The timing of this event does not appear to have been set. Most likely a tonsure was performed whenever it was expedient for both parties. Nonetheless, the head priest of Busshuji performed the tonsure, indicating that it was an important event.

It was fairly common for members of the medieval elite to make known their preferences regarding their funerals by writing a letter or by orally confiding their desires (*yuigon*) to a priest or close friend or relative. Generally, these *yuigon* specified the individual's preference for burial or cremation, noted whom they wished to perform certain parts of the funeral, and sometimes stipulated which sutras they wanted read.

Kanmon gyoki mentions that *nenju* were to be recited during the cremation. *Nenju* are declamations that may include passages from sutras (*kyōmon*), the sacred name of a buddha (*myōgō*), and mantras (*shingon*) that were recited to elicit divine protection.[28] Such phrases were used in many situations where protection was desired, but particularly when someone died. In relation to death, *Kichiji shidai* indicates that priests and close retainers of the deceased recited *nenju*, burned incense (*meikō*), and used vinegar (*su*) as means to protect the corpse from harm immediately after death.[29] Although *Kichiji shidai* does not mention the recitation of *nenju* during cremation, this entry in *Kanmon gyoki* verifies that these utterances were used then as well to evoke special protection, probably because cremation was a dangerous time during which the deceased was permanently separated from the living and the body from the spirit.

Ōei 23 (1416) 11.22: Condolence Calls and Preparations

Important visitors, including senior monks from imperial temples, nuns from Shinjōin, and a number of government officials, called at the palace and made offerings of incense on Yoshihito's behalf. A group of forty-five Zen monks arrived from Fukakusa to read sutras for the deceased.[30]

Ōei 23 (1416) 11.23: Moving the Corpse

As Yoshihito had died in the Daily Life Palace of the Fushimi Palace, his body remained there for three days until it was moved to Daikōmyōji in a secret ceremony (*mitsugi*) that took place between three and five a.m. (*tora no koku*) on 11.23.[31] Before moving the corpse to the temple, the monks prepared the body (*songi*)[32] and placed it in the palanquin (*koshi*).[33] While this was being done, lit incense was offered. The bamboo blinds (*misu*) of the palanquin were rolled up so Yoshihito's face (*songan*) could be viewed. Sadafusa carefully recorded that there was no change in the color of his father's face and that his eyes appeared "as if he were sleeping." These signs of "normalcy" were important as indications to those present that no evil spirits had caused the death, and also because they sanctioned speculation that the prince would have a good rebirth.

That the blinds of the palanquin were rolled up so Yoshihito's face could be clearly seen by those present at the preparation of the corpse may have been a continuation of an older tradition in which the deceased was treated as if he were still alive (*heizei no gi*; also *nyozai no gi*).[34] For example, in 1188, the deceased Fujiwara no Yoshimichi, son of Kujō Kanezane, was transported in a special type of carriage with lattice windows (*ajiroguruma*).[35] Carts with windows are appropriate for those who can see out of them; their use to transport the corpse suggests that the deceased was being treated as if still alive and needing to see (or be seen).[36] But although rolled-up blinds might have signified that Yoshihito was "as if" still living, it is more likely that the blinds were raised to enable relatives to ascertain that malign spirits had played no role in his death.

The palanquin with the corpse was carried out from the south side of the Daily Life Palace, watched by Yoshihito's heir, Haruhito (1374–1417), and by his second son, the diarist Sadafusa, and other lords who crouched down in the garden as the bier passed. The palanquin stopped briefly under the gate, then backed up and passed through it again. The text says that this procedure was followed in compliance with precedent.

The body was transported to nearby Daikōmyōji, where it was encoffined (*nyūgan*) and placed in the Jizō Hall. Placing the body in this hall rather than in the monastery's Lecture Hall was one of the signifiers of a lay funeral.[37] Priests then read sutras that had been requested for the deceased by his family and friends. It is clear that Yoshihito's encoffining took place at the temple, representing a break with earlier court tradition according to which, more often than not, the body was put in the coffin at the residence. For example, the body of Fujiwara Michinaga's daughter Kishi (d. 1025) was placed in the coffin in her home, where she had died; her coffin was also sealed at that time.[38] Encoffining the body at the temple, however, was recommended for Zen-style funerals, and Yoshihito's funeral seems to have followed the Zen style in this aspect.

Ōei 23 (1416) 11.24: The Funeral Procession and Cremation

On 11.24 the members of the funeral procession gathered in the Abbot's Quarters of Daikōmyōji between five and seven p.m.[39] Outside the east gate of the temple, pine (*matsu*) and cryptomeria (*sugi*) trees were cut down and a space cleared for the construction of a rough cypress (*hinoki*) fence and the erection of a torii (Shinto-style gate) made of trees stripped of their bark.[40] The site was sanctified through adornment (*shōgon*), perhaps by wrapping the fence with raw-silk cloth and by setting up a temporary altar complete with the appropriate Buddhist ritual implements. Two wide platforms (*sajiki*) were constructed in front of the gate, one on either side: the southern platform was for imperial relatives of the deceased; other high-ranking courtiers sat together on the northern platform.

The Buddhist service was conducted at the Jizō Hall in front of the coffin. At the appropriate moment the deceased's sons, Haruhito and Sadafusa, and others offered incense before the corpse in the hall. The priest in charge of the ceremony then entered the platform area and the removal of the deceased to the cremation site began: a gong was struck, signaling the funeral procession to begin. Two monks (*gyōja*) led off carrying lanterns (*tōshoku*), followed by four temple attendants (*jisha*) carrying four banners (*hata*). Then came the gong and drum, followed by the deceased's memorial tablet (*ihai*) and the coffin. Following the coffin came the senior priests and over one hundred monks chanting the *Great Spell of Amida* (*Amida no daiju*).[41] The large number of monks was indicative of Yoshihito's exalted position; clearly men of high rank merited larger funerals.

At the site the cremation ceremony (*dabi no gi*) was held. A monk from Kongōin touched the lit torch to the coffin, while prayers and sutras were chanted aloud by the priests and nuns. After the coffin and corpse were reduced to ashes, Haruhito, Sadafusa, and the women returned home. Sadafusa commented that the funeral was very dignified and moved everyone to tears. Later he heard from some people who had attended the cremation that they saw the spirit (*tamashii*) of the deceased fly out of the enclosure (probably along with the cremation smoke). This was considered a strange but exceptionally positive sign.

That Yoshihito was cremated marks a change from the fourteenth-century practice of the Nakahara family, but this change probably cannot be attributed wholly to the new Zen style of funerals. The term used in *Kanmon gyoki* for cremation, *dabi*, translates the Sanskrit term for cremation, *dhyāpayati*. Cremation was recognized as an Indian Buddhist practice. Incidences of cremation in Japan appeared in the eighth century, most notably for Empress Jitō (645–703) as well as for other members of the aristocracy. It does not follow, however, that because Jitō was cremated the funeral ceremony had to have been Buddhist. It is unclear when Buddhist ceremonies became central to imperial funeral rituals, although most scholars agree that they were probably entrenched by the mid-eighth-century funeral of Emperor Shōmu.[42] Archaeological evidence indicates that cremations unconnected to Buddhism were practiced in Japan from as early as 6000 to 5000 BCE.[43] Nonetheless, certainly by the twelfth century, cremation was viewed primarily as a Buddhist ritual favored by the imperial family and a small circle of high-ranking aristocrats. The prestige of this custom was related to the Buddha himself having been cremated. By following his model, the elite believed that they were accruing merit, a means to "becoming a buddha" (*jōbutsu*).[44] Thus, whereas families of the status of the Nakahara (officials serving the court) might have been undecided about the efficacy of cremation in the mid-fourteenth century, cremation was firmly traditional for imperials like

Yoshihito, whose father, Emperor Sukō, had been cremated. The written records more often than not give few clues about the reason(s) for a given choice, but the most frequently cited one is family tradition or precedent. Either or both together may well have determined the choices made by both the Nakahara and Prince Yoshihito.

Sadafusa uses the term *songi* twice in this section about his father's death and funeral. On 11.23, he says, "the *songi* was prepared by the priests, placed in the palanquin, and moved secretly to Daikōmyōji at night," and on 11.24, "the *songi* was moved to the cremation site." *Songi* means "exalted form," and is a word used in reference to images of buddhas and bodhisattvas, to portraits of aristocrats, and as an honorific term for the deceased's memorial tablet. In context, then, did *songi* here refer to Yoshihito's portrait? Two other terms—notably *miei* (revered shadow) and *shin* (true form)—were routinely used in the fifteenth century when referring to the portraits of the Ashikaga shoguns and their wives, but neither appears in this text. Descriptions of later funerals give indisputable specifics about the function of the portrait at the cremation site during Zen-style funerals, telling us that it was hung in the temple in front of the coffin during the service and again outside at a temporary altar at the cremation site. From Sadafusa's account of the *songi* being moved to the cremation site on 11.24, the word could have meant either portrait or corpse, or even memorial tablet, because we know that all three were processed to the cremation site. But in his narration of 11.23 Sadafusa writes, "the *songi* was prepared by the priests, placed in the palanquin, and moved secretly to Daikōmyōji at night," making it unlikely that he was talking about the portrait or the tablet. Rather, in *Kanmon gyoki* Sadafusa seems to use *songi* as an honorific for his deceased father, perhaps because it implied that his father had already become a buddha or bodhisattva. If my interpretation is correct, there is no mention of Yoshihito's portrait during his funeral, although it has been described by Bodiford as a typical Zen-style funeral, at which the portrait is one of the most distinguishing features.

Kanmon gyoki's account of 11.24 is also important because it concisely describes how the cremation site was constructed. First a space had to be cleared outside the east gate of Daikōmyōji; then a cypress fence and a Shinto-style gate (one or more) were assembled. Similar fences and gates were set up for Ashikaga Yoshimochi's cremation about a decade later in 1428, but no platforms were erected for that event. The special techniques used in constructing this type of fence (*aragaki*), as well as the configuration of the cremation site and its symbolism, will be discussed in Chapter 3.

Yoshihito's Memorials

The term *chūin* (also *chūu*), often translated as "intermediate shadow," refers to a transitional state lasting approximately forty-nine days (or seven sevens) between death and the next life. During this time the deceased was believed to be in a condition related to this life but not of it. An appropriate analogy might be that the deceased was viewed somewhat like a photo negative—an imprint of the real person, but one lacking color and substance, and one in which every feature was reversed. That the dead are even today viewed this way in Japan is supported by many customs that require opposite acts to be performed for the deceased—shoes put on backward, garments sewn with visible stitches, offerings made of raw rather than cooked rice, and so forth. Furthermore, it was thought that the actions of the living could actually affect the circumstances of the deceased. Thus, special prayers, sutra readings, and offerings were made during this time to enable the deceased to attain a good rebirth—or, most hopefully, the Pure Land.

The schedule for Yoshihito's seven memorial, or offering, services was slightly irregular. The text notes the reason: it was paramount to speed things up in order to complete them before the New Year. Therefore, the first memorial was held only two days after the funeral on 11.26, the day Yoshihito's cremated remains were retrieved from the pyre and laid to rest.[45] A Yin-Yang Master was in attendance on this day, but he did not seem to have much influence over the events. In the evening those close to Yoshihito, including the diarist himself, gathered in the platform area near the cremation site to hear the Buddhist service and to burn incense in front of the torii gate. The monks waited in front of the gate for the incense offerings to be completed, then they too entered the platform area. While the head priest performed the special service, Yoshihito's remains were retrieved. Afterward, all the monks recited sutras. Yoshihito's remains were carried to Shonyōhachiji and laid to rest in the Abbot's Quarters. The monks again chanted sutras, this time in the garden in front of the Abbot's Quarters, while Haruhito, the diarist, and others listened from the temple's Jizō Hall. Each individual made offerings of incense in front of the deceased's memorial tablet.

The remaining memorial ceremonies for Yoshihito were held on 12.2 (second), 12.7 (third), 12.12 (fourth), 12.17 (fifth), 12.21 (sixth), and 12.25 (seventh), averaging closer to four rather than seven days apart.[46] Thus, there were actually only thirty-two days between the time of Yoshihito's death on 11.20 and the final ceremony on 12.25, far fewer than the customary forty-nine days recommended for mourning. Buddhist priests conducted all of the memorial services.[47]

Additional ceremonies also were performed during this period. For example, an offering ceremony was held for Yoshihito's remains (*shari kōshiki*) on his second seventh-day memorial (12.2). At the fifth (thirty-fifth day) memorial service (12.17), a number of scrolls were dedicated on Yoshihito's behalf, including a hanging scroll of Jizō Bosatsu painted by Haruhito, a copy of the *Perfect Enlightenment Sutra* (*Engaku kyō*) written by Sadafusa, and calligraphy scrolls of the *Brahma's Net Sutra* (*Bonmō kyō*) and the *Juryō-bon* (the sixteenth chapter of the *Lotus Sutra*) written by Yoshihito before his death. On the sixth seventh-day memorial (12.21), Yoshihito's memorial tablet was moved to a pagoda at the Buddha Hall of Daikōmyōji. Haruhito and Sadafusa went to the temple to hear sutras being read.

Concluding prayers (*ketsugan*; read *kechigan*) for Yoshihito were held on 12.25.[48] A day earlier, on 12.24, preparations for the final memorial had begun. At that time folding screens were arranged in the Nurigome[49] and a revered image (*honzon*), a painting of Shaka, was displayed above a pedestal altar table; on the west side was hung a painting of Amida. An altar cloth of very fine semiopaque fabric similar to muslin (*tōchirimen*) was spread on top of the table and a short curtain (*mizuhiki*) covered its sides. Yoshihito's memorial tablet was installed on this altar along with other implements for the offering ceremony—flower vases, censers, and candle stands.

The Buddha altar (*butsudan*) was also prepared; a Thousand-armed Kannon, kept in a portable shrine (*zushi*) and revered by generations, was installed on the altar. The Kannon was needed to perform special sutra readings for repentance. A folding screen was placed in the Fourth Chamber, located along one side of the altar room, and a painting of Fudō was hung on its east side. The entire south side of the Fourth Chamber and the two rooms flanking it were hung with green bamboo blinds (*suiren*) to create a space for people to sit and listen to the service. That evening the Kannon repentance ceremony (*Kannon senbō*), dedicated to the Kannon image in the small shrine, was performed. This was, in fact, the most significant part of the final seventh-day ceremonies.

On the basis of the information given in the text, it is difficult to envision the arrangement of these rooms and the placement of the Buddhist images. *Kanmon gyoki* indicates two main areas of activity for Yoshihito's final memorial service: one, the small interior room, the Nurigome, where the Shaka and Amida paintings were displayed behind a temporary altar holding Yoshihito's memorial tablet; the other space, probably the Jibutsudō, a small Buddhist chapel in the residence, contained the main altar with the specially installed Kannon image. These two rooms were adjacent to each other and the guests sat in abutting rooms. I have contrived a rough approximation of the physical arrangement that Sadafusa described for his father's seventh seven-day memorial service in Figure 2.1.

An incense offering (*nenkō*) was held on 12.25, on which date Sadafusa noted that without doubt his father had attained deliverance from the world of transmigration![50] Notwithstanding that 12.25 was officially the final day (*jinshichinichi*) of the forty-nine-day mourning period, many of the ceremonies had already been held on the previous day. Sadafusa's description of the events of 12.25, therefore, is almost anticlimactic. Other than the incense-offering ceremony, the only other activities on this day were sutra readings and a light meal

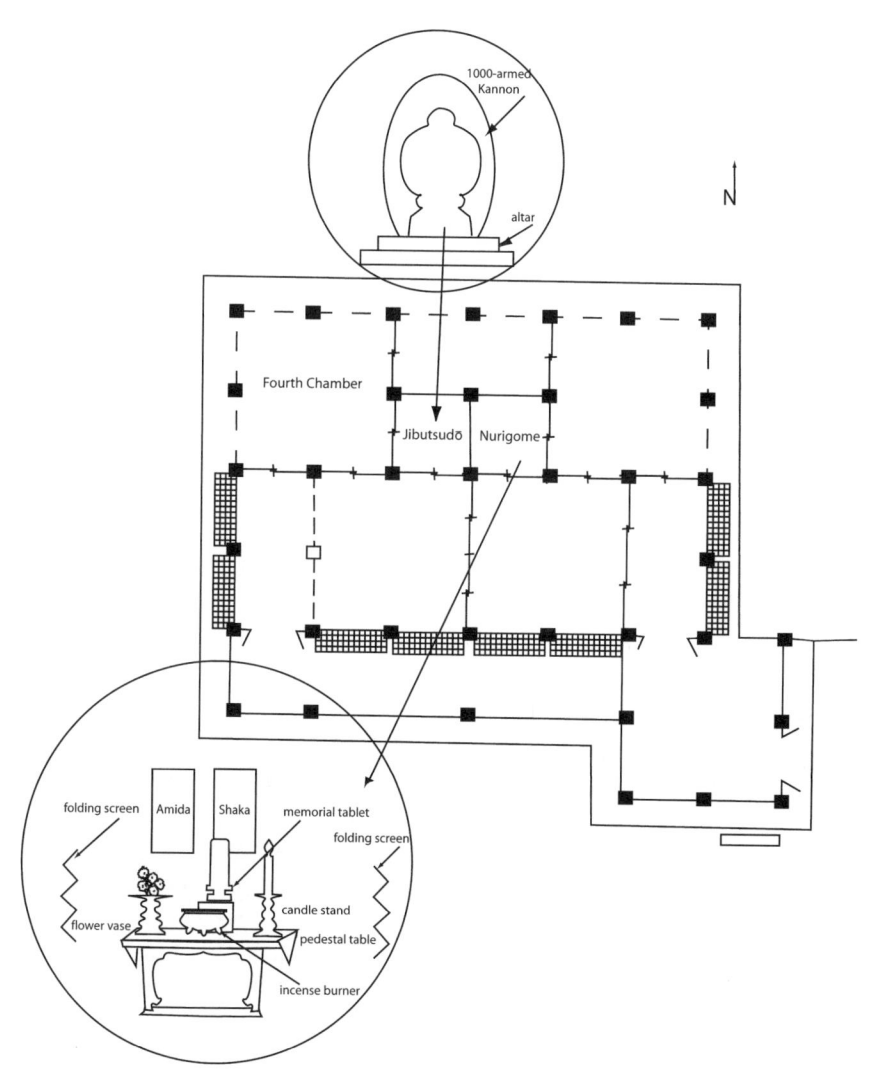

Figure 2.1. Physical arrangement for Prince Yoshihito's seventh seven-day service.
Source: Drawing by Ruthe Karlin.

and tea served to those in attendance. As stated earlier, some of the ceremonies were performed ahead of the usual schedule because the year was rapidly drawing to a close. Other than the shortening of the time frame and the lack of any mention of Yoshihito's portrait, the mourning rituals for Yoshihito were fairly standard. An even fuller picture of the complex rituals of Zen-style funerals emerges from the following accounts of the funerals of three Ashikaga shoguns and a woman who was the wife and mother of two shoguns.

Ashikaga Yoshimochi (1386–1428; Shogun 1394–1423)

The fourth Ashikaga shogun, Yoshimochi, fell ill rather suddenly and died on Shōchō 1 (1428) 1.18 at the age of forty-three. His funeral took place five days later at Tōjiin, a Rinzai Zen temple in northwest Kyoto that had been established in the fourteenth century by Ashikaga Takauji (1305–1358), founder of the Ashikaga line of shoguns.[51] Courtier Madenokōji Tokifusa (1394–1457)[52] in his diary *Kennaiki* (also read *Kendaiki*)[53] offers superb details of Yoshimochi's funeral, including the salient features of the ceremonies conducted during the funeral itself and at the cremation. Tokifusa was not a member of the Ashikaga family, but he had a great deal of personal contact with Yoshimochi and the Ashikaga through his official position as *nanto tensō*, which entailed his handling communications between the court and the bakufu.

After Yoshimochi died, preparations immediately began for his funeral (1.18).[54] As was customary, priests gathered around the body and chanted sutras and made incense offerings incessantly. Relatives and officials paid mourning calls to the residence, and the schedule for the funeral was discussed at length, including who would fill the various roles. No mention is made of the participation of a Yin-Yang Master in the scheduling. On the day after he died (1.19), Yoshimochi's body was placed in a special palanquin (*ajirogoshi*) and taken to Tōjiin, accompanied by a procession of high-ranking priests, feudal lords, and family members, whose clothing and accouterments are described in minute detail.[55] This type of palanquin had thin, black-lacquered slats of bamboo or wood attached over the ceiling and windows.[56] Upon arrival at the temple, the body was placed in the west chancel of Tōjiin's Buddha Hall, where offerings of incense and sutra readings continued for the deceased and where a large number of Yoshimochi's loyal retainers took the tonsure on 1.22, renouncing the world as an expression of their grief and devotion.

The greater part of the five days between Yoshimochi's death and his funeral was occupied by discussions among the higher-ranking members of the government about who would succeed him as shogun. Yoshimochi's son, Yoshikazu (1407–1425), had served as shogun for only two years before he died unexpectedly in 1425 at the age of seventeen. Yoshimochi himself was only forty years old when Yoshikazu died, so he filled the position a second time upon his son's death, but without taking the title of shogun. Now, with Yoshimochi's death, it was imperative to find a successor immediately. But who should fill the position? Apparently Ashikaga Mochiuji (1398–1439), the Kantō deputy, was expecting to be chosen.[57] Although Mochiuji had some supporters, Yoshimochi's younger brother Yoshinori (1394–1441) was chosen as the new shogun by lottery. Yoshinori was the sixth son of Ashikaga Yoshimitsu. He was serving as a Tendai abbot at Enryakuji before his brother died, because he had not been expected to succeed as shogun. Thus, he became the new shogun quite by chance (and politics).

Shōchō 1 (1428) 1.23: Buddhist Rite of Affixing the Coffin Lid; Buddhist Rite of Hanging the Portrait; Buddhist Rite of Moving the Corpse to the Cremation Site

Early on the morning of 1.23 everyone donned white, raw-silk robes (*jō-e*) and went to the temple.[58] When the funeral was to begin, those attending, wearing silk gauze over the shoulders of their short jackets (*dōfuku*) and straw sandals (*waragutsu*) on their feet, entered the Buddha Hall (*butsuden*) and offered incense before the coffin, which rested in the west side of the hall. The officials proceeded to stand behind the coffin in the northwest corner for the duration of the service. Note that in this account we are told exactly where the coffin was placed in the Buddha Hall.

The newly appointed shogun, Yoshinori, entered the hall through a door in the northwest corner and went and stood on the west side of the coffin. A special rite was conducted for affixing the lid to the coffin (*sagan butsuji*), followed by a ceremony for hanging the deceased's portrait (*kashin butsuji*). Yoshimochi's portait (*miei*), drawn by the well-known early fifteenth-century court painter Tosa Yukihiro (fl. 1406–1434), was displayed directly in front of his coffin; we are told that everything about the image was superbly beautiful. Next, a ritual for moving the coffin to the cremation site (*kigan butsuji*) was performed. When this had been completed, attendants carrying brocade banners (*kinpan*), cymbals (*hatsu*), drums (*tsuzumi*), and paper-covered oil lanterns (*andon*) formed a procession and set out from the temple. Two family members followed, carrying Yoshimochi's memorial tablet and his portrait; both walked in front of the coffin. Then, workers connected to the temple (*rikisha hōshi*)[59] picked up the coffin, assisted by loyal warriors, and carried it out of the temple on their shoulders. The new shogun lifted the white silk cords (*tsuna*)[60] attached to the front of the coffin and rested them on his shoulders.[61]

From this passage we can identify three funeral rituals not mentioned in the earlier texts; all are connected specifically to the funerals of Chan/Zen priests. *Sagan butsuji* is a special Buddhist ceremony, accompanied by sutra chanting, that was performed when the lid was put on the coffin. The ritual is not described in detail in the text, and *Bukkyōgo daijiten* defines it only as a special Buddhist ceremony that began when the corpse was moved from the residence to the Dharma Hall (*hattō*) (usually located behind the Buddha Hall) and ended with the closing of the coffin.[62] This ceremony likely involved sutra chanting, incense offerings, and the ritual action of closing the coffin.[63]

In contrast to *Kanmon gyoki*'s account of Yoshihito's rites, we are not told where Yoshimochi was encoffined, only that his body was moved to the temple the day after he died. Presumably the body rested there in the coffin, uncovered, until the coffin-closing ceremony took place in the Buddha Hall immediately before the body was transported to the cremation site. Thus, the corpse lay in state at the temple for four days, from 1.19 to 1.23—a very different scenario from that of Yoshihito, who was kept at the palace for three days until, on the night before the funeral, his body was finally moved to the temple. Written records suggest that it was more common in the Heian period for members of the imperial family and high-ranking members of the court to keep their dead in the residence until the funeral procession. Thus, for Yoshihito's family the pull of this ancient precedent may have overridden the newer Zen funeral tradition of moving the corpse to the Buddhist temple soon after death. It should also be noted that the time of lying-in-state, whether at the residence or at the temple, for both Yoshihito and Yoshimochi was rather long (four days for Yoshihito and five days for Yoshimochi). This was possible only because both died in winter (the eleventh and first months respectively), making preservation of the bodies for that length of time feasible.

Since Yoshimochi was to be cremated, the lid was probably not actually affixed to the coffin but simply placed on top of it for easy removal at the cremation site, where firewood would be inserted to facilitate the burning. For burials, the lid was usually nailed to the coffin, each nail pounded in with a heavy stone. Traditionally, each nail was struck only once. Fujiwara Teika observed in *Meigetsuki* that his father Shunzei's (d. 1204.11.30) coffin lid was held in place by ten nails, each pounded in place by a single stroke with a rock.[64] Hikaru Suzuki's study shows that even today it is still common for families in rural Japan to use stones rather than hammers to nail the coffin shut, probably following tradition.[65]

The second new ritual presented in *Kennaiki* is the ceremony for hanging the portrait before the corpse (*kashin butsuji*) during the funeral. The same phrase appears often in later funeral records, reinforcing our understanding of the practice as one of a series of Buddhist rituals commonly performed during Zen-style funerals for the military elite in the fifteenth century. In Japan, records as early as the late eleventh century mention portraits being dedicated at memorial services.[66] During the funerals, however, portraits were not commonly displayed until sometime in the twelfth century, when the practice became standard at the funerals of Zen priests. It is often said that this convention was then quickly adopted by members of the court and became particularly popular with the top tier of the warrior class. Yet it is difficult to judge how rapidly the practice spread or how common it really was. Although records confirm that portraits of important Buddhist priests were present at the funeral and cremation site as early as 1309,[67] the documents I examined (admittedly only a sample) suggest that the practice was not very popular with either the court or military elite in the fourteenth century. The mid-fourteenth-century *Moromoriki*, for example, makes no mention of portraits at the funerals of either Morosuke or Kenshin, only later at their memorial services. Likewise, there is no evidence that portraits were part of Ashikaga Takauji's funeral in 1358, although they were used for his memorials as well. *Kanmon gyoki* makes no clear mention of a portrait at Prince Yoshihito's funeral in 1416 either—neither at the temple or cremation site nor in the funeral procession. Thus, it may be that throughout the fourteenth and early fifteenth centuries, the practice of displaying a portrait of the deceased at the funeral was more limited than has been previously thought.

Kigan butsuji, the third ritual to appear in *Kennaiki*, was performed before the body could be moved from the temple to the cremation site. The need for this ritual confirms that it was still believed that moving the corpse was fraught with danger. Although the reason for this trepidation is not explained in the text, it may well have been apprehension that, once the body was moved, the spirit might be unable to find its way back to it. Even today in Japan there is a general belief that a person's soul hovers near the corpse after death until it can become sufficiently separated. People also feared that pollution from the body could more easily contaminate the living if it was moved. Thus, moving the body anywhere—from the residence to the temple or from the temple to the cremation or burial site—required special rituals to counteract the risk.

Kennaiki's description of Ashikaga Yoshimochi's cremation suggests a rite similar to but more sophisticated and detailed than Prince Yoshihito's, which took place some twenty years earlier. Unfortunately, we cannot be sure if the increased complexity was due to developments in funeral rituals, or to the different status levels of the two deceased individuals, or to differences in the interests and observations of the two writers themselves.

Kennaiki also offers additional details about the various physical structures that were constructed near Yoshimochi's cremation site and about some of the rituals performed there. For Yoshimochi's funeral, narrow wooden platforms several yards long were built outside of the Buddha Hall on its west side, and a crematory (*hiya*) enclosed by a cypress fence wrapped in white raw silk was constructed about a hundred yards (1 *chō*) to the west of the hall. The coffin was carried and a black horse led around the cremation site three times.[68] Members of the deceased's family, including the shogun designate (Yoshinori), followed the coffin in its circumambulation. Yoshinori then put down the white cords that he had been carrying and entered the enclosure; the diarist Tokifusa and the other participants did not enter the fenced area, but watched the cremation from nearby.

Shōchō 1 (1428) 1.23: Buddhist Rite of Offering Tea; Buddhist Rite of Offering Water; Buddhist Rite of Lighting the Cremation Fire

Kennaiki relates that a portrait of the deceased was hung about three yards (1 *jō*) in front of the entryway to the crematory, near the temporary altar where the mortuary tablet and three Buddhist ritual implements (*mitsu gusoku*) were placed. At this point, a ritual offering of tea was made to the deceased (*tencha butsuji*), followed by an offering of water (*tentō butsuji*). Then came the final rite—the lighting of the cremation fire (*ako butsuji*). Priest Genchū lit the fire with a long pine torch (*taimatsu*).[69] As a column of smoke arose from the pyre, everyone wept, wiping the tears from their faces. The nuns faced south and offered prayers. The diarist Tokifusa described the row upon row of nuns, priests, and abbots from important Gozan temples as "numerous as clouds and mists."

Three new rituals are elucidated in the above section of text—the final offerings of tea and water to the deceased and the ritual for lighting the cremation fire. None of these ritual actions were specifically named in *Kanmon gyoki* for Prince Yoshihito's funeral; rather, that text made only the most general reference to a cremation ceremony (*dabi no gi*). Although *Kennaiki* does not elaborate, for the *tencha butsuji* and *tentō butsuji* rites libations of tea and hot water were poured into small Buddhist offering bowls and placed on the temporary altar. After these rites came the frightening part of the funeral when the body was set afire, ending all hope for the bereaved that the deceased could somehow return to the world of the living. The special ritual (*ako butsuji*) that accompanied this action, probably involving the recitation of special spells while the lit torch was being raised, undoubtedly did much to ameliorate the intense anxiety felt by all who witnessed it.

During the cremation, the priests chanted sutras (*fugin*) while circumambulating the pyre.[70] The new shogun, Yoshinori, offered incense before his brother's mortuary tablet and then retired to the Abbot's Quarters of the temple. Other members of the court and military elite also made offerings of incense. Then they removed their straw sandals near the temple gate by stamping on their heels (to avoid using their hands), put on shoes without outer soles, and got into their palanquins. The *aozamurai* (also *aosaburai*) (samurai of the sixth rank attached to *kuge* houses) purified themselves by sprinkling salt over their bodies and then stood outside the gate, facing north, while a ceremony to remove the pollution (*harai*) brought on by their proximity to the deceased was performed. When they returned home, they faced north again, took off their sandals, and washed their feet (by washing one foot with the other), thus completing the purification.[71] This passage makes it clear that hands were not to touch either shoes or feet that had trod upon the cremation ground. It is unclear, however, why the participants faced north while performing these actions. Why directions were significant in Japanese rituals is a question that merits further research.

The Schedule of Memorials

The rituals of the forty-nine-day mourning period for Ashikaga Yoshimochi began on the day after the funeral (1.24) with his first seven-day memorial.[72] On the next day (1.25) the Buddhist ceremony for his remains (*shikkotsu/shūkotsu butsuji*) was held at Tōjiin. The head priest of Shōkokuji performed the Buddhist service. Sutras were chanted and ceremonial walking (*gyōdō*) was performed accompanied by cymbals and drums. The head of Tōjiin carried the ex-shogun's remains into the Buddha Hall in a box wrapped in a brocade cover, followed by the new shogun Yoshinori, various daimyo and close retainers, and the heads of the Gozan temples. There they performed a special ceremony after which the monks recited sutras while performing ceremonial walking. Yoshimochi's remains were placed inside a pagoda.[73]

Only a few additional memorial services for Yoshimochi appear in *Kennaiki*. The second was held just three days later, on 1.28; we are told that the date was moved back, but no reason is given.[74] On this day a ceremony was performed and incense was offered, but no further details are divulged. On this day the date for the final memorial was revealed; it was to be held the following month on 2.19 (the account of this final memorial no longer exists). No mention is made of the third memorial, but the fourth was held on 2.6.[75] Of his fifth and sixth memorials we have no account at all, because several entries around this period are missing.

Hino Shigeko (1411–1463)

The funeral of Hino Shigeko[76] is described in *Inryōken nichiroku*,[77] a lengthy record covering about thirty years that was written by two Zen monks, Kikei Shinzui and Kisen Shūshō; Kikei wrote the entries on Shigeko's funeral. Hino Shigeko, who died on 1463.8.8, was a member of a family of court bureaucrats. During the Nanbokuchō period (1336–1392) the family was divided, with some Hino clan members supporting Go-Daigo and the Southern line and others siding with the Northern line. The division caused the family's fortunes to decline, but they were restored when the family managed to marry a daughter to Shogun Yoshimitsu (1358–1408; shogun 1368–1394), starting a tradition of providing wives to the Ashikaga shoguns.

Shigeko, the daughter of Hino Shigemitsu, became the wife of the sixth Ashikaga shogun Yoshinori (1394–1441; shogun 1429–1441), making her also the sister-in-law of Yoshimochi, whose funeral has already been discussed. Two of her sons also became shoguns: Yoshikatsu (1434–1443; shogun 1442–1443) became the seventh Ashikaga shogun, and Yoshimasa (1436–1490; shogun

1449–1473) succeeded him at age fourteen as the eighth shogun. Shigeko wielded significant political power as an adviser to Yoshimasa, because he inherited the title of shogun at such a young age. Her funeral would probably not have been given the attention it received in *Inryōken nichiroku* had it not been for her important role as Yoshimasa's advocate and adviser.

The funeral service for Hino Shigeko (referred to as Takakura-dono in the text) took place almost forty years after Yoshimochi's, but was nevertheless in many respects very similar to her brother-in-law's; it was even held at the same temple, Tōjiin, the Ashikaga mortuary temple. It was unusual for women, much less a woman from outside the Ashikaga family, to be accorded the honor of a funeral at the Ashikaga family temple (*bodaiji*), but Shigeko was no ordinary consort.

Shigeko died at her residence, the Takakura Palace, on 1463.8.8, and her funeral was held just three days later, on 8.11. On the night of her death, her body was bathed, sutras were chanted, and incense offerings were made. Incense was also offered in front of her portrait (*shin*). Immediately that same night, plans were made for her funeral and cremation.[78] Priest Kikei Shinzui, author of this section of *Inryōken nichiroku*, figured importantly in setting the schedule of events for the funeral, but her son Yoshimasa, the current shogun, demanded to be consulted on the details.

On 8.10 numerous people paid condolence calls at the Takakura residence. Although the shogun was unable to be present, he sent a messenger to speak on his behalf. Apparently Shigeko was administered the tonsure posthumously, because she received a Buddhist title given to an ordained noble (*ingō*)—Shōchiin, first rank, Manzan Daizenjōni. On the day of her funeral, she received her posthumous name (*imina*), Shōju.[79]

Kanshō 4 (1463) 8.11: The Funeral Procession

The funeral began very early on the following day (8.11), between three and five a.m.[80] The palanquin bearing Shigeko's corpse traveled from her residence to Tōjiin, located at Kyoto's Kitamachi in Kita-ku. Instead of taking the most direct route along the main road, the procession followed a narrow, winding path to avoid passing Kitano Shrine. This was probably to avoid polluting the shrine precincts. Twelve temple laborers (*rikisha hōshi*)[81] wearing white robes bore the palanquin into Tōjiin's Buddha Hall. There the body was placed in the coffin, which was installed in the hall's west side; there it remained until its cremation, scheduled for later that day. Shigeko's body, like Prince Yoshihito's, had remained at the residence for almost three days before it was moved to the temple, and only then was it encoffined.

While the body was in transit, the shogun and other elite guests began arriving at the Abbot's Quarters of Shinnyoji, a Zen temple located just east of

Tōjiin. There they took off their official robes and exchanged them for white mourning robes in preparation for the funeral. They then climbed back into their carriages and traveled to Tōjiin, descending outside the outer Sōmon (gate) and entering through it.[82] The guests entered the Buddha Hall from the south door on the east corridor, passing along the east side of the altar and arriving at the Imperial Chamber (*gosho no ma*) of the Abbot's Quarters. There they put on straw sandals, reentered the Buddha Hall, and stood on the west side in front of the Buddha image. Priest Jikuun *oshō*,[83] serving as chief mourner (*moshu*), recited *nenju*,[84] and another priest, Jikka, chanted *nenju* in front of the coffin. Priest Gessen stood on the right side of the corpse to perform the ceremony for the closing of the coffin lid (*sagan butsuji*). This was followed by the ceremony for moving the body out of the temple (*kigan butsuji*). Following the two rituals came more Buddhist chanting, while the white-robed attendants raised the coffin onto their shoulders. Priest Kikei (the diarist) presented the cloth cords to Shogun Yoshimasa. Because they were long and thick, an attendant tied them for him, and the shogun then placed them over his right shoulder.

The description that follows of the procession to the cremation site is almost identical to the 1416 account of the procession at Prince Yoshihito's funeral, suggesting that its form was fairly standard. Four priests beating drums and four playing cymbals led the cortege. A senior priest (*zōsu*)[85] followed them, carrying Shigeko's memorial tablet. Temple attendants (*jisha*) came next, bearing the flower vase, censer (*kōro*), candle stand (*shokudai*), hot water (*yu no ki*) and tea (*chasan*) containers, and four brocade banners (*kinpan*). Four other attendants made paper flower offerings (*setsuryū*) as the procession moved along to the cremation site.[86] When it reached the pyre, the coffin was carried around it three times and was set down. Yoshimasa handed the cloth cords to Priest Kikei and went and stood on the north side of the cremation pit, facing south. Kikei went and stood on the shogun's left. The attending courtiers lined up to his (Kikei's) left, while those who had close connections to the shogun were lined up on the shogun's right.[87] The *monzeki* of Sanbōin, Shōgoin, Jōdoin, and the other imperial monasteries stood to the left of the courtiers, and nuns (*bikuni*) lined up on the north and south sides of the funeral pyre.

The cremation ceremony finally began between five and seven a.m. when the head mourner, Jikuun, requested the ceremony of offering the hot water (*tentō butsuji*) to the deceased. The ceremony was performed while Priest Ien chanted the proper words (*hōgo*). Next, Jikuun commanded the offering of ritual tea to the deceased (*tencha butsuji*) and priest Kyūen chanted. The chief mourner then requested the special ceremony for lighting the fire (*hinko butsuji*),[88] which was performed while another priest chanted a buddha's name. When the three rituals were completed, the faggots were laid and the fire lit. Various sutras and spells were recited, including the Spell of Great Compassion (*Daihiju*) at the end.[89] The monks dispersed, and Shogun Yoshimasa entered the Abbot's Quarters to wait for the ritual of retrieving the remains (*kikotsu butsuji*). There he removed his mourning robe and put on the robe he had arrived in. He then read sutras (*kankin*) and ate a small meal.

Between three and five p.m. a gong sounded, and the monks gathered for the ceremony to retrieve Shigeko's remains. The shogun put on a mourning robe (*kyōfuku*) and straw sandals (*waraji*) and went to the cremation site. He picked up a single bone fragment and went outside the cremation area where everyone was seated in the same order as for the cremation. The chief mourner, Jikuun, chanted the special ceremony for retrieving the remains, which were gathered up, wrapped in paper, and handed to a temple official. One of the priests then consecrated the remains and Jikuun's chanting ended. Led by one priest, the monks chanted the sutras that had been offered by the family on the deceased's behalf. After this Buddhist service to transfer merit (*ekō*), the monks began to disperse. The shogun and other mourners climbed into their carriages and returned to the Abbot's Quarters of Shinnyoji, where they removed their mourning robes, put on their black court robes, and returned home.

At the end of the entry for 8.11 we are told that the golden screens that had been placed around the coffin were returned to Shigeko's residence, whence they had been borrowed. Although the screens are not mentioned earlier in the text, they were probably set up flanking the coffin as it rested in Tōjiin's Buddha Hall before the funeral. The function of golden folding screens in death rituals is discussed in greater depth in Chapter 3.

Five of the six Buddhist rites performed for Yoshimochi's funeral—closing the coffin lid (*sagan*), moving the corpse (*kigan*), offering hot water (*tentō*), offering tea (*tencha*), and lighting the torch (*ako/hinko*)—were also performed at Shigeko's; only the rite of hanging the portrait (*kashin butsuji*) was not mentioned. There is no evidence that any of these rituals were performed at the funerals of the Nakahara in the mid-fourteenth century. Certainly none of the terms mentioned in the current account can be found in *Moromoriki*. Even three-quarters of a century later, in 1416, none of these rites was mentioned by name in Sadafusa's chronicle of the funeral of Prince Yoshihito, although some of the same actions were described. Thus, the funerals of the Ashikaga, including Shigeko's, clearly present more elements of a typical Zen-style funeral than either Prince Yoshihito's or the Nakahara's. Although only the vaguest of generalizations should be made on the basis of this small sample, it does appear that the imperial family and those associated most closely with it retained more traditions from ancient funeral practices, whereas the Ashikaga, staunch supporters of Zen Buddhism from the start, were more eager to adopt the new style of funerals associated with Zen.

It would be useful to compare Shigeko's funeral with other funerals conducted for elite laywomen in the fifteenth century, but little work has been done on this topic. In one of the few studies to address the subject of medieval funerals for women, Bodiford states, astonishingly, that a majority of the lay funerals in the Sōtō Zen sect were held for women.[90] This statement does not appear to apply to lay funerals for the elite, at which it was paramount for the ceremonies to reflect the high public status of the deceased. Obviously those in positions of power and wealth were primarily males, and their funerals were more often recorded. It has been suggested that, because women faced a number of obstacles on the path to salvation related to their gender, they had a greater need, not only for funerals, but also for special sermons and sutras to save them.[91] Yet few gender-specific rites or sutras appear in the records of either Nakahara Kenshin (14th c.) or Hino Shigeko (15th c.). The only differences noted for Kenshin's rites were that her grave marker was cut slightly shorter than her husband's, the *Lotus Sutra* was the predominant sutra recited at her ceremonies (Esoteric sutras accompanied her husband Morosuke's), and the family held fewer monthly memorial services over time for Kenshin than for Morosuke. But how can we interpret these differences? At that time social status was significantly determined by gender, making it difficult to decide whether specific differences in the treatment of a given woman were purely gender-related. On the surface, Shigeko's funeral appears to have been much like those of the Ashikaga shoguns, but because the sutras chanted were not named in *Inryōken nichiroku*, we cannot tell if they were different from those chanted for Ashikaga shoguns. Clearly this is an area for further research.

Ashikaga Yoshimitsu (1358–1408; Shogun 1368–1394)

I have chosen to discuss the funeral of Ashikaga Yoshimitsu (d. 1408.5.6) last because of two pivotal diagrams that illustrate precisely and effectively how the various objects and implements discussed in the previous sections were arranged. The diagrams are presumed to have been produced at the time of Yoshimitsu's death in 1408, but have come down to us in a later document, *Jishōindono ryōan sōbo*, written by the Zen priest Genryū Shūkō (1458–1491) when the eighth shogun, Ashikaga Yoshimasa, died in 1490.[92] Along with his own report of Yoshimasa's funeral, Genryū included remnants of the earlier archive on the funeral of the third shogun, Ashikaga Yoshimitsu, which comprised brief written notes plus the two very valuable diagrams of the funeral procession and the cremation site. We do not know who was responsible for this earlier material, but Genryū likely included it in order to preserve it, and also because the diagrams served as important models for Yoshimasa's funeral.

The diagrams of Yoshimitsu's funeral procession and cremation site, though of considerable importance, provide scant information about other aspects of his funeral, such as the schedule. But *Noritoki kyōki* (Record of Lord Noritoki), a chronicle by Yamashina Noritoki, supplies an outline.[93] According to Noritoki's account, the third Ashikaga shogun, Yoshimitsu (1358–1408), died on Ōei 15 (1408) 5.6, at the age of fifty-one. His body was moved to Tōjiin that same day. On the following day (5.7) the diarist Noritoki paid a condolence call on his successor, Shogun Ashikaga Yoshimochi. A number of priests and other important members of the court and military government also came to pay their respects that day and over the next few days. On 5.8 Noritoki went to Tōjiin to make incense offerings. Yoshimitsu's funeral and cremation were held on 5.10, four days after his death, and his remains were retrieved in the early morning of 5.11.

Noritoki kyōki says little else about Yoshimitsu's funeral, but the display and positioning of the coffin and the various ritual implements, as well as the seating arrangements of the funeral participants on 5.10 are of great interest and are explained in the following diagrams and Genryū's notes in *Jishōindono ryōan sōbo*.[94]

The manner in which the ritual objects were arranged in the procession as it left Tōjiin's Buddha Hall and moved to the cremation site is revealed in Figure 2.2. The arrangement was such that the corpse in its coffin rested on the west side of the Buddha Hall, as it would do in the funerals of Ashikaga Yoshimochi (1428) and Hino Shigeko (1463). When the Buddhist service was over, a golden cloth with paulownia crests (the Ashikaga family crest) woven into it with threads of blue and red was placed over the coffin. The coffin was then lifted up and, with the deceased's head pointing west, was moved out through a door on the west side of the hall. Yoshimochi (the current shogun), his brother, the Shogunal Deputy (*kanrei*),[95] Lord Uramatsu, and two young boys (*chigo*) all carried the cord (*nawa*),[96] with Yoshimochi holding the section closest to the coffin. The other participants chanted for Yoshimitsu's rebirth in a buddha land (*ōjō*).[97]

All of the other ritual implements for the funeral noted in the diagram were transported either by close relatives of the deceased or by temple priests and attendants. An uncle of the deceased shogun, for example, carried Yoshimitsu's memorial tablet. Eight novices (*shami*) from Shōkokuji stood to the right of the tablet. It was their job to carry and scatter the paper flowers (*setsuryū*) during the procession to the cremation site. The heads of the major Zen temples (*seidō*) conveyed the musical instruments and banners, while attendants to priests (*jisha*) carried the portrait of the deceased, the hot water and tea containers, flowers, candles, and banners. Attendant novices (*gyōja*) were responsible for transporting the lanterns.

The banners led the procession from the temple, followed in order by the

Funerals in the Fifteenth Century 73

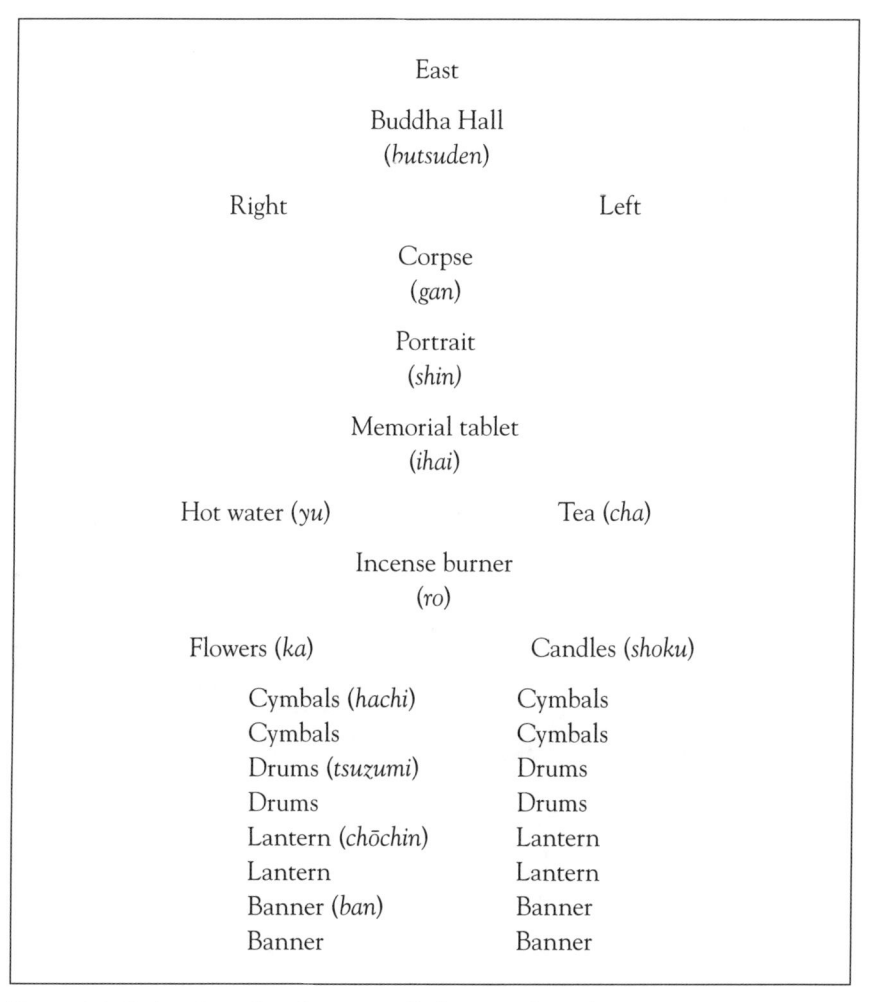

```
                        East
                     Buddha Hall
                      (butsuden)
      Right                                Left
                        Corpse
                         (gan)

                        Portrait
                        (shin)

                    Memorial tablet
                        (ihai)

    Hot water (yu)                    Tea (cha)

                     Incense burner
                         (ro)

      Flowers (ka)                   Candles (shoku)
         Cymbals (hachi)              Cymbals
         Cymbals                      Cymbals
         Drums (tsuzumi)              Drums
         Drums                        Drums
         Lantern (chōchin)            Lantern
         Lantern                      Lantern
         Banner (ban)                 Banner
         Banner                       Banner
```

Figure 2.2. Order of ritual implements in Yoshimitsu's funeral procession.
Source: Translated and modified from *Jishōindono ryōan sōbo*, in *Dai Nihon shiryō*, vol. 7, pt. 10, ed. Tōkyō Daigaku Shiryōhensanjo (Tokyo: Tōkyō Daigaku Shuppankai, 1930–1985), after diagram on pp. 10–11.

individuals carrying the lanterns, instruments, ritual implements, memorial tablet, portrait, and finally, the corpse. At the cremation site, those at the front of the procession stopped first at designated areas outside the fenced enclosure that surrounded the funeral pyre. Figure 2.3 reflects the grouping of the ritual implements at the cremation site.[98]

At the cremation site the decorated gold coffin cover was taken off and suspended as a canopy, and the coffin itself was lowered onto a specially con-

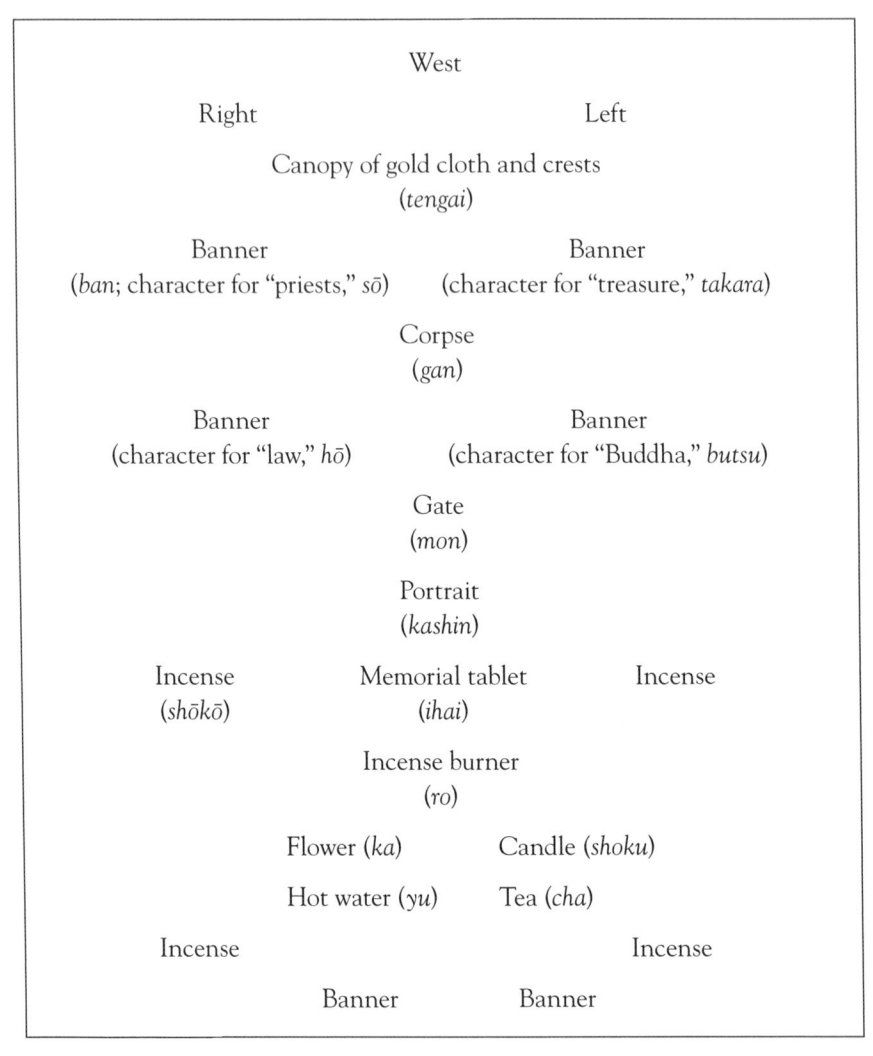

```
                              West
        Right                              Left
               Canopy of gold cloth and crests
                          (tengai)

           Banner                        Banner
 (ban; character for "priests," sō)  (character for "treasure," takara)

                           Corpse
                            (gan)

           Banner                        Banner
  (character for "law," hō)     (character for "Buddha," butsu)

                            Gate
                           (mon)

                          Portrait
                          (kashin)

       Incense         Memorial tablet        Incense
       (shōkō)             (ihai)

                       Incense burner
                            (ro)

                Flower (ka)      Candle (shoku)

                Hot water (yu)   Tea (cha)

       Incense                               Incense
                   Banner        Banner
```

Figure 2.3. Order of ritual implements at Yoshimitsu's cremation site.
Source: Translated and modified from *Jishōindono ryōan sōbo*, in *Dai Nihon shiryō*, vol. 7, pt. 10, ed. Tōkyō Daigaku Shiryōhensanjo (Tokyo: Tōkyō Daigaku Shuppankai, 1930–1985), after diagram on pp. 10–11.

structed hearth. The current shogun and his brother sat to the right of the corpse, attended by Yamashina (Noritoki) as sword bearer (*kenyakusha*). These three individuals were the only ones, other than the officiating priests, permitted inside the enclosed cremation area. The daimyo were seated just outside the gate.

Comparisons of Fifteenth-Century Funerals

The fifteenth-century records add much to our understanding of the various components of the medieval funeral and how they were put together. Although not every step of the funeral appears in every record, all of the funerals comprised similar elements and their differences were usually of degree (number of attendants, ranks of priests, etc.).

One of the most interesting comparisons that can be made among these examples relates to timing and scheduling. Certain actions required a certain amount of time. For example, after a death a waiting period was observed before the body was bathed and the robes changed. The length of time is nowhere specified, but the attending priests usually waited a few hours before proceeding, presumably in order to ascertain that the deceased's spirit had indeed permanently left the corpse. During the waiting period planning for the funeral got under way, suggesting that no one really expected the deceased to revive. Close relatives were immediately summoned to the residence and high-ranking priests gathered to discuss the schedule of events and to designate the participants for the funeral and for the memorials. In the fourteenth-century Nakahara family funerals, the Yin-Yang Master still controlled the funeral schedule, with the Ji sect monks wrangling for equal say in Kenshin's case. There is no mention of Zen Buddhism, Zen temples, or specifically Zen-style rituals in the account of the Nakahara funerals. By the fifteenth century, however, Zen Buddhist priests were determining the schedules for all four funerals discussed above, all four of which were held at Zen temples, confirming the extent of influence Zen Buddhism had gained over funerals in fifty years. It is also possible that the differences may only indicate the individual preferences of two families, the Nakahara and the Ashikaga, and have little bearing on the general practices of their successive centuries. To make broader generalizations, we need more accounts to examine.

When the corpse was transferred, first to the temple and then to the cremation site, was also significant. It is instructive to consider what reasons influenced the time when the corpse was moved. The four individuals discussed in this chapter were all cremated—Ashikaga Yoshimitsu and Prince Yoshihito four days after their death, Ashikaga Yoshimochi five days after, and Hino Shigeko three days. A number of considerations might have influenced the amount of time it took to prepare a funeral and cremation. Paramount among these was the status of the deceased. It is likely that the high status of the two shoguns and Prince Yoshihito entailed additional planning for more elaborate funerals. Other events of national import also influenced the timing of mortuary rites. For example, the five-day interval between Ashikaga Yoshimochi's death on 1428.1.18

and his funeral and cremation on 1.23 was due in part to the length of time it took to choose a new shogun to succeed him. Finally, the time of year materially affected the timing of the funeral: warmer months necessitated quicker funerals. This clearly accounted, at least in part, for the scant three days between Hino Shigeko's death on 1463.8.8 and her funeral and cremation on 8.11. The heat of summer no doubt mandated that cremations take place soon after death. Nonetheless, the average amount of time between death and cremation in the fifteenth century seems to have been about four days.

In all four cases, the deceased was moved from home to a Zen temple for a time ranging from a few hours to four days before cremation. The amount of time the corpse lay in state at the temple varied for several reasons (Table 3). For instance, the bodies of the two Ashikaga shoguns, Yoshimitsu and Yoshimochi, lay in state at Tōjiin longest—four and three days respectively. Presumably, this was because of their strong religious affiliations with this temple and also because of their public status. Large numbers of daimyo and government officials were expected to travel to make condolence calls on the relatives of the deceased and to make incense offerings at the temple. Three or four days were necessary for them to arrive and pay their respects. Prince Yoshihito, a member of the imperial family, lay in state at Daikōmyōji for only one day. His brief lying-in-state period at the temple may have been related to the strong influence of older imperial traditions, according to which the corpse remained in the residence for condolence calls. Although Yoshihito was a devout follower of Zen Buddhism, his funeral also retained many elements associated with earlier imperial funerals. Hino Shigeko, on the other hand, rested at Tōjiin for only a few hours before she was cremated, probably because she was female and not a public official. Both circumstances (and the summer heat) would have encouraged a quicker funeral.

The Zen-style funeral designed for abbots comprised nine special rituals, only eight of which were typically performed for the funerals of lay individuals in the fifteenth century.[99] In some instances, a ritual action was performed, but the author of the account did not record the specific Buddhist term for it, even when he was a Zen priest. Table 4 designates the ritual actions considered appropriate at any of the four funerals discussed in this chapter and indi-

Table 3. Length of Time between Death, Lying in State, and Burial

Ashikaga Yoshimitsu	d. 1408.5.6	Corpse moved 5.6	Funeral 5.10
Prince Yoshihito	d. 1416.11.20	Corpse moved 11.23	Funeral 11.24
Ashikaga Yoshimochi	d. 1428.1.18	Corpse moved 1.19	Funeral 1.23
Hino Shigeko	d. 1463.8.8	Corpse moved 8.11	Funeral 8.11

Funerals in the Fifteenth Century 77

Table 4. Ritual Actions Recorded and Performed at Funerals

	Yoshimitsu (d. 1408)	Yoshihito (d. 1416)	Yoshimochi (d. 1428)	Shigeko (d. 1463)
nyūgan butsuji (placing body in coffin)	No	Yes	Yes	Yes
igan butsuji (moving coffin to temple)	No	Yes (term not used)	Yes (term not used)	Yes (term not used)
sagan butsuji (closing coffin)	No	No	Yes	Yes
kashin butsuji (hanging portrait)	Yes (term not used)	No	Yes	Yes (term not used)
kigan butsuji (moving coffin to cremation site)	Yes (term not used)	Yes (term not used)	Yes	Yes
tencha butsuji (offering of tea)	Yes (term not used)	No	Yes	Yes
tentō butsuji (offering of water)	Yes (term not used)	No	Yes	Yes
ako, hinko butsuji (lighting pyre)	No	Yes (term not used)	Yes	Yes (called *hinko butsuji*)

cates whether or not the prescribed actions of the ritual were performed. Where a rite was performed but not recorded by its Buddhist name in an account of the funeral is indicated in parentheses.

For Ashikaga Yoshimitsu's funeral (1408), none of the special phrases were used. Nonetheless, it is clear from the diagram in *Jishōindono ryōan sōbo* that the coffin was carried to the cremation site (*kigan butsuji*) and that appropriate ritual implements for three of the rituals—a portrait for the *kashin butsuji*, a teabowl for the *tencha butsuji*, and a water bowl for the *tentō butsuji*—were included in the funeral procession. It is likely, then, that the rituals associated with these objects were performed. It is also probable, because Yoshimitsu's was clearly a Zen-style funeral, that the rituals for putting the corpse in the coffin (*nyūgan*), affixing the coffin lid (*sagan butsuji*), moving the corpse to the temple (*igan butsuji*), and lighting the cremation fire (*ako butsuji*) also took place. Our problem with this example is that we have two diagrams that detail the arrangement of the objects for Yoshimitsu's funeral but no text to explain what actions took place.

Kanmon gyoki uses only one of the special phrases (*nyūgan*), placing the body in the coffin (11.23), in describing Prince Yoshihito's funeral (1416). But it describes moving the corpse to Daikōmyōji (11.23), moving the corpse to the cremation site (11.24), and lighting the torch (11.24). These are the only four rituals that we know for certain were performed. The coffin lid was undoubtedly closed, but whether this was done ritually is not known. More important, there is no mention of a portrait, and we have no evidence that tea and water libations were offered. Of the four funerals discussed in this chapter, Prince Yoshihito's seems the least affected by Zen rituals, although it is often cited as a representative example of a Zen-style funeral.

Of the four funerals examined, Ashikaga Yoshimochi's in 1428 is the most typical example of a Zen-style funeral. Seven rituals are referred to by their special terms in *Kennaiki* and one additional action (moving the body to the temple) is described. Yoshimochi's corpse was moved to the temple on 1.19 and encoffined on 1.20; the other six rituals—*sagan butsuji, kashin butsuji, kigan butsuji, tencha butsuji, tentō butsuji,* and *ako butsuji*—all took place on 1.23. *Kennaiki* is the only source that gives particulars about the placement of the portrait—that it was displayed directly in front of the coffin in the temple and that it was also hung in front of the entryway to the crematory above a temporary altar.

Hino Shigeko's 1463 funeral, as described in *Inryōken nichiroku*, was very similar to Yoshimochi's, but with a few differences in the timing of two of the rituals. The first one may be significant. When Shigeko's portrait was hung (the term *kashin* was not used), it was at her residence immediately after she died (on 8.8), and incense offerings were made in front of it at that time. This suggests that a portrait was immediately available; it had not been necessary to have one made. That her portrait was not displayed at either the temple or at the cremation site may reflect reservations about a public funeral for her; although she was important to the Ashikaga as the wife and mother of shoguns, she herself was not a public figure. The other, smaller change is that the hot water libation was offered at her funeral before the tea offering, a reverse of the order of offerings for Yoshimochi. This minor change, however, may not be significant.

Not only did fifteenth-century funerals employ death rituals similar in many ways to each other; remarkably, many of the rituals recorded in these medieval texts are still practiced in Japan today. Studies of contemporary Japanese death practices reveal that similar ceremonies are still performed at or about the time of death, including ceremonies for calling back the soul of the deceased (*tamayobi*), turning the deceased's head to the north (*kitamakura*), bathing and changing the robes, arranging golden folding screens (*kin byōbu*) upside down or reversed near the bedside to ward off malevolent spirits, placing a message on the gate of the house where the individual died to inform others of danger from death pollution (*monoimi fuda*), chanting sutras, and offering incense. In her descriptions of funeral practices, Hikaru Suzuki mentions contemporary practices such as sutra recitations and incense offerings, viewing the deceased for the last time, using a stone to drive the nails into the coffin lid, serving food to those attending before and after the funeral (*otoki*), turning the coffin three times before it is cremated, using pine torches to lead the funeral processions along with banners, dragon-headed staffs, memorial tablets, death flowers, canopies over the coffin, cloth cords extending from the coffin, and so forth. The seven sevens are also still practiced today, much as they were in the medieval period, with the forty-nine-day period of mourning considered typical and most crucial, followed by the special memorial services held during the Festival of the Dead (*bon*), at the New Year (*shōgatsu*), and as part of equinox (*higan*) celebrations, as well as monthly (*gakki*), annual (*nenki*), and periodic (*onki*) memorials for the deceased.[100]

Notable in their absence from contemporary funerals, however, are painted portraits. Suzuki confirms that today temporary altars are set up in front of the coffin, complete with incense burners, offering vessels, and vases for flowers; at the same time she states emphatically that "no photo of the deceased was placed on the altar until funeral companies introduced the practice."[101] While she is obviously right that photographs were not used in the medieval period, painted portraits of the deceased surely were. As these fifteenth-century examples prove, the display of an image of the deceased at the funeral was not a new practice introduced in modern-day Japan.

THE MATERIAL CULTURE OF DEATH

OBJECTS OF SEPARATION AND CONTAINMENT 3

In medieval Japan an astounding variety of forms and materials were used to enclose the body after death so as to separate the dead from the living. Few have been preserved, for the obvious reason that they were generally buried, burned, or otherwise destroyed. Fortunately, some basic knowledge about what materials were used can be reconstructed from funeral manuals and records in medieval diaries of the funerals of elite members of society. What some of these objects looked like can be seen in illustrated handscrolls of the same period. This chapter examines the series of containers and enclosures—including clothing and coverings, coffins, folding screens, fences, screen curtains, and special buildings—that were essential in dealing with death; it also assesses how each of these functioned at successive stages in the process of separation.

Enclosures and containers are related concepts, but whereas an enclosure is an area sealed off by a barrier, a container is a particular type of enclosure used for holding or transporting something. Enclosures can be used to distinguish what is private from what is public, and they can be used to bar that which is undesirable, violent, or harmful. Containers function in the same way, separating what is inside from what lies outside. Both enclosures and containers can also be used to conceal and to deflect harm, making them structures well suited for dealing with death, which, being considered unique and frightening in Japanese society, impels the survivors to contain it and to separate themselves from it. From the moment dying begins until well after the body has disintegrated, efforts are made at every step to contain and separate the deceased from the world of the living.

What follows is a general summary of the most common types of containers and enclosures and an explanation of how they were utilized in medieval and earlier death practices; it is not intended to be comprehensive, nor would all the types of containers or enclosures be used for any one individual's death. The synopsis covers the containment practices prevalent among Japan's elite—the imperial family, the court, and high-ranking members of the military—over a broad span of time.

Separating and Containing the Dead

In Japan, as in most cultures, the process of separation began on the deathbed. As death approached (if there was warning), a folding screen was placed at the foot of the dying.[1] The screen did not completely separate the dying individual from the living, but initiated the process by encircling the area around the feet. The head of the dying person was oriented toward the north, with the screen positioned around the feet at the south, the direction long associated with light and the afterworld in ancient China and Japan. The placement of the screen, in effect, partially separated the ailing person, who was still in this world, from the next world, in the hope, perhaps, that he or she might be prevented from passing over to the other side. When it became clear that the spirit had departed, attempts were sometimes made to call it back to the body through a special ritual called *tamayobi* (also *tamayobai*),[2] but this action was not common in the medieval period. Once death had been ascertained, the body was placed in a series of enclosures and containers that gradually removed it farther from its loved ones and from the world it had left.

Upon death, the deceased was washed and his or her robes changed. The corpse was covered with a shroud and placed inside a wooden coffin that formed the first fully enclosed physical barrier between the deceased and the living. Later, the coffin was placed inside yet another container—a carriage or palanquin. For imperial deaths, as the corpse made its journey to the grave or cremation site another layer of separation was added. White silk screens carried by attendants were held up around the vehicle, effectively concealing it from view every step of the way and simultaneously protecting the living from the pollution of the body.[3] As in the West, the color of death in Japan is envisioned as "black," with death often being referred to as a "black shade" (*kuroi kageri*) or "black pollution" (*kuro fujō*). Today and in medieval times the use of white cloth hangings and white clothing for funerals, as well as white paper to cover the household shrine altar (*kamidana*), are intended to counteract the dangers of "black death" by protecting the living and the gods from death pollution.[4]

After the funeral procession reached the cremation site, the bier, the officiating priests, and the immediate family proceeded through one or more Shinto style gates to enter a roughly fenced enclosure that had been specially constructed and wrapped in panels of white raw silk. At this point the coffin was removed from the carriage and placed inside a roughly constructed wooden hut for the cremation. The crudity of the fenced enclosure and hut was probably intended to highlight their difference from the more finished structures built for the living. The roughness might also have signified impermanence, as both the hut and the enclosure were burned after the funeral, or the use of common materials might have been purely economical. At all times, from the moment of leaving the residence to the time it was laid on the pyre, the body was confined within multiple containers and enclosures—clothing, shroud, coffin, carriage, white silk screens (for the imperial family), cloth-wrapped fence, and hut. By the time of cremation at least six layers had been put in place to separate the corpse from the living. If the body was buried instead of cremated, similar procedures were followed; the deceased was placed inside a carriage, taken inside an enclosure, and sealed under the earth or in a special building. Whether the body was cremated, buried, or entombed, a grave was prepared and a fence constructed around it. Thus, the remains were carefully tended at the site of the cremation or burial, and the encircling and separating continued at the gravesite.

The discussion of containers and enclosures in this chapter is intended to facilitate a better understanding of their appearance and construction and their function in death rituals. Some of the objects will be familiar from the previous chapters, but many were not written about by medieval observers, probably because they were too commonplace to merit description. A few, such as the moving cloth screens, were used only for imperial funerals. Examining the objects used to contain the corpse through the lenses of diaries, funeral manuals, and medieval illustrations allows us to appreciate their fundamental importance in elite funerals.

Wrapping the Body

The corpse was first separated from the living by wrapping it and encasing it in robes and covers. The deceased was typically dressed in white hemp robes (*kyō katabira*), like a pilgrim on a journey to gain Buddhahood, with a triangular white headcloth (*zukin*), hand wraps (*tekkō*), knee protectors, and Japanese-style white socks (*shiro tabi*). After it was placed in the coffin, the corpse was then covered with a shroud (*hikiōi*) on which special Sanskrit letters were written.[5] The letters represented protective phrases.

In the diaries examined in this volume there are few details about the clothing for the deceased other than the changing of the robes or the shrouding of the clothed body. Earlier records, however, are more instructive. For Retired Emperor Shirakawa's funeral on 1129.7.8, for example, a shroud called a *nogusagoromo* (loosely translated as a "garment of field grass") was placed over his corpse.[6] It has been suggested that the word *nogusagoromo* may have originated in the early Heian period (9th–11th c.), when corpses were customarily tossed into fields and hidden in grassy areas as a way of removing them and the accompanying pollution from populated areas.[7] A *nogusagoromo* for Retired Emperor Toba's funeral on 1156.7.2 was described as made of white glossed silk (*neriginu*) eight *shaku* (slightly under eight feet) in length, with Sanskrit syllables or words thought to possess special power (mantras) written on the outside from head to foot and covering the entire body. After the shroud was drawn up over Emperor Toba, his deathbed robes were removed and an official court robe (*sokutai*) was laid inside the coffin.[8] This description of the process of removing the deceased's clothing is similar to instructions found in the contemporary *Kichiji shidai* (Order of auspicious affairs; late 11th–12th c.) by Shukaku Hosshinō (1150–1202), Emperor Go-Shirakawa's second son. The text instructs that in the summer the robe worn by the deceased was to be removed by pulling it down over the feet after the shroud had been drawn up over the body.[9] Sometimes paper rather than cloth was used as a cover for the body, as in Fujiwara Shunzei's funeral on 1204.12.1. Sanskrit phrases were written on this paper cover.[10] Writing special words or phrases on the shroud was believed to facilitate salvation or ensure a good rebirth, much as sprinkling sand over the body did in the Kōmyō Shingon sand ritual (*dosha kaji*).[11] A fourteenth-century illustrated handscroll, *Yūzū nenbutsu engi* (Origins of the Yūzū sect) shows a white shroud with letters written in ink in two long vertical rows covering the recumbent corpse of the priest Ryōnin in his wooden coffin (Figure 3.1).

Coffins

After the deceased was bathed (*mokuyoku*) and dressed, the body was placed in a wooden coffin.[12] Historical sources seldom offer detailed descriptions of the coffin, but *Kichiji shidai* reports that an average coffin in the twelfth century was about six feet long, less than two feet across, and about a foot and a half high.[13] Two wooden runners attached horizontally along the coffin's bottom acted as "feet" and a long vertical skid attached on top of the lid aided in lifting and lowering. *Kichiji ryakki* further reveals that the inside and outside of the lid and the bottom of the coffin were to be lacquered to prevent fluid seepage from the body. Sometimes a diviner chose an auspicious day and ordered the coffin on that day when an individual was still living.[14] More often, however, the coffin was ordered after death, in which case there was often not sufficient time to add the many coats of lacquer.[15] Indeed, many diaries refer to the coffin being ordered on the afternoon of the encoffining, which usually took place in the evening of the day of death. Although the information given in *Kichiji ryakki* suggests that the size of the coffin was rather standard, it appears that each was designed for a specific individual. That coffins were not

Figure 3.1. Ryōnin's coffin.
Source: *Yūzū nenbutsu engi* in *Zoku Nihon no emaki*, vol. 21, ed. Komatsu Shigemi (Tokyo: Chūō Kōronsha, 1992), after image on p. 53.

Figure 3.2. Shinran's coffin.
Source: *Zenshin shōnin Shinran den-e*, in *Zokuzoku Nihon emaki taisei: Denki, engi hen*, vol. 1, ed. Komatsu Shigemi (Tokyo: Chūō Kōronsha, 1994), after image on p. 102.

made ahead of time in great numbers suggests that strong taboos or superstitions surrounded the process.

A number of images of coffins appear in medieval handscrolls, and they generally conform to the written descriptions. *Yūzū nenbutsu engi* (14th c.), *Hōnen shōnin e-den* (14th c.), and *Zenshin shōnin Shinran den-e* (late 13th c.) all depict rectangular coffins as simple, unlacquered wooden boxes. In the scene where Priest Shinran lies dying we can see a simple, unlacquered coffin ready and waiting in the background, hidden from the ailing priest by a folding screen (Figure 3.2).

In the two other illustrations the corpse is already inside the coffin. *Hōnen shōnin e-den* shows a stone coffin that has been dug up for reburial. As a priest removes the lid and pulls down a white shroud, everyone is astounded to see that Priest Hōnen's appearance is exactly as it had been when he was living (even though he has been buried for fifteen years; Figure 3.3). In *Yūzū nenbutsu engi*, a white shroud completely covers the body of Priest Ryōnin (1073–1133;

Figure 3.3. Hōnen's coffin.
Source: *Hōnen shōnin e-den*, in *Zoku Nihon no emaki*, vol. 3, ed. Komatsu Shigemi (Tokyo: Chūō Kōronsha, 1990), after image on p. 49.

see Fig. 3.1). Two parallel lines of ink, probably Sanskrit prayers, can be seen running the length of the shroud from head to toe.

Folding Screens and Hanging Cloth Screens

Folding screens (*byōbu*) and screens made of fabric hung from a frame (*kichō*) not only functioned as temporary room partitions and decorative backdrops in the residences of the elite, but also served as protective enclosures for the dying and the recently deceased. Scenes from *Hōnen shōnin e-den* (Figure 3.4) and *Zenshin shōnin Shinran den-e* (Figure 3.2) show the priests Hōnen and Shinran on their deathbeds, lying on their right sides facing the viewer and the west, the direction of Amida's Western Paradise.

Both priests can be seen reclining on straw mats, thick robes covering their bodies and six-panel folding screens encircling their feet, showing the

Figure 3.4. Hōnen on his deathbed.
Source: *Hōnen shōnin e-den*, in *Zoku Nihon no emaki*, vol. 3, ed. Komatsu Shigemi (Tokyo: Chūō Kōronsha, 1990), after image on p. 2.

typical preparations taken in the medieval period for high-ranking priests and elite members of society as death approached. In cases of sudden death, similar arrangements would have been made immediately after the last breath was drawn.

Written sources confirm that the corpse was prepared in much the same manner in the medieval period as in the Heian period. After Retired Emperor Toba died on 1156.7.2, we are told, his head was forthwith turned to the north and his face to the west, then the robe he had been wearing was taken off and a new one placed over the body.[16] The straw mat that Toba was lying on was then removed,[17] folding screens were set up around him, and a light, probably candles or a lamp, was placed near his body; finally, incense was lit.[18] Although various texts mention that the garments the individual was wearing at death were changed, it was uncommon to actually dress the body in the new garment. Rather, the new robe was generally laid over the corpse, covering it from head to foot. So the two priests in Figures 3.2 and 3.4 are shown near death; if they had already died, we would expect their heads to have been covered up and the mats on which they rested to have been removed.

In the illustrations depicting Shinran's and Hōnen's death scenes, the painted sides of the screens face the recumbent priests, also verifying that they are still alive. It has been generally assumed that after death the screens were reversed, with the painted side facing out, as it is customary in some areas of Japan to reverse the screens in this manner when someone dies even today. None of the medieval diaries or handscrolls that I examined explicitly confirm that the screens around a corpse were reversed, but there is some evidence that the practice predated the fourteenth century. *Kichiji ryakki* gives instructions that after death the screens around the body were to be reversed.[19] The eleventh-century *Eiga monogatari* comments that when Kishi, a consort of Emperor Go-Suzaku died in 1025, both the folding and hanging screens had to be "changed."[20] The text does not say clearly that they were reversed, but some scholars assert that even at this time it was customary to reverse the curtains and screens in the room when someone died.[21] It is likely, therefore, that this custom began in the early Heian period, or perhaps earlier, and persisted throughout the medieval period and later.

It is unclear why the practice of reversing the screens is so seldom discussed in medieval diaries and why it is hardly ever illustrated. Hōnen and Shinran are pictured first still alive on their deathbeds and then dead in their coffins, but not in the moments after they died with the screens reversed. It may be because the moments before death and the encoffining of the corpse are seen as the more important events in the Buddhist world. The final moment of one's life can influence one's fate after death, and in the Pure Land tradition "right mindfulness at the last moment" (*rinjū shōnen*) is crucial for experiencing Amida's descent to lead one to the Western Paradise. Placing the corpse in the coffin, which involved special ritual actions and chanting (*nyūgan butsuji*), was likewise a pivotal moment when the deceased was removed from the sight (and world) of the living. The handscrolls can be enormously helpful in recovering information, but their other hagiographic or doctrinal aims preclude telling us more about these folding screens. How were they decorated? Were certain subjects and styles considered particularly appropriate to death and dying? In the illustrations above, the painted sides of the screens are at best barely visible, making the answers to these questions unobtainable.

Written sources, however, are more forthcoming about the subjects and styles of screens used at funerals. In particular, *Inryōken nichiroku*, the fifteenth-century record compiled by Rokuon'in priests Kikei Shinzui (dates unknown) and Kisen Shūshō (d. 1493), includes a number of references to the death-related uses of screens.[22] This source does not specifically deal with screens set up around dying individuals, but it does give particulars on how screens were used to surround the corpse during funeral rituals.

One type, the gold-leaf folding screen (*kinbyōbu*), was placed behind the coffin as the body lay in state and also behind the funerary tablet after burial or cremation. The gold-leaf screens mentioned in *Inryōken nichiroku* were painted with flowers and plants. On 1463.8.11, for example, we are told that golden screens had been borrowed from the Takakura Gosho and positioned behind the coffin of Ashikaga Yoshimasa's mother, Hino Shigeko (1411–1463; Buddhist name Shōchiin) as she lay in state at Tōjiin.[23] The screens were decorated with designs of azaleas under pine trees (*matsu no shita ni tsutsuji hana*) on gold-leaf gound.[24] Likewise, after the ninth Ashikaga shogun, Yoshihisa (d. 1489.3.26), was cremated, a pair of golden screens painted with bamboo were set up behind his mortuary tablet at Tōjiin.[25] Yet another source mentions a pair of golden screens covered with fan paintings arranged on either side of Ashikaga Yoshiharu's (1511–1550) casket, with their painted sides turned away from the body.[26]

Several entries state that such screens were used in accordance with custom or precedent, suggesting that by the fifteenth century golden screens with paintings of plants and flowers were conventional accouterments for death ceremonies of the elite. Golden screens and memorial tablets with golden letters appear in textual contexts in which the remains of the deceased and the living occupy the same space. The records imply that this combination of plant motifs and gold somehow purified the scene or had a prophylactic effect on the pollution that accompanied death, making it possible for the living to interact with the dead safely in the same space.

The prevalence of flower and plant motifs on these gold-leafed screens is related to paradise imagery in the *Taima mandara* and in Pure Land Buddhism.[27]

In Buddhism the lotus flower in particular has special associations with the enlightened Buddha, but flowers in general are linked to the paradise imagery in many Pure Land sutras, such as the *Dai muryōju kyō* and *Jōdo sanbukyō*. Accordingly, plants were reminders of Amida's Pure Land and served to assure the believer that the deceased was enjoying that peaceful and blossom-filled paradise. The Ashikaga shoguns, of course, were devotees of Zen Buddhism, but medieval Japan saw a considerable intermingling of Pure Land and Zen beliefs. Indeed, the examination of the death rituals of the Nakahara family in Chapter 1 suggests an even greater eclecticism in medieval death rituals at this time than has been suspected, with rituals drawn from ancient yin-yang practices as well as from more conventional Esoteric, Pure Land, and Zen Buddhist traditions.

It is also clear that the gold leaf on the screens had special meaning for death practices in medieval Japan. Gold appears in Pure Land sutras, always with implications of "preciousness, purity, and radiance."[28] According to ancient texts, one of the distinctive signs of the Historical Buddha was his golden body (*kinjin*). Gold pigments or leaf applied to his images allude to the Buddha himself. In descriptions and depictions of Pure Land Buddhism, the Buddha Amida appears suffused with a golden radiance, which also represents his purifying light. Buddhist devotees, therefore, equated gold with the historical Buddha and with Amida's special powers of purification, and believed that gold (representing Amida) could ameliorate the pollution of death and protect them from defilement.

What was the fate of these golden screens after they were used in funeral rituals? In Japan the personal effects of the deceased were traditionally burned after cremation or burial of the corpse. For example, after Emperor Go-Ichijō's funeral in 1036 the various lacquer boxes and the emperor's personal items that they contained, such as his comb stand and hat, were burned. In addition, anything used specifically for the deceased during the funeral, including the low table for food offerings and the utensils for washing the body, was likewise burned, including the carriage that carried the corpse to the cremation site.[29] If personal carriages were destroyed, why not the folding screens that surrounded and protected the body? It seems, however, that they were not—even when the screens were the personal property of the deceased. For example, the golden screens of azaleas and pines used for Hino Shigeko's funeral were said to be her personal property, yet twenty-eight years later they are mentioned again in the same diary, indicating that they had not been burned.[30] The incinerated items belonging to Emperor Go-Ichijō were all wooden objects, as are screens, but the gold painted or applied to their surfaces seems to have exempted them from being destroyed in accordance with the popular death taboos. In fact, the prophylactic quality attributed to the gold may explain why they could even be reused. We also do not know whether families only recycled certain gold screens for use at later funerals, or whether the screens were returned to daily use. It would be convenient if one screen could be followed throughout its lifetime, and how and when it was used could be accurately tracked, but the documents needed for such research are difficult to find. We can only wonder how many of the medieval-period golden screens displayed in museums and prized by collectors today were originally intended for funerary use. It is certainly a good possibility that some, at least, were used in this manner, yet our current reading of these screens remains largely secular. Their brilliant gold and bright polychromy mesmerizes us, and we immediately envision them framing important personages at banquets and ceremonies. Seldom do we imagine them as backdrops for corpses and coffins.

Examples of gold used for other objects connected with death are numerous. Buildings that housed mummies or other types of human remains, or structures that were simply associated with someone's death, were sometimes covered with gold leaf. The Konjikidō, conceived as a hall of worship for Amida and as a tomb, was entirely overlaid with gold leaf by Fujiwara no Kiyohira (1056–1128) to counteract, it was believed, the impurity of entombing his mummified body and those of his son and grandson inside altar daises.[31] Other, later, buildings were also sheathed in gold. The most famous, of course, is the glittering Golden Pavilion (Kinkakuji) built between 1397 and 1407 by the third Muromachi shogun, Ashikaga Yoshimitsu (1358–1408). Constructed originally as a private Amida chapel at Yoshimitsu's Kitayama estate, the Golden Pavilion was designated as a reliquary (*shariden*) when the villa was converted into a Zen temple, Rokuonji, after Yoshimitsu's death. The first floor of the Golden Pavilion held carved images of Amida, Kannon, and Seishi, as well as a portrait statue of Yoshimitsu and a portrait of priest Musō Soseki, suggesting that mortuary rituals were held at the site.[32] Later examples include a spirit hall (*tamaya*), covered inside and out with gold-and-black lacquer, that was built for Nanbu Toshiyasu (d. 1631), a daimyo from Mutsu (Aomori), Kōdaiji, a memorial temple built for Toyotomi Hideyoshi, and a spirit hall built for Sanada Nobuyuki (1566–1658).[33] Only the interiors of the two latter structures were decorated with floral subjects on gold-leaf backgrounds, but the idea is the same: gold was employed to mitigate and purify any pollution associated with death.

Gold pigments were also applied to memorial tablets (*ihai*) for the same purpose (Plate 2).[34] These long, narrow wooden plaques stood upright on a base and were housed in family temples during the medieval period, though today they are generally kept on Buddhist altars (*butsudan*) in family homes. After the funeral, a priest, important family member, or prominent artist or calligrapher was requested to write the deceased's Buddhist name (*kaimyō*)[35] and the date of death on the tablet in gold. For example, in 1487 the painter Kano Masanobu (1434–1530) was commissioned to write *kaimyō* in gold paint on eight memorial tablets of former Ashikaga shoguns, and in the following year he was ordered by Kisen Shūshō to add gold characters to another.[36] These tablets, much like painted or sculpted portraits, were understood to serve as receptacles for the deceased's spirit. The gold letters helped purify the object, making it safe for placement in a temple and for contact with the living.

There are other examples of gold being used in unusual ways in connection with death. A case in point is the special golden oxcart decorated with colored cords (*itoge no kuruma*) that carried Fujiwara Teishi (d. 1000.12.16), daughter of Michitaka (953–995), to her resting place south of the Toribeno burial ground.[37] As a consort of Emperor Ichijō, Teishi had been elevated to imperial status, making this type of carriage appropriate for her rank. But the use of gold may suggest a singular need for additional protection in transporting her body to its final resting place because Teishi died during childbirth, which was considered a particularly "impure" death. It may be that the gold was intended to offer additional protection when a death had been problematic.[38]

Moving Screens

During the Heian period two other types of cloth screens, inner screens (*gyōshō*; also *kōshō*) and outer screens (*hoshō*), were employed as moving curtains to conceal the coffin as it progressed to the grave or cremation grounds (Figure 3.5).

These screens were generally made of white raw silk attached to wooden or bamboo frames. The cloth screens were primarily used at imperial funerals and to conceal court women when they traveled. No known paintings show how they were used for funerals, probably because the funerals of emperors were seldom illustrated. Existing written records, however, do mention the

Figure 3.5. Moving screens (*gyōshō/hoshō*).
Source: *Jingihaku sōmoki* in *Nihon kyōiku bunko*, vol. 10 (*shūkyō*), ed. Kurokawa Mamichi (Tokyo: Dōbunkan, 1910–1911), after image on p. 692.

screens. The best description is of Emperor Go-Ichijō's funeral in 1036: we are told that sixteen inner screens (*gyōshō*) concealed the palanquin that held his coffin and, along with four long silk outer screens (*hoshō*) on each side, accompanied the emperor's body on its trip to the cremation site.[39] Each inner screen, measuring a little over five feet long (5 *shaku*), was made of white silk and carried on a white staff by a single attendant.[40] Thus, in total, sixteen attendants supported the *gyōshō* surrounding Go-Ichijō's palanquin, arranged as five screens on each side and three each concealing the front and rear. Although there may well be other symbolism to this number, sixteen has great significance in Buddhism: there are sixteen arhats (*jūroku rakan*) who protect the Buddhist law, sixteen contemplations on Amida (*jūrokkan*), sixteen great kingdoms in India at the time of Buddhism (*jūroku daikoku*), and sixteen protective deities (*jūroku zenjin*).

Surrounding the *gyōshō* was another set of even larger movable screens called *hoshō*, which provided additional concealment and protection. Four of these outer screens were carried on each side of Go-Ichijō's palanquin flanking the inner screens, bringing the total number of *hoshō* to eight. The use of four outer screens per side relates to another pivotal number in Buddhism, and there are a multitude of terms related to Buddhism that use this number.[41] The number four (*shi*) is also a homonym for death (*shi*) in Japan, offering yet another possibility why four of these screens were chosen to flank each side of the coffin (sixteen is also a multiple of four). The outer screens were similarly made of white silk, but each was extraordinarily large, measuring approximately sixty feet (6 *jō*) long, and required five people to carry it. Thus, in total, fifty-six attendants were needed to carry the two layers of inner and outer screens as the procession moved along its journey to the burial or cremation grounds.

The purpose of the movable silk enclosures in imperial funerals was obviously to conceal the coffin, but from whom? As funerals generally took place in the middle of the night, spectators would have been few, and anyone who attended could not have seen much because of the darkness. Nevertheless, a living emperor would never appear without a barrier—a screen or bamboo blind—between him and others, so it is reasonable that his corpse also needed to be separated and protected by the movable cloth screens. Moreover, the protective white silk screens were essential in safeguarding those who accompanied the body from the pollution believed to emanate from the corpse. As suggested earlier, white screens and white clothing for Japanese funerals served to purify, counteracting the dangers of death and protecting the living from pollution. Movable screens were not mentioned in any of the later sources on funerals that I examined. Whether they continued to be used for the funerals of royals in the medieval period is a topic for further study.

Enclosures for Cremation: Fences and Curtains

One of the most astounding visualizations of a medieval funeral procession and cremation is that of Priest Nichiren depicted in *Nichiren shōnin chūgasan*, a set of five handscrolls compiled by Enmyōin Nitchō (1441–1501) and illustrated by a little-known Kyoto artist, Kubota Muneyasu (Plate 3). Indeed, because the Nichiren scrolls were produced in the late fifteenth or very early sixteenth century, several hundred years after Nichiren's death in 1282, the images are representative of funerals of that era rather than those of the thirteenth century. Not surprisingly, then, the details match closely those found in written sources documenting the fifteenth-century funerals of the Ashikaga shoguns. Two other, earlier, scrolls, notably *Hōnen shōnin e-den* (14th c.) (Plate 4) and *Zenshin shōnin Shinran den-e* (late 13th c.) (Plate 5), also illustrate the cremations of medieval priests, albeit in much simplified form. My interest in these images is for the visual data they can provide about fourteenth- and fifteenth-century funerals; I do not intend to suggest that they accurately represent the funerals of these priests. Rather, when taken together with information available in earlier texts like *Kichiji ryakki* and *Sakeiki*, these important paintings allow us better to understand both how the arrangement of the cremation site changed over time and yet how very consistent it remained. The pictures are particularly compelling because they illustrate structures no longer used and little remembered today, while the written sources offer valuable details, including their actual sizes and construction.

For the funerals of the elite from at least the Heian period on, it was common to construct either one or two rough-hewn fences (*aragaki*), made of woven strips of either cypress bark or bamboo, around the cremation site.[42] The use of common, rough, unfinished materials is significant because it was another way to distinguish structures made specifically for the dead from the more finished constructions built for the living or designed for buddhas and *kami*. Although the size of the cremation enclosure must have varied somewhat according to the deceased's social and economic status and the historical period, one source tells us that the fence measured about 120 yards (36 *jō*) around, was a little over 6 feet (6 *shaku*) high, and had four unfinished wooden torii-style gates built into each of its four sides, which faced the cardinal directions.[43] The fence and the gates were specially constructed to avoid inserting any pillars into the earth, so as not to violate ancient taboos associated with digging into the ground, believed to be the realm of powerful earth deities. This type of construction was called *kirikake*, which literally means to "cut and hang."[44] To support the vertical pillars, horizontal slats were attached to the vertical posts like wainscoting.[45] Because these slats were set very close together, such an enclosure effectively concealed its occupants. For this reason, a similar type of fence was placed near exterior walls of the imperial palace compound to keep outside prying eyes from seeing the royal occupants. Indeed, it is likely that for the funerals of emperors, the enclosures surrounding their cremation sites were more substantial, constructed of wood, and not unlike those at the palace.[46] At cremation sites for people of less than imperial status, however, such as those for priests and shoguns in the fifteenth century, enclosures were probably similar to those seen in the Nichiren scroll (Plate 3). Both types were effective in concealing the coffin, the cremation, and the private grief of the mourning family from outsiders. Although the fifteenth-century enclosures were probably not as large as those for earlier imperial cremations, the general arrangement described in the twelfth-century *Kichiji ryakki* is very similar to the image depicted in the sixteenth-century handscroll of Nichiren's cremation.

For the cremations of emperors and imperial princes in the Heian period, it was common to construct an identically shaped smaller precinct inside the outer fence. This type of labor-intensive double enclosure was constructed when Emperor Go-Ichijō was cremated in 1036. His double enclosure comprised an outer fence almost 360 feet (36 *jō*) in circumference and about 6 feet (6 *shaku*) high, and a slightly smaller inner fence (*uchi gaki*) approximately 240 feet in circumference (24 *jō*) and about the same height as the outer fence. Raw silk was draped over both fences and white sand was sprinkled on the ground between them. The double enclosure had two gates, with the second torii erected on the south side of the inner fence, identical in size and position to a torii on the south side of the outer fence. Both gates were about 13 feet tall (1 *jō*, 3 *shaku*) and nearly as wide (1 *jō*, 2 *shaku*).[47] When Emperor Go-Ichijō's funeral procession reached the cremation site, the long moving screens would have been positioned flanking the pathway from the south torii to the fenced area. As the coffin was removed from the palanquin and carried inside the enclosure, it would have been totally concealed from view by the cloth screens on both sides and by the curtains on the gate at the end. The construction of two matching fences, one inside the other, augmented the sacredness of the inner ritual area where the cremation took place and also distinguished it as a special imperial site. The greater the number of enclosures or barriers created between the living and the dead, the more protection was afforded to both. But such protection came at a high cost and appears to have been available only to members of the imperial family and high-ranking members of the court.

Two enclosures may originally have communicated higher status, but by the medieval period the single-enclosure configuration had become the norm, as illustrated in both *Nichiren shōnin chūgasan* (Plate 3) and *Hōnen shōnin e-den* (Plate 4), where only a single palisade surrounds the priests' funeral pyres. Yet the cremation sites depicted in the Nichiren and Hōnen handscrolls are very similar to the one described for Emperor Go-Ichijō's cremation in the eleventh century, except for single enclosures rather than double. In the illustration of Hōnen's cremation, four strips of white cloth (*manmaku*) were wrapped horizontally and affixed to slender black poles to form a fence. At least some of the poles must have been inserted directly into the ground, because no horizontal boards or anything else stiff enough to hold them upright are in evidence. This type of enclosure could be quickly constructed to accommodate the need for a quick funeral, or it might have been a simplification contrived by the artist. However constructed, all the enclosures served the same purpose and were equally effective in concealing from view everything but the flames and smoke of the cremation fire. The wrapped enclosure at the cremation site generally had the same purpose as the moving screens in the funeral procession—to protect the viewers from the body's pollution.[48] The cloth-hung poles that serve as Hōnen's cremation enclosure look as if they could have been carried as protective screens in his funeral procession; there is no evidence, however, that this was done. Both *Sakeiki* and *Kichiji ryakki* describe double enclosures with silk curtains hung from both the inner and outer torii, and special handmade white curtains wrapped horizontally around the outsides of both the encircling fences.[49] The handscroll of Nichiren's funeral (late 15th–early 16th c.) illustrates only a single enclosure, but it clearly shows us the fence wrapped with white silk. It does not, however, show any silk cloth hanging from the south gate (Plate 3).

In the picture of Nichiren's funeral, the enclosing fence is intersected by four gateways, each with its name written on the wooden plaque hanging from its crossbeam—Hosshinmon (Gate to Awaken Aspiration for Enlightenment) on the south gate, Shugyōmon (Gate of Asceticism) on the west, and Bodaimon (Gate of Repose of the Dead) on the north. The writing on the east gate cannot be read, but a second large torii, standing to the south of the enclosure, has Nehandō (Nirvana Hall) written on its plaque. This basic structure consisting of an enclosure and four gateways has ancient roots in Asia, recalling the arrangement of Aryan villages in India, a layout that was later appropriated for enclosing stupas holding relics of the Buddha. The four gateways at Japanese cremation sites are "Shinto-style" torii, but they are not dissimilar to the early Indian gates seen at the Great Stupa at Sanchi. According to Gorai Shigeru, gates of this same configuration and type were used in ancient Japan at *mogari no miya* (temporary interment palaces), and later the four gates were incorporated into Buddhist funerals in Japan.[50] Other scholars, however, see their symbolism as deriving from the "four gates of Buddhism" (*shimon*), which represent the four stages of Buddhist practice: (1) awakening aspiration (Hosshinmon, east); (2) practice (Shugyōmon, south); (3) enlightenment (Bodaimon, west); and (4) nirvana (Nehanmon, north). It has been suggested that the gates might have come into use for funerals in Japan through their

NORTH
Nehanmon

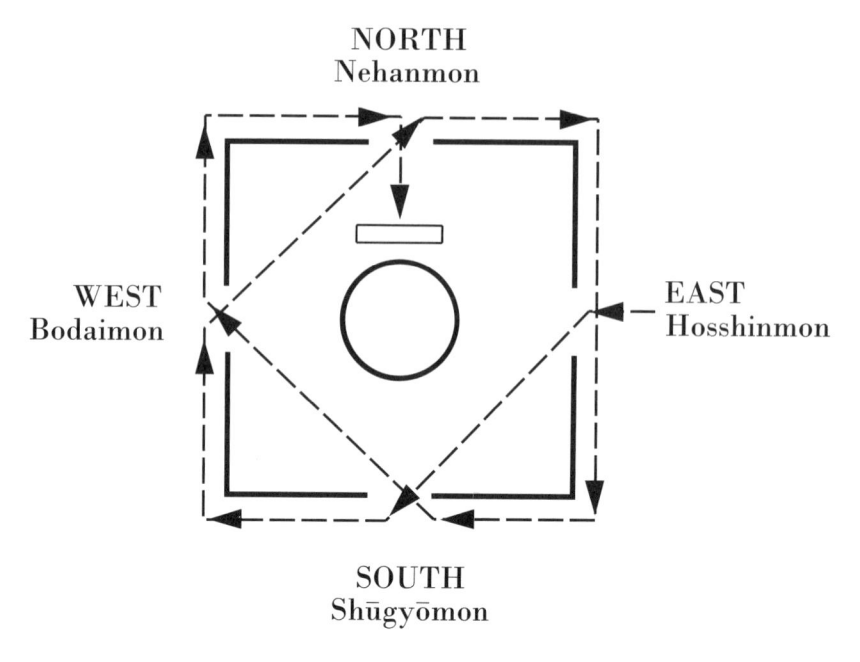

WEST
Bodaimon

EAST
Hosshinmon

SOUTH
Shūgyōmon

Figure 3.6. Movement of corpse at cremation site.
Source: Drawing by Adriana Maguina-Ugarte. Adapted from Bernard Faure, *The Rhetoric of Immediacy: A Cultural Critique of Chan/Zen Buddhism* (Princeton, NJ: Princeton University Press, 1991), p. 199.

association with a Shingon ritual for the dead in which the coffin was taken in and out of them following a particular sequence.[51] Indeed, Hosshin, Shugyō, Bodai, and Nehan are terms associated with the four directional gates of the Esoteric mandala, correlating with the directions east, south, west, and north, respectively.[52] In the traditional Buddhist mandala the correlation between the names of the gates and the cardinal directions differs from the correlation at Nichirin's cremation site. This aberration in the Nichiren handscroll may be interpreted as another instance of the artist slightly altering the normal sequence for artistic (or other) reasons.

In Zen-style funeral rituals the four gates had another purpose. The coffin was carried clockwise around the cremation ground three times, entering first through the east gate and then passing through each of the other three gates.[53] Thus, the coffin entered the Hosshinmon (Present), exited through the Shugyōmon (Ten Worlds), reentered through the Bodaimon (Future), and exited through the Nehanmon (Past), symbolizing the four stages of a Buddhist's life, from delusion to nirvana.[54] The first circumambulation signified the ven-

Plate 1. Ten kings of hell and scenes of punishment. Artist unknown. 14th century. Pair of hanging scrolls.
Source: Idemitsu Bijutsukan, ed., *Eigakareta gokuraku to jigoku: Bukkyō kaiga meihin ten* (Tokyo: Benridō, 2002), after pp. 20–21, plate 2.

Plate 2. Memorial tablet (*ihai*). Source: Tōjiin, Kyoto. Photo by R. Scott Van Zant.

Plate 3. Nichiren's cremation. Source: *Nichiren shōnin chūgasan*, in *Zokuzoku Nihon emaki taisei: Denki, engi hen*, vol. 2, ed. Komatsu Shigemi (Tokyo: Chūō Kōronsha, 1993), after image on pp. 72–73.

Plate 4. Hōnen's cremation. Source: *Hōnen shōnin e-den*, in *Zoku Nihon no emaki*, vol. 3, ed. Komatsu Shigemi (Tokyo: Chūō Kōronsha, 1990), after image on p. 52.

Plate 5. Shinran's cremation.
Source: *Zenshin shōnin Shinran den-e*, in *Zokuzoku Nihon emaki taisei: Denki, engi hen*, vol. 1, ed. Komatsu Shigemi (Tokyo: Chūō Kōronsha, 1994), after image on pp. 106–107.

Plate 6. Nichiren's funeral procession—torch, lotus flower, banners, dragon-head banner hooks. Source: *Nichiren shōnin chūgasan*, in *Zokuzoku Nihon emaki taisei: Denki, engi hen*, vol. 2, ed. Komatsu Shigemi (Tokyo: Chūō Kōronsha, 1993), after image on p. 71, bottom panel.

Plate 7. Nichiren's funeral procession—censers, musical instruments, flower vase, candle holder, scrolls, sutra tables. Source: *Nichiren shōnin chūgasan*, in *Zokuzoku Nihon emaki taisei: Denki, engi hen*, vol. 2, ed. Komatsu Shigemi (Tokyo: Chūō Kōronsha, 1993), after image on p. 70, bottom panel.

Plate 8. Nichiren's funeral procession—offering trays and vessels, memorial tablet, shoes, cloth cord. Source: *Nichiren shōnin chūgasan*, in *Zokuzoku Nihon emaki taisei: Denki, engi hen*, vol. 2, ed. Komatsu Shigemi (Tokyo: Chūō Kōronsha, 1993), after image on p. 71, upper panel.

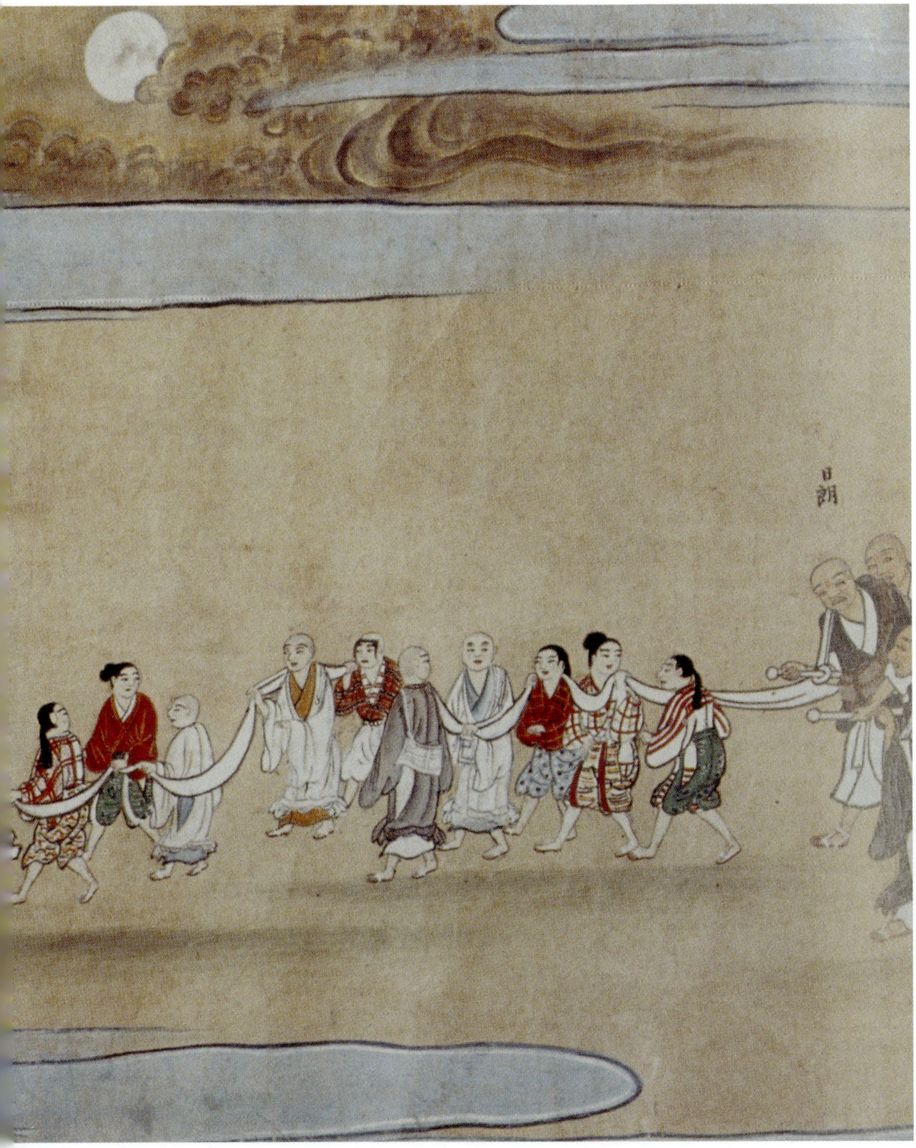
日朗

Plate 9. Nichiren's funeral procession—palanquin, canopy, helmet, sword, riderless horse.
Source: *Nichiren shōnin chūgasan*, in *Zokuzoku Nihon emaki taisei: Denki, engi hen*, vol. 2, ed. Komatsu Shigemi (Tokyo: Chūō Kōronsha, 1993), after image on p. 70, upper panel.

Plate 10. Nichiren's funeral procession—Kamakura warriors.
Source: *Nichiren shōnin chūgasan*, in *Zokuzoku Nihon emaki taisei: Denki, engi hen*, vol. 2, ed. Komatsu Shigemi (Tokyo: Chūō Kōronsha, 1993), after image on p. 69, bottom panel.

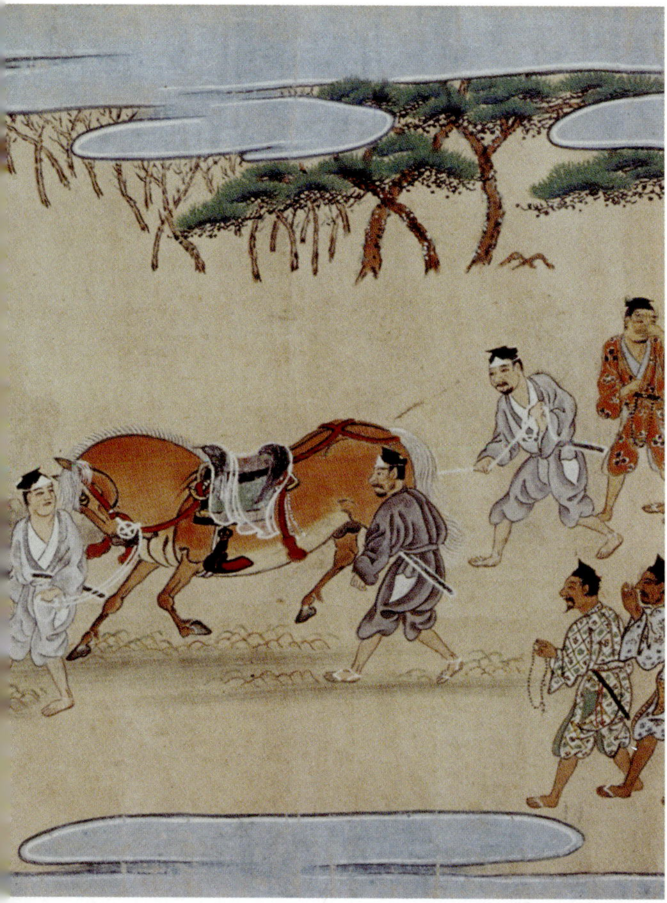

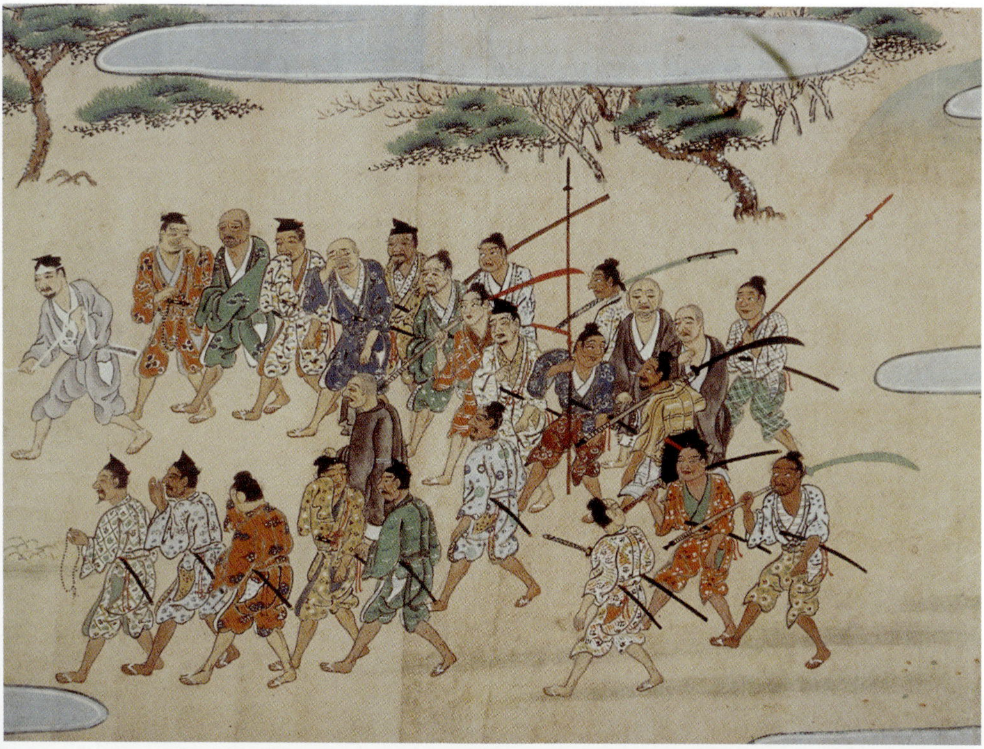

Plate 11. Hōnen's seventh memorial service. Source: *Hōnen shōnin e-den*, in *Zoku Nihon no emaki*, vol. 3, ed. Komatsu Shigemi (Tokyo: Chūō Kōronsha, 1990), after image on p. 29.

eration of the Buddha, the second the elimination of illusions, and the third the attainment of sublimation.[55] The three rotations of the coffin around the cremation site are said to correspond to the three circumambulations that devout Buddhists make around the stupa, symbolizing the creation of a buddha (here, the deceased) at the center. Other symbolism of the gates is related to the "four encounters" that Sakyamuni experienced during his spiritual quest. Four times he left the palace and entered the royal city, and on successive visits encountered a sick man, an old man, a corpse, and an ascetic. After each chance meeting, he left the city through a different gate on its east, south, west, or north sides.[56]

This circumambulation ritual was performed at two of the fifteenth-century Zen-style cremations that I examined—that of shogun Ashikaga Yoshimochi on 1428.1.23 and of his sister-in-law Hino Shigeko on 1463.8.11.[57] There is little evidence to support the performance of the circumambulation ritual for burials, or with any great regularity for any of the other Ashikaga cremations in the fifteenth century. Naming the gates, as described above, was likely a common practice in the late medieval period, notwithstanding scant mention of the practice in written records. Therefore, the illustrated handscroll of Nichiren's funeral provides an unparalleled record of late medieval cremation practice.

In the *Nichiren* scroll, the gateways on the north and east sides are "wrapped" in white silk, making entry and exit inaccessible, while the south and west gateways remain open for entry and egress. Thus Nichiren's coffin was probably brought into the cremation site through the south gate, possibly because this was the direction associated with entering the afterworld, according to ancient Chinese cosmology. After the ceremony, his cremated remains were then likely removed through the west gate, the direction of the Western Paradise. This procedure would have been different from the traditional circumambulation described above, but it reveals a strong sense of directional symmetry: at the time of death the body was positioned with its head pointing north; the corpse was removed from the residence through the eastern wall of the compound;[58] the body was brought into the cremation site from the south; and the cremated remains were taken out through the west gate. The texts that discuss the Ashikaga cremations do not mention which gates the coffin passed through or the order, only that the coffin was processed around the site three times.

A temporary four-posted mourning "hall" (*sōjōden/sōbadono*) was sometimes used at imperial funerals as a place to set down the coffin after taking it from the palanquin or carriage and before the cremation began. This type of structure is not illustrated in the handscrolls nor described in medieval texts. *Sakeiki*'s account of Go-Ichijō's funeral in the fifth month of 1036 explains that his hall measured about seven or eight feet (7–8 *shaku*) on each side and was just under eight feet (8 *shaku*) high. It was constructed just west of the outer gate. Silk curtains were hung from its roof down the four sides, and rectangular straw mats (*nagamushiro*) were installed over the wooden flooring throughout.[59] The coffin was placed in the center on three special tatami mats decorated with brocade borders (*kōraiberi*).[60]

Another shelter (*kishoya*; also *uwaya*, or *hiya*), composed of four pillars and a roof with a rectangular hearth pit (*ro*) in the center, was built in the middle of the cremation area defined by the inner fence. The *kishoya* for Emperor Go-Ichijō's cremation was very large, roughly twenty feet long (2 *jo*), fifteen feet wide (1 *jo*, 5 *shaku*), and twelve feet (1 *jo*, 2 *shaku*) high.[61] *Kichiji ryakki* gives the standard measurement for a hearth as about nine feet long (9 *shaku*), three feet wide (3 *shaku*), and two and a half feet deep (2 *shaku*, 5 *sun*), with the narrow ends oriented to the north and south.[62] The roof of the structure was draped with white silk curtains that hung down over its four sides.[63]

A cremation hut is illustrated in the *Nichiren* scroll, but it is much smaller and architecturally less complex than those for earlier imperial funerals described in *Kichiji ryakki* and *Sakeiki*, and it lacks silk curtains (Plate 3). The simple structure depicted in the scroll is comprised of four vertical posts supporting a makeshift roof of wood planks uneven in width. Beneath its eaves hangs a plaque bearing the word *tōgaku* (the Buddha's enlightenment or enlightenment equal to the Buddha's), signifying that the deceased about to be cremated, in this case Priest Nichiren, was enlightened. In the illustration, we can see that a shallow pit has been dug into the earth and lined with wooden planks for the hearth.

The construction of the hearth to hold imperial coffins was quite complicated, including various layers of different materials placed in its boxlike form. First two rough mats (*komo*)[64] were laid directly on the earth, followed by two more mats (*mushiro*).[65] Charcoal (*tan*) was piled on top of the mats, then firewood (*maki*) was added. Stacks of firewood, charcoal, pine branches, and straw to fuel the flames were prepared and placed on all sides of the cremation hut.[66] A slightly different arrangement for the construction of Emperor Go-Ichijō's cremation pit is described in *Sakeiki*, where mats (*mushiro*) formed the initial layer, followed by handmade cloth spread over them, then silk cloth, and finally piles of kindling. The four sides of this hearth box were covered with white cloth, and large buckets of water were placed in the four corners of the cremation hut, each with a ladle and a broom.[67] The various layers separating the ground from the coffin had both prophylactic and practical functions: protecting the corpse from earth spirits that might have been angered by the digging of the hole, raising the coffin off the ground to allow for better burning, and also providing combustible materials for the cremation.

Two additional tent-like structures (*aku* or *aku no ya*) were constructed outside the outer gate, one on the right side and one on the left, to accommodate the elite persons who attended Emperor Go-Ichijō's cremation.[68] Commonly used for special court rituals or festivals, such structures were composed of four pillars set into the ground to form a square with another pillar in the center. The structure on the right was reserved for members of the court and had the additions of a roof and wooden floor planking (*itajiki*) covered with mats of miscanthus reed; long strips of white silk were draped from the roof to form a four-sided tent. The structure on the left was also tented with white silk, but it had no wooden floor, only straw mats covering the bare ground; this was where the Buddhist priests connected to the palace (*gozensō*) sat during the cremation.[69] The materials used in the building of these structures—wood, straw, and silk—are burnable, and the structures were presumably destroyed after the cremation. The two different types of flooring distinguished the status of the two groups—courtiers and priests.

Although such viewing platforms are not depicted in any of the later illustrated handscrolls, various chronicles attest that similar structures were still used at funerals in the fifteenth century. According to *Kanmon gyoki*, two wooden platforms (*sajiki*) were built in front of the torii gate for Prince Yoshihito's cremation in 1416. In that text the platform on the south side accommodated the deceased's family and the one on the north side was for other elite guests.[70] According to *Kennaiki*, a wooden platform was constructed along the west side of Tōjiin's Buddha Hall for Ashikaga Yoshimochi's funeral in 1428,[71] presumably to accommodate the shogun's family. No platforms are recorded for Hino Shigeko's funeral (1463.8.11), perhaps because her funeral and cremation took place just three days after she died and there would not have been sufficient time to construct them. Although none of the above texts mention cloth strips forming a tent, the platforms they describe surely had the same function—as mourning areas for those attending. They also served to elevate the participants above the ground at the cremation site, which would have been polluted by the corpse. The only individuals who actually entered the enclosed area demarcated by the fences were the corpse, the attendants who carried the coffin, officiating priests and nuns, and members of the immediate family. Others waited in the tents or on the platforms outside the enclosure. *Sakeiki* and *Kichiji ryakki* contain clear descriptions of the fenced enclosures, gates, and other graveside structures, proving that these edifices were not unique to later Zen-style funerals, nor to the medieval period, but rather were continuations of centuries-old imperial cremation practices now utilized by important Buddhist priests and military elite for their own funerals.

Enclosures for Burials: Spirit Hall

Most emperors and some members of the court were cremated during the late Heian and medieval periods. Still, a surprising number in the twelfth through fourteenth centuries requested burial, including emperors Toba (1103–1156) and Go-Shirakawa (1127–1192) and the famous poet Fujiwara Shunzei (1114–1204). The great majority of those who chose burial, however, were female, many the wives and mothers of emperors. Most requested burial in written wills or through oral testaments. In the medieval records examined earlier, the one unquestionable burial was that of a woman, Nakahara Kenshin, in the fourteenth century. It may be that the idea of putting an intact body either into an earthen grave or an aboveground burial chamber was somehow more bearable and felt less physically final than cremation. At least one eleventh-century mourner (male), however, seems to have found consolation in the smoke and fire of cremation, saying, "Had it been the usual cremation, he [Emperor Ichijō] might have hoped for a glimpse of smoke hanging over the plain, but now even that consolation would be denied him."[72] Why females favored burials over cremations is unclear, but burials certainly made it possible to avoid witnessing the finality of the body going up in flames and the disposal of the charred remains. Unfortunately, records describing burials are not as detailed as those for cremations. Perhaps that is because burials were not as common among the elite, but it may also be because they were not as vivid or exciting to write about. Because neither textual nor visual sources in the medieval period provide much that is helpful, the following section leans on earlier records to facilitate our general understanding of how the body was separated and contained during burials.

Many sources suggest that enclosures were as essential in burials as in cremations. In the case of burials, it was common for the body to be interred in an area enclosed by a fence. *Sankaiki* (1180.10.3), for example, relates that a daughter of Takamatsu Chūnagon (Fujiwara Sanehira) died at age sixty-seven and was interred near Hosshōji at a site surrounded by a single bamboo fence.[73] Although the text uses the term *dosō*, which is generally interpreted to mean that the body was buried, that word was used rather broadly in premodern Japan, and included interments in other types of containers and enclosures. In short, any disposal of the body other than cremation was considered a burial, or *dosō*.

In the eleventh century it became common practice to inter individuals, usually females, inside specially constructed edifices called Spirit Halls (*tamadono/tamaya*), which were then sealed tight.[74] For example, Fujiwara Teishi (d. 1000.12.16), empress of Emperor Ichijō, had requested she not be cremated, so her remains were carefully entombed inside a Spirit Hall at Toribeno. Teishi's body was surrounded and protected by at least five different layers of enclosures: it was wrapped in cloth, encoffined in a wooden casket, placed inside a wooden carriage, and interred inside a small wooden building that was then further enclosed by a wall of earth or a wooden fence.[75] Such enclosures—the shroud, coffin, carriage, and fences—were also typically used during cremations. In 1025, when the wife of courtier Fujiwara Nagaie died in childbirth, she and her dead child were placed together in the coffin.[76] A carriage transported them to the area north of the great gate of Hosshōji, where the entire carriage was interred in a Spirit Hall roofed with cypress bark and surrounded by a roofed mud wall (*tsuiji*).[77]

Even more details are available regarding the burial of Empress Seishi in 1025.[78] A burial chamber was made for her inside a cypress-roofed Spirit Hall built within an earthen-walled enclosure located northwest of Urin'in's Western Cloister (*nishi-in*). The chamber was beautifully furnished and illuminated with oil lamps. It is not clear whether just the coffin or both the coffin and the carriage box were entombed in the building.[79] In the above examples it is seldom made clear whether the Spirit Hall was used as a final resting place or as a site of temporary interment, but *Sakeiki* suggests that the structure for Empress Seishi was a temporary resting place.[80] In temporary burials the body was entombed in a hall and later moved and either buried in the ground or placed in a larger, permanent structure. Temporary burials were common for Japanese rulers of the pre-Nara period, where significant time was needed to construct fittingly large tombs (*kofun*), but the tradition may also have continued into the early eleventh century.

Other edifices, such as pagodas, Lotus Halls, and Amida Halls, came to replace the Spirit Hall. Although some of the details of the burials changed, these structures functioned in much the same way as the Spirit Halls. For example, we are told that in 1145 Fujiwara Shōshi (Taikenmon'in; consort of Emperor Toba) was interred in a stone chamber underneath a special Lotus Hall built for this purpose at Hōkongō-in.[81] When Fujiwara Sōshi, wife of Fujiwara no Tadamichi, died in 1155 at the age of sixty-one, her body was placed in a carriage and taken to the mountains east of Hosshōji, where a pagoda had been newly constructed to hold her corpse. The coffin was lifted out of the carriage and brought into the pagoda through the south door, with the head of the deceased positioned to the north, and was placed beneath the Buddhist altar through a hole made by taking off the front boards of the dais. A new lid was made for the coffin from a large wooden plank, and an enormous stone, measuring approximately seven feet long by four feet wide, was pulled into place with ropes. Small pebbles and white sand were mixed together to fill up the space above the stone. Lime was spread on top, and the boards of the altar were replaced, sealing the casket inside. Presumably, such precautions were taken to prevent the smell of decay from permeating the temple. A three-foot standing image of Shaka, said to be the same image Sōshi had venerated when she was dying (she had held five strings attached to it), was centered on the altar directly over the body.[82] Although specially constructed halls were often used as sites to bury the cremated remains of the dead, this entry confirms that some uncremated bodies of high-ranking women were also interred inside the altars of such halls.

Indeed, interring the intact corpse rather than cremated remains under an altar seems to have been a common practice for both males and females in the twelfth century. Yiengpruksawan noted several other examples—a consort of Emperor Horikawa was interred uncremated in the dais of Urindō (1114), and—the most famous example—Fujiwara Kiyohira's mummified body was placed inside a gilt-wood coffin and enclosed under the altar of the golden Konjikidō about 1129; he was joined by the mummies of his two sons in 1157 and 1158.[83]

Why it would be appropriate for either the cremated remains or the corpse itself (the vast majority of which were court women) to be interred under a Buddhist altar remains somewhat of a mystery. In medieval Europe, of course, only the privileged—saints, high-ranking clerics, and royalty—were permitted burial in tombs inside the church proper, with the most important being buried nearest the holiest areas. Similar considerations of status may have influenced burials in temple altars in medieval Japan as well. Certainly the economic reality in Japan was such that only members of the court, and later the very top echelon of the military, could afford to bury their dead beneath an altar, for generally this meant that the family in large part subsidized or even controlled that temple. The act of burying a body under an altar also seemed to serve, in a general way, as a reenactment of the original placement of the Buddha's remains in containers within stupas, and therefore may exemplify a wish to create relics rather than simply to entomb a body. Interring the body under the altar may be likened to enshrining hair or other body relics inside an icon. Just as the relic is worshipped along with the image, so the remains or corpse beneath the altar received the worship held in that space. Furthermore, those who entered the temple or joined in worship services before the altar would presumably remember the individual entombed within and include him or her in their prayers. Also, if the purpose of Buddhist funeral rituals was to aid in ridding the corpse of its pollution and to protect the living from it, then by extension placing the body in close proximity to the gilt Buddhist image would prove even more efficacious in eliminating its impurities.

The need to rid the body of death pollution may also explain in part why the bodies of females were more likely to be interred in altars than those of males. Since it was believed to be more difficult for females to be reborn directly into a Buddhist paradise, some survivors may have sought to assist their female deceased by placing them beneath an altar. The closest a corpse could get to the purity of the Buddha was under the altar and directly beneath the principal icon. Proximity to the image must have been credited with a very powerful prophylactic effect. This interesting practice of entombing the coffin, sometimes complete with its carriage, in a special hall, or of placing the coffin beneath an altar in a hall or pagoda became less common in the late medieval period, as more people eschewed burial in favor of cremation.

Grave Enclosures and Tablets

Whether the body was cremated, buried in the earth, or interred inside a building, grave markers were set up at the spot where the remains were finally laid to rest. Although well before the medieval period efforts were made to mark the graves of the elite with stone monuments, wooden markers, and small fences, in those earlier periods the living did not return regularly to the burial site after the interment, and gravesites quickly fell into ruin and were forgotten. Throughout the medieval period, however, the grave functioned as a gathering place for the family, a place for sutras to be read, and a place for offerings to be made on behalf of the deceased throughout the forty-nine-day period. In the discussion of the memorial services held for Nakahara Morosuke and his wife, Kenshin (Chap. 1), for example, we noted that temple priests, nuns, officials, and family members traveled to the grave on the morning of each of the seven memorial services to offer incense and chant sutras. Only after performing the rituals at the grave did the mourners move to the family chapel at the Nakahara residence for the memorial ceremony. By the mid-fourteenth century the grave had become a location that remained closely connected with the person of the deceased.

Typically, those who could afford to bury the bodies or cremated remains of their dead constructed graves enclosed by a low fence called a *kuginuki*, a structure composed of a series of square pillars held upright by two or three sets of horizontal braces (*nuki*).[84] Several illustrations show us what these fences looked like. One of the best and earliest is the late twelfth-century illustrated handscroll *Gaki zōshi*, which depicts several varieties of grave enclosures (Figure 3.7). On one of the graves (lower left) we see a stone grave marker in the form of a five-storied pagoda (*gorintō*), set atop a square mound of earth supported by rocks, and enclosed by a wooden fence. The fence is rectangular, having five wooden vertical stakes on each of two facing sides and four on the other two, and it is just high enough to reach the top of the earthen mound.

The same scroll depicts three other graves marked in three different ways. The mound on the upper center looks like a natural hillock, with large and small trees and grass growing on it; there is no sign of a fence or man-made markers. The grave in the center is also unfenced, but has three tall vertical tablets called *sotoba* propped up by rocks in the center of the knoll. The third grave, on the far right, is similarly structured, but the mound is lower, its top is

108   The Material Culture of Death

Figure 3.7. *Kuginuki, gorintō, sotoba, zushi*. Source: "*Gaki zōshi*." 12th century. Reproduced in *Ōemaki ten*, ed. and comp. Kyoto National Museum (Tokyo: Yomiuri Shinbunsha, 2006), after p. 43, plate 3.

leveled, and it is supported by rocks around its base. A small wooden shrine (*zushi*), holding three miniature Buddhist images (probably Amida, Kannon, and Seishi), is set in the middle of the mound, flanked by two large vertical tablets; those three structures are surrounded by a myriad of thin pointed stakes set into the earth and supported by rocks at their bases.[85] Several theories about the different types of graves and what they mean have been proposed.[86] It is most likely that, in the twelfth century, the three grave types marked the different statuses of the individuals buried in them, with the highest level, emperors and courtiers, having well-constructed graves with fences and either wooden or permanent stone markers. Contrariwise, the scene may also show different stages of decay, with tablets and shrines marking the newer graves, on which relatives had more recently made offerings of *sotoba* on the deceased's behalf, and those lacking markers and offering tablets being older graves that time had restored to their natural tree-and-grass-covered forms.

    The vertical wooden stakes, both large and small, have protective phrases written on them in Sanskrit. Family members typically wrote these phrases on the tablets and presented them as offerings to increase merit for themselves and for their deceased relatives in the afterlife. A great number of *sotoba* are so tightly packed around the top of the grave on the right that they form a fence, functioning, in a sense, as a *kuginuki*. We can see that the tips of the stakes are darkened, suggesting that they were painted. The fourteenth-century court

Figure 3.8. Enclosure at Shinran's grave.
Source: *Zenshin shōnin Shinran den-e*, in *Zokuzoku Nihon emaki taisei: Denki, engi hen*, vol. 1, ed. Komatsu Shigemi (Tokyo: Chūō Kōronsha, 1994), after image on pp. 108–109.

official Nakahara Moromori (Chap. 1) noted that when the *kuginuki* was set up around his father's grave on his one-month death anniversary, the five Buddhist colors (*goshiki*: blue, yellow, red, white, and black) were spread on the upper parts of the fence.[87] Although I have found no other written evidence for this convention, several other medieval handscrolls show graves with *kuginuki* with darkened tips, suggesting that this was a common practice.

Figure 3.9. Enclosure at Nichiren's grave.
Source: *Nichiren shōnin chūgasan*, in *Zokuzoku Nihon emaki taisei: Denki, engi hen*, vol. 2, ed. Komatsu Shigemi (Tokyo: Chūō Kōronsha, 1993), after image on p. 74.

In *Zenshin shōnin Shinran den-e* (late 13th c.), another variety of grave enclosure is shown encircling Priest Shinran's grave at Ōtani in Higashiyama, Kyoto (Figure 3.8). This fence is also rectangular, with four posts on two facing sides and three on the other two. The fence appears to rest on top of either leveled ground or a large flat stone and surrounds a single stone grave marker with an umbrella-shaped top, called a *kasatōba*. The fence is made of thin slats of bamboo or some other light material, and the tips of the posts appear painted.[88] This image is thought to represent Shinran's grave in the first decade or so after he died.[89] Today, however, a stone fence, more substantial and permanent, surrounds his grave in Higashiyama. In the case of a less prominent individual, the wooden fence would have decayed and the occupant of the grave been forgotten over time. Only because Shinran's followers were determined to remember and honor him as the founder of a new sect of Pure Land Buddhism was the fence well maintained and eventually reconstructed in stone.

Nichiren shōnin chūgasan (16th c.) offers a later example of a *kuginuki*, this one around the priest Nichiren's grave (Figure 3.9). Like the others, this enclosure is also rectangular and constructed of thin white vertical slats held together by horizontal strips near the top and bottom. All the posts are tipped with black. Nichiren's grave is unusual because a gabled roof of thin wooden slats, resting on four wooden posts, has been built over the stone marker. Unlike the more substantial Spirit Halls (*tamadono*) described above, which had four walls and held the body in a sealed environment, the four sides of this structure are open. The visitors to Nichiren's grave are seated outside the fenced area, suggesting that the roof was not intended to provide a place for them to worship, but rather was built to protect the grave from the elements and probably to mark the tomb as that of someone important.

Demarcating the Dead

It is clear that in medieval times in Japan a substantial number and type of enclosures and containers were essential elements in the process of death to demarcate and separate the dead from the world of the living. Indeed, every time a corpse was moved, another enclosure or container was added, further emphasizing the growing physical and spatial gap that was opening between the two worlds. Near the end of life, the dying individual was moved either to a room separated from the main living area or sometimes to a nearby temple. This removal was the first spatial and physical layer of separation. Next, his or her head was positioned to the north with the face to the west, and a folding screen was placed around the feet, thus furthering the partitioning process. After death was confirmed, the body was washed, dressed in fresh robes (or covered with the new robe), then covered with a shroud, and finally encoffined. After the coffin lid was put in place, the corpse was fully circumscribed by the casket, and was enclosed yet again by the carriage in which the coffin was placed. In the medieval period the coffin was then transported to a temple, where it remained for a few days before the corpse was buried or cremated. Along the route to the cremation site, the corpse was enclosed in its carriage and, in some imperial funerals, further protected by two layers of silk screens. Once at the site, a fence covered with white silk cloth protected it from the eyes of viewers.

After the remains were interred, they continued to be enclosed and separated from the normal world by the grave mound itself and by the wooden or stone enclosures that surrounded it; wooden tablets and stone monuments marked the site. These multiple encasings of the body and gradual shifts away from the residence and everyday life are important markers of an ever-widening separation between deceased and survivors. The final act of detachment was the burial or cremation; beyond that point, the living and the dead were permanently separated, and the living could never again see or be with the deceased. Even at the cremation the corpse continued to be encircled by silk-wrapped fences and marked by its position at the center of all the human activity.

In addition to symbolizing separation and the transition to other physical and spatial environments, the series of enclosures and the gradual stages of movement away from the sphere of normal life activity had the effect of physically transporting the pollution of death farther and farther from the living, and also of mitigating its effects. Moreover, while providing the living with material layers of protection from the pollution of the corpse, enclosures and containers also came to represent the new status of the deceased. Although there is some evidence that the tendency to "enclose" both the corpse and the grave declined over the centuries, in general, the highest-ranking individuals continued to be identifiable as such by this form of special marking.

The materials used for the containers and enclosures connected to death and funerals were unremarkable enough, consisting of rough, readily available, inexpensive materials such as raw silk, debarked cypress, pine or bamboo, and mud (for walls). Indeed, few of the appurtenances directly connected to the corpse in medieval funerals were ornately decorated or made of costly or rare materials; no decorated lacquer, rich ornament or color, no gold or silver metalwork, no carved cenotaphs or friezes appeared until much later. All of the materials associated with the containment of death were easily accessible and exceedingly perishable. In essence, these materials of death resonated with the Buddhist notion of impermanence.

RITUAL IMPLEMENTS FOR FUNERALS AND MEMORIALS 4

The implements that accompanied Japanese funeral rituals and death memorials are still plentiful; they were produced by workshops to be durable and to perform particular functions. Bronze candleholders and many other intriguing appurtenances of religious practices are housed today in major museums. The usual label identifies an implement by type but says little or nothing about its religious function. Extracted from their original contexts, religious paraphernalia in a museum cannot reveal where or how they were once used, let alone the meanings they had held for participants in religious rituals. Until recently, modern scholarship has added little to the information on the labels because—save for sculpture, painting, and architecture—the implements of ritual were consigned to the "minor arts" and therefore mostly ignored. Unlike traditional grave goods in early China, implements had not been owned by the deceased when alive or been made especially for a given deceased individual after death. Beyond revealing generally that the deceased was sufficiently wealthy and high-ranking, most objects used at funerals and death memorials in medieval Japan demonstrate very little about the particular social or political status of the deceased.

In his discussion of early Chinese ritual paraphernalia (*liqi*), Wu Hung claimed that ritual objects can be distinguished from similar-appearing ordinary tools and mundane wares by their costly manufacture: they are made of precious materials and/or exhibit specialized craftsmanship requiring an unusual amount of human labor.[1] This theory applies also, to some degree, to medieval Japan where Buddhist ritual implements, many of which derived from the forms of ancient Chinese bronze vessels, were also made of bronze, an expensive material used almost exclusively for ceremonial objects. Lacquered wooden implements, which are also tremendously labor-intensive, were also popular for religious ceremonies and rituals.

As we have seen, death rituals in medieval Japan required the use of special objects, the meaning of which lay in their roles in funerary and memorial ceremonies. Clearly, one of the best ways to understand how they were used in the past is by examining the illustrations that remain from the period in question. That particular ritual implements are so carefully depicted in these illustrations suggests that they were indeed recognized as important to the performance of the rituals. Because the funerals and memorial services of the secular elite in the medieval period were not generally illustrated, however, this chapter will look at the types of ritual objects depicted in funeral scenes in illustrated biographies of important priests (kōsō den-e) dating from the fourteenth through the early sixteenth centuries. In particular, I shall concentrate on the types of ritual implements that attended Priest Nichiren's (1222–1282) funeral procession in the Nichiren shōnin chūgasan handscroll (early 16th c.), and those that accompanied Priest Hōnen's (1133–1212) seven seventh-day death memorials in Hōnen shōnin e-den (early 14th c.), with examples from other medieval scrolls introduced where useful. By employing this methodology, I am not suggesting that the scrolls provide historically accurate illustrations of how implements were used for the funerals and memorials of Nichiren or Hōnen, as neither scroll is contemporary with the time of death of its subject. Rather, the pictures show the types of objects commonly employed for mortuary rites associated with high-ranking priests and elite members of society in late medieval Japan, a fact borne out by the fifteenth-century records of the funerals of the Ashikaga shoguns discussed in Chapter 2. Illustrated handscrolls allow us to "see" which ritual implements were used when and how they were positioned (information only rarely provided in written records), and may help to foster new thinking about their original function in funerary rituals.

Ritual Implements in Funeral Processions

About the funeral of Nichiren, who died in 1282, we have only a few details. More than two centuries later an extensive visualization of that important event appeared in the form of an illustrated biography called the Nichiren shōnin chūgasan (Annotated paintings of Nichiren shōnin).[2] Priest Enmyōin Nitchō (1441–1510), about whom little is known,[3] began work on this project late in his life, probably after 1506. The illustrations for the scrolls (five in all) were commissioned by the Provisional Senior Assistant High Priest Nissei,[4] a priest of Kyoto's head Nichiren sect temple, Honkokuji, who selected the little-known Kyoto artist Kubota Muneyasu to paint them; the images were completed in 1536. From start to finish, the entire production took some twenty-six years, and the length of time is reflected in the minute detail of the work.

The fact that an official biography of Priest Nichiren was not commissioned immediately after his death raises some interesting questions, especially given that illustrated biographies of other priests who founded important religious sects during the Kamakura period were completed within decades of their demise. For example, *Denpō-e*, an illustrated biography of Priest Hōnen, was finished in 1237, just twenty-five years after he passed away; and *Zenshin shōnin-e* was ready in 1295 for Shinran's thirty-third death anniversary.[5] Many such biographies of the founders of new sects were created in the late Kamakura period by their disciples, both to signify their veneration of the founders and to legitimate their roles as successors. There is some evidence that these illustrated biographies were recited at the memorial services for the founding priests and also circulated by traveling priests as objects of worship and tools of proselytization.[6] But according to Wakasugi Junji, creating a biography of Nichiren was less important to his followers, because the Nichiren sect, unlike those founded by Hōnen and Shinran, focused on venerating written phrases, such as sutra titles, venerable names, and special letters. Furthermore, Nichiren and most of his followers were not members of the elite, a class associated with handscrolls for centuries, nor did they interact with them. These circumstances, according to Wakasugi, may explain why Nichiren sectarians did not immediately choose the handscroll format to venerate Nichiren.[7]

Why one of his distant disciples chose to create an illustrated biography of Nichiren's life and death over two hundred years after the master's passing may be related to growing differences within sects in the fifteenth century, which might have spurred Priest Nitchō to reaffirm the link between his branch of the sect in Kamakura and the main lineage in Kyoto. Whether Nitchō arranged with Nissei for the illustrations before he died in 1510, or whether Nissei himself decided to illustrate the biography, is not known. Nonetheless, the resulting production, written by Nitchō in Kamakura with illustrations organized by Nissei at the founder's temple, Honkokuji, in Kyoto, effectively united these two older lineages. Furthermore, by the fifteenth century, patronage of the Kyoto branch of the Nichiren sect had changed, and aristocratic and elite warrior patrons had become the main supporters of the Kyoto temple. Therefore, in addition to the handscroll being the most practical and popular format for an illustrated biography at this time, it was also a format familiar to Honkokuji's new high-ranking patrons.[8] While studying the detailed drawings of Nichiren's funeral procession, we must keep in mind that, because of the great lapse in time between Nichiren's death and their creation, they cannot be interpreted as representative of his actual funeral. Rather, the images are typical of funeral processions of the time in which they were created—the late fifteenth/early sixteenth century—which serves our study well.

Nichiren shōnin chūgasan portrays Nichiren's funeral procession as a lengthy parade: following behind a torchbearer are over sixty religious and secular followers carrying banners and ritual objects (Plate 6). Thirteen priests bear the essential Buddhist ritual implements (Plate 7). After them, and immediately preceding the palanquin with Nichiren's coffin, are ten adolescent acolytes and young samurai holding a white cloth cord attached to the top of the palanquin that carries the corpse (Plate 8). The palanquin, in turn, is borne by eighteen black-robed priests and followed by a single attendant holding a canopy over it. Other participants walk behind the coffin, carrying Nichiren's great sword, his armor, and his helmet. A disciple leads the priest's riderless horse (Plate 9). Many of Nichiren's devoted followers who aided and protected him during his life bring up the rear of the procession (Plate 10).

The size of the procession, including the number of ritual implements, priests, attendants, and mourners, is intimately related to the status (real or constructed) of the deceased and to the time.[9] Early Chinese canonical sources, such as the *Li ji* (Book of rites) and *Yi li* (Ceremonies and rites), prescribed details for the proper number of hearse pullers, banners, mourners, and so forth for the funeral processions of each rank or status of persons, from the emperor on down. In early Japan processions were similarly regulated. But what was the purpose of the procession itself in Buddhist funerals? In his study of European medieval liturgical processions, Clifford Flanigan describes processions as incorporating encoded displays of power relationships that "serve to authenticate and authorize the prevailing order in ways that seem 'natural,' beyond comment, and virtually beyond conscious observation."[10] Japanese medieval diarists never seemed to question or comment on the necessity or importance of the funeral procession, perhaps because, as Flanigan suggests, processions were so basic to medieval rituals that they were simply taken for granted.[11] Several levels of analysis of the procession are possible, but the most obvious explanation is that funeral processions, with their large numbers of participants and plethora of sacred banners, bronze and lacquered vessels, flowers, scrolls, and musical instruments, were symbolic displays of power that also represented the social position of the deceased's family, his followers, and the community.

Controlling the performance of death rituals was an important expression of political power in ancient cultures. The Japanese court seized this power as early as the seventh century, issuing regulations on how people could bury their dead in *Hakusōrei* (646 CE).[12] Rules on how to mourn the dead were promulgated in a special section of the eighth-century Yōrō Code (717–724 CE). Over the centuries Buddhist priests gradually took over the duty of burying the dead, an undesirable job and dangerous because of the innate pollution of the corpse, until in the fourteenth century the power to regulate funeral rituals rested almost completely in their hands. It was the officiating clergy, chosen by the family from among temples to which they had close affiliations, who organized the funeral, possessed and cared for the ritual implements, and whose numbers dominated the cortege. Although the priesthood created and directed the spectacle, it was careful to spotlight the deceased visually in the procession. The *Nichiren shōnin chūgasan* illustrates this, depicting the encoffined corpse at the very center of the procession, enclosed and protected by a phalanx of black-robed monks who frame and present the deceased to the mourners.

The ritual of the funeral procession, at the same time as it conveyed the deceased (presumably in safety) to the afterworld, also reaffirmed the strength of the community. Communal participation in the procession helped the deceased to move through time and space along its final journey. Many meanings can be attached to this processional movement—a journey through life, a passage from the profane to the sacred, a movement toward the heavenly realms—all were persistent themes in death rituals. It was also the final journey that participants and deceased would take together. As such, it reaffirmed, one last time, the deceased's position within the family and the community. The participants in the funeral procession also symbolically completed the journey, the physical movement transforming them along with the deceased. Likewise, the lavish vessels, fragrant flowers and pungent incense, musical instruments, and other ritual implements that accompanied the deceased in the procession were transformational, changing this world into another realm, the Pure Land.

Nichiren's funeral cortege falls into three natural sections, with the assembly of priests carrying Buddhist ritual implements constituting the core of the first section. The ritual objects conveyed in this section were those typically found in Buddhist temples and commonly used in most Buddhist rituals, such as incense burners, musical instruments, candles, flowers, and lanterns. Here, they represent Nichiren's vocation as a Buddhist priest. For lay funerals, this part of the procession probably symbolized the deceased's affiliation with Buddhism and connection with a particular temple.

The second section of the procession is centered on Nichiren's corpse, which rests in a coffin placed inside an elaborately decorated palanquin borne along on long poles carried by fellow priests. The body in the coffin represents the very essence, the heart, and the visual focus of the procession. Preceding the coffin is the group of young acolytes and boys.

In the final section, a few of Nichiren's close attendants follow the coffin, bringing various possessions that symbolized his life as a warrior—his great sword, his helmet and armor, and his horse. Last of all is a throng of his followers, men who revered Nichiren as their spiritual and military leader.[13] This final section of the procession, therefore, consists of the deceased's personal belongings and his associates from many walks of life who had converted in order to follow his teachings.

In the *Nichiren shōnin chūgasan* handscroll, several visual indicators, including physical proximity to the casket and manifest expressions of grief, suggest which participants were personally attached to Nichiren. Those who walked closest to his casket were most devoted to him during his life. Indeed, the individuals who conveyed his personal effects and carried the ritual objects that most directly represented him, such as his memorial tablet and portrait, were likely relatives and temple officials who had befriended Nichiren during his life. The expressions on the faces of the participants are also telling. The monks leading Nichiren's funeral procession seem comparatively stoical, whereas the priests carrying his coffin and those following immediately behind it appear to be moved by extreme grief, their faces twisted and contorted with strong emotions.

In addition, small handwritten characters representing the names of the participants were inscribed above some of the figures in the funeral procession. That the named persons are nearest to the coffin further supports the premise that these were individuals known to the deceased as well as to Nitchō, who wrote the text.[14] Thus, in many ways the order of the medieval funeral procession both simulated and preserved the deceased's position in society. In death as in life, Nichiren was a fulcrum between the Buddhist establishment and his unorthodox beliefs and teachings.

Torches and Headbands

Some of the ritual objects visible in the handscroll are little known today, which is one reason why the paintings are such a valuable source of information about medieval funerals. Leading the funeral procession is a low-ranking samurai wearing a short gray robe over knee-length pants, a folded black cap, and a white triangular headband (*hokaku*), and carrying an enormous torch (*taimatsu*) made of long sticks of pine (or bamboo) bound together by thick white rope (Plate 6). Because funeral processions typically took place at night, torches were necessary to light the way for the mourners to the grave or cremation site. Holding the funeral in the dead of night was related to ancient beliefs that a corpse remained in a liminal, vulnerable state until it was permanently buried or cremated, and was especially vulnerable while it was being moved. Early in Japanese funeral history torches were placed around the *mogari no miya* (palace of temporary interment) to protect the corpse from malevolent spirits and at the same time to keep the pollution of death from harming the living.[15] In medieval Japan moving the corpse secretly at night by torchlight was thought to lessen both possibilities for harm. Although seldom mentioned in written texts, torches were therefore central components of funeral processions, and they are in evidence in many of the funeral scenes depicted in medieval handscrolls.[16] As further proof that the procession is taking place by night, we have not only the flaming torch but also the full moon visible behind swirling clouds just above the group of acolytes and young samurai who precede the coffin. Torches were also used more generally for travel by night; they were not unique to funerals.

All of the figures wearing short gray robes and knee-length trousers are distinguished by triangles of white cloth tied around their foreheads. These individuals are Nichiren's relatives and personal associates, many of whom carry his personal belongings. According to *Sōhōmitsu* (Esoteric funeral practices), an early medieval record of Shingon funerals, the white squares of raw silk, folded diagonally, were called *hokaku* and were worn around the foreheads of those responsible for placing the firewood into the coffin for the cremation.[17] *Hokaku* also appear in earlier illustrations of funerals, such as the thirteenth-century illustrated handscroll of the *Kitano Tenjin engi*, where two men wearing white cloth triangles can be seen bearing the coffin.[18] In contrast, except for the priests, those carrying the coffin, the young children preceding it, and the samurai disciples bringing up the rear, everyone in Nichiren's procession wears a white headband. Clearly, by the early sixteenth century, when the illustrations for this set of scrolls were completed, the white headbands designated participants, usually relatives or close friends of the deceased, not just the individuals who carried the coffin or deposited firewood into it.[19]

Paper Flowers and Banners

In the same illustration, four charcoal-robed participants hoisting long poles follow directly behind the torchbearer (Plate 6). The first carries a pole topped with a large red-and-blue paper lotus flower (*ō renge*; also *setsuryū*), its multicolored petals gently drifting down around the bearer. Long a potent symbol of the Buddha's purity and perfection, the lotus may here represent the Pure Land, where it was believed Nichiren would be reborn.[20] The use of paper flowers in funeral processions, however, probably stems from Chinese Chan (Zen) funerary traditions, at which, typically, four paper flowers were planted at the four corners of the grave, symbolizing the flowering sala trees under which the Buddha lay in death.[21] Four paper flowers for funerals was customary in Japan as well, although only one flower is represented here in Nichiren's funeral procession.

Atop the other three poles are white cloth banners (*ban*), affixed by metal rings to intricate dragon heads (*ryūzu sao, tatsugashira*; Figure 4.1).[22] It is common knowledge that dragon heads on long poles were used at funerals, but the history of ritual dragons has not been well explained. Numerous folktales relate how dragons came to be associated with death in Japan. The most plausible explanation, however, is that in ancient times the character for *ryō* (spirit or soul) was pronounced *ryū*, a homonym for the word dragon; thus, the dragon became conflated with the spirit of the deceased. Gorai tells us that, before

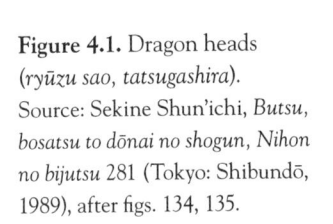

Figure 4.1. Dragon heads (*ryūzu sao, tatsugashira*). Source: Sekine Shun'ichi, *Butsu, bosatsu to dōnai no shogun, Nihon no bijutsu* 281 (Tokyo: Shibundō, 1989), after figs. 134, 135.

banners were used, "pouches for the spirit" (*tamashii bukuro*), intended to contain the spirit and keep it from floating away after death, were hung from the carved dragon's mouth. The dragon form was only later adopted by Buddhism and employed for funeral processions.[23]

Dragon heads were sometimes made of bronze, but more often of split green bamboo or wood brightly painted. Hundreds and thousands of these must have been made for funeral ceremonies during the medieval period, but only a few have survived. The dragon heads shown in the Nichiren scroll might have been made of bronze, but more likely of wood or bamboo. Dragon heads are still used in modern death rituals in some parts of Japan. For example, in Kita-Kyushu the person who leads the coffin to the graveyard still traditionally carries two dragon-head staffs, one male and one female.[24]

The three ritual banners attached to these dragon heads appear in the first section of the procession. The one large and two small banners are composed of small triangles of unadorned white fabric to which are attached long cloth rectangles. Appended are eight long, thin cloth streamers (*ban soku*)—one on each side of the triangle and at the midpoint of the lower portion, and four more along the lower edge of the rectangle. Banners, too, have a long association with mortuary rites in Japan.[25] At the ruler's place of temporary interment in ancient Japan, four ritual banners (*shihonban*), along with "silk thread" flowers (*hanakazura*) were positioned in the four cardinal directions.[26] According to *Jingihaku sōmoki*, three of the banners represented the lineage of the deceased's father, of his mother, and the deceased's own position in the family, while the fourth bore information about the cause of death and the date of the funeral.[27]

Banners have an equally long history of serving to elevate the magnificence of Buddhism. According to the Vimalakirti Sutra (*Yuima kyō*), banners were an ancient Indian adaptation from battle standards and were intended to signify Buddhism's triumph over demons.[28] The eighth-century *Nihon shoki* (552.10) says that, in the sixth century, cloth banners (*hata*) as well as sun shades (*kinugasa*) were brought to Japan from Korea along with Buddhist images and sutras.[29] In Japan they have been made from a wide variety of fabrics, including plain silk, brocade, figured twill, and gauze. Some very elaborate banners were even fabricated of gilt bronze, such as Hōryūji's seventh-century ordination-ceremony banner (*kanjō ban*).[30] Banners were among the many articles (*shōgongū*) required to adorn the sacred space occupied by buddhas and bodhisattvas in the Buddha Hall for services and ceremonies. This fourteenth-century illustration (Figure 4.2) shows five multicolored banners (*goshiki ban*), hanging one per pillar, at a ceremony for choosing the priests for important positions in the temple system. Banners also adorned the precincts of Shinto shrines, hung on the outside of the building high up on an exterior wall because they were not permitted inside buildings that housed *kami*.[31]

Figure 4.2. Banners of five colors (*goshiki ban*).
Source: *Hōnen shōnin e-den*, in *Zoku Nihon no emaki*, vol. 3, ed. Komatsu Shigemi (Tokyo: Chūō Kōronsha, 1990), after image on p. 106.

Examples of banners used in conjunction with Buddhist mortuary rituals in Japan abound. In the mid-eighth century ten enormous banners, each measuring over fifty feet in length, were displayed in commemoration of the first death anniversary of Emperor Shōmu (701–756).[32] In 1036 a banner of yellow silk inscribed with a Buddhist mantra was carried on a white pole (made of cypress or cryptomeria) at the head of Emperor Go-Ichijō's funeral.[33] Other illustrations from the fourteenth century show a narrower type of banner constructed of five cloth strips in the "five Buddhist colors" of blue, yellow, red, white, and black (*goshiki ban*), which was grasped on one end by the hands of the dying believer as death approached.[34] The pure whiteness of the banners carried in Nichiren's funeral procession, however, was specifically meant to protect both humans and gods against the pollution of death.[35]

Lanterns, Censers, and Musical Instruments

Following the banners are two young attendants carrying tied bundles of sticks. These faggots would be used to light the cremation fire from the larger torch. Behind them two Buddhist acolytes carry lanterns (*chōchin*), their glowing red candles inside, suspended from short sticks. These were to provide additional light for the procession, as were two other lanterns seen about midway through the procession.

Following the lanterns are eight black-robed priests, some carrying long-handled censers (*egōro*) and others playing ritual musical instruments (Plate 7). Both the lanterns and the censers are modifications of more elaborate arrangements that date back to early imperial funerals. For Go-Ichijō's well-documented interment, instead of being hand-carried, the lamps and censers were placed on special litters—one litter held a burning lamp (*hi no koshi*), another a censer and vases of flowers (*kō no koshi*).[36] The lamps used in Nichiren's funeral were a type of *kagochōchin* or "basket-woven" lantern. Usually such lanterns were constructed of lightweight bamboo and covered with paper to facilitate their being carried by hand. The two examples near the front of Nichiren's procession, however, appear to be made of bronze and may have belonged to a temple. The two long-handled incense burners are of an ancient type used for making offerings before the Buddha. Incense was placed in the bowl-shaped part, lit, and presented to the deity. The fragrance of incense was often said to have transformative powers that purified the worship space and those in attendance, as well as simulating the beautiful scents believed to permeate the Western Paradise. Incense also played a practical role in funerals by helping to conceal the odor of the decaying corpse; as embalming was not practiced in medieval Japan, decomposition was a serious problem, necessitating immediate burials and cremations, especially in the summer months.

Ritual music for Nichiren's funeral was provided by four monks playing cymbals (*nyōhachi*) and striking a metal gong (*shōko*) and bowl (*kinsu*) with wooden mallets. All of these instruments were easy to carry and play while walking, and all were primarily percussive. The sounds produced by musical instruments were designed to attract the deity's attention and to entertain him during the ritual, but they also provided a rhythm for the participants to follow as they walked to the cremation site. The tones created by striking the metal implements were a type of music associated with the unparalleled sound of the Buddha preaching, as well as with the glorious sound of heavenly music that would be playing throughout the Pure Land.[37] Like incense, music was intended to purify the senses. During the funeral, music also produced a necessary cadence for the participants and solemnized the proceedings.

Three Offering Vessels

Following the musicians, three Buddhist monks carry white carved trays upon which rest the three essential Buddhist offering vessels (*mitsu gusoku*)—a flower vase (*kebyō*), a tortoise-and-crane candleholder (*tsurukame shokudai*), and an incense-filled censer (*kōro*) (Plate 7).[38] As conventional equipment for Buddhist ceremonies, they are commonly found on Buddhist altars, containing offerings to the deities of flowers, light, and incense, respectively. The three Buddhist offering vessels were also important ritual objects in the performance of medieval funerals and memorial services, and many early records mention them in that context. We are told that the three were placed on a temporary altar at the entrance to the crematory for Ashikaga Yoshimochi's funeral in 1428, and they are mentioned again as objects carried in the procession for Hino Shigeko's funeral in 1463.[39] Although they do not appear in the section on Prince Yoshihito's funeral, the vessels are also duly noted in the description of his memorial service in 1416, at which Yoshihito's memorial tablet was installed on an altar with a flower vase (kebyō), censer (kōro), and candle stand (shokudai).[40] In the illustration of Nichiren's funeral, we can see vessels holding a lotus flower, a lit red candle, and burning incense.

The tradition of making offerings to the deities is modeled after an ancient Indian custom of presenting flowers and gifts of incense, unguents, food, drink, and light (candles) to high-ranking guests. Ritual offerings were a part of early Buddhist practice in Japan, as attested to by the Shōsōin's collection of vessels for holding flower petals, which date from as early as the eighth century.[41] According to Japanese popular belief dating from the pre-Heian period, burning incense and candles served to keep evil spirits from entering the body of the deceased.[42] That belief may explain why lighted lamps were placed on either side of the body immediately after the corpse was washed and dressed in fresh robes, and also why torches and lanterns were needed to accompany the corpse to the burial or cremation grounds. The appearance of the *mitsu gusoku* marks the end of the first section of the procession, where the ritual objects carried by the priests were for the glorification of the Buddha.

The focus of the next section shifts from more traditional Buddhist ritual implements to mortuary objects specific to Nichiren's funeral: Nichiren's portrait, copies of sutras, two wooden trays (hokai) holding offering vessels, his mortuary tablet (ihai), and a pair of silk Chinese-style shoes (kutsu) worn by high-ranking Buddhist priests on formal occasions are conveyed in this section of the procession. All of the items in this section would have been placed on or near a temporary altar that was constructed at the cremation site.

Scrolls and Sutras

The priest following the bronze censer carries a scroll written on indigo-dyed paper and wrapped in white silk, the ends of which are tied around his neck (Plate 7). This priest walks alone, the only solitary figure in the funeral procession, and the prominence that this confers suggests that the scroll he is carrying is of utmost importance. Is it a painted Buddhist icon or perhaps a portrait of the deceased? Either is possible, but the scroll is most likely a portrait of the deceased that is being transported to the cremation site for display at the temporary altar. I found no evidence that Buddhist icons were conveyed to the site, but a number of written sources from the fifteenth century confirm that portraits of the deceased were carried in procession to the cremation site and displayed there.[43]

Relatives, friends, and disciples of the deceased typically wrote and dedicated phrases from sutras in order to accumulate merit for him or her in the afterworld, and several of these inscribed offerings can be seen in Nichiren's funeral procession. Following the individual with the portrait scroll are two attendants conveying two small wooden sutra tables (*kyōzukue*); on one table are three books and on the other eight small indigo-dyed handscrolls. The three books are probably sutras, or possibly the temple's death records (*kakochō*).[44] The eight scrolls are almost certainly the eight fascicles of the Lotus Sutra, as Nichiren had declared that sutra superior to all others. The books and scrolls may be Buddhist sutras written by the deceased himself before he died or phrases copied by his relatives and dedicated on Nichiren's behalf to increase his merit in the next world.

Offering Trays, Memorial Tablet, and Shoes

After the books and scrolls, two more banners herald two priests carrying white offering trays with shallow wooden bowls and two attendants with lanterns (Plate 8). The two offering bowls and the trays are made of unfinished wood, probably Japanese cedar (*sugi*), based on their white color. The shallow bowls were used for the final offerings of hot water (*tentō*) and tea (*tencha*) to the deceased. In the fifteenth century such ritual offerings were typically prepared for shoguns and members of their family, including Ashikaga Yoshimitsu (1408.5.10), Yoshimochi (1428.1.23), and Hino Shigeko (1463.8.11).

Before the procession began, Nichiren's posthumous name (*hōgō* in the Nichiren sect) would have been written in black ink on a wooden memorial tablet (*shiraki ihai*). This plain wooden tablet was carried in the procession and would have either been cremated along with the body or placed on the grave. After the forty-nine-day period of mourning ended, a black-lacquered tablet (*hon ihai*) was placed on an altar at the deceased's family temple. Later, a priest would rewrite the posthumous name on this permanent tablet in gold ink.[45] The offering dishes, the memorial tablet, and, presumably, the silk slippers, which were symbolic of Nichiren's achievement of high rank within the temple, were usually burned during the cremation.[46]

Palanquin and Coffin

The next section of the procession features the coffin itself, enclosed inside an exquisitely decorated palanquin and carried by mourning monks. Many written records mention carriages and palanquins as a means to transport coffins to the gravesite, but none tell us much about their appearance. Therefore the illustrations in *Nichiren shōnin chūgasan* are especially important for what they can tell us about their appearance and role in funeral rituals.

A group of ten young boys, four acolytes dressed in white priests' robes (one is actually very light gray) and six young male attendants in multipatterned robes, lead the palanquin by a long white strip of cloth called a *zen no tsuna* (rein of virtue), which is tied to the decorative ball on top of the palanquin (Plate 9).[47] The origin of this unusual custom is not known, but similar procedures are recorded in a number of medieval sources.[48] For Ashikaga Yoshimochi's funeral procession in 1428, as already mentioned, the newly appointed shogun, Ashikaga Yoshinori, picked up the white silk cords attached to Yoshimochi's coffin and placed them on his shoulders.[49] Some sources suggest that the cords symbolized leading the deceased to the afterworld or paradise, while others propose a more practical original function—that of helping to pull the palanquin and its coffin up hills.[50] In a modified form this practice was continued for funeral processions in the Edo period and is performed even today in some parts of Japan.[51]

The palanquin carrying Nichiren's coffin is unlike earlier images and descriptions of coffin-bearing vehicles. Rather than being rectangular and of undecorated wood with slatted bamboo windows,[52] this palanquin is small, square, and windowless, with gilded metal on its black-lacquered wooden supports and a small blue-and-white banner (*ban*) flowing from each of the four corners of its roof (Plate 9). The body of the palanquin is covered with patterned brocade of white, blue, and green chrysanthemums against a deep-orange background; a green cloth has been draped just below the roof.[53] Seventeen priests wearing black robes carry the palanquin along on two long white poles.

Nichiren's funeral carriage is similar to the *sōkaren*, or "onion-flower palanquin," so named because of the golden ball on its roof.[54] *Sōkaren* were used to convey deities during shrine and temple festivals and also to transport the emperor to and from the festivals.[55] But at least one scholar believes that the carriage shown in this scroll is better identified as a *gan*.[56] That character usually referred to a niche or alcove for a Buddhist image, but also came to allude to a box with a roof in which the death flower (*shikabana*) was placed during funerals. According to Katsuda, the placement of the corpse in a *gan* mimics the placement of a Buddhist image in a niche; the action in effect treats the deceased as a buddha.[57] Over time the term further evolved to describe the type of funeral conveyance shown in the *Nichiren shōnin chūgasan* scroll; the term also referred both to the coffin and to the corpse itself. There may be some connection between the two types of palanquins because both originally provided space for a deity. Thus, both the *gan*-type palanquin and the *sōkaren* were considered vehicles for superior beings.[58] The artist's intent in drawing the special palanquin was clearly to highlight Nichiren's importance, and perhaps even to imply his godlike status. Considering Nichiren's humble beginnings as the son of a fisherman, the decision to portray his final conveyance as one of the highest rank undoubtedly reflects a conscious effort on the part of the scroll's commissioner, a Nichiren-sect priest himself, to elevate the founder of his sect.

In size and shape the coffin inside must have corresponded to the shape of the palanquin, so we can assume that the coffin was a round, cask-like container. This form forced the corpse to be placed in a sitting posture with legs folded in meditation pose.[59] This type of tall coffin rarely appeared in earlier handscrolls, such as *Hōnen shōnin e-den* (early 14th c.) or *Zenshin shōnin Shinran den-e* (late 13th c.), which favored the more familiar rectangular wooden box, but it seems to have been popular for elite burials in the sixteenth and seventeenth centuries.[60] The choice of the type of palanquin and coffin represented in the Nichiren handscroll, therefore, is a product of the period in which the handscroll was created. The illustration shows a type of funeral popular with elite warriors in the Sengoku period (1467–1568) and later, and is probably not representative of the type of funeral actually held for Nichiren centuries earlier.

Canopy

A single attendant wearing a pale-gray robe can be seen walking behind the coffin, holding over it a decorative canopy attached to a long pole with an ornate dragon head (Plate 9). The shape of the canopy replicates the top of the palanquin. It has the same design and is covered with identical brocade fabric, displays a golden ball at its peak, and has four banners streaming from its four corners (these banners are orange rather than blue). Canopies do not appear in the funeral processions depicted in earlier illustrated handscrolls. But the diagram preserved in *Jishōindono ryōan sōbo* records that a canopy was used for Ashikaga Yoshimitsu's funeral (d. 1408.5.6). Notations written on that plan mention a gold brocade cloth with paulownia crests on it, suspended over Yoshimitsu's coffin for the procession.[61] From the text and the illustration we may presume that canopies were integral to funerals of the secular elite at least by the early fifteenth century, and that they were suspended over the corpse during the procession and again at the cremation site itself.

In Asia the canopy was an ancient emblem of royalty, dating back to the second millennium BCE in India. Indian Buddhism adopted the canopy as a general sign of elevated status, and ornamental canopies came to be suspended over Buddhist statues in temples and sometimes held above the heads of priests in processions. Canopy-like forms (*kinugasa*) made of clay were even found on the surfaces of ancient tombs (*kofun*) in Japan, along with clay swords and banners—all thought to signify high status and also to have magical properties to aid and protect the deceased. Thus, the use of canopies during funerals is an ancient one and persists even today in some parts of Japan.[62] The canopy suspended over Nichiren's corpse was intended to denote his high status as an important priest. By illustrating the canopy, the high-status palanquin, and even the large size of the procession, the artist quite intentionally suggested the high degree of the sect's founder at a time when it was important to emphasize that prestige as related to high-ranking patrons of the Nichiren sect in Kyoto.

Following the coffin and the canopy are individuals and objects with personal ties to Nichiren. His armor, helmet, and great sword are draped with white gauze, as is the saddle of his riderless horse (Plate 9). Nichiren's most beloved attendant, Ryūōmaru, his face covered in sorrow, can be seen here walking behind the coffin, wearing white mourning dress that signifies his deep grief as Nichiren's closest living friend and disciple. About a dozen individuals in the procession, including Ryūōmaru, are identified by their names written above their figures.[63] Bringing up the rear of the procession is a large group of the warriors from Kamakura who had embraced Nichiren's dictum to follow the teachings of the Lotus Sutra (Plate 10).

Most participants in this procession are monks wearing black or gray garments, but various other colors are also to be seen. In general, the color and type of robe tell us something about the wearer's relationship to the deceased.[64] All the Buddhist priests in the illustrations, distinguishable by their shaved heads, wear long black or gray priests' robes with white surplices and straw sandals, presumably because they were present in their official capacity as priests. Most other participants, presumably relatives and friends of the deceased, are wearing short jackets (*suō*),[65] gray in color, with gray pants rolled up to the knees, folded black caps (*samurai eboshi*), and white triangular headbands (*hokaku*). A few individuals wear white or near-white clothing, attesting to their close relationship to the deceased during his life. For example, the person carrying the canopy over the palanquin and the two men handling Nichiren's horse wear very light-gray, almost white, jackets and pants, suggesting they had a special relationship with the priest. Nichiren's closest friend, Ryūōmaru, wears a white jacket and rolled-up pants, both with red stripes at the hems, and over them a gauzy white robe. The six boys holding the coffin cord wear jackets and rolled-up pants of patterned red, green, and white, and the four young acolytes with them wear long white or gray priests' robes. The warriors bringing up the rear of the procession have not donned special mourning robes, but have all rolled up their pants, probably to prevent their touching the ground polluted by the corpse.

Rules of propriety for mourning dress in Japan are very complex and the colors of the robes worn by the elite for mourning have changed over the centuries. Mourning apparel for relatives of the deceased around the seventh century, for example, consisted of plain unbleached (white) garments made of hemp.[66] Early eighth-century mourning and funerary laws (*Yōrō sōsō ryō*, 718) directed those above a certain court rank to wear dark-gray or black (*shakujo*) hemp robes for mourning, a custom that continued throughout the Heian period.[67] In the medieval period, high-ranking members of the court still generally wore black robes for mourning but other groups favored white mourning garments. The reason for this change is unclear, but unbleached robes were easier and more economical to produce. From the Sengoku period on, around the time the *Nichiren* scrolls were made, families and close retainers of deceased warriors generally mourned their dead wearing white robes. This trend continued for centuries until the late nineteenth century when the imperial family, influenced by royal European mourning customs, adopted black mourning robes for their funerals. The practice caught on with the general populace after mid-century, and today most mourners wear black kimono or Western suits.[68]

Few illustrated examples of funeral processions remain from the medieval period to allow further comparison. The procession for Priest Hōnen's funeral in *Hōnen shōnin e-den* (early 14th c.), for example, is much shorter and simpler than Nichiren's, but here too the priests and temple attendants who carry the coffin wear long robes ranging from black to gray and brown, while both Hōnen's brother and another close relative following the coffin on horseback wear pure-white mourning robes. Thus, the general rule that relatives and friends closest to the deceased wear white robes seems to have held more or less constant during and since the medieval period.

Written sources provide more details on the standard of mourning dress. In the fourteenth-century *Moromoriki*, the deceased's two sons, Moroshige and Moromori, put on white robes to visit their father's grave (1345.2.19). A special clothes-changing ceremony had taken place earlier that day, in which the two sons exchanged their black court robes and hats for white robes. For women, however, the rules were different. The deceased's wife did not change into mourning clothes, being already tonsured and hence clad in the traditional garments of a nun—a short black robe with half sleeves and a Buddhist surplice, tied with a plain silk sash. The deceased's daughter changed from a plain black robe to a short Chinese-style jacket of black-dyed hemp fabric.[69] For this family of court officials in the mid-fourteenth century, white robes were worn by men of the family and black robes by the women during the forty-nine-day period of morning. About the dress worn for the funeral itself, the account is not clear. Surviving illustrations of funeral processions confirm the color of the robes worn by males, but since they show no women, we have no visual verification of the written record of their dress.

At the Ashikaga funerals, proximity to the corpse seems to have been a determinant of the color of the robes. For Shogun Yoshimochi's funeral, on 1428.1.23, his younger brother and shogun-elect Yoshinori (whose priestly name was Gien before being named shogun) donned short jackets of soft white silk (*shiro neriginu*) with white silk gauze over them.[70] For Hino Shigeko's funeral

(1463.8.11), we are told that the men carrying her corpse wore white robes (*hakui*), and also that the elite guests participating in the funeral exchanged their everyday robes for special white ones (*jōe*); everyone wore sandals to the cremation site.[71] These examples suggest that immediate family members and those who had direct contact with the corpse wore white, presumably because that color offered the most protection against pollution to the ones who most needed it.

Ritual Implements for Memorial Services

Various types of ritual implements (*kuyōgu*) were also essential for the Buddhist rituals that accompanied the forty-nine-day period of mourning following death. These were the seven seventh-day periods, counted from the day of death, during which mourners visited the grave, heard Buddhist sermons (*seppō*), read and copied sutras that they then dedicated on behalf of the deceased (*ekō*), and participated in offering services (*kuyō*)[72] for the repose of the deceased's soul. Contemporary written sources are not very useful in describing the ritual setting or, for the most part, the objects used for the memorial services, nor do they explain where they were placed. Probably because these implements were essentially the same ones used for most Buddhist services, everyone knew what they were, and therefore they did not warrant detailed accounts in diaries. For those who do not know, pictures are invaluable.

One set of illustrated medieval handscrolls—the *Hōnen shōnin e-den* (Illustrated biography of Priest Hōnen; early 14th c.)—is particularly valuable in this regard.[73] The forty-eight scrolls, owned by Chion'in in Kyoto, are essentially what the title calls them but also contain information about his disciples and his important teachings. It is said that Retired Emperor Go-Fushimi (1288–1336) issued an imperial order to Shunjō (or Shunshō), the chief priest of Kudoku'in on Mount Hiei, to compile several earlier biographies into this comprehensive illustrated set.[74] The work was undertaken in 1307 and completed almost ten years later, probably to commemorate Hōnen's one-hundredth-year death anniversary (but a few years late), with many different artists contributing sections of text and pictures. Thus, these illustrated handscrolls were produced approximately a century after Hōnen's death.[75]

Hōnen was certainly important enough in the Buddhist religious world to justify the elaborate production. He began his career studying Tendai Buddhism on Mount Hiei for thirty years, but around 1175 underwent a conversion experience that impelled him to abandon the temple and become an itinerant monk, preaching the recitation of Amida's name as the only way to be reborn in his paradise. Although his ideas were roundly criticized by the monks of Mount Hiei's main temple, and he and his disciples were often persecuted, Hōnen managed to survive various attacks and died of illness in his eighties. For us, the il-

Ritual Implements for Funerals and Memorials 131

lustrated scrolls' importance lies in their detailed illustrations of the seven memorial services that followed Hōnen's death; these show us which ritual implements were used for each service and how they were arranged on the altars. The only caveat is that the pictures are rather small, some of the paintings are damaged, and some of the reproductions are not distinct.

First Memorial

According to the text preceding the images, on his deathbed Hōnen left instructions stipulating that no hall should be built to memorialize him and no ceremonies should be held on his behalf.[76] Instead, he requested his followers to chant the *nenbutsu*. Despite his express wishes, his follower Priest Hōrenbō Shinkū felt that propriety demanded the performance of the traditional seven memorial rituals on Hōnen's behalf. The services of another priest, Shinrenbō, were secured for the first memorial (*shonanoka*), and an im-

Figure 4.3. Hōnen's first memorial service.
Source: *Hōnen shōnin e-den*, in *Zoku Nihon no emaki*, vol. 3, ed. Komatsu Shigemi (Tokyo: Chūō Kōronsha, 1990), after image on p. 20.

Figure 4.4. Set of Buddhist ritual implements. Bronze. 13th century. Fujita Bijutsukan.
Source: Ōchō no butsuga to girei: Zen o tsukushi, bi o tsukusu, ed. Kyoto National Museum (Kyoto: Kyoto National Museum, 1998), after p. 92, plate 36, bottom.

portant court official, Fujiwara Sanemune,[77] sponsored the event. Each memorial was conducted by a different priest and had a different sponsor.

All seven of Hōnen's Buddhist memorial ceremonies appear to have been held in the same hall. Although not identified in the handscroll, the location is probably the site of the Seishidō chapel at Chion'in, where Hōnen passed away. For the first service, two low ceremonial tables stand on a section of bare wooden flooring (Figure 4.3). Shinrenbō sits on a low dais (raiban) in front of the larger red-and-black lacquer table, which serves as an altar and holds the ritual implements for the ceremony. The smaller table beside it (waki tsukue) holds the overflow of objects. Around this space is tatami matting for the comfort of those attending. A painted scroll hangs on a standing screen (tsuitate) placed opposite the seated priest. Even in this small picture it is clear that the subject of the scroll is Fudō Myōō, whose image was also hung for Nakahara Morosuke's first memorial. At opposite ends of the longer table are two bronze flower vases holding white flowers (most likely lotus blossoms) that symbolize death (and rebirth). Along the front of the table are six small, wide-mouthed bronze offering vessels in a row, three on each side of a lidded incense burner (kasha kōro) (Figure 4.4). Although not visible here, the six small vessels (rokki) typically contained offerings such as flowers, perfumed unguents (zukō), water for the Buddha (aka), and food and drink (onjiki).[78] In most Buddhist rituals they were offered to the Buddha as the honored guest; here they were offered on behalf of the deceased. Several of the offering dishes in the picture appear to hold green sprigs of shikimi (star anise), a plant often grown around graves and commonly used as an offering to the Buddha. The bronze vessels arrayed on the main table, originally associated with Esoteric Buddhist rituals, were commonly found in temples of all sects by the fourteenth century.

The two objects on the side table are more difficult to identify. The one in the center appears to be a round lacquered (*makie*)[79] container with a lid and the other a long, thin scroll, perhaps a sutra scroll, or it might be a folded letter, possibly one requesting the priest to recite special sutras on behalf of the deceased (*fujumon*). Such letters were generally written by mourners close to the deceased and given to the officiating priest, who then chanted the requested sutras at the service. The priest, in turn, received alms as payment from the requester. Priest Shinrenbō, clothed in black mourning robes, sits facing the altar, and we can well imagine the sonorous chanting and the wafting incense as he intones sutras and raises the long-handled censer (*egōro*) in front of the scroll of Fudō Myōō. Scores of mourners listen and weep. The officiating priests and family members sit inside the room for the ceremony; other mourners gather on the veranda.

The precise—and highly similar, if not identical—arrangement of the ritual implements confirms their pivotal roles in the rituals surrounding death in medieval Japan. Proper ritual was deemed necessary to affect the karmic balance of the soul as it passed through the crucial forty-nine days after death, then to attain Amida's paradise or to be reborn in another form. Similarly, it was essential that the correct implements be accompanied by appropriate offerings and ritual phrases.

Proper conduct of the seven memorial ceremonies was absolutely crucial to the deceased's well-being because, it was believed, the soul was examined by one of the Ten Kings on the first day of each of the seven seventh-day periods after death. Each king was a secondary manifestation of a primary buddha (*honji butsu*) who embodied the promise of salvation. Therefore on each seventh-day a different Buddhist icon, each embodying also a different judgment king, was displayed.[80] When the painting of Fudō Myōō was brought out for Hōnen's first memorial, it functioned as the principal object of veneration (*honzon*) of that day's Buddhist service, since Fudō also embodied King Shinkō, who judged the soul on that first seventh day. All of the offerings made to the deity were intended to persuade him to be lenient with the deceased.

Second Memorial

The setting for Hōnen's second memorial service (*futananoka*) is almost identical to the first. The offering cups hold *shikimi*, but the flower vases are empty and the *makie* lacquer container has disappeared from the side table; in its place are two folded letters or perhaps rolled scrolls (Figure 4.5). In place of the Fudō Myōō is a painting of a standing Amida.[81] Priest Gubutsubō officiated at this service; a descendant (perhaps a grandson) of the *bettō nyūdō* (title) provided the funds.[82]

Figure 4.5. Hōnen's second memorial service.
Source: *Hōnen shōnin e-den*, in *Zoku Nihon no emaki*, vol. 3, ed. Komatsu Shigemi (Tokyo: Chūō Kōronsha, 1990), after image on p. 22.

Third Memorial

Unfortunately, a large door panel hinders our view of the offering table at the third-week memorial (*minanoka*); on its near end we can see a single vase filled with branches of *shikimi*, which conceal most of the hanging scroll suspended behind the vase (Figure 4.6). We can see that the scroll has been

Figure 4.6. Hōnen's third memorial service.
Source: *Hōnen shōnin e-den*, in *Zoku Nihon no emaki*, vol. 3, ed. Komatsu Shigemi (Tokyo: Chūō Kōronsha, 1990), after image on p. 22.

changed, but we cannot identify its subject. No small side table is in evidence, and only one modest offering vessel is visible on the far right end of the larger table; in it is a green leaf (*shikimi*). Nonetheless, although not visible, the main ritual implements for this service were undoubtedly the same as for the previous memorials. The text tells us that the officiating priest on this day was Jūshinbō and the donor Shōshinbō Tankū. It also mentions that a wooden plaque (*mokuhan*) with a poem by Ōgishi (C. Wang Xizhi, 307–365) was offered on this day.

Fourth Memorial

For the fourth memorial (*yonanoka*) the officiating priest was again Hōrenbō, shown seated with his back to the viewers and holding a folding fan with carved ribs (*eribone sen*; Figure 4.7). Several of the ritual implements on the exquisite *makie* table are visible,[83] but the side table is absent. It is impossible to see what is in the two vases, but *shikimi* leaves are evident in the small offer-

Figure 4.7.
Hōnen's fourth memorial service. Source: *Hōnen shōnin e-den*, in *Zoku Nihon no emaki*, vol. 3, ed. Komatsu Shigemi (Tokyo: Chūō Kōronsha, 1990), after image on p. 24.

ing dishes. Nothing of this day's hanging scroll can be seen except a portion of its lotus-petal base, because the image is almost completely obscured by the open window lattices. The text for this section includes several phrases from the letter read by the sponsor of the service, Ryōsei; though they refer to Amida ("the excellence of singular faith in [A]mida," and the "*raigō* cloud"), this reference seems to relate generally to Amida descending at the time of death, rather than the trope of a particular image of Amida.

From the unusual angle, which clearly shows one side of the small altar, near Hōrenbō's right shoulder we can glimpse a new object, a gilded bronze chime (*kei*). It hangs from a wooden stand lacquered in black with gold flecks.[84]

Ritual Implements for Funerals and Memorials 137

The chime would have been struck to emphasize important phrases chanted during the service and to notify the participants when certain actions should be performed.

Fifth Memorial

The ritual setting for the fifth memorial (*itsunanoka*) is very similar to that of the first (Figure 4.8). All the implements can be clearly seen—vases hold pink-tipped lotus flowers and in the offering containers sprigs of *shikimi*. On the small side table are a tied letter or scroll and a black lacquer box. Assistant Master of Discipline (*gon no risshi*) Ryūkan is the officiating priest, and the donor, Seikanbō Genchi. Ryūkan raises a long-handled censer, undoubtedly before a hanging scroll, but a wall panel blocks our view of it.

Figure 4.8. Hōnen's fifth memorial service.
Source: *Hōnen shōnin e-den*, in *Zoku Nihon no emaki*, vol. 3, ed. Komatsu Shigemi (Tokyo: Chūō Kōronsha, 1990), after image on pp. 24–25.

Sixth Memorial

Two prominent persons participated in Hōnen's sixth-week memorial (*munanoka*)—as officiating priest, Hōin Seikaku, and as donor or sponsor, Jien. Seikaku (also Shōkaku, 1167–1235) was a Tendai priest noted for the eloquence of his Buddhist sermons. Late in life he is said to have become a follower of Hōnen.[85] Signifying his high status in the religious community is the Buddhist surplice of pieced gold brocades that Seikaku wears over the black of his mourning robes (Figure 4.9). Jien (1155–1225), head abbot (*bettō*) of the Tendai temple Tennōji, is nowadays better known as a *waka* poet. He sits closest to

Figure 4.9. Hōnen's sixth memorial service.
Source: *Hōnen shōnin e-den*, in *Zoku Nihon no emaki*, vol. 3, ed. Komatsu Shigemi (Tokyo: Chūō Kōronsha, 1990), after image on p. 27.

Seikaku, wearing simple priestly robes and surplice. Two lacquered tables and the requisite ritual implements are present, but both vases are empty and the offering vessels cannot be clearly seen. Clearly depicted in the hanging scroll is a monk wearing an elaborate surplice and holding a staff in one hand and a jewel in the other, the iconic appurtenances of Jizō Bosatsu.

Seventh Memorial

The seventh and final memorial service (*shichinanoka*) in the forty-nine-day period of mourning is the most important and traditionally the most elaborate (Plate 11). By this day, it was hoped the soul of the deceased had been approved by all seven kings and had moved on, either to the Pure Land or to another and better rebirth. After the seventh memorial, abbreviated memorial services were typically held every month on the date of death, with longer services on the annual death date.

Kōin, abbot of Miidera, officiated at this final service, and Hōrenbō Shinkū was the sponsor. Kōin, wearing brown monk's robes, sits before two low tables that serve as the altar. Behind the tables is a single-panel standing screen with a black-lacquered frame, on which is mounted a hanging scroll of the Diamond World Mandala. In place on the altar are the regular implements: two flower vases holding branches of *shikimi* and a row of six small bronze offering vessels, with a round incense burner standing in the middle of the row. Kōin holds a long-handled censer in his right hand. On the smaller side table, we can see a handscroll, but the pillar of the building blocks our view of the table's center, perhaps hiding the lacquer box visible in other scenes. Just to the priest's right, the upper part of the lacquered stand for the bronze chime is visible.

Ritual Implements in a Memorial Context

Despite problems of flaking paint and scenes with obstructive doors and windows, it is readily apparent that the seven Buddhist memorial services for Hōnen were all held in the same location and utilized the same furniture and ritual implements. The location was the small chapel at Chion'in where Hōnen died, although it is also possible that a grave hall was built and designated for this purpose. The pieces of furniture needed for memorial rituals were few and included only a low dais for the officiating priest, two low lacquered tables—an oblong one that served as an altar and a smaller square side table that held additional objects needed to perform the services—and a large standing screen placed behind the tables. The screen served as a backdrop upon which the seven painted images were hung, one at each seventh-day memorial.

Using low lacquered tables as temporary altars was a common practice in

Figure 4.10. Ritual implements on Gokurakuin's altar.
Source: *Boki ekotoba*, in *Zoku Nihon no emaki*, vol. 9, ed. Komatsu Shigemi (Tokyo: Chūō Kōronsha, 1990), after image on p. 66.

the medieval period, one undoubtedly dictated by limited space and the need for portability. In other handscrolls we see them employed for Buddhist ceremonies other than memorial rituals. For example, in the illustrated biography of Priest Kakunyo (1270–1351), *Boki ekotoba* (14th c.),[86] a similar lacquered table holds the ritual implements for the tonsure of Shūshō (Kakunyo's childhood name).[87] In this same handscroll a larger table holding a formal arrangement of ritual objects functions as the main altar (*shumidan*) in front of Amida at Gokurakuin (Figure 4.10). Thus, low tables served as altars for various Buddhist ceremonies.

Much the same can be said about the ritual implements displayed for Hōnen's seven memorial services. Vessels used to present offerings to the Buddha on behalf of the deceased and those holding offerings to the Buddha for other purposes are the same, or of the same type. In the hair-cutting scene (immediately above) are an incense burner (lower right), six small offering cups, a long-handled censer (left), and a small open book. We can see a more complete arrangement of offering vessels on the table in front of the large golden Amida in *Boki ekotoba*: two flower vases filled with green-leafed branches (probably *shikimi*); six offering cups, some holding green leaves; a round footed incense burner in the center; and two bronze offering bowls mounded with white rice. Except for the rice offerings, the ritual implements for Hōnen's memorial services were identical—two vases of green sprigs, six small bronze offering cups, and an incense burner. I found no evidence that rice was offered to the deceased at any memorial services held during the forty-nine day period. Thus, like the altar table, the Buddhist ritual implements shown in the illustrations of Hōnen's memorials were standard offering vessels.

Save for Hōnen's memorial services, at which *shikimi* (*illicium religiosum*; Japanese star anise) was used as an offering and sometimes as a replacement for flowers, there is little information regarding the types of offerings presented at these events. In Japan from very early times *shikimi* was used to mark sacred places and, later, as offerings to Buddhist icons. Because it is aromatic, *shikimi* was placed in coffins, buried with corpses, and placed on top of graves to neutralize the odor of decay.[88] *Shikimi* was also planted around graves and cemeteries for the same purpose. For this reason the plant has a long and close association with death and Buddhist death rituals. Furthermore, because the plant is a type of evergreen, its leaves stay green after the branch is cut, making it an attractive "living" offering. The fragrant bark and leaves of the plant were also important components of the incense that was burned at funerals and memorial rituals. It was the most important offering at Hōnen's memorial services, as attested by its repeated appearances in *Hōnen shōnin e-den* (Table 5). Although a well-known offering at traditional Buddhist ceremonies as well, the plant seems to have had special importance for medieval death rituals and was perhaps the most common offering at memorial services.

The ritual chime (*kei*), positioned at the officiating priest's right side at Hōnen's fourth and seventh memorials (see Figure 4.7, Plate 11), also had strong associations with Buddhist death rituals in Japan. Chimes in medieval Japan were made of bronze and were suspended from lacquered wooden frames, but their origin can be traced back to stone chimes (*qing*), which were used for

Table 5. Plants/Flowers Offered at Hōnen's Seven Memorials

	Memorial	Contents of vases	Contents of offering cups
1st	shonanoka	white flowers	shikimi
2nd	futananoka	empty	shikimi
3rd	minanoka	shikimi	shikimi
4th	yonanoka	not visible	shikimi
5th	itsunanoka	lotus	shikimi
6th	munanoka	not visible	not visible
7th	shichinanoka	shikimi	shikimi

Figure 4.11. Priest striking the chime for Ryōnin's death.
Source: *Yūzū nenbutsu engi*, in *Zoku Nihon no emaki*, vol. 21, ed. Komatsu Shigemi (Tokyo: Chūō Kōronsha, 1992), after image on pp. 54–55.

ritual music in ancient China, and have been found there in tombs.[89] The instrument was struck at certain points in Buddhist services, and it was often used to accompany the chanting of sutras at the approach of and following death. In the illustrated handscroll of the *Yūzū nenbutsu engi* (14th c.), for example, after priest Ryōnin (1073–1132) passed away, several priests mourned him by striking the chime in rhythm with their chanted prayers (Figure 4.11). As they chanted, Amida and a heavenly host of bodhisattvas and musicians descended to receive Ryōnin into the Western Paradise. The tale implies that the music of the chime played a role in this heavenly manifestation.

Among the more fascinating accompaniments to Hōnen's memorial services are the seven painted Buddhist icons that were suspended from the standing screen behind the altar table. Only three of the seven images can be identified definitely—the Fudō Myōō (first memorial), Jizō (sixth), and the Diamond World Mandala (seventh). Two others can only conjecturally be identified as Amida (second) and Shaka (third). The images for the fourth and fifth memorials cannot be seen clearly. Still, the order of the identifiable images differs from that in other fourteenth-century records of memorial ceremonies (Table 6).

Ritual Implements for Funerals and Memorials 143

Table 6. Comparison of the Order of Buddhist Images for Memorial Services

	Hōnen scroll	*Moromoriki*	*Ten Kings* scrolls
1st	Fudō Myōō	Fudō Myōō	Fudō Myōō
2nd	Amida?	Yakushi	Shaka
3rd	Shaka?	Shaka	Monju
4th	?	Kannon	Fugen
5th	?	Jizō	Jizō
6th	Jizō	Fugen	Miroku
7th	Diamond World	Amida	Yakushi

Moromoriki (Chap. 1) gives the order of images for Nakahara Morosuke's memorial services as Fudō Myōō, Yakushi, Shaka, Kannon, Jizō, Fugen, and Amida Buddha. And both *Moromoriki* and *Hōnen shōnin e-den* present different orders from the one depicted in a fourteenth-century pair of hanging scrolls of *Ten Kings of Hell and Scenes of Punishments* (Plate 1), which show the order as Fudō Myōō, Shaka, Monju, Fugen, Jizō, Miroku, and Yakushi.[90] As all three of these sources date to the same century, the differences lead us to conclude that either the order was not yet set at this time or that it varied according to sectarian preferences.

The Diamond World Mandala, hung for Hōnin's seventh memorial, was an exception to custom, as mandala were generally not displayed during the forty-nine-day period. More commonly, offerings were made to individual buddhas and bodhisattvas at the first seven memorial ceremonies, in an appeal to their counterpart kings to be lenient in their judgments of the soul during the crucial forty-nine days after death. Not only was the order of displaying the images not set at this point in history, the particular buddhas and bodhisattvas seem also to have varied. Five of the seven buddhas in *Moromoriki* appear in the *Ten Kings* handscroll, but Kannon and Amida appear in *Moromoriki* and Miroku and Monju in the *Ten Kings* scroll. The information in the Hōnen scroll is sparse, but only two of the confirmable images appear in the other examples.

Examples from other medieval handscrolls further confirm that the types and arrangements of the ritual implements depicted in Hōnen's memorials were standard for death-related ceremonies in medieval Japan and also for most other types of Buddhist ceremonies. An illustration in *Yūzū nenbutsu engi* (14th c.) shows an altar set with ritual objects next to a woman who is preparing for her own death.[91] According to the text, the daughter of Izumi no Senji Dōkyō took Buddhist vows and became a nun under Priest Ryōnin's tutelage. She then confined herself to a hermitage, where she passed her days practicing a concentrated recitation of the Nenbutsu (*nenbutsu zanmai*).[92]

Figure 4.12. Death of a nun, with scrolls of Amida Triad, *myōgō*, and teacher's portrait. Source: *Yūzū nenbutsu engi*, in *Zoku Nihon no emaki*, vol. 21, ed. Komatsu Shigemi (Tokyo: Chūō Kōronsha, 1992), after image on p. 66.

When she felt death approaching, she hung three scrolls on the wall above a rectangular table altar (Figure 4.12). The middle scroll is an Amida Triad; the right scroll is a calligraphic rendering of that deity's sacred name (*myōgō*); and the left scroll is a portrait of her teacher, Ryōnin. The ritual bronze implements—two (empty) flower vases, six small offering vessels, an incense burner, and two additional cuplike vessels—stand on the large altar table in front of the paintings. The nun also prepared a long-handled censer and two books of sutras on another small, low lacquered table in front of the altar. All of the implements here are familiar to us from texts and images documenting other death-related services.

Another scene in the same scroll depicts a special Nenbutsu service (*betsuji nenbutsu*) held for an ailing individual.[93] In a bare, wood-planked room the family is gathered before a large gilt image of a seated Amida Nyorai, on an ornate lotus pedestal (Figure 4.13).

An altar table and another lower table are placed in front of the icon, with the proper ritual implements—the flower vases, six offering vessels, and

Figure 4.13. Special Nenbutsu ceremony.
Source: *Yūzū nenbutsu engi*, in *Zoku Nihon no emaki*, vol. 21, ed. Komatsu Shigemi (Tokyo: Chūō Kōronsha, 1992), after image on p. 80.

an incense burner—arranged on the altar table and sutra scrolls on the lower table. Thus, we may assume that these were typical for Buddhist ceremonies in the medieval period.

Zen-Style Funerals and Ritual Implements

The structure of post-Heian-period funerals was strongly influenced by China through the transmission of Zen Buddhism in the late twelfth century. Funerals and death-related ceremonies in medieval Japan closely followed the Chinese monastic codes produced during the Song dynasty (960–1279).[94] The progressive effect of these codes in Japan was to make funeral rites more popular and affordable to individuals outside the circle of the imperial family.

The new Zen-style funerals clearly must have spurred the production of funeral implements in Japan, many of which—banners, incense burners, flower vases, and offering containers—had been used for services long before Buddhism began to take over the funeral industry. Yet, given the growing numbers of individuals who were not only Buddhist devotees but also able to afford elaborate funerals, processions, and memorial services in the medieval period, production necessarily increased at this time. Indeed, the vast majority of mortuary implements still extant in Japan date back no earlier than the thirteenth century. Their production has been little studied and would benefit from further research. But it is clear that the need and criteria for these implements were not chiefly aesthetic; rather their importance lay in the roles they played in the rituals.

Funeral processions and memorial services were crucial because they not only helped to guide the deceased on their journey through the afterlife, but also the mourners and community to come to terms with their loss. Processions were active, colorful, and loud. They took place in darkness by dramatic lamplight, and the ritual implements were imbued with an impressive symbolism. The procession and the seven memorial rituals touched all of the mourners' senses. Seeing the robes and banners, smelling the pungent incense, hearing the music and chanting—all combined to reach and heal the mourners' grief. The evidence gathered here indicates that, although the specifics of the funeral procession and memorial services were not strictly codified, they did follow a general pattern that was considered efficacious in helping the deceased to separate from the living and move on to a new level of existence.

PORTRAITS OF THE DECEASED 5

Portraits as Instruments and Objects of Mortuary Rituals

The common view of a portrait is that it represents a specific individual, either historical or legendary. A portrait, however, is that and more.[1] The making of portraits in the West has been described as "a response to the natural human tendency to think about oneself, of oneself in relation to others, and of others in apparent relation to themselves and to others," which suggests that the development of Western portraiture has been driven by concepts of the self and the individual.[2] This statement applies mainly to the modern period of portraiture. Historically, portraiture in the West was also meant to engage its viewers in a wide range of considerations, including social status and political authority, cults of fame, and didactic purposes.[3] In premodern East Asia, however, these considerations were less important. Rather, a primary function of portraits in China, Korea, and Japan was to serve as proxies of the ancestors in rites of ancestral veneration. Mortuary portraits were created specifically as stand-ins for the deceased in funerals and memorial rituals. As such, the images were viewed as living manifestations of the deceased, who shared in the essence of that person when alive. Therefore these portraits should be considered as both instruments in and objects of mortuary rituals.

In medieval Japan portraits of the deceased were indeed considered ritual implements essential to Buddhist funerals and to the offering services performed on behalf of the deceased (*tsuizen kuyō*).[4] In these two contexts they were consecrated images through which the presence of the deceased could be invoked. Although they were used as ritual objects in mortuary services, portraits differ significantly from the types of objects discussed in Chapter 4. Some of the distinctions are obvious. For example, the implements discussed in the previous chapter were made of long-lasting bronze or lacquered wood, and those very implements, or others of the same types, were used in other religious rituals performed in Buddhist temples. Mortuary portraits, on the other hand, were either hanging scrolls painted with ink and color on paper or silk, or wooden sculptures with polychromy. The most important difference, however, is that portraits of the secular deceased were never used in conventional Buddhist ceremonies. Both painted and sculpted portraits of laypersons were stored in family temples (*bodaiji*). Painted images would be specially brought out from storage for display on the deceased's death anniversaries; sculpted images, being nearly life-size, usually stood permanently positioned in niches or in particular sections of the family temple. Portrait sculptures were made only for people who held important political positions and were therefore uncommon, but they functioned in the same way as painted portraits in rituals commemorating the deceased.[5] Portraits of the secular elite in medieval Japan are therefore unique among the essential ritual objects used in Buddhist mortuary ceremonies, because they were intimately associated with a particular individual and family.

Despite the pivotal role played by painted portraits in funerals and memorial ceremonies throughout Japan's medieval period, today they are seldom found in temples and are even more rarely used for ceremonies honoring the dead.[6] Many contemporary anthropological studies on early funerary and mortuary customs in Japan mention portraits only in passing or not at all.[7] Indeed, it is generally stated that the custom of placing a picture of the deceased on the funeral altar began in the early Shōwa reign period (1926–1989).[8] Even elderly Japanese to whom I have spoken seem wholly unaware that many of the famous medieval portraits now in museums once hung above funeral altars. By the early twentieth century photographs had replaced paintings, presumably for reasons of cost and convenience, but concomitant changes in the status of the likeness must also have occurred. Today, a photograph of the deceased is placed on a special altar during the wake and at the funeral, but the function of the photograph appears to be different from that of a painting or sculpture and reflects a change in the popular conception of mortuary images that should be examined.

Once a painted portrait ceased to play its original role, it was lost or discarded over time, as memory and recognition by the descendants faded. Some of the surviving hanging-scroll portraits were acquired by museums, which effectively removed them from their original context and presented them as works of art. Scholars became interested in portraits of famous historical figures, portraits inscribed by notable individuals, and those made by known artists, seeking what such representations could reveal about these people and about Japan's history. Although the beauty of hanging-scroll portraits would seem to call for equal interest in their aesthetic qualities, their original function was not primarily aesthetic. But because of these surviving portraits' displacement, their mortuary function has not received serious study.

Because in the early twentieth century most studies on portraiture were undertaken by historians of art and other aspects of Japanese civilization, who focused on describing and identifying the subject of the portrait and, less often, on identifying the painter or calligrapher, the favored methodologies were connoisseurship and stylistic analysis.[9] These methods furthered an understanding of the subject, the artist, and the cultural and historical context, helping to place the work in time and to assign it to a school or individual. The need to identify the individual portrayed was further driven by a newly invigorated commercial art market and the concomitant increased value of the portrait if the subject was known.[10]

In this chapter I shall not attempt to analyze specific portraits or seek to identify their subjects, nor will I utilize portraits as sources of historical or social information;[11] both approaches have been well explored. Likewise, scholars have already reassessed the function of portraits of Buddhist priests (chinsō), arguing that they should not be understood as certificates of enlightenment or proofs of dharma inheritance, but as ritual objects that functioned within the larger ritual context of Buddhist funerals and memorial rites.[12] My intent is to carry this reappraisal a step further by examining portraits of Japan's medieval lay elite as ritual objects, figuratively removing them from their current homes in art museums and resurrecting their original ritual context.[13] This chapter, therefore, examines how portraits were displayed for mortuary rites. Furthermore, it considers several specific questions that have not been satisfactorily answered—what defines a mortuary portrait? when were these portraits commissioned and by whom? when and where were they hung during the ceremonies? who actually saw them? what rites were performed before them? and how were they perceived by the living?

Portraits and Buddhist Mortuary Rituals

Portraits used in conjunction with Buddhist services for the dead have a long history in China, dating from at least the fourth century CE and continuing through about the fourteenth century.[14] During this period portraits of esteemed monks were typically sculpted or painted for use in mortuary rites; there are also rare instances of portraits of eminent monks venerated prior to death.[15] Although Buddhism traditionally negates the material world and the human body, early on its devotees and missionaries adopted visual representations in order to aid the transmission of Buddhism by embodying, and thus vivifying, its message. Images of the Buddha, bodhisattvas, and arhats (holy monks who attain "conditional" nirvana in this life and full extinction after death) were created as concrete reminders to believers of their special powers, and also of their place in the transmission of the Buddhist Law. According to one scholar, painted portraits of monks derived from the tradition of arhat paintings in China, similarly serving as reminders of the monk's achievements and his position in the lineage of transmission.[16]

The picture becomes more complex in the late Tang period (9–10th c.), when Buddhist practices inspired the use of portraits in Chinese ancestor rituals. By the late tenth century a confluence of Buddhism and ancestor worship had emerged, wherein Buddhist monks and nuns conducted memorial services for deceased ancestors of the elite in Buddhist temples.[17] Although in China many of the rituals associated with the veneration and memorialization of ancestors were later taken over by Daoist and Confucian ritual specialists, the practices that were transmitted to Japan and that influenced mortuary rites for the Japanese elite throughout the fourteenth and fifteenth centuries arrived in the form of Zen Buddhist death rituals.

Examination of Tang and pre-Tang Buddhist sources reveals that portraits were most commonly used in mortuary and commemorative rites, in which they served four important functions: (1) as resting places for the departed spirit; (2) as the focus for ritual offerings to the deceased; (3) as images to memorialize the deceased; and (4) as a way of identifying the tomb.[18] This list encompasses most of the functions of portraiture in medieval Japan.

Although some quasi portraits or portrait-like images associated with the corpse existed in pre-Buddhist Japan, we do not know how these images were interpreted or how they functioned as objects.[19] It was not until Buddhism, with its by then rich store of images and literature, became entrenched in Japan that portraits of the deceased began to play roles recognizable to us in rituals connected with death.

Among the earliest forms of mortuary portraiture in Japan were wooden sculptures of Buddhist masters that served as substitutes for their mummified bodies. An immigrant monk from China, Ganjin (C. Jianzhen, 688–763), was an early proponent in Japan of this concept. The idea developed from a Chinese practice whereby the bodies of a few notable spiritual monks, such as Huineng (638–713), were mummified as "buddhas in the present body" (*sokushin jōbutsu*). The practice was based on the belief that the bodies of devout monks, who had practiced rigorous austerities and meditation, might be preserved without decay after death (albeit generally with the help of desiccation and a generous coating of lacquer). The priest's actual mummified body thus became an image of veneration for his disciples. The degree of success of the mummification was considered a measure of the deceased's high level of spiritual attainment. It then became common to sculpt or paint images of priests after death and to place them in special worship halls. Ganjin was un-

Portraits of the Deceased

Figure 5.1. Portrait sculpture of Enchin (Okotsu Daishi).
Source: *Fushichō no tera Miidera: Chishō daishi issen hyaku nen go-onki kinen*, with editorial assistance from Shinshūsha (Ōtsu City: Sōhonzan Onjōji (Miidera), 1990), after plate 2.

doubtedly familiar with this practice, for upon his death in 763 a life-size, hollow dry-lacquer portrait statue was made and enshrined in a chapel at his retirement temple, Tōshōdaiji in Nara.

Jimon denki horoku describes an unusual wooden portrait sculpture made to venerate the Tendai abbot Enchin (Chishō Daishi, 814–891).[20] According to the text, soon after Enchin's death a "reflected image" (*eizō*) was made and

Enchin's ashes and bones were placed inside it. Thereafter, the image, known as Okotsu Daishi (Great Master Honorable Bones), became an object of mortuary veneration.[21] Depositing the remains of priests in their portrait sculptures followed the ancient practice of placing the supposed bodily remains of the Buddha within his images.[22] Enchin's image is one of the earliest examples in Japan of a portrait sculpture that functioned as both a relic urn and a devotional image, a practice well documented in Tang and pre-Tang China.[23] Enchin's bones and ashes inside this image affected the way in which the statue was perceived and venerated. The portrait, being three-dimensional and nearly life-size, gave a physical impression of the deceased; the bodily relics inside supplied an added dimension of Enchin's presence. With the remains inside, the image was not just a man-made object: it was imbued with Enchin's holiness. Countless likenesses of other eminent Buddhist priests were sculpted in the centuries after Enchin, fulfilling a number of important functions related to the Buddhist way of death in Japan: providing resting places for their spirits, serving as objects for rituals and offerings, and supplying visual prompts for remembering the dead.

Although it is generally assumed that early sculpted portraits of priests were part of mortuary and other temple ceremonies, it is not clear that all of these images were used during the priests' funerals. Unless a statue was commissioned well in advance, it was unlikely to be completed in time for the funeral, because sculpted or dry-lacquer portraits took much longer to create than the few days usually intervening between the death and the funeral.

Among the earliest painted portraits associated with Buddhism in Japan are lineage portraits (*soshizō*), such as the famous set of five hanging scrolls of the founders of the Shingon school of Buddhism that were brought from Tang China by priest Kūkai (774–835) and are now preserved at Tōji in Kyoto. Ritsu sect lineage portraits (*Risshū soshizō*) and portraits of Zen priests (*chinsō*), both of which developed later, in Song dynasty (960–1279) China, also came to be known in Japan and were used in a variety of Buddhist ceremonies, such as celebrating the foundation of the lineage, special Esoteric Dharma transmission ceremonies, master–disciple transmission, funeral services, and for Buddhist memorial ceremonies.

Written proof that portrait paintings were used for mortuary rituals connected to the *secular* elite came later in Japan. Numerous diaries chronicle the role portraits played in imperial memorial rites during the eleventh and twelfth centuries, but little evidence exists that the images were used during their funeral services at this time. The eleventh-century *Eiga monogatari*, for example, documents all manner of imperial funerals, including a long and detailed entry on Emperor Go-Ichijō's interment in 1036, but no portraits are mentioned.[24] But we are told that at a memorial service for Go-Ichijō in 1088, more than fifty years after his death, his portrait (*miei*) was hung in a hall (the Sanmidō) and venerated.[25] All evidence suggests that, in the late Heian period, portraits were created for and displayed at memorial services for emperors and members of the imperial family but played no role in funerals. It is often said that these high-level individuals resisted having portraits painted during their lifetimes because of strong taboos based on the fear that such images could be used to lay curses on the sitter.[26] It was only after the twelfth century, probably encouraged by Buddhist priests, that emperors permitted their portraits to be drawn while they were living.

There is also little proof that painted portraits were used for mortuary rites of other elite segments of society, primarily members of the court and military elite (other than Buddhist priests), until about the thirteenth century, suggesting that these classes of society did not assimilate the custom much before the Kamakura period. Indeed, this has been tacitly assumed, because early diaries and records hold very little information about the practice for groups other than the imperial family.[27] The discovery of a portrait presumed to be of courtier Fujiwara no Tadahira (880–949) offered tantalizing hope for an earlier date, but unfortunately it has been impossible to ascertain that the portrait in question is indeed Tadahira. All we have is a record in *Okanoya kanpakuki*,[28] which says that in 1246 a life-size painting of a seated courtier was found in poor condition in the back part of a hall at Hosshōji.[29] There was, apparently, considerable discussion even in the thirteenth century about this portrait and general disagreement about the identity of the sitter. Nonetheless, even if the image is not Tadahira (10th c.), its discovery does seem to suggest that portraits of persons other than immediate members of the imperial family were created, probably for display at memorial rituals, before the mid-thirteenth century.

Terminology and Ritual Function

Before discussing the function of portraits in the funerals and memorial services of Japan's medieval elite, it is important to know how the various terms for portraits have traditionally been understood in China and Japan, because it will reveal when and why particular images came to be made and suggest how certain images functioned ritually. Close examination of the various terms can help us interpret how portraits were conceived and received in medieval Japan.

Two terms for portraits, *izō* and *juzō*, generally differentiate between posthumous images and paintings made from life, respectively, and suggest, to some degree, their functions. Both types are associated with mortuary rituals in medieval Japan. The terms originated in China as *yixiang* and *shouxiang*, respectively, with *izō/yixiang*, portraits made after the subject's death, considered to be the earlier practice. But the terms changed meanings over time, and traditionally they have been somewhat differently understood in China and Japan. Furthermore, scholars writing about portraiture have employed the terms differently when discussing religious and secular portraits.

In China, *yixiang*, or "portrait left behind," most properly referred to an image commissioned near the end of a person's life for the purpose of veneration after death, although the term was also sometimes used for images commissioned posthumously by disciples or family members.[30] The Song monastic codes, for example, mandated that an abbot's portrait be painted as he approached death to ensure that it would be ready for his funeral rites and annual memorial services; such portraits were generally termed *yixiang*.[31]

In contrast, *shouxiang*, "longevity image," referred to a portrait made a number of years before the subject's death. At first, such images were probably not venerated until after the subject died, but by the Song dynasty they were hung in patriarch halls for veneration during the abbot's lifetime, alongside images of deceased abbots.[32] The practice of making *shouxiang* portraits before death was developed in response to the increasing mobility of eminent monks. As monks began to move from one abbacy to another, it became no longer practical to wait until they were near death to draw their portraits, because by that time the abbot might no longer be in residence, making it difficult to obtain his image for enshrinement in the patriarch hall.[33] Thus, in China the only real difference in the implication of the two terms seemed to revolve around the number of years the portrait was made prior to death, *yixiang* referring to portraits made just before the sitter's death, and *shouxiang* to those made many years prior to the death.[34]

In Japan the characters rendered the literal meanings identical to those in Chinese—"portraits left behind" (*izō/yixiang*) and "longevity portraits" (*juzō/shouxiang*). But in historical documents and diaries their connotations appear to be quite different. In Japan, *izō* generally referred to portraits that were made after the subject's death and *juzō* to portraits drawn at any time during the subject's lifetime. The distinction between the two is also related to the reason each was commissioned. *Izō* were made specifically for use as mortuary portraits—presumably because no earlier images existed—and members of the deceased's family generally commissioned their production. *Juzō* were made during the subject's lifetime, often for purposes originally unrelated to death, such as to celebrate a birthday, long life, or a worldly achievement; the subject himself would often commission the portrait. This latter type of portrait seems to have developed later in Japan and can be documented only from about the thirteenth century,[35] perhaps reflecting a new focus in the Kamakura period on recording and visually memorializing individual achievements.

Sometimes the circumstances of production were not so straightforward:

portraits actually painted after death could be copied from an existing portrait that had been painted or sculpted during the subject's life. Do we call such images *izō* because they were posthumous, or *juzō* because they copied an image made from life? Ashikaga Yoshimasa's (1436–1490) funeral portrait is a case in point. Four days after Yoshimasa's death, sketches were brought to his relatives so that they could choose one from which a painting would be made for the funeral.[36] We do not know when these sketches were made. It may be that they had been produced some years earlier, while Yoshimasa was still alive, and were only brought to the family for their selection after his death.[37] Quitman Phillips notes that several completed portraits of Yoshimasa already existed by 1490, and that those images could also have been used for the painter's sketches.[38] Or might the painter have made the sketches after viewing Yoshimasa's corpse? In China, drawing a portrait of the deceased was not uncommon, but whether it was also done in Japan we do not know.[39] This is just one example of the uncertainties that complicate our understanding of the terms *izō* and *juzō*.

Portraits also exist that were commissioned during the subject's life expressly to accumulate offerings and merit for transfer to the portrait's subject upon death.[40] This interesting practice, called *gyakushu*, was a deliberate preparation for one's own death. In the portrait one's living self became as one of the honored dead, and in that guise one would receive merit through special rites and offerings made by oneself before that portrait. The offerings were like those made during the seven seventh days, but performed before death. It was believed that such offerings made in advance to the Ten Kings would encourage their favorable judgments after one died. Such rites were popular because the merit generated before death was thought to be seven times stronger than the merit requested on one's behalf postmortem by one's relatives. This practice developed in association with Ten Kings beliefs in China and was known in Japan from the late ninth century.[41] A case in point is the portrait of himself that the Retired Emperor Go-Tsuchimikado (1442–1500) ordered painted in 1489 in anticipation of his death and had installed in the Sanmai'in subcloister of Hanjūin.[42] How should we categorize such a portrait? Phillips states that, in the fifteenth-century portrait inscriptions that he examined, the designation *juzō* always refers to images produced during the sitter's life, regardless of when they were put to ritual use.[43] So perhaps this was the criterion that the medieval Japanese themselves used.

As there are no discernable visual differences between *izō* and *juzō*, looking at the images themselves certainly does not help us to determine whether they were painted before or after death or for what original reasons. But it is sometimes possible to identify an image as *izō* or *juzō* from temple records or from information written on or, in the case of sculpture, inside the image. Temple records and documents found inside the wooden portrait sculpture of

Priest Eison at Saidaiji revealed that the statue was completed on 1280.8.26 as a *juzō* to celebrate his eightieth birthday.[44] This *juzō* was later appropriated for mortuary rituals, even though that was not its original purpose. Only such inscriptions or documents can tell us definitively whether or not an image was made for a secular purpose prior to death.

Thus, in medieval Japan portraits commissioned at various times in the subject's history and for diverse reasons could be used in mortuary rituals. If a suitable portrait already existed, that image was often used for the funeral rituals and for the weekly memorial ceremonies that took place in the forty-nine days that followed. If no suitable portrait of the deceased existed, the family or temple commissioned one, usually based on other existing portraits or sketches or, if none were at hand, following verbal descriptions. It is likely that the practice of producing portraits during one's life to celebrate old age or achievement (*juzō*) was stimulated as much by the need to have a portrait ready when death approached as by the desire to commemorate the importance of one's human accomplishments.

At first, pondering the definitions of these terms appears not to be a useful exercise, since both types often ended up as mortuary images regardless of their original purpose. Yet the very existence of the two terms seems to suggest that the Japanese thought the distinction important. Despite an underlying assumption in the medieval period that any existing portrait might later be put to use in mortuary rites, those created specifically for that purpose may have had special significance as "remnants" of the individual, much like physical relics. Furthermore, from approximately the fifteenth through the nineteenth century, portraits were needed both for the funeral and for the many subsequent memorials. From this we may surmise that the vast majority of portraits from this period that have come down to us today had mortuary functions in their own times.

If the terms *izō* and *juzō* tell us generally whether the image was made pre- or postmortum, other terms for portraits commonly found in Japanese medieval records, such as *miei/goei/gyoei*, *katashiro* (C. *xingshi*), *zō* (C. *xiang*), and *shin* (C. *zhen*), apprise us more specifically of the portrait's meaning and function. These terms, too, derive in full or in part from China and are difficult to define because their usage changed over time and geographical space. It is possible, however, to outline their history and to attempt to elucidate some of the attitudes held by medieval Japanese toward portraits and death.

In their discussion of Chinese portraiture, T. Griffith Foulk and Robert H. Sharf addressed the two latter terms. *Xiang* (J. *zō*) is an ancient word for images made to represent the attributes of select phenomena and observed forms. *Xiang* are understood to subsume the sense of mystery that once accompanied the early iconic replication of things in ancient China. Thus, *xiang* are perceived as concrete forms or images expressing generally formless concepts. The other term, *zhen*, emphasizes the formless aspects of concrete entities, such as representations of the intangible aspects of the Buddha or humans. This term appeared in China as early as the Six Dynasties period (220–589) in reference to portraits judged to accurately depict the "spirit resonance" or "true" appearances of their subjects. *Zhen* was most commonly used in medieval Buddhist sources and was preferred for portraits drawn or sculpted from life (or believed to be) that attempted to capture the "essence" (i.e., spirits or souls) of living, historical figures.[45] The official histories of Han China, namely the *History of the Han* (*Han shu*) and *History of the Latter Han* (*Hou Han shu*), generally referred to portraits as being either *xiang* (image) or *xing* (shape/form).[46]

Quitman Phillips framed his chapter on Japanese portraiture with a discussion of two different but related terms—*shōzō* (C. *xiaoxiang*) and *eizō* (C. *yingxiang*)—which he found in abundance in Japanese diaries and records of the late fifteenth century.[47] *Shōzō* may be translated literally as an "image [that] resembles" and *eizō* as an "image [that] reflects." In China both of these terms were more often used for ancestor portraits than for portraits of Buddhist priests, suggesting that "resembling" and "reflecting" were concepts of greater import for ancestor images. My research suggests that the same was true in medieval Japan, where diarists, primarily members of the court who lived outside monastic communities, seemed to favor the terms *shōzō* and *eizō* when writing about portraits, whereas Buddhist monks more often used the term *shin* (C. *zhen*; true appearance).

Miei, *goei*, and *gyoei*, all translated as "revered or noble reflections," appear to be uniquely Japanese terms, although similar meanings are expressed through slightly different characters in China—*yingxiang* for ancestor portraits and *yurong* for imperial portraits. Although the kanji are identical for all three terms in Japanese, *miei* and *goei* are generally considered the correct designations for portraits of *kami*, buddhas, and deceased individuals (roughly equivalent to *yingxiang*, the term for ancestor portraits in Chinese).[48] *Gyoei* is used more specifically for painted portraits and photographs of emperors and the imperial family (similar to *yurong*). Because these distinctions can only be determined if the words are spoken or if the character is glossed to indicate pronunciation, their use in early periods cannot be easily verified.

The meaning of *katashiro* is similarly ambiguous. Although generally it referred to human forms made of wood or paper that were used for purification ceremonies or as objects to temporarily accommodate the spirit or soul of a *kami*, the term was sometimes used to refer to portraits of the deceased, probably because of the latter nuance. An example of this latter meaning appears in *Moromoriki* on 1345.8.26. We are told that Moromori went to the Jizōdō of Hōjiji at Shijō Bōmon, where Kenshin's body had been taken the evening before the burial, to make offerings to Amida and to the sacred images (*katashiro*) of his father, Morosuke, mother, Kenshin, and deceased sister, Gakumyō.[49] This term *katashiro* (substitute form) usually referred to paper images of humans used by the Yin-Yang Master (*onmyōji*) for purification ceremonies, but it might also be used to denote an object in which the spirit of the deceased takes up temporary residence. It was often used interchangeably with *yorishiro* (possessed form). In this case, it is most likely that the term pertains to portraits of the deceased, where the spirit was believed to reside when the portrait was hung for veneration.[50]

In summary, the various terms for portraits may originally have had unambiguous meanings and the portraits to which they were applied distinct uses, but when employed by writers in medieval Japan who were not monks, their meanings became imprecise and began to overlap. Writers of medieval diaries and records used all of the terms rather loosely and often interchangeably. For example, in the mid-fourteenth-century *Moromoriki*, author Nakahara Moromori referred to his parents' memorial portraits as *ei*, *eizō*, and *miei*. In a few instances, he also referred to them as *katashiro* (see entries for 1345.8.26 and 1346.3.23). Madenokōji Tokifusa, the author of *Kennaiki*, called a portrait of Ashikaga Yoshimochi a *miei* (1428.1.18). Priest Kisen Shūshō, writing in *Inryōken nichiroku*, mentioned two different portraits of Ashikaga Yoshimasa, referring to one as *eizō* (1490.1.7) and one as *shin* (1490.2.5). Moreover, the term for the special Buddhist service for displaying the portrait of the deceased in front of the coffin is *kashin butsuji*, "the Buddhist service for hanging the *shin*," suggesting that *shin* was the proper Buddhist term. Although I have examined only a small sample of medieval texts, these confirm that Buddhist priests used *shin* more often than secular writers. And although the terms discussed above seem to have been used as near equivalents for portraits of the deceased in medieval Japan, it is likely that the writer's social position influenced which term he was likely to use. This suggests another area for further research.

Who Commissioned Memorial Portraits?

Who commissioned portraits for funerals and death memorials is a question that has not been thoroughly examined. In his discussion of portraits Quitman Phillips offers useful hints on how this may have been determined, but I wish to consider and expand on his statements.[51] The general principle that determined who should commission a portrait of the deceased was relatively straightforward: it should be commissioned by the person or persons closest to the deceased. Thus, for high-ranking Buddhist priests, close followers or disciples of the deceased planned the funeral and commissioned the image. For medieval courtiers and military elite, family members shared responsibility for the planning of the funeral and memorial services with the Buddhist priests who would officiate at those ceremonies, often with some input from the Yin-Yang Master. But the portrait was usually ordered by a member of the immediate family or, in the case of a military leader, sometimes by a close follower.

Information in medieval diaries suggests that a distinct hierarchy governed Japan's elite, and that the order of the survivors within that hierarchy dictated who was responsible for commissioning the deceased's memorial portrait. Family organization and general social structure in medieval Japan were essentially Confucian in nature, with males and older members occupying positions of reverence or respect. These Confucian underpinnings had been added to the Buddhist ritual system very early in China, perhaps as early as the eighth century, and were then passed on to Japan.[52] In medieval Japan, therefore, portraits were most often made *of* individuals who were worthy of respect within the Confucian hierarchy—male spouses, parents, teachers, and rulers—and *by* the individuals who owed them devotion—wives, children, pupils, and subjects. In general, therefore, more portraits were made of males and commissioned by females, mainly in their capacities as wives, children, or mothers of predeceased sons.

Diaries provide abundant references to portraits commissioned according to these rules of Confucian hierarchy, and these references exemplify how the system worked. Although the proper order was occasionally varied, for the most part it was followed. When the male head of a high-ranking family died, his wife, sons, or loyal retainers, generally in that order, were responsible for obtaining portraits for the Buddhist services. A case in point is the Nakahara, a low-ranking Kyoto court family whose head held the hereditary title of Senior Secretary. When the head of the family, Morosuke, died in 1345, his wife, Kenshin, ordered a portrait of him be dedicated at his seventh-week memorial service.[53]

When a son died before his parents, the mother, rather than the father, typically commissioned the portrait. When Shogun Ashikaga Yoshihisa died at the age of twenty-four in 1489, his mother, Hino Tomiko, and a trusted retainer, Akamatsu Masanori, ordered a memorial image of Yoshihisa riding to battle.[54] Within the Confucian system of relationships it was the responsibility of inferiors to generate merit for their superiors. This is why it was not appropriate for Yoshihisa's father, the retired shogun Yoshimasa, to order a portrait of his son. When an adult shogun died, often a personally close follower participated in plans for the portrait, illustrating the devotion a subject owed his ruler. After Ashikaga Yoshimasa died the following year (1490), the artist showed sketches to his personal attendant Horikawadono, who then picked out the one he thought best represented his lord. That sketch was shown to Yoshimasa's wife for her approval, and was then presumably used to create the final portrait.[55]

Figure 5.2. Portrait of Ashikaga Yoshimitsu. Artist unknown. 14th century Rokuonji, Kyoto.
Source: Takagishi Akira, *Muromachi ōken to kaiga: Shoki Tosa-ha kenkyū* (Kyoto: Kyōto Daigaku Gakujutsu Shuppankai, 2004), after plate 1.

Certainly more than one person could and often did commission portraits for the purposes of *tsuizen* services and later veneration. The act itself brought merit to the commissioner, the artist, and the deceased, so creating multiple images had the happy effect of improving everyone's chances for a high rebirth. In general, the more important the deceased, the more portraits were made and dedicated. Only a small number of the images that remain today, however, can be assigned to a specific patron, either by searching through diaries or by examining portrait inscriptions. Even when a diary names a person who commissioned a portrait for a funeral or memorial service, there is no way to match that name with an uninscribed image. And, unfortunately, relatively few of the remaining portraits, even those inscribed with the name of the deceased, bear sufficient data about who ordered them or when. For example, of the three known inscribed images of Ashikaga Yoshimitsu, we can link only one to the individual who ordered it.[56] Its inscription tells us that his brother Yoshimochi dedicated the portrait at the end of the sixth month of Ōei 15 (1408), probably for Yoshimitsu's seventh (final) memorial service (Figure 5.2). At the top of the second portrait are poems written on colored squares, but nothing about the patron.[57] The third portrait, dedicated in Ōei 31 (1424), bears an inscription by Genchū Shūgaku,[58] but this painting is believed to be a copy.[59] Of the three extant portraits, therefore, we can be certain about the patron of only one. Such problems make patronage studies of mortuary images very difficult indeed.

Portraits for Funerals

One of the most significant changes that took place in mortuary rituals between the fourteenth and fifteenth centuries was the dramatic increase in Zen-style funerals held for secular individuals. One of the major modifications in this new style was the refocusing of the funeral service around the deceased's portrait and memorial tablet. Portraits had been important features of memorial ceremonies for elite laypeople for centuries in Japan, but there is no evidence that they were displayed during their funerals until sometime in the Kamakura period. Over time, high-ranking patrons of the Zen monasteries were exposed to the new rituals while attending funerals for deceased abbots. There they saw the priest's stately painted portrait and his wooden memorial tablet venerated in the context of a rich array of banners, lanterns, incense, and offerings, all of which must have made the funeral rituals available to them seem puny, if not downright shabby, by comparison. Soon courtiers and military elite alike, for a variety of reasons, became devotees of this new sect and began regularly to request funerals of the style accorded abbots. The monks obliged, undoubtedly seeing this trend as a means to extend their influence in Japanese society

One of the most crucial changes brought about by the new funerary practices was that now images of the deceased were needed immediately at death. This, of course, affected when portraits were painted. As mentioned earlier, there are few records of *juzō* (paintings produced to celebrate a birthday, a long life, or a worldly achievement) being made much before the thirteenth century. One reason for their newfound popularity in the thirteenth century may therefore be related to the growing need for portraits for funerals. Whereas previously portraits could be commissioned and painted in time for the one-month or forty-ninth-day anniversary, now the artist had to produce an image for the funeral, generally held only a few days after the death. It was most unlikely that an image could be commissioned, sketched, approved, and turned into a finished painting in those few days. Therefore it is at least plausible that people would have begun to order their own portraits, which could be used to celebrate long life or achievement and then, eventually, would be available for their funerals.

A crucial component of the Zen funeral was the display of the deceased's portrait on a specially prepared altar placed in front of the corpse. In the fifteenth-century funerals discussed in Chapter 2, the portrait was typically hung twice—once in front of the coffin as it rested inside the temple before and during the funeral service and again, later, above a temporary altar constructed near the entryway to the cremation site.[60] After the funeral service at the temple was over, the portrait, the temporary altar, and the other ritual objects were transported to the cremation site in a grand procession, and the altar with its portrait and was set up once again in front of the entry gate to the cremation grounds.

If a portrait had not been made during the deceased's life, speed in portrait making was essential, because medieval funerals were generally held within a week after death, although much longer preparation periods are documented for emperors and some shoguns. If no previous portrait existed, one had to be ordered quickly. An artist was called to the residence by the deceased's relatives a few days after the death; he either brought sketches with him or received the commission for the portrait at that time. When Retired Shogun Ashikaga Yoshimasa died on 1490.1.7, Kano Masanobu (1434–1530) brought seven or eight sketches (*kamigata*) of the shogun to the house four days later, on 1.11.[61] On 1.17, a multitude of details relating to the funeral were decided, including who would have the honor of carrying the portrait, and who the memorial tablet, in the procession. The portrait was ready for the funeral on 1.23, less than two weeks later.[62] But two weeks was a very long time to wait for cremation in medieval Japan, where preservation of the body was not practiced; it was possible in this case only because Yoshimasa died in winter.[63] The amount of time that elapsed between a death and a funeral depended primarily on the amount of preparation needed, which was related to the deceased's position within the family, their status in society, and, to some degree, the season; funerals were organized more speedily in warmer months to preclude decomposition of the body.

Since the amount of preparation required for a funeral correlated closely with the deceased's status in society, the funeral of a retired shogun obviously required great preparation. Preparations for Yoshimasa's funeral took more than two weeks, mostly to allow time for a new portrait to be made. When the low-ranking courtier Nakahara Morosuke died on 1345.2.6, his funeral was held only three days later, on 2.9, the brevity of the interval to some extent reflecting that family's modest social and economic position in the mid-fourteenth century and perhaps also the general political climate of upheaval in Kyoto.[64] But would three days have been enough time to commission a new portrait? Because the text for the two intervening days is missing, we do not know if the family ordered a portrait during that time, although the text does confirm that other, Buddhist, images for the subsequent seven memorials were commissioned on 2.9, the day of the funeral. It is likely that Pure Land monks performed Morosuke's funeral service;[65] at any rate, there was little to suggest that it was a Zen-style funeral. Whether Buddhist sects other than Zen used portraits at funerals in the fourteenth century is a topic that needs additional study.

Moromoriki also describes the funeral of Morosuke's wife, Kenshin, just six months later, on 1345.8.23. No portrait was requested for her funeral either, and the text is clear that Ji sect monks handled her burial. Seasonal temperatures undoubtedly influenced the family's decision to hold the funeral quickly; Kenshin was buried with all possible haste during the early hours of the night after she died. This entry does seem to suggest that a portrait of Kenshin was available soon after she died, implying that the image must have been made before her death; certainly this was possible, because she had been ill for almost three months before succumbing. If hers had been a Zen-style funeral, the image would have been hung above a special altar at the Jizōdō where Kenshin had been taken the evening of 8.23. But Moromoriki says nothing about an image being used during her funeral or before it, suggesting that the practice of displaying portraits at funerals was likely not a component of this fourteenth-century Ji sect funeral.

The placement of the deceased's portrait during a medieval funeral service is most precisely described in Kennaiki, a diary written by the courtier Madenokōji Tokifusa (1394–1457). Tokifusa's meticulous description of the funeral of the fourth Ashikaga shogun, Yoshimochi (1386–1428) illustrates how faithfully this funeral followed its Chan models. Yoshimochi died on 1428.1.18; his funeral was held five days later on 1.23 at Tōjiin, a Rinzai Zen sect temple and the Ashikaga family mortuary temple in northwest Kyoto.[66] On the day of the funeral the coffin was brought in and placed on the west side of Tōjiin's Buddha Hall (butsuden), just as had been done for Chan abbots in Song-period China.[67] After the ceremony for placing the lid on the coffin (sagan butsuji) was performed, a portrait (miei) of Yoshimochi, painted by Tosa Yukihiro,[68] was hung in front of the coffin (kashin butsuji). This step, too, closely followed the Chinese practice of suspending the portrait of the abbot above the dharma seat in the Dharma Hall. Kennaiki does not describe a temporary altar, but one was typically set up in front of the portrait to hold flower vases, incense burners, candles, and offertory vessels. Offerings of incense from all the participating monks and the close relatives of the deceased were presented, one by one, in front of the portrait. Funeral banners were placed flanking the coffin, and perhaps a folding screen was set up behind it.[69] In China a casket screen was typically placed at the foot of the banners, but the *Chanyuan qinggui* gives no further explanation about this object.[70]

After the Buddhist service a special ritual was performed before moving the coffin out of the Buddha Hall (*kigan butsuji*) in a procession of relatives and attendants carrying brocade banners, cymbals, drums, the memorial tablet, and the portrait of the deceased.[71] Once the procession arrived at the crematory, which was enclosed by a cypress fence located a little over one hundred yards to the west of the Buddha Hall, the portrait, the mortuary tablet, and the three important ritual implements (*mitsu gusoku*)—flower vase, candleholder, and censer—were set up on a temporary altar about three yards in front of the entry. After the last offerings of tea (*tencha butsuji*) and water (*tentō butsuji*) for the deceased, the head priest used a pine torch to light the fire and cremate the corpse (*ako butsuji*).

All of the actions documented in *Kennaiki* closely followed a set of ritual prescriptions developed centuries earlier in China. One small difference is that in China the portrait was carried to the cremation site on its own special litter, whereas in Japan it was hand-carried by a blood relative or close follower of the deceased. That a funeral service for a shogun in fifteenth-century Japan so closely resembled that of an abbot in twelfth-century China speaks to the tremendous importance of maintaining traditional forms and to the belief that rituals were effective only if the proper sequence of actions was strictly followed.

The sequence of the rituals described in *Kennaiki* raises several important points about the function of the portrait and the memorial tablet in the funeral. The deceased's portrait was unrolled and presented only after the lid had been firmly placed on the coffin[72] and the body concealed from view, suggesting that the image took on a special role at this point. What the medieval Japanese made of this juxtaposition of body and image is not discussed in secular diaries, but it is accepted that they viewed the portrait and the memorial tablet as substitutes for the physical body in this sense: they both provided the spirit with a place to reside and also, to some extent, embodied the deceased when alive. Portraits and memorial tablets functioned similarly in both secular and monastic contexts in China as well. In secular funerals, it was only when the corpse had been sealed in the casket that the portrait became "home" to the soul of the deceased. In a monastic context, when the portrait occupied the abbot's meditation seat and received incense offerings at the funeral, it was acting as the abbot himself had during his lifetime.[73]

The memorial tablet was another specifically death-related implement imported from China along with portraits and Chan Buddhism.[74] Generally constructed of wood, memorial tablets were all oblong. The Buddhist name of the deceased (*hōmyō*, dharma name; also *kaimyō*, precept name) and his or her death date were usually written on the front, with the secular name and birth date on the back, although there were many variations of this format depending on the sect of Buddhism to which the deceased belonged. In China, wooden tablets were initially associated with Confucian funerals and ancestor worship as early as the second and third centuries CE, when they were placed on the altar directly in front of the portraits.[75] The practice was adopted for use in Chan patriarch halls late in the Southern Song period (13th c.).[76] In Japan, however, most written references to *ihai* occur much later, dating from the latter decades of the fourteenth century.[77] The description of Ashikaga Yoshimochi's funeral (1428) in *Kennaiki* and the diagram of the third Ashikaga shogun Yoshimitsu's (1408) funeral in *Jishōindono ryōan sōbo* clearly demonstrate that in Japan, too, the tablet was placed in front of the portrait, both in the temple and at the cremation site.

The portrait and the mortuary tablet essentially became surrogates for the deceased and the objects of the family's offerings during the funeral and the memorial ceremonies that followed. The portrait and tablet, therefore, functioned much as the soul cloth had in ancient China and the Chan portrait later on, representing an astonishing continuity in mortuary beliefs in the two countries over a long span of time.[78]

Portraits for Memorial Rituals

Buddhist memorial services, like those for Confucian ancestors in China, were timed to coincide with death anniversaries. A complex system for memorializing the dead through offerings on major and minor anniversaries was well developed in Japan by the fourteenth century. The most important memorials were those held within the first year after death—the seven seventh days (the weekly services for the first seven weeks [49 days] after death, referred to as the *chūin* period), the monthly memorials (*gakki*), and the one-year anniversary (*ikkai ki*). Each memorial typically included trips to the deceased's grave, Buddhist services at the residence or temple, incense offerings made on behalf of the deceased, alms presented to the presiding priests, and small repasts prepared for the participants.

The memorial rituals for deceased abbots or temple patriarchs in China centered on hanging the portrait of the deceased abbot on the lecture platform; in Japan, the portrait was more often suspended in front of a small screen or wall panel in a room or hall at the deceased's family temple. The image received offerings of incense, which were intended to "raise the enlightened spirit to a more exalted status" in the realm of the ancestors; in turn, these offerings would have the effect of elevating the status of the lineage and the temple.[79] Sutra recitations also produced merit, which was believed to benefit both the giver and the recipient, the deceased's spirit. It is clear that portraits of abbots and patriarchs in this context took the place of the person himself in the rite, with the portrait receiving the oblations as the abbot himself would have done. In China, portraits were hung only for the memorial services of abbots-qua-Buddhas, an elite group of "venerables" that was conceived of in Song- and Yuan-period China; ordinary Chinese monks did not merit memorial portraits.[80]

Surprisingly, few medieval Japanese handscrolls illustrate portraits being displayed for the important seven seventh days, whether of secular figures or of Buddhist priests. All of Priest Hōnen's seven seventh days, for example, are illustrated in *Hōnen shōnin e-den*, but no portraits of him can be seen. The omission can not be ascribed to the artist's carelessness, for each memorial is rendered with enough detail to show the appropriate painted Buddhist icons suspended above a small altar table, furnished with the requisite ritual implements.

Nonetheless, though neither the text nor the illustrations in *Hōnen shōnin e-den* confirm that portraits of Hōnen were displayed during his seven seventh days, one image shows his close disciple and successor Ku-amidabutsu performing an offering service at a much later date before a very lifelike portrait (*shin-ei* or "true shadow") of Priest Hōnen (1133–1212) (Figure 5.3).[81] The portrait scroll can be seen displayed against a wall of a small room, with offerings of flowers, incense, and what appears to be rice set on a low lacquered table directly in front of it. Ku-amidabutsu is in the act of performing the service from a raised platform (*raiban*) facing the image. In his right hand he holds a large bronze censer, and a bronze gong rests near his right knee. Other attending priests are seated according to rank on raised mats behind Ku-amidabutsu and to his right. In the painted portrait Hōnen is shown seated on a raised mat (*agedatami*), clothed in deep-brown monk's robes and holding prayer beads in both hands. The image in the handscroll bears a striking resemblance to the famous portrait of Hōnen owned by Nison'in in Kyoto, although the text of *Hōnen shōnin e-den* says that the image shown was installed at Chion'in (Figure 5.4).[82] The Nison'in portrait (commonly referred to as the *ashibiki no miei*) is thought to be the earliest extant image of Hōnen and is dated to the thirteenth century. Although it is difficult to say whether the Nison'in and Chion'in images were the same or one was a copy of the other, some reasonably similar portrait was sufficiently well known in its own time for the artist to reproduce a fairly accurate copy in this handscroll.

Figure 5.3. *Shin-ei* of Priest Hōnen.
Source: *Hōnen shōnin e-den*, in *Zoku Nihon no emaki*, vol. 3, ed. Komatsu Shigemi (Tokyo: Chūō Kōronsha, 1990), after image on p. 109.

Memorial services for elite secular figures held during the *chūin* period (before the forty-ninth day) appear not to have required portraits. There are plentiful mentions in diaries of portraits dedicated or displayed for memorial ceremonies held many months or years after the funeral, but surprisingly few references to their display before the seventh week after death. In *Moromoriki*, for example, Nakahara Morosuke's portrait is first mentioned on 1345.3.25, the forty-ninth day after his death.[83] On that date Kenshin offered a letter requesting sutras be read on her husband's behalf, noting in it that she was also dedicating a portrait scroll (*miei*). That image was perhaps displayed on subsequent monthly anniversaries or, more likely, on Morosuke's one-year death anniversary (1346.2.6), when, we are told, portraits (*eizō*) of the deceased parents (Kenshin died on 1345.8.23) were hung above an altar upon which two sculptures of an Amida *sanzon* and a Nyoirin Kannon were displayed.[84] For Morosuke's third-year memorial (1347.2.5), portraits (*eizō*) of both parents were again hung, accompanied by the same two wooden icons.[85] Regrettably, precise descriptions of how the images were arranged are not present in this text.

Figure 5.4. Portrait of Hōnen (*ashibiki no miei*). Artist unknown. 13th century. Nison'in, Kyoto.
Source: Kajitani Ryōji, *Sōryō no shōzō* [*Nihon no bijutsu* 388] (Tokyo: Shibundō, 1998), after plate 11.

About Kenshin's portrait the data are ambiguous. The only clear reference to a portrait during the forty-nine-day period after her death is an entry made on 1345.8.26, three days after she was buried, stating that Moromori went to the Jizōdō to make offerings to an Amida Triad and to images (*katashiro*) of his father, Morosuke; mother, Kenshin; and deceased sister, Gakumyō.[86] There is no mention of a portrait at Kenshin's funeral or at any of her seven seventh days, also held in the Jizōdō. Nonetheless, the image that Moromori made offerings to on 8.26 was hung in that same hall. It is reasonable to suppose, therefore, that it was available for Kenshin's funeral and for her seven memorial services. But we have no way to confirm that it was part of the rituals, and given what we know of Morosuke's funeral and seven seventh days, it is unlikely.

If the purpose of the portrait was to stand in for the deceased, as it did in China, it would seem that an image would be required immediately after death. That the portrait was not important until on or after the forty-ninth day in the instances discussed above, suggests that a stand-in for the deceased was not mandatory. But why not? The status of the deceased seemed to change dramatically on the forty-ninth day. The absence of a portrait prior to that day implies that there was some uncertainty about the status of the soul throughout the forty-nine days following death—possibly that it was difficult for the soul to inhabit an image until it had successfully passed the judgment of the Ten Kings. Herman Ooms offers a different but related explanation in his analysis of modern Japanese ancestral rites and beliefs. He says that the purpose of the funeral is to free the soul from the body and that, in the seven weeks that follow, it was thought that a "power" was released that could only be brought under control by the service on the forty-ninth day, when the soul finally left for the grave.[87] Thereafter, it was believed, after the final seventh-day memorial the spirit could not return and was no longer a danger to the living. It may be, then, that it was too dangerous to invoke the spirit to return to an image until there were certain assurances in place that it could be controlled; these assurances could apparently be established by the series of Buddhist services that ended on the forty-ninth day.

After the forty-ninth day, Kenshin's and Morosuke's portraits received offerings regularly at two different temples on their respective monthly and yearly death anniversaries. On 1345 (Jōwa 1) 10.23, two months after Kenshin died and just days after her forty-ninth-day memorial, her son Moromori presented offerings to portraits (*eizō*) of his parents and sister Gakumyō at Shōunbōji (Seiunbōji?), located at Shijō Takakura.[88] On 1347.2.5, at Morosuke's third-year death anniversary (actually the second year after death), an Amida and portraits of the parents were dedicated.[89] On the following day (2.6, Morosuke's "proper" anniversary), offerings were made to the same (or a similar) image or set of images at Shōunbōji, and also on 2.23 (Kenshin's monthly anniversary) at Hōjiji's Jizōdō at Shijō Bōmon.[90]

Thus, plentiful written records help us verify that portraits were displayed for the memorial services of the elite (other than Buddhist priests) throughout the Heian period and through the mid-fourteenth century, but they offer little evidence for the use of portraits during the forty-nine-day period. Even for Ashikaga Takauji (1305–1358), the first mention of a portrait dedication dates from about the time of his one-year death memorial on 1359 (Enbun 4) 4.24. On 4.22, just days before this anniversary, a portrait (iei, "posthumous shadow") was dedicated at Kōyasan's An'yōin, where a part of Takauji's remains were interred.[91] Other portraits of Takauji exist, both painted and sculpted, but none can be documented as having been used for services prior to the forty-ninth day after his death.[92] Although Pure Land and other Buddhist sects are said to have adopted the new Zen-style funerals soon after their introduction, there is every indication that they had not made a complete change by the mid-fourteenth century. Even Ashikaga Takauji, whose regime promoted Zen Buddhism during the fourteenth century, was still personally very attached to Pure Land beliefs. Numerous records attest to his devotion to Jizō Bosatsu, a Buddhist avatar of compassion, and state that he consistently relied on dreams of Jizō to guide his actions throughout his life. It is not surprising that, although he generously patronized Zen monks and supported the construction of Zen temples, scholars doubt his personal commitment to Zen practice.[93] It is also not unexpected, then, that his funeral did not strictly follow the traditional Zen format.

Although the information, both documentary and visual, concerning the use of portraits at memorial rituals in the fourteenth century appears to be fairly consistent, the small number of existing examples makes it difficult to draw any firm conclusions beyond the observation that the portrait was usually dedicated on the forty-ninth day. Nonetheless, this suggests that the portrait functioned differently in the fourteenth century than it did in the fifteenth century, when it was displayed in conjunction with the corpse in the temple. In that juxtaposition the portrait served as an immediate proxy for the deceased, suggesting that the soul moved from the corpse to the portrait even before cremation, whereas in the fourteenth century the portrait was apparently viewed as a receptacle to house the spirit's return only after it had been judged and pacified and had moved on to another stage in the afterlife. The emphasis in Zen Buddhism on cremation, with its immediate and complete destruction of the physical body, may have created a sense of immediacy to the provision of a new "home" for the spirit; both the portrait and the memorial tablet fulfilled this need. The two ways of utilizing the portrait in the rituals—hanging it in front of the corpse versus displaying it only after the spirit had been safely brought under control—seem to reflect two systems of thought—Zen and Pure Land respectively. Throughout the tumultuous fourteenth century it is apparent that the older Pure Land and other beliefs associated with death in early Japan continued strongly to impact the choices the elite made in their personal lives and about their deaths.

Accounts in *Inryōken nichiroku* of Ashikaga Yoshimasa's (d. 1490.1.7) seven seventh days offer a glimpse of the new and very different role portraits played in Zen-style ceremonies almost a hundred and fifty years later. Because Yoshimasa's first and second seventh-day death memorials were held on 1490.1.13 and 1.18 respectively, both actually took place before his funeral (1.23). This was exceptional, but no doubt related to the extraordinary length of time—sixteen days—it took to prepare for that important event. No portrait is mentioned in this source for either the first or second memorial (1.13 and 1.18).[94] But it appears that the portrait was already in progress, as the official shogunal painter, Kano Masanobu, had been called to Yoshimasa's villa on 1.11 to submit a number of preparatory sketches.[95] We know that a portrait was ready for his funeral on 1.23, because on that day the "hanging of the portrait" ritual took place.[96] Yet *Inryōken nichiroku* does not mention the image when relating the third (1.25) and fourth seventh-day (date not given) memorials. Finally, for the fifth memorial on 2.5 we are told that incense was offered before his portrait (*shin*), and likewise on the forty-ninth day (2.24), at the final seventh-day memorial.[97] Nonetheless, it is likely that Yoshimasa's portrait was displayed at all seven of his death memorials. The presumptive lack of consistency in the written record may have occurred because the services were held at Tōjiin, and the diary's author, Kisen, was a priest of Rokuon'in, a subtemple of Shōkokuji. Although Kisen attended all of the memorial services, he was not the ritual specialist in charge of the services for Yoshimasa at Tōjiin, and he may not have thought of his diary as an official record. Written records are not always, for whatever reason, precise.

Sometimes the surviving images themselves can reveal when they were made and how they were used. On a portrait of Ashikaga Yoshimitsu (1358–1408) at Rokuonji, an inscription written by his eldest son and successor, Yoshimochi (1386–1428), tells us that the portrait was completed in the latter part of the sixth month of 1408 (Ōei 15; Figure 5.2).[98] As Yoshimitsu's final seventh-day memorial was held on 6.25 (he died on 5.6), it is likely that this portrait was dedicated at his forty-ninth-day ceremony at Tōjiin. Inscriptions and temple records confirm that multiple images were dedicated to Yoshimitsu on many subsequent death anniversaries. A few examples include a portrait sculpture unveiled on his first death anniversary in 1409 (Ōei 16), a painted portrait dedicated at Tōjiin in 1424 (Ōei 31), another at Saihōji in 1476 (Bunmei 17), and a sculpted image offered in 1427 by the sixth shogun, Yoshinori (1394–1441). Because the inscriptions on each image bear the date of its dedication, we can say with certainty that all were dedicated after Yoshimitsu's forty-ninth day.[99] Using inscriptions in tandem with texts produces the maximum information. For example, although none of the inscriptions on these extant portraits of Yoshimitsu declares that it was used for his funeral, a diagram in *Jishōindono ryōan sōbo* verifies that a portrait was displayed. Thus, images and texts work together to provide the fullest possible picture of the ritual use of such images.

Unfortunately, the countless diaries and illustrated handscrolls that record deaths and funerals for Japan's medieval elite offer relatively meager information regarding the portraits used in their mortuary rites, making it decidedly difficult to state precisely how and when those portraits were used. Both written and visual sources corroborate Chinese Chan and Japanese Zen ritual texts that say portraits were to be carried in funeral processions, but only *Kennaiki* offers substantive evidence about where the portraits were positioned while the body awaited burial or cremation. There is no satisfactory source of information about when and where the portrait appeared throughout the seven seventh days, and only irregular data about its use for later memorial ceremonies.

Furthermore, other sources that include information about funerals and mourning services had different agendas and often do not provide the desired answers. For example, the earliest legal code for funerals, *Sōsōryō* (Laws governing funerals and mourning), a chapter of the Ritsuryō legal statutes established in the seventh century, primarily addressed regulations for mourning clothing and the length of time of mourning proper for the deceased of each rank.[100] Imperial manuals of funerary rituals, such as *Kichiji shidai* and *Kichiji ryakki* from the late eleventh century, do not mention portraits at all, although they faithfully record the use of folding screens and supply all kinds of facts about the handling of the body, proportions of the coffin, and details of the funeral. Likewise no mention of portraits can be found in *Sōhōmitsu* (Secret Buddhist precepts for funerals), a record of Shingon funerals from the early medieval period, although it gives a good description of other procedures in use at the time.[101]

Why was the portrait so underreported in both textual and visual sources? Was it precisely because portraits were so essential to funeral and memorial ceremonies and so integral to the ceremonies that they were unquestioningly accepted and understood, hence requiring little special notice by the diarists? For some, this may be true. Indeed, it often seems that status-conscious diary writers devoted far more space to the names of noteworthy individuals who attended the funerals than to the minutiae of their physical surroundings. Illustrated scrolls, on the other hand, were rather good at detailing the surroundings of their narratives, and I can think of no good reason why there are no renditions of a body lying in state other than that the images did not survive. Surely, if the corpse can be shown being placed in the coffin (as in several scrolls), there should be an image somewhere of a body lying in state at the temple. Portraits of laypersons, it seems, were displayed for funerals and during the seven seventh days only during or close to the fifteenth century and later. Portraits were dedicated by descendants at later memorial ceremonies from at least the eleventh century, but they do not seem to have been used in those early centuries during either funerals or the seven seventh days. This is one of the important changes that Zen Buddhism brought to Japanese funeral rituals.

Portraits and Rituals

Although we know that, for many in medieval Japan, the portrait was an integral part of the complex experience of death, how exactly did it function within the context of the rituals surrounding death and the disposal of the body? A basic definition of a ritual is that it comprises a sequence of fixed acts or events that follow a prescribed order. Thus, the place of the portrait within the sequence of events surrounding the death of an individual in medieval Japan bears further scrutiny.

Kennaiki identifies a special Buddhist ceremony for unrolling the portrait scroll and displaying it near the coffin (*kashin butsuji*), which takes place immediately after the ritual action of placing the lid on the coffin (*sagan butsuji*). The sequence of actions is important, because it suggests that the portrait became a focus for the living only after the body was sealed from view. Through the ceremony that accompanied the hanging of the portrait, the image was in some way transformed into a substitute for the no longer visible, encoffined body; in some sense, it embodied the deceased himself. From this point on, the portrait seems to have functioned as a proxy of the deceased, and acts performed by the living were directed toward it, rather than toward the corpse. For example, when offerings of flowers or incense were made during subsequent memorial services, they were placed on the altar before the portrait of the deceased. The only time the portrait was in close proximity to the corpse was when it hung directly in front of it immediately after the encoffining—as if that proximity could encourage or facilitate the proper transference of the spirit to the image. Exactly when it was believed the spirit left the body is an interesting question, one that has no single answer. However, in one early fifteenth-century account, a number of laypeople who attended the cremation of the imperial prince Yoshihito (d. 1416), a son of Emperor Sukō, were overheard to say that when the smoke rose from the cremation fires, they felt his soul (*tamashii*) ascended with it.[102] Undoubtedly, everyone held different views, and opinions must have varied considerably, depending on religious sect, social class, and period.

According to *Kennaiki*, when Yoshimochi's body was moved from the hall to the crematory, the portrait (and the mortuary tablet) both preceded it in the procession. The illustration of Nichiren's funeral procession in *Nichiren shōnin chūgasan* gives us a good picture of the portrait's physical position vis-à-vis the coffin. In the handscroll a priest carries the portrait (rolled up), walking behind a group of mourners with banners, cymbals, drums, and other ritual implements. Next comes yet another group of mourners carrying banners, offerings, and the mortuary tablet, and, following them, the coffin. Thus, the tablet is positioned far closer than the painting to the coffin in the procession. The tablet was made of plain white wood, usually cryptomeria. Some sources say that it was burned with the corpse, but more often it was placed on top of the grave, where it stood as an object into which the spirit could enter, while a second lacquered tablet was retained in the mortuary temple for use in future memorial services.[103]

That the portrait accompanied the coffin to the cremation site and was displayed there again, this time outside the entryway, further supports its new and altered status as another receptacle for the spirit, whose former abode, the body, was about to be destroyed. While the body continued on beyond the gate to the pyre and extinction, the portrait remained outside as the deceased's *locum tenens*. *Kennaiki* is precise about how far in front of the enclosure the portrait was hung—one *jō*, or about three yards. The distance was intended to separate and protect the embodying image from the impurity of the corporeal body and the act of cremation, but the purpose or meaning of that particular distance I do not know. Its placement outside the enclosure also ensured that Yoshimochi could be "seen" (as his earthly body no longer could) by the mourners who, except for the priests and immediate family members, remained outside the enclosure.

The mortuary tablet and important ritual implements were also carried to the cremation site and set up near the portrait on a temporary altar. Offerings of incense and sustenance—tea and hot water—were presented to the deceased. The text does not make it clear whether the offerings were directed to the mortuary tablet or to the portrait or both, but perhaps the distinction was not important.[104] The funeral culminated when a priest touched the pine torch to the cremation pyre. These same ritual actions were typically performed at the Zen-style funerals of the Ashikaga shoguns from the fourteenth century on.[105]

Portraits of the deceased were also displayed on each seventh-day memorial for forty-nine days after death and for subsequent monthly and annual memorial ceremonies marking the day of death. Sometimes the same portrait was used, but new images were generally commissioned for the major memorials. The importance of a memorial was determined in part by whether the spirit was undergoing a crucial change on that date. For example, it was believed that on the forty-ninth day the soul received its final judgment and would be reborn into one of the six realms or "paths" (*rokudō*)—the realm of celestials, the realm of titans or warriors, the human world, the state of animals, the limbo of hungry ghosts, and the various hells.[106] Therefore it was common, on this and other crucial memorial dates, to have additional sutras performed and a new portrait made, or to contribute to the creation of new Buddhist images or temple buildings, in hope of gaining sufficient merit to help the deceased gain a better rebirth.

The sequence of actions at a typical memorial ceremony in medieval Japan is well documented and not very different from today's ritual. In Western cultures, death memorials focus on the act of remembering, but in Japan continued interaction between the living and the deceased is of paramount importance; thus, the Buddhist service revolves around making offerings of food and water, incense, flowers, and sutras, which simultaneously gained merit for both the deceased and the living.

Accurate Depiction and Efficacy

One final aspect to consider is the relationship between accuracy and efficacy in portraits. How important was it for a portrait of the deceased to be an accurate rendition of its corporeal subject? This question forces us to suppress a tendency to judge these images on the basis of our modern perceptions of what constitutes competent mimesis. Furthermore, ours is a judgment unlikely to escape distortion by the access to easy and perfect replications made possible today by cameras and photocopying machines. Nowadays we fail to find the act of exact replication unusual or particularly powerful; in our world, accurate copies are the expected outcomes of modern technology. Thus, when we look at medieval portraits in museums today, we cannot help perceiving a singular lack of individuality. We can see that clothing patterns and styles are different and, upon closer examination, that facial features also differ from one image to another. Nonetheless, to our modern eyes, the figures do not appear convincingly plastic. Although sculpted images are more convincing by virtue of their three-dimensionality, we still feel dissatisfied—the image is not quite life-size, the head is too large, the lack of color is distracting. We cannot, as David Freedberg says, "purify ourselves either of our past or of the insistent present," nor can we bring ourselves to give these images "their full weight as reality and not merely as representation."[107] Therefore, although the earliest known portraits in China were no more than line-drawn stick figures shown in profile, it is important to consider that their third-century BCE viewers must have experienced them as very much alive and real.

The development of portraiture and the importance of verisimilitude in

China are of interest to us for what they tell us about the need to paint accurate portraits in Japan.[108] In China, the earliest generalized depictions from the Neolithic period developed into more individualized linear drawings of figures during the Warring States period, from the beginning of the fifth to the end of the third century BCE. In the Han period (206 BCE–220 CE), artists developed an interest in physiognomy and began to correlate an individual's moral fiber with the bone structure and pigmentation of the face. Nonetheless, extant Han portraits do not begin to approach our own criteria for personalized images. By the Tang period (618–906), however, significant advances had been made in mimetic representation, which seems to have appeared first in memorial portrait sculptures of Buddhist abbots and later in painted portraits. Portraits created at this time were required to reproduce more than just the sitter's appearance; it was equally important to convey "spirit vitality" (*shen qi*), the "life energy" of the sitter.[109] By the late eleventh century, two types of portraits—those accurately rendering appearance and those reflecting the unique character or spirit of the individual—were formalized. Thereafter, formal likenesses were favored for memorial veneration, while the latter type of portraits were prized as secular objects.[110]

Although the development of Japanese portraiture was inextricably tied to these changes in Chinese portraiture, the Japanese never stressed the importance of verisimilitude to the same extent as did the Chinese. Rather, although medieval Japanese seem to have paid lip service to the issue of likeness, perhaps because it was such an intrinsic part of their heritage from China, they did not pursue it in their portraits beyond striving to make them look sufficiently like the deceased to be recognizable by the living. This was a very different approach from that of the Chinese, who emphasized likeness as the only means by which the living could recognize the deceased and perform the proper rituals for them. For Confucian rituals, the faithful representation of the subject was absolutely imperative, to the extent that "if only one hair [in a portrait] is not correctly rendered, the sacrifice will be for another man, which is most inconvenient."[111] Quitman Phillips thoroughly covered the subject of likeness in medieval Japanese portraits, and he too commented upon what appears to be a marked disconnect between finished portraits and textual accounts of individuals ordering countless sketches just to find one that resembled them satisfactorily.[112] Those textual accounts notwithstanding, I did not find much—either in written sources or in the portraits themselves—to suggest that likeness was considered particularly important for Japanese mortuary portraits. We cannot know whether one sketch was really more lifelike than another, nor can we know whether the criterion for choice was something else entirely.

The role of portraiture in the medieval Japanese funeral was at once like that of any other ritual implement and yet different. The use of portraits was always linked to funeral and memorial services, but their production was often initially directed to other occasions, such as birthdays and secular accomplishments—albeit with an eye to their eventual use at the time of death. Tracing their appearance through the diaries and records of the elite reveals that the function of portraits changed radically from the fourteenth through the fifteenth centuries. Initially, they seem to have played little role in the actual funeral and were only of effective use after the seventh seven-day memorial rite, when it was believed that the soul had been safely reborn into its next life. Later, under the influence of Zen (and Chinese traditions), the portrait assumed a central role in the funeral itself and in the seven seventh days, along with the memorial tablet. Portraits also functioned differently from other ritual objects used in Japanese medieval funerary practices because they represented an individual. Even if the verisimilitude of the image does not satisfy our modern criteria, it more than fulfilled the expectations of medieval mourners. Not only did the portrait hold the lost loved one in memory, it also acted as the repository for the soul.

Ultimately, when enough generations had passed so that no one was left who remembered the deceased, the portrait was retired and placed in the storage room of the family temple, and later of the residence. Only portraits of very important individuals, such as major abbots or shoguns, continued to be viewed regularly, because they formed part of a divine lineage and their visages became symbolic rather than specific. Indeed, painted portraits of the most significant early Ashikaga shoguns were once hung in the Buddha Hall of Tōjiin as lineage portraits, following the same sequence as Zen (and Chan) Buddhist lineage portraits, with the temple founder in the center (Musō Soseki), flanked by the first (Takauji), third (Yoshimitsu), and fifth (Yoshinori)[113] Ashikaga shoguns on his left (viewer's right), and by the second (Yoshiakira) and fourth (Yoshimochi) shoguns on his right.[114] Portraits no longer needed for mortuary rituals or as lineage images would eventually become treasured again, but not as memorial objects. Rather, they would be valued for their artistic beauty and, when possible, as part of the historical record. Most modern-day viewers may see them only thus, but we should remember that most medieval portraits were primarily made for and used in rituals intended to help the deceased to make a transition and the living to remember and then to move on.

NOTES

Introduction

1. See, for example, F. Max Müller, *Lectures on the Science of Languages* [1861] (New York: Scribner, Armstrong & Co., 1967); Edward B. Tylor, *Primitive Culture* [1871]; Arnold van Gennep, *The Rites of Passage* [1909], ed. Monika B. Vizedom and Gabrielle Caffee (Chicago: University of Chicago Press, 1960); Emile Durkheim, *The Elementary Forms of the Religious Life: A Study in Religious Sociology* [1912], trans. Joseph Ward Swain (London: Allen & Unwin, 1915); S. H. Hooke, ed., *The Labyrinth: Further Studies in the Relation between Myth and Ritual in the Ancient World* (London: Society for Promoting Christian Knowledge, 1935); S. H. Hooke, ed., *Myth and Ritual* (London: Oxford University Press, 1933); Mircea Eliade, *Cosmos and History: The Myth of the Eternal Return*, trans. Willard R. Trask (New York: Harper & Row, 1949).

2. See S. J. Tambiah, "A Performative Approach to Ritual," *Proceedings of the British Academy* 65 (1979): 113–169; Catherine Bell, *Ritual Theory, Ritual Practice* (New York: Oxford University Press, 1992).

3. Jessica Rawson, "Ancient Chinese Ritual as Seen in the Material Records," in *State and Court Ritual in China*, ed. Joseph P. McDermott (Cambridge: Cambridge University Press, 1999), pp. 20–49; 23.

4. Cornelius Osgood, *Ingalik Material Culture* (New Haven, CT: Yale University Press, 1940), p. 26.

5. See discussion in John Kieschnick, *The Impact of Buddhism on Chinese Material Culture* (Princeton and Oxford: Princeton University Press), pp. 19–23.

6. See Hayami Akira, *Kinsei nōson no rekishi jinkōgaku teki kenkyū* (Tokyo: Tōyō Keizai Shinpōsha, 1973); Wakita Haruko, "Muromachi-ki no keizai hatten," in vol. 7 of *Iwanami kōza Nihon rekishi* (Tokyo: Iwanami Shoten, 1976); Wakita Osamu, *Kinsei hōkensei seiritsu shiron* (Tokyo: Tōkyō Daigaku Shuppankai, 1977); John W. Hall, Keiji Nagahara, and Kozo Yamamura, eds., *Japan before Tokugawa: Political Consolidation and Economic Growth, 1500–1650* (Princeton, NJ: Princeton University Press, 1981).

7. For example, see Susan B. Hanley, *Everyday Things in Premodern Japan: The*

Hidden Legacy of Material Culture (Berkeley, Los Angeles, and London: University of California Press, 1997).

8. *Kokuhō Daigoji ten: Yama kara orita honzon*, comp. Tokyo National Museum, Daigoji, Nihon Keizai Shinbun, Inc. (Tokyo: Benridō, 2001).

9. Anne Nishimura Morse and Samuel Crowell Morse, "Introduction," in *Object as Insight: Japanese Buddhist Art and Ritual* (exh. cat., Katonah Museum of Art, 1996), pp. 8–11; p. 9.

10. Kawada Sadamu with Anne Nishimura Morse, "Japanese Buddhist Decorative Arts: The Formative Period 552–794," in *Object as Insight: Japanese Buddhist Art and Ritual*, pp. 26–31; p. 26.

11. Michael R. Cunningham, with essays by John M. Rosenfield and Mimi Hall Yiengpruksawan, *Buddhist Treasures from Nara* (exh. cat., Cleveland Museum of Art, 1998).

12. Ibid., p. viii.

13. Robert H. Sharf and Elizabeth Horton Sharf, eds., *Living Images: Japanese Buddhist Icons in Context* (Stanford, CA: Stanford University Press, 2001), p. 4.

14. More recently, Sharf called for art-historical research to address the actual function of images. See Sharf and Sharf, *Living Images*, p. 4.

15. *Hakusōrei* (Orders for burials) was formulated as part of the larger Taika Reform Code. That such an edict was thought necessary does not necessarily imply that such behaviors were widespread. The language of the early codes was often borrowed directly from Chinese legal codes. Fragments of the contents are only known today through excerpts in the *Nihon shoki*; J. E. Kidder, *The Lucky Seventh: Early Hōryūji and Its Time* (Tokyo: International Christian University/Hachiro Yuasa Memorial Museum, 1999), p. 57, 62.

16. Many of Kōtoku's remonstrances appear to have been against Han dynasty burial practices, suggesting that they were the norm in Japan before the reform. *Nihongi: Chronicles of Japan from the Earliest Times to A.D. 697*, trans. W. G. Aston (Rutland, VT, and Tokyo: Charles E. Tuttle Company, 1975), pt. 2, pp. 217–218.

17. Interestingly, funerary extravagance does not seem to have been regulated again in Japan until the Edo period, when the Tokugawa shoguns issued proscriptions that funerals be kept "modest." See Andrew Bernstein, *Modern Passings: Death Rites, Politics, and Social Change in Imperial Japan* (Honolulu: University of Hawai'i Press, 2006), pp. 32–33.

18. Shukaku Hosshinō, *Kichiji shidai*, in *Shinkō gunsho ruijū* (*zatsubu* 77), ed. Hanawa Hokinoichi and Kawamata Keiichi (Tokyo: Meicho Fukyūkai, 1977–1978), pp. 684–688.

19. Reproduced in *Shinkō gunsho ruijū* (*zatsubu* 77), pp. 689–695. *Kichiji* means "auspicious," which funerals are not. But, it may have been standard to give such texts an "auspicious" title as a way to write about the taboo subject of death without activating the malignant spirits. Later in the Edo period, *kichiji* also came to mean "malignant" or "calamity" and was used to refer to funerals. *Nihon kokugo daijiten* (*shukusatsuban*) (Tokyo: Shogakkan, 1982), vol. 3, p. 615.

20. *Sōhōmitsu*, in *Nihon kyōiku bunko*, vol. 10 (*Shūkyō*), ed. Mamichi Kurokawa (Kyoto: Dōbunkan, 1911), pp. 683–689.

21. *Daizōkyō* was published in many editions beginning in the eighth century. I consulted the standard edition, *Taishō shinshū daizōkyō*, ed. Takakusu Junjirō and Watanabe Kaigyoku (Tokyo: Taishō Issaikyō Kankōkai, 1924–1934; rpt. 1967), vol. 81, pt. 5, pp. 624–687.

22. A postscript to that text informs us that Shukaku performed funerals and discussed specific points of ritual with the lay priest Kishin, who was the (retired) director of the Ministry of Military Affairs (Hyōbushō). The synopsis (*kaidai*) in *zatsubu* 4 claims that details surrounding the death and funeral of Go-Shirakawa's eldest daughter, Inpumonin (also called Ryōshi), in Kenpō 3 (1215), 4th month, were appended to this document. *Shinkō gunsho ruijū*; *zatsubu* 4, pp. 16–17. This information, however, does not appear in the text I used. Furthermore, according to *Nihonshi daijiten*, this daughter died in 1216 (Kenpō 4.4.2) (Tokyo: Heibonsha, 1992), vol. 1, p. 669.

23. In *Zoku gunsho ruijū* (*hoi 2*) (Gunsho Ruijū Kanseikai, 1930–1985). Most scholars today refer to this text as *Kanmon nikki*, but the title as it appears on the text in *Gunsho ruijū* is *Kanmon gyoki*, so I will use that designation. The name for this text has been the subject of considerable discussion. The editorial organization that produced the *Gunsho ruijū* version preferred *Kanmon gyoki*, because that title appears on the text. But some scholars have suggested that the title *Kanmon gyoki* was not original to the text, but was added by the Archives and Mausolea Department of the Imperial Household (Shoryōbu Kiyō), the document's owner. For more discussion, see Yokoi Kiyoshi, " 'Nikki' to 'gyoki' no aida," *Bungaku* 52, no. 7 (1984): 69.

24. The Hino had supported the Northern court, and when the Southern line rose to power, the family's fortunes declined. This they remedied by marrying one of their daughters to shogun Yoshimitsu (1358–1408; r. 1368–1394), which began a custom of selecting a wife from the family.

25. James H. Foard suggested that the greatest impact of Kamakura Buddhism on the general population occurred in the Muromachi period; "In search of a lost reformation: A reconsideration of Kamakura Buddhism," *Japanese Journal of Religious Studies* (hereafter *JJRS*) 7, no. 4 (1980), pp. 261–291; 283.

26. However, Bodiford's research into *goroku* "recorded sayings" of the Sōtō sect of Zen Buddhism suggests that funerals were popular in rural Japan in the medieval period and were performed predominantly for people of low social status; William M. Bodiford, *Sōtō Zen in Medieval Japan* (Honolulu: University of Hawai'i Press, 1993), pp. 196–199. *Goroku*, however, only document that conducting funerals was one of the duties of the Sōtō monks and do not tell us much about the form of these funerals for commoners.

27. Collections of stories, such as *Konjaku monogatarishū*, said to date from the late Heian period, include mention of funerals. But these were not necessarily commoner funerals, especially because the authors were usually courtiers or priests. Sakakura Atsuyoshi, Honda Giken, and Kawabata Yoshiaki, eds., *Konjaku monogatarishū, honchōzokubu*, 4 vols. (Tokyo: Shinchōsha, 1978–1984), vol. 3, pp. 110–114.

28. Archaeological data from cemetery excavations might be another source that could be utilized to shed light on the burial customs of other classes.

29. See William M. Bodiford, "Zen in the Art of Funerals: Ritual Salvation in Japanese Buddhism," *History of Religion* 32, no. 2 (November 1992): 146–164; 150–151.

30. Even calibrated incense was used to keep time in Chinese Buddhist monasteries. See Silvio A. Bedini, *The Trail of Time: Time Measurement with Incense in East Asia* (Cambridge: Cambridge University Press, 1994), pp. 81–92.

Chapter 1: Death in the Fourteenth Century

1. A. van Gennep. *The Rites of Passage*, trans. M. B. Vizedom and G. I. Caffee (Chicago: University of Chicago Press, 1960), p. 3.

2. There are many Buddhist paradises, each with a different buddha presiding. The "Pure Land" (*jōdo*), also called the Western Paradise, is Amida's paradise. The popularization of Amida worship in the Heian period solidified the prominence of this paradise in Buddhist literature throughout the medieval period.

3. For example, Tendai funerals incorporated two special meditative practices, the *Hokke zanmai* and the *Jōgyō zanmai*, Shingon funerals focused on the *Kōmyō shingon* (a powerful mantra), and Pure Land on the *Nijūgozanmai kō*, a group meditation practice that has its roots in the Tendai *Jōgyō zanmai*; Tamamuro Taijō, *Sōshiki bukkyō* (Tokyo: Daihōrinkaku, 1971), pp. 100–113.

4. For example, the account of Emperor Go-Ichijō's funeral in 1036 included *nenbutsu* performances (associated with Pure Land sects), an Esoteric ritual called *dosha kaji* (consecrated sand sprinkled over the cremation site), and burial of his remains at Jōdoji, a Tendai temple. See *Sakeiki* (*ruijū zatsurei*), entry for Chōgen 9.5.19, in *Zōhō shiryō taisei*, ed. Zōhō Shiryō Taisei Kankōkai (Kyoto: Rinsen Shoten, 1975), pp. 439–441.

5. For further information on the development of Zen funeral rituals in Japan, see William M. Bodiford, "Zen in the Art of Funerals: Ritual Salvation in Japanese Buddhism," *History of Religion* 32, no. 2 (November 1992): 146–164. In Japanese, see Tamamuro, *Sōshiki bukkyō*, pp. 121–130.

6. For more on death rituals in China, see Michael Loewe, "The Imperial Way of Death in Han China," and David L. McMullen, "The Death Rites of Tang Daizong," in Joseph P. McDermott, ed., *State and Court Ritual in China* (Cambridge: Cambridge University Press, 1999); also James L. Watson and Evelyn S. Rawski, eds., *Death Ritual in Late Imperial and Modern China* (Berkeley and Los Angeles: University of California Press, 1988).

7. According to *Chanyuan qinggui* (Rules of purity for the Chan monastery), funerals for ordinary monks and those for abbots differed primarily in their size and in their use of portraits for abbots but not for ordinary monks. See Yifa's translation of this text in *The Origins of Buddhist Monastic Codes in China: An Annotated Translation and Study of the Chanyuan qinggui* (Honolulu: University of Hawai'i Press, 2002), pp. 206–207 and 217–219. For more on the significance of Confucian elements in Chan funerals, see Alan Cole, "Upside Down/Right Side Up: A Revisionist History of Buddhist Funerals in China," *History of Religions* 35, no. 4 (May 1996): 307–338.

8. Tamamuro, *Sōshiki bukkyō*, pp. 121–122; Cole, "Upside Down," p. 329.

9. Confucians did not believe in rebirth, hells, or paradises, but identified the afterlife with family life, wherein cremation was an unfilial act. For further discussion of Confucian beliefs, see Andrew Bernstein, *Modern Passings: Death Rites, Politics, and*

Social Change in Imperial Japan (Honolulu: University of Hawai'i Press, 2006), pp. 43–47. A more complete discussion of Chan ideology concerning death can be found in Bernard Faure, *The Rhetoric of Immediacy: A Cultural Critique of Chan/Zen Buddhism* (Princeton, NJ: Princeton University Press, 1991), pp. 179–208.

10. See Andrew Bernstein's discussion of how Buddhist monks made themselves indispensable in the exchange of offerings that linked ancestors and descendants in the Chinese ghost festival; *Modern Passings*, pp. 22–23.

11. Alan Cole, "Upside Down," p. 314.

12. The nine rituals are discussed in numerous sources. For English, see Faure, *Rhetoric of Immediacy*, p. 193; for Japanese, see Tamamuro, *Sōshiki bukkyō*, p. 123.

13. Bodiford notes that all Japanese schools of Buddhism except Nichiren and Jōdo Shinshū follow ceremonies described in the Zen monastic codes (*shingi*). Bodiford, "Zen in the Art of Funerals," p. 150.

14. For a detailed discussion of the funerals of monks of the Sōtō sect, such as Gikai (d. 1309) and Meihō (d. 1350), see William M. Bodiford, *Sōtō Zen in Medieval Japan* (Honolulu: University of Hawai'i Press, 1993), pp. 191–193.

15. Throughout I have used *Shiryō sanshū: Moromoriki*, 11 vols. (Tokyo: Gunsho Ruijū Kanseikai, 1968; hereafter *Moromoriki*).

16. The Nakahara were an important Kyoto court family of the fourth rank who held the hereditary title of Senior Secretary (*dai geki*). Moromori's father and his older brother both lived on the east side of Kyoto at Rokkaku Ōji, while Moromori himself lived just a few streets north, at Oshi no Kōji. For details about the Nakahara lineage, see Imae Hiromichi, "Hōke Nakahara shi keizu kōshō," *Shoryōbu kiyō*, vol. 27 (1975), pp. 18–38.

17. Because the section from Kōei 3.9.? to Kōei 4.2.7 in *Moromoriki* has been lost, the information about Morosuke's death can only be found in *Entairyaku*, the diary of Tōin Kinkata, son of Fujiwara Saneyasu. The record covers about fifty years of the Nanbokuchō era, from 1311 to 1360. *Entairyaku, Shiryō sanshu kokirokuhen*, 8 vols. (7 vols. published) (Tokyo: Zoku Gunsho Ruijū Kanseikai, 1967–); Jōwa 1 (1345) 2.6, vol. 1, p. 243.

18. *Entairyaku*, Jōwa 1 (1345) 2.6, vol. 1, p. 243.

19. See also Mitsuhashi Tadashi, "Rinshū shukke no seiritsu to sono igi," *Nihon shūkyō bunkashi kenkyū* 1, no. 1 (1997).

20. *Entairyaku*, Jōwa 1 (1345) 2.6, vol. 1, p. 243.

21. *Moromoriki*, vol. 2, p. 269ff.

22. Ryōzen is an abbreviation of Ryōjusen, the Japanese reading of the Sanskrit term for Vulture Peak, the mountain where the Buddha expounded many sutras.

23. Somewhat surprisingly, more Japanese were buried than cremated prior to the 1930s. Andrew Bernstein, "Fire and Earth: The Forging of Modern Cremation in Meiji Japan," *JJRS* 27, nos. 3–4 (Fall 2000): 297–334; 297.

24. The Japanese words in parentheses in Chaps. 1 and 2 are those from the original text of *Moromoriki*.

25. The text says that this was not done for funerals in the Enkyō (1308–1311) and Shōwa (1312–1317) eras (for funerals of earlier generations).

26. *Nihongi: Chronicles of Japan from the Earliest Times to A.D. 697*, trans. W. G. Aston (Rutland, VT, and Tokyo: Charles E. Tuttle Company, 1972), pp. 21, 28.

27. Edward J. Kidder, Jr., *Japan before Buddhism* (New York: Praeger, 1959), p. 191. I am grateful to Moonsil Lee Kim for directing me to this information.

28. There is also a mythological "hearth god" in China, Zao Shen (also Zao Jun). Traditionally, paper effigies of Zao and his wife were hung above the family hearth and offerings of food and incense made to the couple on special days.

29. *Nihonshi daijiten*, ed. Shimonaka Hiroshi, 7 vols. (Tokyo: Heibonsha, 1994), 2:367.

30. Catherine Bell notes that, in Hindu societies, offerings are made to a sacred fire during the marriage ceremony, and traditionally that fire is taken back to the couple's home, where it is kept burning throughout the marriage and then used to light the funeral pyre at death. *Ritual Perspectives and Dimensions* (New York and Oxford: Oxford University Press, 1997), pp. 99–100.

31. *Heihanki*, Kyūju 2 (1155) 9.21 in *Zōho shiryō taisei* (Tokyo: Rinsen Shoten, 1980), vol. 2, p. 11. For other examples, see also the entry for Hōgen 1 (1156) 7.2 in *Zōho shiryō taisei* (1980), vol. 2, p. 111, and *Meigetsuki*, Tenpuku 1 (1233) 9.30 in *Kunchū meigetsuki*, 8 vols., comp. and annot. Inamura Eiichi (Matsue: Imai Shoten, 2002), vol. 6, p. 146.

32. Katsuda Itaru, *Shishatachi no chūsei* (Tokyo: Yoshikawa Kōbunkan, 2003), p. 98.

33. Suitō Makoto, *Chūsei no sōsō, bosei: Sekitō o zōryū suru koto* (Tokyo: Yoshikawa Kōbunkan, 1991), p. 11.

34. In a conversation on June 3, 2007, Gene Phillips suggested that the *kamadogami* might have been used as a surrogate (*nademono*), to take on the impurities of the deceased or the impurities put on the family by the death itself.

35. Tanaka Hisao, *Sosen saishi no kenkyū* (Tokyo: Kōbundō, 1978), p. v.

36. *Kanmon* (also *kan*) refers to a thousand copper coins strung together through a central hole in each.

37. According to at least one scholar, Buddhist sutra chanting and the presentation of offerings replaced the earlier Japanese custom of ritual lamentations and eulogies for the deceased at some time during the ninth century. See Edmund T. Gilday, "Bodies of Evidence: Imperial Funeral Rites and the Meiji Restoration," *JJRS* 27, no. 3–4 (2000): 273–296; 276.

38. For lack of a better word, I have used the term "memorial," which in English generally means a ceremony that honors someone's memory. It should be understood, however, that in Japan memorial services consist of the making of various types of offerings and are intended to affect the posthumous fortunes of the deceased and even to bring benefit to the survivors.

39. The duties of the Bureau of Yin and Yang (*onmyōryō*) were set forth in the Taihō and Yōrō Codes in the early eighth century, modeled after those of its counterpart in Tang China; but yin-yang practices were popular in Japan even earlier. The bureau's job was to advise the emperor and the state on matters of astronomy, the calendar, and time; to interpret climatic phenomena through divination; and, when threatening signs were observed, to deal with them by issuing restrictions and taboos.

By the late Heian period these services were directed to individual courtiers, and later to warriors. For a multivolume series on the topic, see *Onmyōdō sōsho*, 4 vols., ed. Murayama Shūichi et al. (Tokyo: Meicho Shuppan, 1993). For a discussion in English, see David Bialock, "The Yin and Yang of Power," in *Eccentric Spaces, Hidden Histories: Narrative, Ritual, and Royal Authority from The Chronicles of Japan to the Tale of the Heike* (Stanford, CA: Stanford University Press, 2007), pp. 33–64.

40. In India, seven Buddhist services were held for the dead. Three additional services were added in China, and the practice of using images of ten buddhas/bodhisattvas, one for each of the memorial ceremonies, was brought to Japan around the twelfth century. At some point between the twelfth and fourteenth centuries three additional services were created for the seventh-, thirteenth-, and thirty-third-year death memorials. In the sixteenth century, services were also held on the seventeenth- and twenty-fifth-year anniversaries, bringing the total number of services for the dead to fifteen. Tamamuro, *Sōshiki bukkyō*, p. 171.

41. Duncan Williams says the three buddhas were added in the Kamakura period; *The Other Side of Zen: A Social History of Sōtō Zen Buddhism in Tokugawa Japan* (Princeton and Oxford: Princeton University Press, 2005), p. 48. In fact, few Heian- or Kamakura-period images of the Ten Buddhas remain: fourteenth-century and later paintings of the Thirteen Buddhas are more prevalent. See, for example, the painted image of Thirteen Buddhas belonging to Anrakuji (dated to 14th c.).

42. Japanese apocryphal sutras, such as *Jizō jūōkyō* and *Jūō santansho*, are texts for which no Chinese, Sanskrit, or Pali versions exist.

43. For uses in China, see Stephen Teiser, *The Ghost Festival in Medieval China* (Princeton, NJ: Princeton University Press, 1988), pp. 182–184. Quitman E. Phillips notes that sutras on the Ten Kings emphasize the practice of making ritual offerings to oneself in advance of death (*gyakushu*) and suggests that these paintings may have been used for such services; "Narrating the Salvation of the Elite: The Jōfuku Paintings of the Ten Kings," *Ars Orientalis* 33 (2003): 121–145; 127. See also Motoi Makiko, "Jūōkyō to sono kyōju: gyakushu, tsuizen butsuji ni okeru shōdō o chūshin ni," pts. 1, 2, *Kokugo kokubun* 766 (June 1998): 22–33, and (July 1998): 17–35.

44. Assisting the dead through offerings was not motivated solely by filial devotion but also by the desire to protect oneself and one's descendants from retribution by vengeful spirits (*onryō*).

45. Kūichibō was the head priest of Hōkōinji (also called Higuchidera because it was located on Higuchi no Kōji, just south of Gojō); this was the Nakahara family temple (lineage of the eldest son).

46. Hisao Inagaki's *A Dictionary of Japanese Buddhist Terms: Based on References in Japanese Literature* (Kyoto: Nagata Bunshodo, 1988) translates *fuse* (Skt. *dāna*) as a "gift," whether cash or goods, given to a person, especially a priest. The term is frequently translated as "gifts" and "donations." I will use the latter.

47. *Mon* is a term for one of the individual coins of a *kan*.

48. *Danshi* is thick white crinkled paper originally made from the spindle tree (*mayumi*). After the late-Heian period, *danshi* was more often made from mulberry bark (*kōzo*). It is an elegant and costly writing paper favored by poets in Japan.

49. The text does not clarify who received these donations. Presumably they were either divided among the participating priests or given to the priest responsible for the family's temples.

50. See Phillips, "Narrating the Salvation of the Elite," p. 123. Several terms and varying pronunciations are used interchangeably for this site—*myōdo, meido, myōdō, myōkai, meikai, meifu.*

51. Similar methods to obtain salvation developed in medieval Japan and Europe around the twelfth and thirteenth centuries—through mortuary rituals in Japan and through the concept of Purgatory in Europe. Janet Goodwin, "Shooing the Dead to Paradise," *JJRS* 16, no. 1 (1989): 75.

52. This is the order given in *Taishō shinshū daizōkyō*, ed. Takakusu Junjirō and Watanabe Kaigyoku (rpt. 1967), p. 665.

53. This word literally means "day of decline or weakness." According to yin-yang theory, certain dates in the sexagenary cycle, especially the month and year in which a person is born, and certain of that person's ages, are unlucky and require one to be mindful of taboos and avoid certain activities on these days.

54. Sanskrit seed syllables were often used as substitutes for anthropomorphic representations of Buddhist deities.

55. At least since the early twelfth century it had been routine practice to erect such protective talismans. An early example can be found in *Denryaku*, Kōwa 4 (1102) 12.5, in *Dai Nihon kokiroku*, comp. Tōkyō Daikaku Shiryōhensanjo (Tokyo: Iwanami Shoten, 1960–1984), vol. 12, pt. 1, p. 173.

56. See Katsuura Noriko, "Tonsure Forms for Nuns: Classification of Nuns according to Hairstyle," in *Engendering Faith: Women and Buddhism in Premodern Japan*, Barbara Ruch, general ed., Michigan Monograph Series in Japanese Studies No. 43 (Ann Arbor, MI: Center for Japanese Studies, 2002), p. 117.

57. *Hirobuta* usually refers to the lid of a box in which kimonos are stored.

58. Katsuura Noriko has elaborated on the different social and religious implications of each (*Engendering Faith*, pp. 109–129).

59. The *tsune no godei* was an area of a covered connecting corridor. The *nanmen idei* specified in the text was a space for meeting guests under the southern eaves (*minami no hisashi*) of the eastern annex (*higashi no tai*) in a Shinden-style residence. See Koizumi Kazuko et al., eds., *Emakimono no kenchiku o yomu* (Tokyo: Tōkyō Daigaku Shuppan, 1996), p. 20.

60. This temple was located in Kyoto, but nothing is known about it.

61. We are given no biographical information about this priest, but he must have been well known to the Nakahara because he served as one of the *komorisō*.

62. Seclusion upon the death of an important male has ancient roots in Japan, and examples of the practice appear throughout the *Nihon shoki*. Generally, however, women were secluded. Ebersole suggests that ritual seclusion in the seventh century probably meant that the individuals did not appear in public (anywhere outside the residence). See discussion in Gary L. Ebersole, *Ritual Poetry and the Politics of Death in Early Japan* (Princeton, NJ: Princeton University Press, 1989), pp. 165–167.

63. *Tendoku* may simply mean they read the sutra, but it generally refers to the prac-

tice of chanting a few lines or the opening sentences of long sutra chapters (and omitting the rest). Reading part of the text is considered to be as effective as reading all of it.

64. Corridors or rooms (*hisashi*), one in each of the four directions, surround the inner portion (*moya*) of a Shinden-style building.

65. *Nihon kokogo daijiten* offers two possible identifications: *Sōkyoku* may refer to a section of an office where business was conducted or to a narrow room for women within the imperial palace.

66. A notation in the text says this garment was dyed in the *fushikane* technique, as were the other black robes mentioned in this section. The dye was made from young leaves of the lacquer tree; the same substance was a popular component for blackening teeth in ancient Japan.

67. *Sofuku* are plain white clothes, i.e., mourning clothes.

68. It is likely that Moroshige and Moromori faced northwest during this ritual because the family's clan deity at Hirano Shrine was located in that direction; this was the reason given for why Kenshin faced the northwest in the description of her tonsure.

69. Elizabeth Kenney discusses the practice of "standing up the chopsticks" as a component of the food offerings made to the deceased at the grave in Shinto-style funerals. "Shinto Funerals in the Edo Period," *JJRS* 27, nos. 3–4 (Fall 2000): 239–271; 255.

70. Nuns, like priests, wore monastic garments when attending the dead at funerals. Presumably they, unlike laypeople, did not require the added protection from pollution offered by white robes.

71. *Moromoriki*, vol. 2, pp. 184–185.

72. Ibid., vol. 3, p. 7.

73. Originally *sekitō* (also *seki sotoba*) were pagodas constructed for Buddhist relics. Early ones were made of wood, with stone becoming popular some time prior to the eighth century. In the Kamakura period they began to be used to mark graves. These vertical structures may have three, five, seven, nine, or thirteen layered sections, but the most common number in Japan is three. For more on the history of *sekitō*, see Haga Noburu, *Kaitei zōhō: Sōgi no rekishi* (Tokyo: Yūzankaku, 1970), pp. 86–104.

74. Itō Yuishin has suggested that Kūichibō must have had connections to stonemasons in order to procure the grave marker; "*Moromoriki* ni miru chūsei sōsai bukkyō," in *Sōsō bosei kenkyū shūsei: Haka no rekishi*, vol. 5, ed. Uwai Hisayoshi (Tokyo: Meicho Shuppan, 1989), pp. 215–237; p. 219.

75. The *gorintō* is composed of five stacked shapes. The base form is a cube, topped by a sphere, pyramid, hemisphere, with a conventional "jewel" (*dan*) shape on top; these represent the five elements—earth, water, fire, wind, and space—that make up the phenomenal world. The concept of the *gorintō* originated in Esoteric thought, but quickly spread to other sects; Haga, *Sōgi no rekishi*, p. 89.

76. The *hōkyōintō* was designed as the sacred receptacle for written copies of the *Hōkyōin darani*. A *hōkyōin* stupa was said to have been brought to Japan from China in the mid-tenth century; see Sasaki Rizō, "Hōkyōintō," in *Heian jidaishi jiten*, ed. Tsunoda Bun'ei, 3 vols. (Tokyo: Kadakawa Shoten, 1994), vol. 2, pp. 2281–2282. This

type of pagoda was first used on grave mounds in the Kamakura period; Haga, *Sōgi no rekishi*, p. 94.

77. Names of buddhas (*myōgō*), the Lotus Sutra (*Hoke kyō*) and the *Jōdo sanbukyō* (the three canons of Pure Land Buddhism: *Muryōju kyō, Kanmuryōju kyō, and Amida kyō*) were copied onto these tablets.

78. This theory has also been suggested by Itō Yuishin, "*Moromoriki* ni miru chūsei sōsai bukkyō," p. 219.

79. The three canons of Pure Land Buddhism—*Muryōju kyō, Kanmuryōju kyō, and Amida kyō*.

80. Nakahara Yūa would become the fourth head of the Nakahara house after Moroshige. He practiced the Jōdo religion and served as Morosuke's guide (*zenchishiki*) on his deathbed. Itō, "*Moromoriki* ni miru chūsei sōsai bukkyō," p. 220.

81. *Tatebumi* are letters comprised of a strip of paper bearing the message and an outer envelope made of white paper, folded lengthwise and twisted or folded at both ends.

82. *Chōmoku* (bird's eye) is another descriptive term for the Chinese-style coins with central holes used in the Muromachi period. In this text it is used interchangeably with *kan* and *kanmon*. One *kan* equals 1,000 *mon*, or copper coins with holes that were kept on a string; one *hiki* refers to ten coins.

83. See, for example, a thirteenth-century mandala owned by Matsuodera and reproduced in the special exhibition catalog *Ōchō no butsuga to girei: Zen o tsukushi, bi o tsukusu* (Kyoto: Kyoto Kokuritsu Hakubutsukan, 1998), fig. 102.

84. The full title is the *Nyorai juryō-bon*. It is chapter 16 of the *Hoke-kyō* and explains that the Buddha is eternal.

85. The meaning here (*itajiki ni tagane o kakeru*) is unclear, but perhaps the wooden floors that were polluted by the death were planed or replaced so the family could use the rooms safely. In the Heian period the wooden floor planks were removed in the rooms used for mourning. See examples in William H. McCullough and Helen Craig McCullough, trans., *A Tale of Flowering Fortunes: Annals of Japanese Aristocratic Life in the Heian Period* (Stanford, CA: Stanford University Press, 1980), vol. 1, p. 154, vol. 2, pp. 457, 660, 750.

86. No exact dates for these actions were given.

87. This probably refers to a piece of paper folded in half.

88. Ungoji, located in Higashiyama, Kyoto, is also called Kumoidera.

89. The concept of *hinin* changed over time; see Amino Yoshihiko, *Chūsei no hinin to yūjo* (Tokyo: Akashi Shoten, 1994), pp. 25–63. In *Moromoriki* the term probably refers to beggars, pariahs, and social outcasts. Because the *hinin* dealt with corpses, their positions were outside of normal society.

90. Katsuda Itaru, *Shishatachi no chūsei*, pp. 220–222.

91. *Nyūdō* is a term usually used for lay priests.

92. Keibutsu was a nun of the Rokujō sect and the younger sister of the deceased, Morosuke.

93. This is an image of Amida and his two bodhisattvas, Kannon and Seishi. It is unclear from the text if this was a painted or sculpted triad, but most likely it was a

painted scroll, as sculpted images were much more expensive and likely beyond the means of a low-ranking court family.

94. Probably the phrase *namu Amida butsu* was repeated.

95. *Moromoriki*, vol. 3, p. 50.

96. Probably refers to cloth woven from arrowroot vines.

97. See also Williams' discussion of this topic in *The Other Side of Zen*, pp. 45–47.

98. *Moromoriki*, vol. 3, pp. 99ff.

99. Ibid., pp. 274ff.

100. The idea of adorning the temple emulates the adornment of the Pure Land with beautiful objects that embody meritorious acts.

101. The terms—*minami no sokusho* (or *nansokusho*) and *kita no sokusho* (*hokusokusho*)—suggest an area of the Jibutsudō for relaxation, perhaps a waiting area outside the main altar room. It is unclear whether the text refers to two rooms or to the south and north sides of a single room.

102. The *Zuigu darani* appears in the *Zuigu kyō*, an abbreviation of *Fuhenkōmyō shō jōshijō nyoihōin shinmunō daimyōō daizuigu darani kyō*, and is the "wish-fulfilling spell" of the Zuigu Bodhisattva.

103. *Moromoriki*, vol. 4, pp. 25ff.

104. The text mentions that Ryōchi had made the image(s) two years earlier for the first memorial, but he died in the previous year. Sōen was from the same studio. The text is not clear as to whether Sōen made a single painting or three separate ones. Tazawa Hiroshi interprets it as a single image. Tazawa Hiroshi, *Josei no shōzō* (*Nihon no bijutsu* 384) (Tokyo: Shibundō, 1998), p. 22.

105. Ryōshinbō performed the duties previously carried out by Kūichibō, suggesting that Kūichibō was ill or had died.

106. A priest of Gidarinji in Gion began chanting from 4 to 6 a.m., followed by other priests, each of whom chanted for two hours, ending at 2 a.m.

107. *Moromoriki*, vol. 3, pp. 166ff.

108. See note 92.

109. *Chishiki* served as religious guides for the dying, guiding their final repentances and chanting the Nenbutsu on their behalf. For further discussion of the role of the *chishiki*, see Jacqueline I. Stone, "By the Power of One's Last Nenbutsu: Deathbed Practices in Early Medieval Japan," in *Approaching the Land of Bliss: Religious Praxis in the Cult of Amitābha*, ed. Richard K. Payne and Kenneth K. Tanaka, Kuroda Institute Studies in East Asian Buddhism 17 (Honolulu: University of Hawai'i Press, 2004), pp. 77–119.

110. Little is said about this ritual, but it may be a modification of the Chan/Zen practice of auctioning the deceased master's personal belongings after his death.

111. In this and other medieval texts, the phrase *mitsu mitsu [ni] nusumidasu* is used to indicate that it was done secretly.

112. Itō Yuishin, "*Moromoriki* ni miru chūsei sōsai bukkyō," p. 221. In this section, Itō cites Akamatsu Toshihide, *Kamakura bukkyō no kenkyū*.

113. See discussion by Mimi Yiengpruksawan, "The House of Gold: Fujiwara Kiyohira's Konjikidō," *Monumenta Nipponica* 48, no. 1 (Spring 1993): 33–52; 44–45.

114. He did not enter the gate because the residence was infected with death pollution.

115. Shogun Ashikaga Takauji and his brother Tadayoshi paid their respects to the deceased emperor at Tenryūji both on his actual death anniversary on 8.16 and at the larger celebration on 8.29; *Moromoriki*, vol. 3, pp. 164, 169. Tenryūji was the temple that Takauji had dedicated upon Go-Daigo's death in 1339 for the express purpose of placating the deceased emperor's spirit.

116. In the Heian period, 10 *mon* of a *chōmoku* equaled 1 *hiki*; later 25 *mon* was equal to one *hiki*.

117. Morosuke's stone was erected eight months earlier, on 1345.3.6.

118. The intervening time (between 11.16 and 11.28) was a busy one for the Nakahara family. Moroshige's second son celebrated his second birthday on 11.19, and a funeral was held for a son of a branch family on 11.20.

119. Itō cites *Shintōshū*, which states that the offering ceremony for the grave tablet (*sotoba kuyō*) should take place on the thirty-fifth day; "*Moromoriki* ni miru chūsei sōsai bukkyō," p. 220. *Shintōshū* is a collection of fifty short narrative tales (*setsuwa*), nine of which have Buddhist or non-Shinto subjects. It was probably written between 1350 and 1360. Under each story title is the name Agui, but little is known about the author, although some suspect he was a Tendai monk. *Nihonshi daijiten*, vol. 3, p. 1466.

120. Eight people made offerings for Morosuke's ceremony and five for Kenshin's.

121. For scholarship on the market forces of funeral rites in the Tokugawa period, see Williams, *The Other Side of Zen*.

122. The exceptions are the fifth and seventh seventh-day memorials, when the *Myōhō renge kyō* was copied onto the tablets.

123. *Moromoriki*, vol. 3, p. 198.

124. This sutra refers to and is often an abbreviation of the *Lotus Sutra*. Inagaki, *Dictionary of Japanese Buddhist Terms*, p. 219.

125. This refers to the *Muryōju kyō*, an introduction to the *Lotus Sutra* (*Hoke kyō*) and to the *Fugenkan gyō*, which tells how to meditate on Fugen Bosatsu by showing the practical conclusion of the *Lotus Sutra*. Inagaki, *Dictionary of Japanese Buddhist Terms*, p. 163.

126. This refers to a short sutra presenting the general idea of the transcendental wisdom of the void (*hannya*). Inagaki, *Dictionary of Japanese Buddhist Terms*, p. 92.

127. The *Amida kyō* is a basic canon of Pure Land Buddhism, promising that one who recites the sutra will be reborn into the Pure Land. Ibid., p. 6.

128. Several phrases of text are missing in this section. *Moromoriki*, vol. 3, p. 211.

129. In his discussion of funerals for women in the Sōtō Zen sect, William Bodiford notes that gender-specific sutras, notably the *Ketsubon kyō* (Blood Pool Hell Sutra), were often placed in a woman's coffin as protection from that particular hell. This sutra, however, is not mentioned during Kenshin's funeral or memorial services. Bodiford, *Sōtō Zen and Medieval Japan*, p. 206.

130. Some years later, in 1383, Kokua, a Ji sect priest, built an Amida Hall called Shōhōji at Ryōzen, founding what became known as the Ryōzen Ji sect. Itō Yuishin, "*Moromoriki* ni miru chūsei sōsai bukkyō," p. 221.

131. I have not found any information about Higuchidera (also called Hōkōinji) other than that given in the text—that it served as the Nakahara family temple in Kyoto. Its name suggests that it was located on Higuchi no Kōji, a narrow street just south of and parallel to Gojō. It was probably a Tendai temple.

132. Hashimoto Hatsuko, "Chūsei no kuge shakai to onmyōdō ni tsuite: Moromoriki ni miru," in Onmyōdō sōsho: Chūsei, vol. 2, comp. Murayama Shūichi et. al. (Tokyo: Meicho Shuppan, 1993), pp. 67–81; pp. 67–68.

133. The text is really not specific about whether Morosuke was buried or cremated, but it has been generally assumed that he, like Kenshin, was buried. At any rate, their graves were at the same cemetery.

134. This term primarily refers to the thirteenth-year and later memorials (17th year, 25th year, 50th year, and 100th year).

135. Itō Yuishin, pp. 233–234.

136. The lavish funeral held for priest Gikai in 1309 is discussed in Gikai sōki, Meihō Sotetsu Zenji sōki records the funeral for priest Meihō in 1350, and Tsūgen Jakurei sōki documents priest Tsūgen's funeral in 1391; all were Sōtō Zen priests. For details and citations see Bodiford, Sōtō Zen in Medieval Japan, p. 192. Martin Collcutt outlines the Rinzai Zen funeral for an early lay individual, regent Hōjō Tokimune, in 1284; Five Mountains: The Rinzai Zen Monastic Institution in Medieval Japan, Harvard East Asian Series 85 (Cambridge, MA, and London: Council on East Asian Studies, Harvard University, 1981), p. 70.

137. Gukanki, written by the courtier Konoe Michitsugu, in Dai Nihon shiryō, vol. 6, pt. 21, p. 809.

138. According to Gukanki, Takauji's seven seventh days were held on 5.6 (first), 5.13 (second), 5.20 (third), 5.27 (fourth), 6.5 (fifth), 6.12 (sixth), and 6.17 (seventh). In Dai Nihon shiryō, vol. 6, pt. 21, pp. 809–810.

139. Ibid., pp. 864ff.

140. Ibid., p. 812.

141. For example, Ashikaga Tadayoshi (1306–1352) purportedly thought the text had many errors and ordered it to be revised, but he died before it was finished, so his death is recorded in Taiheiki by subsequent authors.

Chapter 2: Funerals in the Fifteenth Century

1. Yoshihito posthumously became the grandfather of Emperor Go-Hanazono.

2. Kanmon gyoki covers the years Ōei 23 (1416) 1.1 to Bunnan 5 (1448) 4.7. I used Kanmon gyoki (pt. 1) in Zoku gunsho ruijū: hoi 2 [supp. 2] (Tokyo: Gunsho Ruijū Kanseikai, 1930–1985), pp. 48–60. Bodiford also summarizes Yoshihito's funeral, but his interpretation differs from mine in a number of details; see William M. Bodiford, "Zen in the Art of Funerals: Ritual Salvation in Japanese Buddhism," History of Religion 32, no. 2 (November 1992): pp. 153–154, and Sōtō Zen in Medieval Japan (Honolulu: University of Hawai'i Press, 1993), pp. 193–194.

3. Bodiford, Sōtō Zen in Medieval Japan, p. 193.

4. *Kanmon gyoki*, Ōei 23 (1416) 11.20, pp. 48–50.

5. *Bikuni* are fully ordained Buddhist nuns. It is interesting that nuns attended the prince's death because in general nuns attended females.

6. Yoshihito was in his sixty-sixth year when he died. *Kanmon gyoki*, Ōei 23 (1416) 11.23, p. 51. He passed away in a small and humble temporary replacement for the grander Fushimi Palace that had been destroyed by fire in the seventh month of 1401; Ichino Chizuko, "Fushimi Gosho shūhen no seikatsu bunka: *Kanmon nikki* ni miru," *Shoryōbu kiyō* 33 (1981): 20–39; 20.

7. Daikōmyōji was completely destroyed during the Ōnin War (1467–1477). It was rebuilt, but when Fushimi Castle was constructed, it was moved to the grounds of Shōkokuji. The site of Emperor Sukō's imperial mausoleum was unknown for hundreds of years, but was rediscovered in 1864 along with the grave of Yoshihito's heir, Prince Haruhito. Takemura Toshinori, *Shinsen Kyōto meisho zue*, 7 vols. (Kyoto: Shirakawa Shoin, 1963), vol. 5, pp. 73–74.

8. *Dabi* is Japanese for *dhyāpayati*, the Sanskrit term for cremation; Andrew Bernstein, "Fire and Earth: The Forging of Modern Cremation in Meiji Japan," *JJRS* 27, nos. 3–4 (Fall 2000): 300.

9. *Kaji* require a trained master to concentrate and extend the Buddha's universal energy to heal a receptive subject. Pamela D. Winfield, "Curing with Kaji: Healing and Esoteric Empowerment in Japan," *JJRS* 31, no. 1 (2005): 107–130; 108.

10. Hisao Inagaki (in collaboration with P. G. O'Neill), *A Dictionary of Japanese Buddhist Terms: Based on References in Japanese Literature* (Kyoto: Nagata Bunshodo, 1988), p. 164.

11. The ancient Japanese world was peopled with spirits. Some were thought to be aspects or functions of *kami*—*aramitama* (violent spirits), *nigimitama* (peaceful spirits), *sakimitama* (benevolent spirits), *kushimitama* (awe-inspiring spirits); others were "roaming spirits" associated with deceased, unappeased ancestors. For ordinary people, Buddhist images and texts provided one means to worship and manage the spirits. See Kuroda Toshio, "The World of Spirit Pacification: Issues of State and Religion," *JJRS* 23, nos. 3–4 (1996): 321–351; 326.

12. Commoners, however, continued to practice this less formal custom of disposing of bodies well into the medieval period. Katsuda Itaru, *Shishatachi no chūsei* (Tokyo: Yoshikawa Kōbunkan, 2003), pp. 45–47.

13. The *chinkon-sai* (*tamashizume no matsuri*), for example, included rituals performed to invigorate the spirit of the emperor and keep it from departing his divine body.

14. Ebersole, however, defines *tamafuri* as a rite to recall the spirit to the body; he does not discuss *tamayobi*; Ebersole, *Ritual Poetry and the Politics of Death in Early Japan* (Princeton, NJ: Princeton University Press, 1989), p. 42. The ritual of "calling back the soul" was first practiced in China; it appears in sections of the *Yi li* (Ceremonies and rites) and the *Li ji* (Book of rites). David L. McMullen, "The Death Rites of Tang Daizong," in Joseph P. McDermott, ed., *State and Court Ritual in China* (Cambridge: Cambridge University Press, 1999), p. 169.

15. The robe then was laid over the corpse and became its shroud. This action also followed Chinese practice; see McMullen, "Death Rites of Tang Daizong," p. 169.

McCullough hypothesized that the ritual might have been used for the first time in Japan at the death of Fujiwara Kishi in 1025. He also traces the history of this ritual back to the *Li ji* (Book of rites) in China and to the eighth-century Tang ritual codes (*Da Tang kaiyuan li*); William H. McCullough and Helen Craig McCullough, *A Tale of Flowering Fortunes: Annals of Japanese Aristocratic Life in the Heian Period*, 2 vols. (Stanford, CA: Stanford University Press, 1980), pp. 784–785.

16. The early Japanese performed a variety of *tamafuri*-type rituals designed to call back the spirit of the deceased; Ebersole, *Ritual Poetry*, pp. 83–85.

17. The inability of the living to comprehend that a person is no longer among them is particularly poignant in the story of Kishi's death; see McCullough and McCullough, *Flowering Fortunes*, pp. 678–679.

18. Ibid., p. 785. An example may be the *sosei* ("revival") ritual that was performed by a priest for Fujiwara Yoshimichi in *Gyokuyō* on 1188.2.19; in Suitō Makoto, *Chūsei no sōsō, bosei: Sekitō o zōryū suru koto* (Tokyo: Yoshikawa Kōbunkan, 1991), p. 1.

19. This was commonly called the *Fushiminomiya rakugai gosho*, or the "Fushimi Palace outside the capital" to distinguish it from the Fushimi Palace located in Kyoto at Ichijō and Higashi Tōin.

20. For a diagram of the rooms of the Fushimi Palace between 1409 and 1435, see Ichino Chizuko, "Fushimi Gosho shūhen no seikatsu bunka: *Kanmon nikki* ni miru," *Shoryōbu kiyō* 33 (1981): 21.

21. *Kichiji shidai*, p. 686. In some texts the shroud is called a *nogusagoromo*.

22. Washing the body and redressing it were actions dictated in pre-Buddhist Chinese texts, the *Yi li* and the *Li ji*. The early ritual codes also recommend cutting the deceased's nails, but make no mention of cutting the hair; McMullen, "Death Rites of Tang Daizong," p. 173.

23. Bodiford suggests this is the case (*Sōtō Zen in Medieval Japan*, p. 193).

24. *Shikimi* leaves were used as offerings in Buddhist rituals and, because they were aromatic, were often placed in coffins, buried with the corpse, and placed on graves. See Patricia Fister, "From Sacred Leaves to Sacred Images: The Buddhist Nun Gen'yō's Practice of Making and Distributing Miniature Kannons," in *International Symposium: Figures and Places of the Sacred* (Kyoto: International Research Center for Japanese Studies, 2003), pp. 75–98; 78–80.

25. The records are seldom precise about which body parts were washed, probably because the purpose was ritual purification rather than cleanliness.

26. Kishi (1007–1025) was the youngest daughter of Fujiwara no Michinaga. *Eiga monogatari zenchūshaku*, ed. Matsumura Hiroji, in *Nihon koten hyōshaku zenshūshaku sōsho*, 9 vols. (Tokyo: Kadokawa Shoten, 1969–1982), vol. 5, pp. 213–214; also McCullough and McCullough, *Flowering Fortunes*, p. 678. *Kichiji ryakugi* also prescribes reversing the screens for the deceased (p. 689). *Kichiji shidai* cautions, however, that if there is already a standing screen (*tsuitate*) in place when the person dies, folding screens should not be used (*Kichiji shidai*, p. 684).

27. *Kanmon gyoki*, Ōei 23 (1416) 11.21, p. 50.

28. Hisao, *Dictionary of Japanese Buddhist Terms*, p. 227. Alternatively, Bernard Faure describes *nenju* as lectures on *darani*, usually the *Senju sengen daihishin darani kyō*

and the *Ryōgonju*; Bernard Faure, *The Rhetoric of Immediacy: A Cultural Critique of Chan/Zen Buddhism* (Princeton, NJ: Princeton University Press, 1991), p. 193, n. 37.

29. *Kichiji shidai*, p. 685; also *Kichiji ryakugi*, p. 689. In summer months, vinegar was placed in bowls and set near the deceased to cover the odor of death.

30. *Kanmon gyoki*, Ōei 23 (1416) 11.22, pp. 50–51.

31. *Kanmon gyoki*, Ōei 23 (1416) 11.23, p. 51.

32. *Kanmon gyoki* does not tell us how the body was prepared. Most likely it was washed and dressed in new robes.

33. *Koshi* were hand-carried palanquins or litters, while *kuruma* were carts with wheels, drawn usually by oxen but sometimes by horses. The Yōrō Code (early 8th c.) stipulated that, for all but the very elite, the wheels and axles were to be detached from the carriages when transporting the dead, and they were to be carried like litters. Illustrations in handscrolls confirm that palanquins were generally used to transport the elite in the fourteenth and fifteenth centuries.

34. Katsuda lists eight distinct conditions that differentiate *heizei no gi* from regular funerals. See Katsuda, *Shishatachi no chūsei*, pp. 102–103.

35. In *Gyokuyō*, 1188.2.22; Suitō, in *Chūsei no sōsō, bosei*, pp. 2–3.

36. Some Heian-period funerals loosely followed Confucian treatment of the dead as if "still living" (*heizei no gi* or *nyozai nogi*). One component of this type of ceremony was the use of a regular carriage rather than one outfitted for transporting a corpse; Katsuda, *Shishatachi no chūsei*, pp. 102–103.

37. Bodiford, *Sōtō Zen in Medieval Japan*, p. 193.

38. *Eiga monogatari zenchūshaku*, vol. 5, pp. 213–214; McCullough and McCullough, *Flowering Fortunes*, p. 679.

39. *Kanmon gyoki*, Ōei 23 (1416) 11.24, pp. 51–52.

40. My translation differs from Bodiford's in a number of details throughout this section. See Bodiford, *Sōtō Zen in Medieval Japan*, p. 194.

41. This refers to the *Muryōju nyorai konpon darani*, which, according to Hisao, "reveals Amida's inner realization, vows, and merit." Hisao, *Dictionary of Japanese Buddhist Terms*, p. 6.

42. W. G. Aston, *Nihongi* (Rutland, VT, and Tokyo: Charles E. Tuttle Co., 1972), pt. 2, p. 423. See also discussions in Haga Noboru, *Sōgi no rekishi* (Tokyo: Yūzankaku, 1970), pp. 28–42, and Edmund T. Gilday, "Bodies of Evidence: Imperial Funeral Rites and the Meiji Restoration," *JJRS* 27, nos. 3–4 (2000): 273–296; 275–277.

43. Cremated remains date from all stages of the Jōmon period, but primarily from the early, late, and final periods. See Junko Habu, *Ancient Jomon of Japan* (Cambridge: Cambridge University Press, 2004), pp. 159, 173, 174.

44. See Andrew Bernstein's discussion of cremation in "Fire and Earth: The Forging of Modern Cremation in Meiji Japan," *JJRS* 27, nos. 3–4 (2000): 297–334; 300–303; also Andrew Bernstein, *Modern Passings: Death Rites, Politics, and Social Change in Imperial Japan* (Honolulu: University of Hawai'i Press, 2006), p. 29.

45. *Kanmon gyoki*, Ōei 23 (1416) 11.26, p. 53.

46. See entries for *Kanmon gyoki*, Ōei 23 (1416) 12.2 (p. 54), 12.7 (pp. 54–55), 12.12 (p. 55), 12.17 (pp. 56–57), 12.21 (p. 57), and 12.25 (pp. 58–59), respectively.

47. Bodiford, *Sōtō Zen in Medieval Japan*, points out that these rites were all performed by monks connected to the family's local temple (p. 194).

48. According to *Kanmon gyoki*, the service was held in the *dōjō*, a general term for a place where the Buddha is worshipped. It is likely that this and the preceding memorials were held in the Jibutsudō of the Fushimi Daily Life Palace where Yoshihito had lived.

49. A *nurigome* is a small, enclosed space used for sleeping or storage in Shinden-style residences. In the medieval period *nurigome* became part of temple architecture, most commonly used for storage in priests' living quarters. In the priest's living quarters at Shōren'in (14th c.), for example, the *nurigome* was adjacent to the Buddhist altar room. A similar arrangement is described in *Kanmon gyoki*, Ōei 23 (1416) 12.24, p. 58. Mitsuo Inoue, *Space in Japanese Architecture*, trans. Hiroshi Watanabe (New York, Tokyo: Weatherhill, 1985), pp. 112–113.

50. *Nenkō* (to take a pinch of incense) means essentially the same as *shōkō* (to burn incense). But the former usually refers to powdered incense and the latter to sticks of incense.

51. *Kennaiki* lists both reign dates, but other sources list only one or the other. Yoshimochi technically died in Ōei 35 because the Shōchō era did not start until 4.27. Tōjiin, located in Kyoto's Kita-ku, is often conflated with another temple, Tōjiji, which was moved by Takauji's brother Tadayoshi from northern Kyoto to the central part of the city near Sanjō Bōmon. In order to differentiate between the two, in the Muromachi period Tōjiin was also called Kita Tōji. Tōjiin served as the Ashikaga mortuary temple and contains wooden portrait sculptures of Takauji, Yoshiakira, and a number of other Ashikaga shoguns.

52. The Madenokōji are nobles (*kuge*) descended from the Northern Fujiwara Kajūji line. The fourth son of Shoryūkan Roji Suketsune founded this branch family in the Kamakura period.

53. *Kennaiki* covers about thirty years from Ōei 21.12 (1414) to Kōshō 1 (1441). My reading of the text is from *Kennaiki* (pt. 1) in *Dai Nihon kokiroku* (Tokyo: Iwanami Shoten, 1963–1987), vol. 14, pp. 41ff.

54. *Kennaiki*, Shōchō 1 (1428) 1.18, pp. 41–43.

55. Ibid. 1.19, pp. 43–46.

56. After Fujiwara Yoshimichi, son of Kujō Kanezane, died in 1188, he was transported in a special type of carriage with lattice windows (*ajiroguruma*). Yoshimochi's vehicle was a palanquin, but it had the same type of windows.

57. In order to control the eastern provinces after he had moved his government to Kyoto, Ashikaga Takauji appointed his fourth son, Motouji, as his deputy, giving him the title *kantō kanryō* (reserving the succession to shogun for his eldest, Yoshiakira). Mochiuji was the fourth *kantō kanryō*, but there were plots to have him replaced until Shogun Yoshimochi ordered the daimyo of the Kantō to support him. Yoshimochi's support may have encouraged Mochiuji to hope to succeed him.

58. *Kennaiki*, Shōchō 1 (1428) 1.23, pp. 49–55.

59. Laborers who took the tonsure and performed such heavy labor as carrying coffins or palanquins for temples.

60. For this ceremony, the cords were made of white figured cloth (*aya*).

61. Generally referred to as *zen no tsuna* (cords of merit), these cords were to lead the deceased to the afterworld or paradise.

62. *Bukkyōgo daijiten*, ed. Nakamura Hajime (Tokyo: Tokyo Shoseki Kabushikigaisha, 1975), vol. 1, p. 440.

63. Faure says that all of these rituals had the same components: tea offering (*tencha*), lecture on dhāranī (*nenju*) and sutras (*fugin*), dedication of merit (*ekō*), and burning of incense. Bernard Faure, *The Rhetoric of Immediacy: A Cultural Critique of Chan/Zen Buddhism* (Princeton, NJ: Princeton University Press, 1991), p. 193. In the medieval texts, however, whenever details are given, usually only sutra recitations and incense offerings are mentioned.

64. *Meigetsuki*, Genkyū 1.21.1, in Suitō, *Chūsei no sōsō, bosei*, p. 7.

65. Hikaru Suzuki, *The Price of Death: The Funeral Industry in Contemporary Japan* (Stanford, CA: Stanford University Press, 2000), p. 46.

66. One of the earliest examples is a portrait offered at Emperor Go-Ichijō's memorial service in 1088; discussed in Yonekura Michio, *Minamoto no Yoritomo zō: Chinmoku no shōzōga* (Tokyo: Heibonsha, 1995), p. 14.

67. Details about the portrait of Priest Gikai displayed at his funeral in 1309, appear in *Gikai sōki*, and are discussed by Bodiford, *Sōtō Zen in Medieval Japan*, p. 192.

68. The symbolism of moving the coffin around the cremation site is further examined in Chapter 3. See also Bernard Faure's discussion of circumambulation in *Rhetoric of Immediacy*, pp. 195–199. According to Hikaru Suzuki, the practice is still common in parts of Japan today (*Price of Death*, pp. 46–47).

69. Yoshimochi's last testament (*yuigon*) had requested that Teiyō (Mitsuakira), Yoshimitsu's younger brother, perform these ceremonies, but because he was ill, they were performed by Genchū, the head abbot of Rokuon'in.

70. The term used in *Kennaiki* is *gyōdō* (ceremonial walking), a practice that usually involves circumambulating a Buddhist altar while chanting sutras. Inagaki, *Dictionary of Japanese Buddhist Terms*, p. 86.

71. Words are missing in this section of the text and the meaning is not clear.

72. *Kennaiki*, Shōchō 1 (1428) 1.24, p. 56.

73. Phrases from this part of the text are missing. The sentence about the pagoda is the annotator's suggestion.

74. *Kennaiki*, Shōchō 1 (1428) 1.28, pp. 58–59.

75. Ibid. 2.5, p. 63.

76. She is also known as Uramatsu Shigeko.

77. The text used for this section can be found in *Inryōken nichiroku*, in *Dai Nihon bukkyō zenshū* (Tokyo: Meicho Fukyūkai, 1980), vol. 133, pp. 414ff.

78. *Inryōken nichiroku*, Kanshō 4 (1463) 8.8, pp. 414–415.

79. The Buddhist title was decided the day she died, but the posthumous name was first mentioned on the day of her funeral. *Inryōken nichiroku*, Kanshō 4 (1463) 8.8 and 8.11, pp. 414–415.

80. *Inryōken nichiroku*, Kanshō 4 (1463) 8.11, pp. 415–417.

81. See n. 59 above.

82. Normally, guests visiting a temple for worship entered through the Sanmon (main gate). For funerals, side gates were used to symbolize that the purpose was not normal worship and to avoid polluting the main entrance.

83. Oshō is a title given to a precept master and also a term used to designate high respect. All of the priests mentioned in this section have this title. For simplicity's sake I shall simply refer to them as priests.

84. This term includes sutras, spells, or a Buddha's name.

85. This title usually refers to the priest in charge of the sutra repository in a Zen temple, but here it probably indicates a senior priest, someone next in rank to the abbot. Inagaki, *Dictionary of Japanese Buddhist Terms*, p. 373.

86. These are probably precursors of the modern death flowers (*shikabana*), which are also made of white paper.

87. Immediately on Keisen's left were Karasuma (father and son), Hino-dono, Hirohashi-dono, Hyoenokami-dono. On the shogun's right were Kanrei Hosokawa-dono Bu-e and others.

88. *Hinko* has the same general meaning as *ako*—to light a torch to cremate a body. However, *hin* refers to a torch made of twisted reeds rather than pine. According to Mujaku Dōchū, there is another difference; *ako* was used when only one funerary service was performed and *hinko* when there were several (Faure, *Rhetoric of Immediacy*, p. 198, n. 47). However, this meaning does not seem appropriate here.

89. This refers to the *Senju darani*, an 82-phrase *darani*, which expounds the merit of Senju Kannon. See Inagaki, *Dictionary of Japanese Buddhist Terms*, pp. 29, 281.

90. Bodiford, *Sōtō Zen in Medieval Japan*, pp. 204–206. He does not give the period to which this statement applies, but the dates of most of his sources suggest the sixteenth century. His statement is based on an analysis by Hirose Ryōkō of the Buddhist titles used for the deceased in Sōtō Zen funerals in "Zensō to sengoku shakai: Tōhoku ni katsudō shita Zenshōtachi o chūshin to shite," in *Sengoku no heishi to nōmin*, ed. Sugiyama Hiroshi Sensei Kanreki Kinen Ronshū (Tokyo: Kadokawa Shoten, 1978), and in *Zenshū chihō tenkaishi no kenkyū* (Tokyo: Yoshikawa Kōbunkan, 1988). Duncan Ryūken Williams, *The Other Side of Zen: A Social History of Sōtō Zen Buddhism in Tokugawa Japan* (Princeton and Oxford: Princeton University Press, 2005) discusses Sōtō Zen funerals for women in the Edo period (pp. 50–58).

91. Bodiford, *Sōtō Zen in Medieval Japan*, p. 206.

92. *Jishōindono ryōan sōbo*, in *Dai Nihon shiryō*, comp. Tōkyō Daigaku Shiryōhensanjo (Tokyo: Tōkyō Daigaku Shuppankai, 1951–1952), vol. 7, pt. 10, pp. 9–12.

93. *Noritoki kyōki* was written by Assistant Middle Councilor (*gon no chūnagon*) Yamashina Noritoki (1328–1410). Most of the diary was destroyed in a fire in 1405 that consumed Noritoki's home. All that remains today are the sections dating from after the fire (Ōei 12–17 [1405–1410]). They are reproduced in *Dai Nihon shiryō* (vol. 7, pt. 10), comp. Tōkyō Daigaku Shiryō Hensanjo (Tokyo: Tōkyō Daigaku Shuppankai, 1951–1952), pp. 7–9.

94. Diagram on pp. 10–11. Note: For the diagram of the cremation site, the cardinal directions were reversed and are corrected in the errata at the end of the volume (unpaginated). I have incorporated the corrections into my diagram (Fig. 2.3).

95. The *kanrei* was a high official of the Muromachi government who assisted the shogun in all important government matters. The post was rotated among the Shiba, Hosokawa, and Hatakeyama families.

96. In other sources this rope or cord is called the *zen no tsuna*. One end is attached to the coffin or to the carriage carrying the coffin, the other is held by relatives of the deceased. For further discussion, see Chapter 4, "Ritual Implements."

97. This information is given on the diagram of the funeral procession in *Dai Nihon shiryō* (no. 7, pt. 10), p. 10.

98. My arrangement is based on the diagram on p. 11, with its orientation corrected according to the errata on the final page of the volume (unnumbered).

99. The ninth ritual, *tairei shōsan*, is a wake in the form of a consultation with the deceased Zen master. Obviously, this ritual could not be performed for lay Buddhists.

100. Suzuki, *The Price of Death*, pp. 39–49.

101. Ibid., pp. 44–45.

Chapter 3: Objects of Separation and Containment

1. Only members of the aristocracy, high-ranking members of the warrior class, and abbots of important temples would have had access to folding screens in the fourteenth and fifteenth centuries.

2. Traditionally this ritual was performed by standing on the roof of the house and calling out the name of the departed. This practice originated in China and is first mentioned in the *Li ji*; it also appears in later eighth-century Tang ritual codes. It was practiced in similar form only occasionally in Japan, and most written records of its performance date from the Heian period. The first recorded use of the "calling back the soul" ritual may be when Fujiwara no Michinaga's daughter Kishi died in 1025. It was performed again in 1027 when Michinaga died. See William H. McCullough and Helen Craig McCullough, trans., *A Tale of Flowering Fortunes: Annals of Japanese Aristocratic Life in the Heian Period* (Stanford, CA: Stanford University Press, 1980), vol. 2, pp. 784–785, supp. n. 88.

3. White silk screens concealing the carriage or palanquin are documented for imperial funerals, but I have not found examples of their use in the funerals of military elite.

4. The Japanese associated white with auspiciousness from ancient times. In early texts such as *Shoku Nihongi* (official chronicle of the period 700–790), auspicious omens were frequently white—white turtles, white deer, white birds, etc. See Felicia G. Bock, *Classical Learning and Taoist Practices in Early Japan with a Translation of Books XVI and XX of the Engi Shiki* (Occasional Paper No. 17, Center for Asian Studies, Arizona State University, 1985), pp. 6–7. In addition, shrines were not visited for one year after a death to avoid polluting the gods.

5. Sanskrit letters or Buddhist phrases might also be written on the deceased's robe.

6. Minamoto no Morotoki, *Chōshūki*, 2 vols., in *Zōho shiryō taisei*, comp. Zōho Shiryō Taisei Kankōkai (Kyoto: Rinsen Shoten, 1974), vol. 1, Daiji 4.7.8, p. 287.

7. Katsuda Itaru, *Shishatachi no chūsei* (Tokyo: Yoshikawa Kōbunkan, 2003), p. 83.

8. Taira no Nobunori, *Heihanki*, 2 vols., in *Zōho shiryō taisei*, vol. 2, Hōgen 1.7.2, p. 111.

9. Shukaku Hosshinō, *Kichiji shidai*, in *Shinkō gunsho ruijū (zatsubu 77)* (1977), pp. 684–688; p. 685.

10. *Meigetsuki* (Genkyū 1.12.1), in Katsuda, *Shishatachi no chūsei*, p. 83.

11. The practice of *dosha kaji* flourished in the Kamakura period, but there are examples of a similar rite of scattering sand over the cremation site as early as Emperor Go-Ichijō's funeral in 1036. See *Sakeiki (ruijū zatsurei)*, written by Minamoto no Tsuneyori (985–1039), in *Zōho shiryō taisei* (Kyoto: Rinsen Shoten, 1964–1974), Chōgen 9.5.19, p. 440.

12. See also Gorai on coffins; Gorai Shigeru, *Sō to kuyō* (Osaka: Tōhō Shuppan, 1992), pp. 292–299.

13. According to *Kichiji shidai*, the length of a typical coffin was 6 *shaku*, 3 *sun*, width was 1 *shaku*, 8 *sun*, height 1 *shaku*, 6 *sun* (p. 685).

14. *Kichiji ryakki*, in *Shinkō gunsho ruijū (zatsubu 77)* (1977), pp. 689–695; 690.

15. Lacquering was very time- and labor-intensive, because many layers of lacquer are needed and each has to dry thoroughly before the next can be applied. If the lacquer had been allowed to dry properly, however, the container would have been fairly impervious to fluids.

16. It is unclear if Toba was redressed or if the fresh robe was simply laid over his corpse.

17. *Meigetsuki*, Fujiwara no Teika's diary, says that the straw mats that had served as the deathbed for a court woman who died giving birth were cut up in small pieces and thrown into rivers; *Kunchū meigetsuki*, comp. and annot. Inamura Eiichi (Matsue City: Matsue Imai Shoten, 2002), vol. 6, Tenpuku 1 (1233) 9.30, p. 146; *Kichiji ryakki*, p. 689, says the mats should be removed and thrown away.

18. *Heihanki*, vol. 2, Hōgen 1.7.2, p. 111.

19. *Kichiji ryakki*, p. 689. *Kichiji ryakki* is presumed to be a twelfth-century document, but the information about reversing the screens was written on the back of the manuscript, suggesting that it may have been added later.

20. *Eiga monogatari zenchūshaku*, in *Nihon koten hyōshaku zenshūshaku sōsho*, ed. Matsumura Hiroji, 9 vols. (Tokyo: Kadokawa Shoten, 1969–1982), vol. 5, pp. 213; also McCullough and McCullough, *Flowering Fortunes*, vol. 2, p. 678, n. 11.

21. Matsumura Hiroji's explanation of this passage is that the folding and hanging screens around Kishi were displayed in a way that was different from normal; *Eiga monogatari zenchūshaku*, vol. 5, pp. 214; see also McCullough and McCullough, *Flowering Fortunes*, p. 678, n. 11.

22. Rokuon'in is a cloister of the Kyoto Zen temple Shōkokuji. For more information on golden screens and their uses in death rituals, see Bettina Klein, "Japanese *Kinbyōbu*: The Gold-leafed Folding Screens of the Muromachi Period (1333–1573)," pt. 1, *Artibus Asiae* 45 (1984): 5–33.

23. *Inryōken nichiryoku*, vol. 133, Kanshō 4.8.11, p. 417.

24. The description of the decorations appears in a later entry for Entoku 3.1.28 in *Inryōken nichiryoku*, vol. 136, p. 387.

25. *Inryōken nichiryoku*, vol. 135, Chōkyō 3.4.8, p. 415.

26. In *Zoku Ōnin [ko]ki* (scroll 5), Tenmon 19.5.7, cited in Takeda Tsuneo, "Kinpeki shōhekiga ni tsuite," *Bukkyō geijutsu*, vol. 59 (December 1965), pp. 105–122; n. 28. Examples of golden screens used at funerals also appear in Takeda, p. 110, and Klein, "Japanese *Kinbyōbu*," p. 15.

27. Klein, "Japanese *Kinbyōbu*," pp. 19ff.

28. Ibid., p. 19.

29. A lengthy and detailed list of items burned can be found in the entry for Chōgen 9.5.19 in *Sakeiki (ruijū zatsurei)*, p. 439.

30. Klein, "Japanese *Kinbyōbu*," p. 15.

31. Mimi Yiengpruksawan, "The House of Gold; Fujiwara Kiyohira's Konjikidō," *Monumenta Nipponica* 48, no. 1 (Spring 1993): 33–52; 35–36.

32. H. Paul Varley, "Ashikaga Yoshimitsu and the World of Kitayama: Social Change and Shogunal Patronage in Early Muromachi Japan," in *Japan in the Muromachi Age*, ed. John Whitney Hall and Toyoda Takeshi (Berkeley, Los Angeles, and London: University of California Press, 1977), pp. 183–204; 201–202.

33. Andrew M. Watsky, *Chikubushima: Deploying the Sacred Arts in Momoyama Japan* (Seattle and London: University of Washington Press, 2004), pp. 112–113.

34. See also Chapter 4, "Ritual Implements for Funerals and Memorial Services."

35. This name is given when an individual accepts the Buddhist precepts. Typically a ceremony took place when the person was still alive, but in the late medieval period precepts were also administered posthumously.

36. *Inryōken nichiryoku*, vol. 134, Bunmei 19.7.12, p. 522, vol. 135, Chōkyō 2.5.11, p. 198.

37. Women typically used this type of cart, which was often decorated with cords dyed blue, purple, or red. McCullough interprets the description as a "string-decorated carriage with fittings of gold"; *Tale of Flowering Fortunes*, vol. 1, p. 232. Katsuda suggests that Teishi's carriage was made of, or possibly covered with, gold; Katsuda, *Shishatachi no chūsei*, p. 132.

38. Another obvious interpretation is that the gold represented imperial status.

39. *Sakeiki (ruijū zatsurei)*, Chōgen 9.5.19, p. 438. Also McCullough and McCullough, *Flowering Fortunes*, vol. 1, p. 373–374; Katsuda, *Shishatachi no chūsei*, pp. 100–101; Gorai, *Sō to kuyō*, p. 155.

40. The term used is *shiraki*, which may refer to wood with the bark stripped off or to light-colored woods such as Japanese cedar (*sugi*) or *hinoki*, a type of cypress tree native to Japan.

41. There are too many terms to list, but a sample includes the four dharma realms (*shihokkai*), the four teachings of the Buddha during his life (*shikyō*), the four bodies of the Buddha (*shishin*), the Four Noble Truths (*shishōtai*), Four Heavenly Kings (*shitennō*), and the four stages of existence (*shiu*).

42. See also Katsuda, *Shishatachi no chūsei*, pp. 106–107; Gorai, *Sō to kuyō*, pp. 586–587.

43. *Kichiji ryakki*, p. 691. Measurements given in feet are only approximate. Japanese measurements varied over time and were not standardized until the nineteenth

century. I have used those standardized measurements for my approximations (1 *jō* = approx. 3.3 yards or 10 feet; 1 *shaku* = approx. 1 foot).

44. This term appears in the early eleventh-century account of Emperor Go-Ichijō's cremation. See *Sakeiki* (*ruijū zatsurei*), Chōgen 9.5.19, p. 440; Katsuda, *Shishatachi no chūsei*, p. 106; Gorai, *Sō to kuyō*, p. 585.

45. The fence in Plate 3 shows diagonal support slats.

46. Katsuda, *Shishatachi no chūsei*, p. 107; Gorai, *Sō to kuyō*, pp. 586–587.

47. *Sakeiki* (*ruijū zatsurei*), Chōgen 9.5.19, p. 440. The dimensions given in *Kichiji ryakki* on p. 692 are identical.

48. Gorai makes this comment in relation to the funeral scene in the *Shōtoku taishi e-den* (14th c.; version not specified), where there is a wrapped-fence enclosure and within that moving screens (*kōshō*); Gorai, *Sō to kuyō*, p. 155.

49. *Kichiji ryakki*, p. 692; *Sakeiki* (*ruijū zatsurei*), Chōgen 9.5.19, p. 440. It was also common for temples along the funeral procession route to cover their gateways with white hanging curtains.

50. According to Gorai, funerals in the early Heian period used only two gates, but late in the period the number was increased to four under the influence of Buddhist ideas; Gorai, *Sō to kuyō*, pp. 575, 588.

51. Katsuda, *Shishatachi no chūsei*, p. 110; see also discussion in Gorai, *Sō to kuyō*, pp. 581–583.

52. Nakamura Hajime, *Bukkyōgo daijiten* (Tokyo: Tōkyō Shoseki Kabushikigaisha, 1975), vol. 1, p. 533. These more traditional directional associations are also confirmed by Bernard Faure, *The Rhetoric of Immediacy: A Cultural Critique of Chan/Zen Buddhism* (Princeton, NJ: Princeton University Press, 1991), p. 195, and Gorai, *Sō to kuyō*, p. 595.

53. Faure uses the term *unyō sansō* (literally, "wind around to the right three times") for the action of carrying the coffin in a clockwise direction three times around the room, but he is unclear about whether or not the weaving in and out of the doors is part of the ritual; Faure, *Rhetoric of Immediacy*, p. 195. A notation written on a drawing in the section on transferring merit (*sho ekō shingi*) says that the coffin was to be turned three times to the *left* before leaving the temple for the cremation grounds and that the coffin was carried around the crematory three times (no direction given); *Taishō shinshū daizōkyō*, T. 81, 2578, p. 663 and T. 81, 2578, p. 661, respectively. For explanations of why some sources state that the coffin was to be moved clockwise and others counterclockwise, see also Faure, *Rhetoric of Immediacy*, p. 195, n. 42.

54. Faure, *Rhetoric of Immediacy*, pp. 195–199.

55. Ibid., p. 197; see also Nancy Falk, "To Gaze on the Sacred Traces," *History of Religions* 16, no. 4 (1977): 281–293; 291.

56. For other interpretations of the symbolism of the four gates, see Faure, *Rhetoric of Immediacy*, pp. 197–198.

57. In *Kennaiki*, Shōchō 1.1.23, p. 49; and *Inryōken nichiroku*, in *Dai Nihon bukkyō zenshū* (Tokyo: Meicho Fukyūkai, 1980), vol. 133, Kanshō 4.8.11, p. 416, respectively.

58. A portion of the east wall was destroyed to allow room for the coffin's exit. Presumably this was done so that the living would not have to use the gateway used by

the corpse, and also as a means to symbolize the changed circumstances of the dead, who can no longer enter and exit as they once did.

59. It is not clear from the text whether the structure had walls or not.

60. *Sakeiki* (*ruijū zatsurei*), Chōgen 9.5.19, p. 440. The special borders on the mats denote the elite status of those permitted to sit, or in this case rest, upon them.

61. *Sakeiki* (*ruijū zatsurei*), Chōgen 9.5.19, p. 440.

62. *Kichiji ryakki*, p. 692.

63. See also Katsuda, *Shishatachi no chūsei*, p. 106.

64. Traditionally these were made of wild-rice straw (*makomo*).

65. This is a general term for woven mats made of any of the following materials: rush (*ashi*), bulrush (*kaba*), straw (*wara*), or bamboo (*take*).

66. *Kichiji ryakki*, p. 692.

67. *Sakeiki* (*ruijū zatsurei*), Chōgen 9.5.19, p. 440. The water was probably both for fire control and to douse the flames when cremation was completed.

68. *Sakeiki* (*ruijū zatsurei*), Chōgen 9.5.19, p. 440.

69. Katsuda, *Shishatachi no chūsei*, p. 106.

70. *Kanmon gyoki*, Ōei 23.11.24, p. 52.

71. *Kennaiki*, Shōchō 1.1.23, p. 49.

72. McCullough and McCullough, *Flowering Fortunes*, vol. 1, p. 233.

73. Nakayama (Fujiwara) Tadachika, *Sankaiki*, vols. 19–21, in *Shiryō taisei*, 30 vols. (Tokyo: Naigai Shoseki Kabushikigaisha, 1935); entry for Jishō 4.11.2-3, vol. 3 (vol. 21), p. 131. Written by Naidaijin Nakayama (Fujiwara) no Tadachika (1131–1195), *Sankaiki* covers the years between 1151 and 1194. For additional examples of Heian-period burials see also Katsuda, *Shishatachi no chūsei*, pp. 129–141.

74. The Spirit Hall may be related to an older type of hall, the *mogari no miya*, constructed to hold the bodies of imperials until a final resting place could be constructed. *Mogari no miya* were also surrounded by walls or fences. See Gary L. Ebersole, *Ritual Poetry and the Politics of Death in Early Japan* (Princeton, NJ: Princeton University Press, 1989), p. 127. See also Katsuda, *Shishatachi no chūsei*, pp. 133–134, and Gorai, *Sō to kuyō*, pp. 126–128.

75. It may be that just the bed of the carriage was entombed; the wheels were likely taken off, according to Katsuda, *Shishatachi no chūsei*, p. 132. McCullough and McCullough, *Tale of Flowering Fortunes*, vol. 1, p. 232, say that only the coffin was taken into hall, as does Gorai, *Sō to kuyō*, p. 126, who also says the Spirit Hall may have been a place where the body lay in state before burial.

76. We are told that Nagaie's wife was the daughter of Fujiwara Tadanobu, but she is not named.

77. *Eiga monogatari zenchūshaku*, vol. 5, p. 309; Katsuda, *Shishatachi no chūsei*, p. 132; Gorai, *Sō to kuyō*, pp. 126–127; also McCullough and McCullough, *Flowering Fortunes*, vol. 2, p. 696–697.

78. Seishi (972–1025) was the empress (*kōgō*) of Emperor Sanjō. She died at age fifty-four on the twenty-fourth day of the third month of Manju 2 and was buried on the fourteenth day of the fourth month.

79. *Sakeiki*, Manju 2 (1025) 4.4, p. 140; *Eiga monogatari zenchūshaku*, vol. 5, pp.

126–132; also McCullough and McCullough, *Flowering Fortunes*, vol. 2, p. 660, and Katsuda, *Shishatachi no chūsei*, p. 132.

80. *Sakeiki*, Manju 2 (1025) 4.14, p. 141. The meaning of a temporary burial or a place for the body to lie in state is suggested in the word *hin*[*sō*] in the text.

81. Mimi Yiengpruksawan, "The House of Gold: Fujiwara Kiyohira's Konjikidō," *Monumenta Nipponica* 48, no. 1 (Spring 1993): 33–52; 44.

82. *Heihanki*, Kyūjū 2 (1155), 9.16, vol. 2, p. 8.

83. See Yiengpruksawan, "The House of Gold," pp. 33–52. Other examples are given in Nishiguchi Junko, "Where the Bones Go: Death and Burial of Women in the Heian High Aristocracy," in *Engendering Faith: Women and Buddhism in Premodern Japan*, ed. Barbara Ruch (Ann Arbor: The University of Michigan Center for Japanese Studies, 2002), pp. 417–439.

84. See Gorai Shigeru, *Sō to kuyū*, pp. 101–106.

85. According to Gorai, the three vertical pillars on top of the grave in this illustration are called *butsugan sotoba*, and they are surrounded by *senbontōba* (also *sasatōba*); Gorai, *Sō to kuyū*, p. 209.

86. See Suitō Makoto, *Chūsei no sōsō, bosei: sekitō o zōryū suru koto* (Tokyo: Yoshikawa Kōbunkan, 1991), pp. 187–194.

87. *Moromoriki*, vol. 3, Kōei 4 (1345) 3.6, p. 7.

88. Komatsu Shigemi, the annotator of *Zenshin Shonin Shinran den-e*, calls this type of grave enclosure a *suigai* or "transparent fence" (p. 108).

89. Shinran died in 1262; the handscroll is dated to the early fourteenth century.

Chapter 4: Ritual Implements for Funerals and Memorials

1. Wu Hung, *Monumentality in Early Chinese Art and Architecture* (Stanford, CA: Stanford University Press, 1995), p. 24.

2. The scrolls are purportedly based on earlier biographical notes and letters written by Nichiren himself, which no longer exist. *Nichiren shōnin chūgasan*, in *Zokuzoku: Nihon emaki taisei: Denki, engi hen*, vol. 2, ed. Komatsu Shigemi (Tokyo: Chūō Kōronsha, 1993), p. 85.

3. Nitchō was a student of the tenth head, Seishūin Nichien, of the main Kyoto temple, Honkokuji. He is associated with various temples, including Enmyōji in Misaki (Kanagawa) in 1479, Myōhōji in Kamakura ca. 1483–1503, and Honryūji in Izu (Shizuoka Prefecture) ca. 1506. It is believed that he completed the text of Nichiren's biography at Myōhōji; *Nichiren shōnin chūgasan*, pp. 86–87.

4. Provisional Senior Assistant High Priest (*gon no daisōzu*) is the second rank (of four) of the second grade in the Buddhist temple hierarchy.

5. *Nichiren shōnin chūgasan*, p. 87.

6. James C. Dobbins, "Envisioning Kamakura Buddhism," in *Re-Visioning "Kamakura" Buddhism*, ed. Richard K. Payne, Kuroda Institute Studies in East Asian Buddhism No. 11 (Honolulu: University of Hawai'i Press, 1998), p. 35.

7. *Nichiren shōnin chūgasan*, p. 87.

8. Jacqueline Stone, "Rebuking the Enemies of the Lotus: Nichirenist Exclusivism in Historical Perspective," *JJRS* 21, nos. 2/3 (1994): 231–259; 237–243.

9. For example, well over a hundred monks, attendants, and relatives participated in the eleventh-century funeral of Emperor Go-Ichijō, including twelve torchbearers. See William H. McCullough and Helen Craig McCullough, *A Tale of Flowering Fortunes: Annals of Japanese Aristocratic Life in the Heian Period* (Stanford, CA: Stanford University Press, 1980), vol. 1, pp. 373–374, supp. n. 14.

10. C. Clifford Flanigan, "The Moving Subject: Medieval Liturgical Processions in Semiotic and Cultural Perspective," in *Moving Subjects: Processional Performance in the Middle Ages and Renaissance*, ed. Kathleen Ashley and Wim Hüsken (Amsterdam and Atlanta [GA]: Rodopi, 2001), p. 147.

11. Processions continued to be prominent elements in funerals through the Meiji period and vanished sometime in the early twentieth century. Murakami Kōkyō, "Changes in Japanese Funeral Customs during the Twentieth Century," *JJRS* 27, nos. 3–4 (Fall 2000): 335–352; 340.

12. J. Edward Kidder, Jr., *The Lucky Seventh: Early Horyūji and Its Time* (Tokyo: International Christian University and Hachiro Yuasa Memorial Museum, 1999), p. 62.

13. Nichiren was not a member of the warrior class (he was, in fact, the son of a fisherman), but throughout his life he was attacked by various local samurai and priests whom he angered by his teachings. Thus, Nichiren and his followers often had to defend their own lives. See Philip B. Yampolsky, ed., *Selected Writings of Nichiren*, trans. Burton Watson et al. (New York: Columbia University Press, 1990).

14. It may be that Nitchō had access to earlier partial biographies and temple records about such details.

15. Gorai Shigeru, *Sō to kuyō* (Osaka: Tōhō Shuppan, 1992), p. 340.

16. For another example, see Shinran's funeral procession in *Zenshin shōnin Shinran den-e*, pp. 104–105.

17. *Sōhōmitsu*, in *Nihon kyōiku bunko*, vol. 10 (*Shūkyō hen*), ed. Kurokawa Mamichi (Tokyo: Dōbunkan, 1910–1911), p. 687. This type of triangular paper headband was called a *shikan* when it was worn in the twelfth century and earlier by Yin-Yang Masters (*onmyōji*) for certain festivals; Gorai, *Sō to Kuyō*, p. 488. The modern terminology for this triangular headgear is *zukin*; Hikaru Suzuki, *The Price of Death: The Funeral Industry in Contemporary Japan* (Stanford, CA: Stanford University Press, 2000), p. 43. See also discussion in Katsuda Itaru, *Shishatachi no chūsei* (Tokyo: Yoshikawa Kōbunkan, 2003), p. 116.

18. *Kitano Tenjin engi* (early 13th c.), scroll 8, p. 40.

19. Hikaru Suzuki reported that in twentieth-century death rituals in Kita-Kyushu a triangular headcloth was also placed on the deceased; *Price of Death*, p. 43.

20. Although the artificial flowers used for funerals today look nothing like this one, the lotus in the handscroll may be a distant forerunner of today's death flower (*shikabana*); ibid., p. 226, n. 6.

21. Gorai, *Sō to kuyō*, pp. 256–257.

22. The same type of banner attached to a golden dragon head precedes a cortege

of priests for Hōnen's funeral procession in *Hōnen shōnin e-den*, vol. 2 (*Zoku Nihon no emaki* 3), ed. Komatsu Shigemi (Tokyo: Chūō Kōronsha, 1990), p. 14.

23. Gorai, *Sō to kuyō*, p. 187.

24. The modern-day dragon heads, however, are made of bamboo and paper; the head of the dragon is carved out of bamboo, and its body is formed by wrapping the stick in white and black paper; Hikaru Suzuki, *Price of Death*, p. 226, n. 7.

25. Funerary banners have a long history in China, predating their use in Japan. Special directives for the size and design of funeral banners can be found in the ancient (probably Warring States–period) books of the *Li ji* (Book of rites) and *Yi li* (Ceremonies and rites); David L. McMullen, "The Death Rites of Tang Daizong," in *State and Court Ritual in China*, ed. Joseph P. McDermott (Cambridge: Cambridge University Press, 1999), p. 174.

26. Gorai, *Sō to kuyō*, pp. 184, 166.

27. *Jingihaku sōmoki* dates from 1798. But the text was copied from a seventh-century manual preserved at Ikuta Shrine that outlined proper procedure for the mourning and funerals of emperors; in *Nihon kyōiku bunko*, vol. 10 (*shūkyō*), p. 696.

28. Kawada, "Japanese Buddhist Decorative Arts: The Formative Period, 552–794," in *Object as Insight: Japanese Buddhist Art and Ritual* (exh. cat., Katonah Museum of Art, 1996), p. 26.

29. Kajima Masaru, "Kondō kanjō ban," in *Nihon no kokuhō*, vol. 043 (December 14, 1997), p. 72; also *Nihongi*, vol. 2, p. 65.

30. This special banner belongs to Hōryūji in Nara but is now displayed in the Hōryūji Kennō Hōmotsukan at the Tokyo National Museum.

31. Michael R. Cunningham et al., *Buddhist Treasures from Nara* (exh. cat., Cleveland Museum of Art, 1998), p. 194.

32. *Object as Insight*, p. 28. These are now preserved in the Shōsōin. The large size of early imperial banners in Japan likely followed Chinese formulas found in the *Yi li*; see discussion in McMullen, "The Death Rites of Tang Daizong," p. 174.

33. McCullough and McCullough, *Flowering Fortunes*, vol. 1, p. 373.

34. An example of this practice is illustrated in *Hōnen Shōnin e-den*, vol. 2, p. 70. The banner might be attached to a Buddhist image, but more often to a nearby pillar.

35. Historically the color white has symbolized purification. Because it is often worn to counteract the pollution caused by death, white is often also associated with death. For example, female shrine assistants (*miko*) wear white robes to protect the deities from impurities (*kegare*), just as a family will often cover their shrine altar (*kamidana*) with white paper to avoid polluting the deity when there is a death in the immediate family.

36. McCullough and McCullough, *Flowering Fortunes*, vol. 1, p. 373.

37. *Object as Insight*, p. 30.

38. Often five offering vessels (*go gusoku*) appear on the altar—two vases, two candlesticks, and an incense burner.

39. *Kennaiki*, Shōchō 1.1.23, p. 50, and *Inryōken nichiroku*, Kanshō 4.8.11, vol. 133, p. 415.

40. *Kanmon nikki*, Ōei 23.12.24, p. 58.

41. *Object as Insight*, p. 30.

42. Saitō Tama, *Shi to mononoke* (Tokyo: Shinjuku Shobō, 1986), pp. 50–54.

43. See examples in *Kennaiki*, Shōchō 1.1.23, pp. 49–50; *Jishōindono ryōan sōbo*, in *Dai Nihon shiryō* (no. 7, part 10), Ōei 5.5.6, pp. 10–11.

44. Records of the deaths of parishioners, along with their secular and Buddhist names (*hōmyō/kaimyō*), were kept at family temples. The earliest extant textual reference to them appears in the thirteenth-century *Heike monogatari*; *Nihon kokugo daijiten*, vol. 2, p. 1209.

45. The giving of posthumous names to lay individuals who took Buddhist vows evolved from the Buddhist ritual in which a new disciple received a Buddhist name when he entered the priesthood (*jukai*); Gorai, *Sō to kuyō*, pp. 630–634.

46. Burning the personal effects of the deceased was an ancient tradition. See, for example, Emperor Ichijō's (11th c.) cremation, when personal items, including an armrest, his shoes, an inkstone box, etc., were burned along with the body. McCullough and McCullough, *Flowering Fortunes*, vol. 1, p. 374.

47. The cloth strip may also be red, white, or even green.

48. The tradition, dating back to at least the Eastern Han, was probably brought to Japan from China. *Tong dian* (Comprehensive compendium), completed in the early ninth century, states that imperial hearses were to be drawn by a thousand guards holding three-ply silk cords. There were to be six cords in all, each a hundred yards in length and seven inches in circumference; McMullen, "The Death Rites of Tang Daizong," p. 186.

49. *Kennaiki*, 1428.1.23, pp. 49–50. I did not, however, find any examples of youngsters carrying the cords.

50. Gorai, *Sō to kuyō*, p. 300.

51. See, for example, the illustrations of Tokugawa Ieyasu's funeral in 1616; in Komatsu Shigemi, ed., *Tōshōsha engi*, *Zokuzoku Nihon emaki taisei: denki/engihen*, vol. 8 (Tokyo: Chūō Kōronsha, 1994), pp. 77, 82. Hikaru Suzuki mentions a similar custom in Kita-Kyushu today: "a long strip of cloth was tied around the coffin and extended behind it; from there it was held by a line of *kumi* women"; *Price of Death*, pp. 46–47.

52. See, for example, the illustration of the palanquin carrying Hōnen's coffin in *Hōnen shōnin e-den*, vol. 2, pp. 50–51.

53. For commoner funerals in the late nineteenth century, paper rather than cloth was used, so that it could be more easily changed for each funeral.

54. The onion flower (*sōka*) was viewed as felicitous because it kept its form for a long time.

55. Emperor Meiji's casket was carried in a *sōkaren* to his mausoleum in Fushimi Momoyama. T. Fujitani, *Splendid Monarchy: Power and Pageantry in Modern Japan* (Berkeley, Los Angeles, and London: University of California Press, 1998), p. 152.

56. Katsuda, *Shishatachi no chūsei*, p. 237. He cites a Muromachi-period dictionary, *Wakan tsūyōshū*, as the source of this definition. The dictionary defines *gan* as a palanquin (*koshi*) for the deceased.

57. Ibid., p. 241.

58. Two sources, *Daikakuji monjo* (1531) and *Chōkōji monjo* (1606), discuss four

different types of funeral carriages and how much rice was paid for each. The *gan* palanquin was the most expensive; Katsuda, *Shishatachi no chūsei*, p. 238.

59. I found several terms for this type of coffin: *marukan* (round coffin), *tatekan* (vertical coffin), and *zakan* (sitting coffin).

60. The illustrations in *Tōshōsha engi* suggest that a very similar type of palanquin carried the corpse of Tokugawa Ieyasu; Komatsu, *Tōshōsha engi*, pp. 77, 82. Furthermore, the graves of many later Tokugawa shoguns buried at Zōjōji and Kan'eiji were excavated after the temples were bombed in World War II; the evidence suggests that all were buried seated in meditation posture inside vertical coffins; see Suzuki Hisashi, *Hone wa monogataru Tokugawa shogun, daimyōke no hitobito* (Tokyo: Tōkyō Daigaku Shuppan, 1985).

61. *Jishōindono ryōan sōbo*, p. 10.

62. For example, Suzuki found that today in parts of Kita-Kyushu canopies are still held over coffins during funeral processions. Hikaru Suzuki, *Price of Death*, p. 46.

63. Komatsu suggests that the artist's knowledge of the names of some participants may have been transmitted through an earlier record, perhaps the *Nichiren sōsō gyōretsu ki*. *Nichiren shōnin chūgasan*, vol. 2, p. 71.

64. This dates back to ancient Chinese Confucian mourning traditions, in which the type of dress worn expressed each participant's relationship to the deceased; Alan Cole, "Upside Down/Right Side Up: A Revisionist History of Buddhist Funerals in China," *History of Religions* 35, no. 4 (May 1996): 334.

65. *Suō* is a type of *hitatare* worn with long pants (*hakama*) by samurai in the early medieval period.

66. *Nihongi*, trans. Aston (1972), pp. I. 277, II. 274. Another section of the *Nihongi* says that the custom for mourning wear in Silla (Korea) was also plain white garments, suggesting continental influence (p. 326).

67. Plain dark-gray (*nibiiro*) silk was prescribed after the death of an emperor and a paler bluish-gray (*usunibi*) silk for other court deaths. The colors were also used to designate the depth of the mourning; black robes were worn for "heavy" mourning when a parent died, and gray for "light" mourning for other relatives. See McCullough and McCullough, *Flowering Fortunes*, vol. 1, pp. 369–370, and vol. 2, p. 718.

68. Hikaru Suzuki's research into community funeral rituals during the first half of the twentieth century confirms that members of the deceased's immediate family wore white robes and more distant relatives and neighbors wore black kimono; *Price of Death*, p. 44.

69. Whether the daughter was married or single, young or old, may also have determined the color of her robe.

70. *Kennaiki*, Shōchō 1.1.23, p. 50. The author notes that it was not really proper for Yoshinori to wear priestly robes on such an occasion, but it was permitted because he had been a priest.

71. *Inryōken nichiroku*, Kanshō 4.8.11, vol. 133, p. 415.

72. *Kuyō* means to worship or venerate through offerings.

73. *Hōnen shōnin e-den* was first called *Shijūhachikan e-den* (Illustrated biography in forty-eight scrolls) and later renamed *Hōnen shōnin gyōjō ezu* (Drawings illustrating

Hōnen's conduct); see *Hōnen shōnin e-den*, vol. 2, p. 118. The more common appellation today is *Hōnen shōnin e-den*, but some scholars still refer to it as *Hōnen shōnin gyōjō ezu*.

74. *Hōnen shōnin e-den*, vol. 2, p. 118. Little is known about the production of *Hōnen shōnin e-den*. Earlier biographies of Hōnen that likely contributed to the project include *Genkū shōnin shinikki* (ca. 1237–1256), *Honchō soshi denki ekotoba* (1237; also known as *Shikanden*), *Hōnen shōninden ekotoba* (before 1301; also known as *Rinnabon*), *Kurodani genkū shōnin denki* (ca. 1283–1295; also known as *Jūrokumonki*), and *Hōnen shōnin gyōjō ezu* (ca. 1311–1323; also known as *Shijūhachikan e-den*). See *Hōnen's Senchakushū: Passages on the Selection of the Nembutsu in the Original Vow*, trans. and ed. Senchakushū English Translation Project (Honolulu: University of Hawai'i Press and Tokyo: Sōgō Bukkyō Kenkyūjo, Taishō University, 1998), pp. 9–10.

75. Go-Fushimi's reasons for sponsoring this project and contributing his calligraphy to it are an important topic for further research.

76. The names and general outline for this section are taken from the text that accompanies the illustrations in *Hōnen shōnin e-den*, vol. 2, pp. 19–27.

77. At this time Sanemune held the titles of lay priest of Ōmiya and Retired Middle Counselor (*Ōmiya nyūdō sakino naidaijin*).

78. These were gifts commonly offered to an eminent visitor in Indian society—garlands of flowers, unguents and incense to perfume the body, and refreshments.

79. *Makie* is a technique in which gold and/or silver flakes are sprinkled over still-wet lacquer and adhere to the surface when the lacquer dries.

80. The traditional pattern was Fudō, Shaka, Monju, Fugen, Jizō, Miroku, Yakushi Nyorai, but the order was not yet fixed in the fourteenth century or varied according to sectarian preferences. See discussion in Chapter 1.

81. The explanatory text in *Hōnen shonin e-den* suggests that the image is Amida; in the original text of the handscroll, however, no deity is mentioned. The painting itself appears to be a golden image with a golden halo. Its hands are joined vertically in an attitude of prayer, a mudra often used by Amida when he assumes the function of a bodhisattva.

82. *Nyūdō* is a title given to a lay priest; *bettō* has numerous meanings, making it difficult to identify a specific person here.

83. In this illustration the flecks of gold on the black lacquer are quite apparent.

84. *Kei* are related to ancient Chinese stone chimes, which were cut in an inverted V and hung from a wooden frame.

85. Seikaku, a grandson of Fujiwara Michinori (Shinzei), was a Tendai monk affiliated with Mount Hiei. There is no proof that he was Hōnen's disciple; rather, according to *Nihonshi daijiten*, he was a disciple of Chōgen (vol. 3, p. 1187).

86. Ten scrolls of *Boki ekotoba* were produced following Kakunyu's death in 1351 and preserved at Honganji. Scrolls 1 and 7 were lost, then repainted around 1482. Komatsu says that Shogun Ashikaga Yoshimasa (1449–1473) borrowed the set and kept them at the Muromachi Gosho until Honganji requested their return in 1481; at that time the two scrolls were missing. *Boki ekotoba*, in *Zoku Nihon no emaki*, vol. 9, ed. and annot. Komatsu Shigemi (Tokyo: Chūō Kōronsha, 1990), p. 1 (unpaginated).

87. Ibid., p. 25.

88. Fister found associations between *shikimi* and death in various early texts, such as *Man'yōshū* (8th c.), *Genji monogatari* (11th c.), and *Makura no sōshi* (11th c.). My information on *shikimi* in this section is based on the research of Patricia Fister, "From Sacred Leaves to Sacred Images," in *Figures and Places of the Sacred* (Kyoto: International Research Center for Japanese Studies, 2001), pp. 78–80.

89. The *kanji* for *kei* is written with the same characters as *qing*.

90. Reproduced in Idemitsu Bijutsukan, *Egakareta gyokuraku to jigoku: Bukkyō kaiga meisakuō* (Idemitsu Bijutsukan, 2002), pp. 20–21, plate 2.

91. See image and text in *Yūzū nembutsu engi*, in *Zoku Nihon no emaki*, vol. 21, ed. Komatsu Shigemi (Tokyo: Chūō Kōronsha, 1992), pp. 66–67.

92. Inagaki defines *nenbutsu zanmai* as "the concentrated practice of reciting the *nenbutsu* whereby the aspirant attains unity with Amida Buddha." Hisao Inagaki, *A Dictionary of Japanese Buddhist Terms: Based on References in Japanese Literature* (Kyoto: Nagata Bunshodo, 1988), p. 226.

93. See image and text in *Yūzū nembutsu engi*, pp. 80–81.

94. William M. Bodiford, "Zen in the Art of Funerals: Ritual Salvation in Japanese Buddhism," *History of Religion* 32, no. 2 (November 1992): 146–164; 150–151. The earliest extant Chinese Zen monastic code is the *Chanyuan qinggui*, compiled between 1099 and 1103. It was brought to Japan in the early 12th century. See Yifa, *The Origins of Buddhist Monastic Codes in China*, p. 108, and Williams, *The Other Side of Zen*, p. 38.

Chapter 5: Portraits of the Deceased

1. I would like to express my thanks to my coinstructor, Evelyn Rawski, and to the members of our seminar (Naoko Gunji, Kristin Harkness, Kathy Johnston-Keane, Azar Rejaie, Miguel Rojas, Hongyu Wu, and Jui-man Wu), "Portraits and Rituals in East Asia" (Fall 2002), for many fruitful discussions that helped shape my ideas about portraits. I am especially indebted to Naoko Gunji for bringing to my attention many obscure Japanese sources on portraits.

2. Richard Brilliant, *Portraiture* (Cambridge, MA: Harvard University Press, 1991), p. 14.

3. See, for example, Max J. Friedlander, *Landscape, Portrait, Still Life* (New York: Schocken Books, 1963), pp. 231–232; Kurt W. Forester, "Metaphors of Rule, Political Ideology and History in the Portraits of Cosimo I de'Medici," *Mitteilungen des Kunsthistorischen Institutes in Florenz* 15 (1971): 65–104; Sheldon Nodelman, "How to Read a Roman Portrait," *Art in America* 63, no. 1 (1975): 27–33; David Freedberg, *The Power of Images: Studies in the History and Theories of Response* (Chicago: University of Chicago Press, 1989).

4. This term generally means "doing meritorious acts," one of which is holding memorial services to increase the merit of a deceased person; *tsuifuku* is also used.

5. Portraits of Zen abbots were treated slightly differently. They were generally kept in the temples in which these men had lived and served. The sculpted portraits

had permanent positions in the hall, while painted ones were displayed on death anniversaries and for other special temple ceremonies.

6. The exceptions are the painted and sculpted images of famous Buddhist abbots who founded a sect or a temple, many of which are still used today during their memorial services.

7. Anthropologists tend to focus on the importance of the memorial tablet and have little to say about the portrait of the deceased, which today is usually a photograph. See, for example, Robert J. Smith, *Ancestor Worship in Contemporary Japan* (Stanford, CA: Stanford University Press, 1974), and Hikaru Suzuki, *The Price of Death: The Funeral Industry in Contemporary Japan* (Stanford, CA: Stanford University Press, 2000); also a special issue of the *Japanese Journal of Religious Studies* 27, nos. 3/4 (Fall 2000), on mortuary rites in Japan. The historian Andrew Bernstein recently published a study on death rituals in imperial Japan but does not mention portraits in his discussion; see *Modern Passings: Death Rites, Politics, and Social Change in Imperial Japan* (Honolulu: University of Hawai'i Press, 2006).

8. Kōkyō Murakami, "Changes in Japanese Urban Funeral Customs during the Twentieth Century," *JJRS* 27, nos. 3/4 (Fall 2000): 335–352; 344.

9. Copious publications exemplify this approach to portraits, including Minamoto Toyomune, "Jingoji zō Takanobu hitsu no gazō ni tsuite no gi," *Yamato bunka* 13 (1954): 10–19; Kuroita Katsumi, "Ashikaga Takauji no gazō ni tsuite," *Shigaku zasshi* 31, no. 1 (1920): 82–83; Tani Nobukazu, "Muromachi jidai ni okeru shōzōga no seisaku katei," *Kokka* 475 (May 1937): 129–133, and 476 (June 1937): 159–162; Ogino Minahiko, "Moriyakebon den Ashikaga Takaujizō no kenkyū," *Kokka* 906 (September 1969): 7–22, and (October 1969): 7–13; Fujimoto Masayuki, "Moriyakebon busō kibazō gazō sairon," *Shigaku zasshi* 53, no. 4 (1984): 25–40; Shimosaka Mamoru, "Moriyakebon kiba mushazō no zōshu ni tsuite," *Gakusō* 4 (1982): 43–59; Katō Hideyuki, "Buke shōzōga no shin no zōshu kakutei e no shomondai," *Bijutsu kenkyū* 345 (November 1989), pp. 159–173, and 346 (March 1990): 1–15; Kuroda Hideo, *Shōzōga o yomu* (Tokyo: Kadokawa Shoten, 1998).

10. The compulsion to establish objects as art is discussed in a Western context by Freedberg in *Power of Images*. Contact with the West in the Meiji period undoubtedly influenced Japan to follow a similar trend.

11. See Murai Yasuhiko, "Josei shōzōga to sono jidai," *Yamato bunka* 56 (1972): 1–11; Takeda Tsuneo, "Kinsei shoki josei shōzōga ni kansuru ikkōsai," *Yamato bunka* 56 (1972): 12–22; Kuroda Hideo, "Shōzōga to shite no Godaigo tennō," in *Ō no shintai, ō no shōzō* (Tokyo: Heibonsha, 1993), pp. 248–265; Andrew Goble, "Vision of an Emperor," in *The Origins of Japan's Medieval World: Courtiers, Clerics, Warriors, and Peasants in the Fourteenth Century*, ed. Jeffrey P. Mass (Stanford, CA: Stanford University Press, 1997), pp. 113–137.

12. T. Griffith Foulk, Elizabeth E. Horton, and Robert H. Sharf, "The Meaning and Function of Ch'an and Zen Portraiture," paper presented at the panel "Likeness and Lineage: Religious Portraiture in Asia," New York City, February 17, 1990; also T. Griffith Foulk and Robert H. Sharf, "On the Ritual Use of Ch'an Portraiture in Medieval China," *Cahiers d'Extrême-Asie* 7 (1993): 149–219. For other essays that examine the way we look at Japanese Buddhist images and the function of icons in religious

life, see Mimi Yiengpruksawa, "In My Image: The Ichiji Kinrin Statue at Chūsonji," *Monumenta Nipponica* 46, no. 3 (Autumn 1991): 329–347; Bernard Faure, "The Buddhist Icon and the Modern Gaze," *Critical Inquiry* 24, no. 3 (Spring 1998): 768–813; Robert H. Sharf and Elizabeth Horton Sharf, eds., *Living Images: Japanese Buddhist Icons in Context* (Stanford, CA: Stanford University Press, 2001).

13. Yonekura Michio's research on portraits and their ritual uses, in *Minamoto Yoritomo zō: Chinmoku no shōzōga* (Tokyo: Heibonsha, 1995), greatly influenced my approach to this topic.

14. Foulk and Sharf cite an early portrait of a monk, Dao-an (312/314–385) that was used as the focus for worship prior to his death; "On the Ritual Use of Ch'an Portraiture in China," p. 163.

15. For examples of portraits used as the focus of worship prior to death, see ibid.

16. W. Chie Ishibashi, "Introduction," in Hisashi Mōri, *Japanese Portrait Sculpture*, trans. and ed. W. Chie Ishibashi (Tokyo, New York, San Francisco: Kodansha International Ltd. and Shibundo, 1977), p. 13.

17. Ebrey gives the example of Emperor Taizu placing portraits of his parents in a Buddhist temple in 968 and having Buddhist monks and nuns pray for their souls; Patricia Buckley Ebrey, "Portrait Sculptures in Imperial Ancestral Rites in Song China," *T'oung Pao* 83, nos. 1–3 (1997): 42–92; 46.

18. Foulk and Sharf, "On the Ritual Use of Ch'an Portraiture in China," p. 164.

19. For example, a number of small figurines (*dogū*) uncovered in pits at tomb sites dating from the late Jōmon period (ca. 1500–ca. 400 BCE), such as those found at Sugisawa in Yamagata Prefecture, are now believed to be funerary objects made to resemble the tomb's occupant. Objects found in pits are problematic, however, because human remains disintegrate quickly in Japan's acidic soil, making it difficult to determine whether the pit was for storage or burial; Sakai Todayoshi and Esaka Teruhisa, "Yamagata-ken Akumi-gun Warabioka-mura Sugisawa hakken no daitō C_2-shiki no dogū no shutsudo jōtai ni tsuite," *Kōkogaku zasshi* 39, nos. 3–4 (1954). Painted images presumed to be of tomb occupants have also been discovered in early Japanese contexts. Groups of individuals, probably the deceased along with attendants at the funeral, were found painted on the interior walls of a number of stone-chambered tombs, following continental models. See, for example, Richard Pearson's discussion of the painted images in the Takamatsu Tomb (late 7th c.) in *Ancient Japan* (New York: George Braziller/Sackler Gallery, 1992), p. 272. Because of the late date of these images, it is difficult to be certain that they were produced without Buddhist influence.

20. The image was originally kept in the Sannō'in on Mount Hiei, where Enchin had lived. It was then moved to the Kara'in at Onjōji in Shiga Prefecture.

21. *Jimon denki horoku* 8 (*Tōbōki*), in *Dai Nihon shiryō*, vol. 1, pt. 1, p. 867. The text is also reproduced in part in Suito, *Chūsei no sōsō*, p. 151.

22. Hisashi Mōri, *Japanese Portrait Sculpture*, p. 26.

23. Foulk and Sharf, "On the Ritual Use of Ch'an Portraiture in China," pp. 163–169. Earlier portrait sculptures exist, such as the dry-lacquer image of Ganjin dated ca. 763, but the Enshin statue is one of the earliest known to contain bones of the deceased.

24. For an account of Go-Ichijō's funeral, see *Eiga monogatari*, chap. 30, pp. 387–395, in *Nihon koten bungaku taikei*, vol. 76, ed. Matsumura Hiroji and Yamanaka Yutaka (Tokyo: Iwanami Shoten, 1965).

25. *Eiga monogatari*, chap. 40, pp. 537–547; 544.

26. Yonekura, *Minamoto no Yoritomo zō*, p. 22, quotes Akamatsu Toshihide's section on "nise-e" in "Kamakura bunka," *Kōza Nihon rekishi*, vol. 5 (*chūsei* 1) (Tokyo: Iwanami Shoten, 1967). Small wooden images made in human forms (*hitogata*), excavated from the moats of the ancient Nara capital, are often offered as one of the proofs that human images were used for casting spells on the humans they represented.

27. Akamatsu Toshihide, however, believes that members of the court below the middle ranks adopted the practice of having portraits painted from life before the imperials. But he is unclear about when this took place; Yonekura, *Minamoto no Yoritomo zō*, p. 22.

28. This text was written by courtier Fujiwara no Kanetsune and covered 1222 to 1251. The original is kept at the Yōmei Bunko.

29. Discussed in Yonekura, *Minamoto no Yoritomo zō*, p. 15. The condition of the painting seemed to suggest that the image was several centuries old when discovered. Hosshōji was built by Tadahira and served as the Fujiwara clan temple, making it likely that the painting, if indeed it was he, had been stored there for his memorial rituals. It could also be an image of another member of the Fujiwara family. See also Suitō, *Chūsei no sōsō*, p. 153.

30. Jan Stuart and Evelyn S. Rawski, *Worshiping the Ancestors: Chinese Commemorative Portraits* (Stanford, CA: Stanford University Press, 2001), p. 94. Foulk and Sharf, in their discussion of portraits of Chan abbots, do not mention the term specifically but seem to refer to it in their statement that "portraits were indeed produced just prior to, or, if need be, soon after an abbot's death"; "On the Ritual Use of Ch'an Portraiture in China," p. 186.

31. Earlier, in the Tang dynasty, it was more common to make the portrait after death. Not until the Song dynasty were portraits commonly painted while the abbot was alive; Foulk and Sharf, "On the Ritual Use of Ch'an Portraiture in Medieval China," p. 186.

32. The patriarch hall is often called an image hall or a portrait hall (*eidō*; also *mieidō*) in Japan. It is a special room or building within the temple complex where the portrait of the founder of the temple is enshrined. Some temples have large halls that are used to enshrine a number of portraits of venerable or important abbots connected with the temple.

33. Foulk and Sharf, "On the Ritual Use of Ch'an Portraiture in China," p. 186.

34. Another related but later Chinese term, *dashou xiang*, "image of great longevity," has been defined very differently. *Dashou xiang* refers to an image of a gravely ill individual, made by a painter called into the sickroom for that purpose. The custom was recorded in the early twentieth century, but probably dates at least from the Ming dynasty. It has been suggested that such portraits might have been made as talismans to help the subject reach old age or, at the very least, as images that had special power to keep the deceased long in the memory of the survivors. As this term was used, its

meaning seems to approximate *yixiang*, an image made just prior to death; Stuart and Rawski, *Worshiping the Ancestors*, p. 94.

35. Kobayashi Takeshi, "Saidaiji Eisonzō ni tsuite," *Bukkyō geijutsu* 28 (1956): 30–37; 37.

36. See, for example, the references to Ashikaga Yoshimasa's funeral portrait in *Inryōken nichiroku* (Entoku 2.1.11), vol. 136 in *Dai Nihon bukkyō zenshū* (1976), p. 1652.

37. This theory was first proposed by Akamatsu Toshihide, "Ashikaga shi no shōzō ni tsuite," *Bijutsu kenkyū* 152 (January 1949): 24–46; 44.

38. Quitman E. Phillips, *The Practices of Painting in Japan 1475–1500* (Stanford, CA: Stanford University Press, 2000), p. 160. Phillips' explanation suggests that the painter was going to make a finished portrait based on sketches he made of preexisting finished portraits.

39. Stuart and Rawski, *Worshiping the Ancestors*, p. 95. Females in China, however, might not with propriety be viewed by outsiders.

40. For further discussion on *gyakushu*, see Quitman E. Phillips, "Narrating the Salvation of the Elite: The Jōfukuji Paintings of the Ten Kings," *Ars Orientalis* 33 (2003): 121–145; 127.

41. Tamamuro cites a late ninth-century *gyakushu ganmon* from *Sugeie monjo*; *Sōshiki bukkyō*, pp. 193–194.

42. Sanjōnishi Sanetaka (1455–1537), *Sanetaka kōki*, 1489.12.23; in Phillips, *Practices of Painting*, pp. 150–151.

43. Phillips, *Practices of Painting*, p. 150.

44. For further details, see Paul Groner, "Icons and Relics in Eison's Religious Activities," in Sharf and Sharf, *Living Images*, pp. 114–150; 142–150.

45. Foulk and Sharf, "On the Ritual Use of Ch'an Portraiture in China," pp. 160–161.

46. See discussion in Audrey Spiro, *Contemplating the Ancients: Aesthetic and Social Issues in Early Chinese Portraiture* (Berkeley and Los Angeles: University of California Press, 1990), p. 22.

47. Phillips, *Practices of Painting*, pp. 152–153.

48. *Nippo jisho* defines *goei* and *mikage* as words for revered painted portraits, with *miei* used for references to *kami* (pronunciations in *katakana*); *Nihon kokogo daijiten*, vol. 4, p. 638.

49. *Moromoriki*, Kōei 4.8.26, vol. 3, p. 168. The three images at the Jizōdō are mentioned frequently in the diary, but it is not clear if they are three separate paintings or one painting of the three family members. It is generally thought that the practice of painting portraits of husbands and wives together or of multiple family members became popular around this time.

50. Itō Yuishin, "*Moromoriki* ni miru chūsei sōsō bukkyō," in *Sōsō bosei kenkyū shūsei*, vol. 5, p. 223.

51. Phillips, *Practices of Painting*, pp. 149–150.

52. Foulk and Sharf, "On the Ritual Use of Ch'an Portraiture in China," p. 175.

53. A portrait was dedicated on Morosuke's final (seventh) memorial service on Kōei 4 (1345) 3.25 (*Moromoriki*, vol. 3, p. 38) by his wife Kenshin; the portrait is listed

in Kenshin's *fujumon* (a letter documenting her offerings on that day), but the text does not say that a portrait was displayed during the final service. No mention is made of a portrait being displayed for a memorial service until one year after his death, on Jōwa 2 (1346) 2.6 (*Moromoriki*, vol. 3, p. 274). Because the section on Morosuke's funeral is missing, we do not know if a portrait was commissioned for his funeral, or who ordered it. When Kenshin herself died six months later, no portrait was made for her funeral. Presumably a previously painted image was used, because we know that her portrait was venerated along with Morosuke's at later monthly memorials.

54. The image was ordered on Chōkyō 3.4.18 (p. 1479), but the sketch for the portrait was not produced for approval until 5.4 (p. 1490), and the portrait was completed on 5.24 (p. 1506). This portrait of Yoshihisa on horseback was presumably intended for a later memorial service, perhaps for his 100th-day memorial on 7.7; *Inryōken nichiroku*, vol. 135 in *Dai Nihon bukkyō zenshū* (1976).

55. *Inryōken nichiroku*, Entoku 2.1.11, vol. 136 in *Dai Nihon bukkyō zenshū* (1976), p. 1652.

56. The three portraits of Yoshimitsu are discussed by Akamatsu Toshihide in "Ashikaga no shōzō ni tsuite," *Bijutsu kenkyū* 153 (1949): 24–45; 32.

57. A notation on the end of the scroll says the poems were written by Asukai Masachika (Eiga), but it is also possible that the writer was Masachika's grandfather, Asukai Masayori (Sōga), who was Yoshimitsu's poetry teacher; *Nihonshi daijiten*, vol. 1, p. 138.

58. This may be the same Genchū, head abbot of Rokuon'in, who lit Yoshimochi's pyre when he died in 1428; see Chapter 2.

59. Rokuonji owns the first two portraits and Shōkokuji the third. Two of the images are reproduced in *Dai Nihon shiryō* 7.10, pp. 148–149; all three images are illustrated in *Nihonshi daijiten*, vol. 1, p. 137.

60. The memorial tablet was displayed at the funeral at the same points in the service as the portrait.

61. *Inryōken nichiroku* refers to Yoshimasa's portrait as *shōkō gohottai*, which translates as the "councilor's portrait as a Buddhist priest"; Entoku 2.1.11, vol. 136 in *Dai Nihon bukkyō zenshū* (1976), p. 1653. Presumably this term is used because Yoshimasa had entered Buddhist orders as a Zen priest in 1485.

62. *Inryōken nichiroku*, Entoku 2.1.7, 2.1.11, and 2.1.17, vol. 136 in *Dai Nihon bukkyō zenshū* (1976), pp. 1648–1661.

63. The time between death and cremation was sixteen days for Yoshimasa. For Ashikaga Yoshihisa, there were thirteen days between the day he died (3.26) and the day of his funeral (4.9).

64. In the mid-fourteenth century Ashikaga Takauji was fighting to establish order in Kyoto and hegemony throughout the country.

65. Although the Nakahara were buried at a Tendai temple, it is thought that the family was more strongly affiliated with the Pure Land Ji sect; Itō Yuishin, "Moromoriki ni miru chūsei sōsō bukkyō," p. 221.

66. For Yoshimochi's funeral, see *Kennaiki*, Shōchō 1.1.23, vol. 14, pp. 49–50.

67. My comments on Chinese practices in this section are based on the discus-

sion of Chan funeral rites in the 12th-c. *Chanyuan qinggui*, in Foulk and Sharf, "On the Ritual Use of Ch'an Portraiture," p. 191; see also Yifa, *The Origins of Buddhist Monastic Codes in China: An Annotated Translation and Study of the Chanyuan qinggui*. A Kuroda Institute Book (Honolulu: University of Hawai'i Press, 2002), pp. 217–219.

68. Yukihiro (active 1406–1434) was an official painter at the imperial court and a member of the Fujiwara family. He took the name Tosa after he was named governor of Tosa Province. He was one of six listed as painters of Seiryōji's *Yūzū nenbutsu engi* (1414).

69. Although not mentioned in this text, in Japan folding screens decorated with flowers and birds on gold ground (*kinpeki-ga*) were commonly used for funerals. For example, a pair of golden screens decorated with bamboo were sent to Tōjiin on 4.8, the day before Ashikaga Yoshihisa's funeral; *Inryōken nichiroku*, Chōkyō 3.4.8, in vol. 135 in *Dai Nihon bukkyō zenshū* (1976), p. 1469. See also my Chapter 3.

70. Foulk and Sharf translate the phrase as "casket screen"; "On the Ritual Use of Ch'an Portraiture," p. 191. Yifa translates it as "curtains"; *Origins of Buddhist Monastic Codes in China*, p. 217.

71. In China the portrait was carried on a litter to the cremation or interment site and again installed on an altar.

72. For burials, the lid was usually nailed on, but for cremations it was left unfastened so that faggots could be placed inside at the cremation site.

73. Foulk and Sharf, "On the Ritual Use of Ch'an Portraiture," p. 192.

74. In China they are generally called "spirit tablets" or "soul tablets" (*shenwei; lingpai*) and sometimes "ancestral tablets" (*weipai*).

75. Nakamura, *Bukkyōgo daijiten*, vol. 1, p. 32.

76. Foulk and Sharf, "On the Ritual Use of Ch'an Portraiture," p. 193.

77. An early mention of an *ihai* in Japan appears in reference to Ashikaga Takauji's death in *Inryōken nichiroku*, Enbun 3 (1358) 6.29, in *Dai Nihon shiryō*, vol. 6, pt. 21, p. 923.

78. In early China, after the body was encoffined and until burial, a strip of cloth placed near the coffin represented the deceased. Wailing and offerings thereafter took place before the soul cloth. See Patricia Buckley Ebrey, trans., *Chu Hsi's Family Rituals: A Twelfth-Century Chinese Manual for the Performance of Cappings, Weddings, Funerals, and Ancestral Rites* (Princeton, NJ: Princeton University Press, 1991), p. xxiii.

79. Foulk and Sharf, "On the Ritual Use of Ch'an Portraiture," p. 193.

80. Ibid., p. 195. It is not clear whether the authors are discussing an annual memorial or one immediately following death. No portrait is noted for funerals of ordinary monks in the *Chanyuan qinggui*'s section on "The Monk's Funeral"; Yifa, *Origins of Buddhist Monastic Codes in China*, pp. 206–209.

81. The handscroll was not produced immediately after Hōnen's death but compiled in the early decades of the fourteenth century to celebrate Hōnen's 100th-year death anniversary.

82. Nison'in is located in Saga in western Kyoto. It was the temple from which Hōnen spread his *nenbutsu* practice, and also the site of his grave.

83. *Moromoriki*, Kōei 4.3.25, vol. 3, p. 38.

84. Ibid., Jōwa 2.2.6, vol. 3, p. 274.

85. Although this date is two years after Morosuke died, the Japanese count his death as the first year; this was therefore his third-year anniversary; ibid., Jōwa 3.2.5, vol. 4, p. 25.

86. Ibid., Kōei 4.8.26, vol. 3, p. 168.

87. Herman Ooms, "A Structural Analysis of Japanese Ancestral Rites and Beliefs," in *Ancestors*, ed. William Newel (The Hague: Mouton, 1976), p. 67. But the way in which Ooms and others have interpreted ideas of the spirit in modern Japan is colored by the results of the conscious separation of "Shinto" and "Buddhist" ideas (*shinbutsu bunri*) that took place in the late nineteenth century.

88. *Moromoriki*, Jōwa 1.10.23, vol. 3, p. 230.

89. Ibid., Jōwa 3.2.5, vol. 4, p. 25.

90. Ibid., Jōwa 3.2.6, vol. 4, p. 34 and Jōwa 3.2.23, p. 45. It is not certain whether the offerings were made to the images that had been dedicated on 2.5. More likely there were several sets of his parent's portraits, one for each temple where offerings were made to their spirits.

91. Takauji's remains were divided among three temples—the Tadain in Ōtsu, Kōfukuji in Tanba, and Kōyasan's An'yōin. On 1359.4.25, one day after the death memorial, a mortuary tablet (*ihai*) was also dedicated; *Dai Nihon shiryō*, vol. 6, pt. 22, pp. 513–514.

92. For recent scholarship on Takauji's portraits, see Miyajima Shinichi, *Shōzōga no shisen: Minamoto no Yoritomozō kara ukiyoe made* (Tokyo: Yoshikawa Kōbunkan, 1996), pp. 29–35; Kuroda Hideo, "Kiba mushazō no zōshu: Shōzōga to *Taiheiki*," in *Shōzōga o yomu*, ed. Kuroda Hideo et al. (Tokyo: Kadokawa Shoten, 1998), pp. 24–52.

93. See Martin Collcutt, "Musō Soseki," in *The Origins of Japan's Medieval World: Courtiers, Clerics, Warriors, and Peasants in the Fourteenth Century*, ed. Jeffrey P. Mass (Stanford, CA: Stanford University Press, 1997), pp. 281–282; Thomas Donald Conlan, *State of War: The Violent Order of Fourteenth-Century Japan* (Ann Arbor, MI: Center for Japanese Studies/The University of Michigan, 2003), pp. 187–188.

94. *Inryōken nichiryoku*, Entoku 2.1.13 and 18, vol. 136, pp. 1656–1661. On 1.13, the corpse was encoffined and moved to Tōjiin.

95. Ibid., Entoku 2.1.11, vol. 136, p. 1652.

96. Ibid., Entoku 2.1.23, vol. 136, p. 1667.

97. Ibid., Entoku 2.2.5, vol. 136, p. 1677 and 2.24, p. 1697.

98. *Dai Nihon shiryō*, vol. 7, pt. 10, p. 148.

99. Ibid., pp. 148ff.

100. In *Kokushi taikei*, ed. Kuroita Katsumi (Tokyo: Yoshikawa Kōbunkan, 1966), vol. 24 (*Ryōshūkai: Kōhen*), pp. 955–973.

101. According to an inscription dated Bunsei 13 (1830) 3.6, *Sōhōmitsu* is believed to be a copy of a guide to Shingon funerals written six or seven hundred years earlier (early 12th or 13th c.). Reproduced in *Nihon kyōiku bunko*, vol. 10 (*shūkyō*), ed. Kurokawa Mamichi (Tokyo: Dōbunkan, 1911), pp. 683–707.

102. *Kanmon gyoki*, Ōei 23.11.24, p. 52.

103. Gorai Shigeru, *Sō to kuyō* (Osaka: Tōhō Shuppan, 1992), pp. 603–610.

104. Some sources mention that sugar or honey was added to the hot water.

105. Among them, Takauji's funeral in 1358, and a similar sequence of actions for the funeral of the second Ashikaga shogun, Yoshiakira, who died on 1367.12.7. In *Dai Nihon shiryō*, vol. 6, pt. 28, pp. 560–561; also Suitō, *Chūsei no sōsō*, p. 81.

106. Those destined for the Pure Land were received there at the moment of their deaths, while those appearing before the kings were doomed to yet another rebirth.

107. Freedberg, *Power of Images*, pp. 431, 438.

108. See, for example, Dietrich Seckel, "The Rise of Portraiture in Chinese Art," *Artibus Asiae* 53, nos. 1–2 (1993), pp. 7–26; Jan Stuart, "Calling Back the Ancestor's Shadow: Chinese Ritual and Commemorative Portraits," *Oriental Art* 43, no. 3 (Autumn 1997), pp. 8–17; Richard Vinograd, *Boundaries of the Self: Chinese Portraits, 1600–1900* (Cambridge: Cambridge University Press, 1992).

109. This quality was thought to be particularly evident in portraits by Zhou Fang (ca. 730–ca. 800).

110. For a more detailed conspectus of Chinese portraiture, see Stuart and Rawski, *Worshiping the Ancestors*, pp. 75–91.

111. Quoted from *Er Cheng ji* (Collected works of the two Cheng brothers, Cheng Hao [1032–1085] and Cheng Yi [1033–1107]), cited in Stuart and Rawski, *Worshiping the Ancestors*, p. 80.

112. Phillips, *Practices of Painting in Japan*, pp. 156–159. Phillips notes that even when a great number of sketches (*kamigata*) were ordered, the verisimilitude of the finished portrait still did not seem enhanced.

113. Yoshikazu was technically the fifth shogun, but he ruled for only two years (1423–1425) before he died, so apparently was deemed of little consequence to the lineage.

114. See Akamatsu Toshihide, "Ashikaga shi no shōzō ni tsuite," p. 28.

LIST OF JAPANESE WORDS

agedatami 上げ畳
ajirogoshi 網代輿
ajiroguruma 網代車
aka 閼伽
Akamatsu Masanori 赤松政則
Aki Nyūdō (Engen) 安芸入道（円源）
ako 下火
ako butsuji 下火仏事
aku/aku no ya 幄・幄の屋
Amida 阿弥陀
Amida kyō 阿弥陀経
Amida no daiju 阿弥陀の大呪
Amida Nyorai 阿弥陀如来
Amida nyorai myōgō 阿弥陀如来名号
Amida sanzon 阿弥陀三尊
andon 行灯
An'yōin 安養院
aosaburai/aozamurai 青侍
aragaki 荒垣
aramitama 荒御魂
ashi/i 葦
ashibiki no miei 足曳御影
Ashikaga Mochiuji 足利持氏
Ashikaga Motouji 足利基氏
Ashikaga Tadayoshi 足利直義
Ashikaga Takauji 足利尊氏
Ashikaga Yoshiakira 足利義詮
Ashikaga Yoshiharu 足利義晴
Ashikaga Yoshihisa 足利義尚

Ashikaga Yoshikatsu 足利義勝
Ashikaga Yoshikazu 足利義量
Ashikaga Yoshimasa 足利義政
Ashikaga Yoshimitsu 足利義満
Ashikaga Yoshimochi 足利義持
Ashikaga Yoshinori 足利義教
ashuradō 阿修羅道
Asukai Masachika (Eiga) 飛鳥井雅親（栄雅）
Asukai Masayori (Sōga) 飛鳥井雅縁（宋雅）
aya 綾
ban 幡
ban soku 幡足
betsuji nenbutsu 別時念仏
bettō 別当
bikuni 比丘尼
bodaiji 菩提寺
Bodaimon 菩提門
Boki ekotoba 慕帰絵詞
bon 盆
Bonmō kyō 盆網經
Bonmō no jūjū 梵網の十重
bukku/buku 佛供
Bunan (era) 文安
Bunei (era) 文永
Bunmei (era) 文明
Bunsei (era) 文政
Busshuji 佛種寺

butsudan 佛壇
butsuden 佛殿
butsugan sotoba 佛龕卒塔婆
butsuji 佛事
byōbu 屏風
byōdō 廟堂
cha 茶
chakufuku no gi 着服の儀
Chanyuan qinggui 禪苑清規
chasan 茶盞
chawan 茶碗
chigo 稚児
chikushōdō 畜生道
chinkon-sai 鎮魂祭
chinsō/chinzō 頂相
Chion'in 知恩院
chishiki 知識
Chishō Daishi 智証大師
chō 丁・町
chōchin 提灯
Chōgen 長元
Chōhakuji 長伯寺
Chōkōji monjo 長香寺文書
Chōkyō (era) 長享
chōmoku 鳥目
chōrō 長老
Chōshūki 長秋記
chūin/chūu 中陰・中有
chūin no gi 中陰の儀
dabi 荼毘
dabi no gi 荼毘の儀
dai geki 大外記
Daihiju 大悲呪
Daikakuji monjo 大覚寺文書
Daikōmyōji 大光明寺
Dai muryōju kyō 大無量壽經
Dainichi 大日
danshi 檀紙
darani 陀羅尼
dashou xiang 大壽像
Denpō-e 伝法絵
Denryaku 殿暦
dōfuku 道服
dogū 土偶

dōjō 道場
dosha kaji 土砂加持
dōshi 導師
dosō 土葬
eboshi 烏帽子
egōro/ekōro 柄香炉
ei 影
eidō 影堂
Eiga monogatari 栄華物語
Eison 叡尊
eizō (C. yingxiang) 影像
ekō 廻向
Enbun (era) 延文
Enchin 円珍
Engaku kyō 圓覺經
Engi (era) 延喜
Enkyō (era) 延慶
Enmyōin Nitchō 円明院日澄
Enmyōji 円明寺
Enryakuji 延暦寺
Enshōbō 円勝房
Entairyaku 園太暦
Entoku (era) 延徳
eribone sen 彫骨扇
eshi 繪師
Fudō Myōō 不動明王
Fudono/Fumidono 文殿
Fugen Bosatsu 普賢菩薩
Fugenkan gyō 普賢觀經
fugin 諷経
Fuhenkōmyō shō jōshijō nyoihōin shinmunōshō daimyōō daizuigu darani kyō 普遍光明清淨熾盛如意寶印心無能勝大明王大随求陀羅尼經
Fujiwara no Kanetsune 藤原兼経
Fujiwara no Kishi 藤原嬉子
Fujiwara no Kiyohira 藤原清衡
Fujiwara no Michinaga 藤原道長
Fujiwara no Michinori (Shinzei) 藤原通憲 (信西)
Fujiwara no Michitaka 藤原道隆
Fujiwara no Nagaie 藤原長家
Fujiwara no Neishi (Kōgimonin) 藤原寧子 (広義門院)

Fujiwara no Sanehira　藤原実衡
Fujiwara no Sanemune　藤原実宗
Fujiwara no Saneyasu　藤原実泰
Fujiwara no Seishi　藤原娍子
Fujiwara no Shōshi (Taikenmon'in)　藤原璋子(待賢門院)
Fujiwara no Shunzei　藤原俊成
Fujiwara no Sōshi　藤原宗子
Fujiwara no Tadahira　藤原忠平
Fujiwara no Tadamichi　藤原忠通
Fujiwara no Teika　藤原定家
Fujiwara no Teishi　藤原定子
Fujiwara no Yoshimichi　藤原良通
Fujiwara-shi no jo　藤原氏女
fūjumon　諷誦文
Funaoka Nishino　船岡西野
fuse　布施
fuse chūmon　布施注文
fushikane　フシカ子 (付子鉄)
Fushimi　伏見
Fushiminomiya Sadafusa (prince)　伏見の宮貞成新王
futananoka　二七日
gakidō　餓鬼道
gakki　月忌
Gaki zōshi　餓鬼草紙
Gakumyō　學妙
gan　龕
Ganjin (C. Jianzhen)　鑑真
geki　外記
Genchū　玄中
Genchū Shūgaku　厳中周㗉
Genji monogatari　源氏物語
Genryū Shūkō　彦竜周興
Gessen　月泉
Gidarinji　祇陀林寺
Gien　義円
Gion　祇園
Go-Daigo (emperor)　後醍醐天皇
Go-Fushimi (emperor)　後伏見天皇
go gusoku　五具足
Go-Hanazono (emperor)　後花園天皇
Go-Ichijō (emperor)　後一条天皇
Gojō　五条

gokai　五戒
gokuraku　極楽
Gokurakuin　極楽院
goma　護摩
goma kechigan　護摩結願
gon no daisōzu　権の大僧都
Gon no risshi Ryūkan　権の律師隆寛
gorintō　五輪塔
Goryō　御霊
goryō　御霊
goshiki　五色
goshiki ban　五色幡
Go-Shirakawa (emperor)　後白河天皇
gosho no ma　御所間
Go-Suzaku (emperor)　後朱雀天皇
Go-Tsuchimikado (emperor)　後土御門天皇
Gozen Onkata　御前御方
gozensō　御前僧
Gubutsubō　求仏房
Gukanki　愚管記
gyakushu　逆修
gyōdō　行道
gyōja　行者
Gyokuyō　玉葉
gyōshō/kōshō　行障
hachi/hatsu　鉢
hakama　袴
haka mairi　墓参り
hakamori hōshi　墓守法師
hakui　白衣
Hakusōrei　薄葬令
hanakazura　花かずら
Hanjūin　般舟院
hannya　般若
Hannya shingyō　般若心經
Han shu　漢書
harai　払い
Haruhito (prince)　治仁親王
hata　旗
hatsu　鉢
Hatsukadō　二十日堂
hattō　法堂
Heihanki/Hyōhanki　兵範記

Heike monogatari 平家物語
heiken 平絹
heizei no gi 平生の儀
hibutsu 秘仏
Hieizan 比叡山
higan 彼岸
Higashiyama 東山
Higodono 肥後殿
Higuchidera 樋口寺
Higuchi no kōji 樋口小路
hijiri 聖
hiki 疋
hikiire 引入
hikiōi 引覆
Hime Goryō 姫御料
hinin 非人
hinko 秉炬
hinko butsuji 秉炬仏事
Hino-dono 日野殿
hinoki 檜
hi no koshi 火の輿
Hino Shigeko 日野重子
Hino Shigemitsu 日野重光
Hino Tomiko 日野富子
hinsō 殯喪
hiōgi 檜扇
hiraginu 平絹
Hirano Shrine 平野神社
hirobuta 広蓋
hisashi 庇・廂
hitatare 直垂
hitogata 人形
hiya 火屋
hōei 法会
hōgo 法語
hōgu 法具
Hōin Seikaku 法印聖覚
Hōjiji 宝持寺
hōjō 方丈
hokai 外居・行器
hokaku 冒額
Hoke kyō 法華経
Hokke mandala 法華曼荼羅
Hōkōinji 法光院寺

Hōkongō-in 法金剛院
Hōkyōin darani 寶篋印多羅尼
hōkyōintō 法篋印塔
hōmyō 法名
Hōnen 法然
Hōnen shōnin e-den 法然上人絵伝
Hōnen shōnin gyōjo ezu 法然上人行状絵図
hon ihai 本位牌
honji butsu 本地仏
Honkokuji 本圀寺
Honryūji 本立寺
honzon 本尊
Hōrenbō Shinkū 法蓮房信空
Horikawa (emperor) 堀川天皇
Horikawadono 堀川殿
Hōryūji 法隆寺
hoshō 歩障
hosshin 發心
Hosshinmon 發心門
Hosshōji 法性寺
Hou Han shu 後漢書
hōyō 法要・法用
Huineng 慧能
Hyōbu Daibu Nyūdō (Ryōen) 兵部大部入道良円
Hyōbushō 兵部省
ichiji nenbutsu 一時念仏
Ichijō (emperor) 一条天皇
iei 遺影
Iekuni 家國
Ien 以遠
igan 移龕
igan butsuji 移龕佛事
ihai (C. *weipai*) 位牌
ikkai ki 一回忌
Ikkō 一向
Ikkō-ha 一向派
Ikkō-shū 一向宗
imina 諱
ingō 院號
Inpumonin (Ryōshi) 殷富門院（亮子）
Inryōken 蔭涼軒

List of Japanese Words

Inryōken nichiroku 蔭涼軒日録
Ippen 一遍
isshūki 一周忌
itajiki 板敷
itoge no kuruma 糸毛車
itsunanoka 五七日
Izanagi 伊邪那岐・伊弉諾
Izanami 伊邪那美・伊弉冉
izō (C. *yixiang*) 遺像
Izu 伊豆
Izumi no Zenji Dōkyo 和泉前司道經
Ji (sect) 時宗
Jibutsudō 持仏堂
Jien (Jichin) 慈円（慈鎮）
jigokudō 地獄道
Jikka 竺華
Jikuun 竺雲
Jimon denki horoku 寺門伝記補録
Jingihaku sōmoki 神祇伯葬喪記
jinshichinichi 尽七日
jisha 侍者
Jishōindono 慈照院殿
Jishōindono ryōan sōbo 慈照院殿諒闇總簿
Jitō (empress) 持統天皇
Jizō 地蔵
Jizō Bosatsu 地蔵菩薩
Jizōdō 地蔵堂
jō 丈
jōbutsu 成仏
Jōdoin 浄土院
Jōdo sanbukyō 浄土三部經
jōe 浄衣
Jōwa (era) 貞和
jūbutsu 十仏
jukai 受戒
jūō 十王
jūrokkan 十六観
jūroku daikoku 十六大国
jūroku rakan 十六羅漢
jūroku zenjin 十六善神
Juryō-bon 壽量品
jūsan butsu 十三仏
Jūshinbō 住真房

juzō (C. *shouxiang*) 寿像
kaba/gama 蒲
kabuse 加布施
kagochōchin 籠提灯
Kagutsuchi no kami 迦具土神
Kaiketsu no nikyō 開結二經
kaimyō 戒名
kaji 加持
kake obi 掛帯
kakochō 過去帳
Kakunyo 覚如
kamadogami 竈神
kami 神
kamidana 神棚
kamigata 紙形
kan 貫
kanjō ban 灌頂幡
kankin 看經
kanmon 貫文
Kanmon gyoki 看聞御記
Kanmon nikki 看聞日記
Kannon 観音
Kannon senbō 観音懺法
Kano Masanobu 狩野正信
kanrei/kanryō 管領
Kanshō (era) 寛正
karaginu 唐衣
kariginu 狩衣
Karyaku (era) 嘉暦
kasatōba 笠塔婆
kasha kōro 火舎香炉
kashin 掛真
kashin butsuji 掛真仏事
katabira 帷子・帷
katashiro (C. *xingshi*) 形代
kebyō 華瓶
kegare 穢
Kegon kyō 華厳經
kei (C. *qing*) 磬
Keibutsubō 經佛房
Kenchō (era) 建長
Kennaiki/Kendaiki 建内記
Kenpō (era) 建保
Kenshin 顯心

Kenshōin Naifu Madenokōji Tokifusa 建聖院内府万里小路時房
kenyakusha 刀役者
kesa 袈裟
Ketsubon kyō 血盆經
ketsugan/kechigan 結願
Kichiji ryakki 吉事略紀
Kichiji shidai 吉事次第
kichō 几帳
kichū 忌中
kigan 起龕
kigan butsuji 起龕仏事
kijitsu 忌日
Kikei Shinzui 季瓊真蘂
kikotsu 起骨
kinbyōbu 金屏風
kinjin 金人
Kinkakuji 金閣寺
kinpan 錦幡
kinpeki-ga 金碧画
kinsu 磬子
kinugasa 衣笠・絹傘・華蓋
kirikake 切掛け
Kisen Shūshō 亀泉集証
kishoya 貴所屋
kitamakura 北枕
Kitano 北野
Kitano Tenjin engi 北野天神縁起
Kiyomizudera 清水寺
Kōdaiji 高台寺
Kōei (era) 康永
Kōfukiji (in Tanba) 光福寺
Kofun (era) 古墳
kofun 古墳
Kōgimonin 広義門院
koginu 小衣
kōgō 皇后
Kōgon (emperor) 光厳天皇
kohon 古本
Kōichibō 行一房
Kōin 公胤
Kojiki 古事記
komo 薦・菰
komorini 籠尼

komorisō 籠僧
Kōmyō (emperor) 光明天皇
Kōmyō shingon 光明眞言
Kongō Dainichi Nyorai 金剛大日如来
Kongōin 金剛院
Konjikidō 金色堂
kō no koshi 香の輿
kōraiberi 高麗縁
kōro 香炉
koshi 輿
kōsō den-e 高僧伝絵
kotsu butsuji 骨佛事
Kōyasan 高野山
Ku-amidabutsu 九阿弥陀仏
Kubota Muneyasu 窪田統泰
Kudoku'in 功徳院
kuge 公家
kuginuki 釘貫
Kūichibō 空一房
Kujō Kanezane 九条兼実
Kūkai 空海
Kunikane 國兼
kuro fujō 黒不浄
kuroi kageri 黒い翳り
kurozome 黒染
kuruma 車
kushimitama 櫛御霊
kutsu 沓・靴・履
kuyō 供養
kuyōgu 供養具
kyōfuku 凶服
kyō katabira 経帷子
kyōmon 経文
Kyōshoden 校書殿
kyōzukue 経机
Kyūen 九淵
lingpai 靈牌
Li ji 禮記
liqi 禮器
Madenokōji Tokifusa 万里小路時房
maki 薪
makie 蒔絵
makomo 真菰
Makura no sōshi 枕草子

List of Japanese Words

manmaku 幔幕
Man'yōshū 万葉集
Manzan Daizenjōni 萬山大禪定尼
marukan 丸棺
matsu 松
matsu no shita ni tsutsuji no hana 松下躑躅花
meifu 冥府
Meigetsuki 明月記
meikai 冥界
meikō 名香
miei/goei/gyoei 御影
mieidō 御影堂
Miidera 三井寺
mikage 御影
miko 巫女
Minamoto no Morotoki 源師時
Minamoto no Tsuneyori 源経頼
minanoka 三七日
Miroku 弥勒
Misaki 三崎
misu 御簾
mitsugi 密儀
mitsu gusoku 三具足
mizuhiki 水引
mo 裳
mogari no miya 殯の宮
mokuhan 木版
mokuyoku 沐浴
mon 文
Monju 文殊
monoimi fuda 物忌札
monzeki 門跡
Moromoriki 師守記
moshu 喪主
Motokuni 元國
motoyui/motoi 元結
moya 喪屋
munanoka 六七日
Muryōju kyō 無量壽経
Muryōju nyorai konpon darani 無量寿如来根本陀羅尼
mushiro 莚
Musō Soseki 夢想礎石

Mutsu 陸奥
myōgō 名号
Myōhōji 妙法寺
Myōhō renge kyō 妙法蓮華経
nademono 撫物・摩物
nagamushiro 長莚
Nakahara Goryō 中原御料
Nakahara Kenshin 中原顕心
Nakahara Morokane 中原師兼
Nakahara Morokō 中原師香
Nakahara Moromori 中原師守
Nakahara Moroshige 中原師茂
Nakahara Morosuke 中原師右
Nakahara Moroyumi 中原師躬
Nakahara Yūa 中原友阿
Nanbokuchō 南北朝
Nakayama (Fujiwara) Tadachika 中山 (藤原) 忠親
Nanbu Toshiyasu 何部利康
nanto tensō 南都伝奏
nawa 縄
Nehandō 涅槃堂
Nehanmon 涅槃門
Nenbutsu 念仏
nenbutsu zanmai 念仏三昧
nenju 念誦
nenki 年忌
nenkō 拈香
neriginu 練絹
nibiiro 鈍色
nichibutsu 日佛
nichibutsu kuyō 日佛供養
Nichiren 日蓮
Nichiren shōnin chūgasan 日蓮聖人註画讃
Nichiren sōsō gyōretsu ki 日蓮葬送行列記
nigimitama 和御魂
Nihongi 日本紀
Nihon shoki 日本書紀
nijūgozanmai 二十五三昧
ninanoka 二七日
ningendō 人間道
Nippo jisho 日葡辞書

nishi-in 西院
nishi men no hidarikata kore o kiru 西面ノ左方切之
Nison'in 二尊院
Nissei 日政
nogusagoromo 野草衣
Noritoki kyōki 教信卿記
nurigome 塗籠
Nyōbō Onkata 女房御方
nyōhachi 鐃鈸
Nyoirin Kannon 如意輪観音
Nyorai juryō bon 如来壽量品
nyozai no gi 如在の儀
nyūdō 入堂
nyūgan 入龕
nyūgan butsuji 入龕佛事
ōban 椀飯
obi 帯
Ōei (era) 応永
Ōgishi (C. Wang Xizhi) 王羲之
ōguchi hakama 大口袴
ōi 覆い
ōjō 往生
Okanoya kanpakuki 岡屋関白記
okibumi 置文
Okitsuhiko no kami 奥津比子神
Okitsuhime no mikoto 奥津比売命
Okotsu Daishi 御骨大師
Ōmiya nyūdō saki no naidaijin 大宮入道先内大臣
onjiki 飲食
onki 遠忌
onmyōdō 陰陽道
onmyōji/onyōji 陰陽師
Onmyōryō 陰陽寮
ō renge 大蓮華
origami 折紙
oshō 和尚
Ōtani 大谷
otoki 御斎
Ōtsu 大津
raiban 礼盤
raigō 来迎
raigō sanzon 来迎三尊

rakuhatsu 落髪
reiji (sahō) kechigan 例時作法結願
reiku 霊供
rikisha hōshi 力者法師
rinjū shōnen 臨終正念
Risshū soshizō 律宗祖師像
Ritsuryō 律令
ro 炉
Rokkakudō 六角堂
Rokkaku Ōji 六角大路
rokki 六器
rokudō 六道
Rokujō Jishū 六条時宗
rokumotsu 禄物
Rokuon'in 鹿苑院
Rokuonji 鹿苑寺
rōsoku 蝋燭
Ruijū zatsurei 類聚雑例
ryō 両
Ryōchi 了智
Ryōnin 良忍
Ryōsei 良清
Ryōshinbō 了心房
Ryōzen 靈山
Ryōzenden 靈山殿
Ryōzen Hōin Chōkan 靈山法印朝観
Ryūōmaru 龍王丸
ryūzu sao 竜頭竿
sadaijin 左大臣
sagan 鎖龕
sagan butsuji 鎖龕佛事
Saidaiji 西大寺
Saihōji 西芳寺
sajiki 桟敷
Sakeiki 左経記
sakimitama 幸魂
saka hinin 坂非人
samurai eboshi 侍烏帽子
Sanada Nobuyuki 真田信之
Sanbōin 三宝院
Sanetaka kōki 実隆公記
Sanjō Bōmon 三条坊門
Sanjonishi Sanetaka 三条西実隆
sankai ki 三回忌

List of Japanese Words

Sankaiki 山槐記
Sanmai'in 三昧院
Sanmidō 三昧堂
Sanmon 山門
sanzon seiyō 三尊聖容
sasatōba 笹塔婆
seidō 西堂
Seikaku/Shōkaku 聖覚
Seikanbō Genchi 勢観房源智
seirei 聖霊
Seiryōji 清涼
Seishidō 勢室堂
Seishūin Nichien 成就院日円
sekitō 石塔
sekitō kuyō 石塔供養
senbontōba 千本塔婆
Senju darani 千手陀羅尼
Senju Kannon 千手観音
seppō 説法
setsuryū 雪柳
Shaka 釈迦
shaku 尺
shakujo 錫紵
shakujō 錫杖
shami 沙弥
shariden 舎利殿
shari kōshiki 舎利講式
shen qi 神氣
shenwei 神位
shi 四
shi 死
shichinanoka 七七日
shichitai gobutsu 七体御佛
shihokkai 四法界
shihonban 四本幡
Shijō Bōmon 四条坊門
Shijō Takakura 四条高倉
Shijūhachikan e-den 四十八巻絵伝
shikabana 死花花
shikan 紙冠
shikimi 樒・梻
shikkotsu/shūkotsu butsuji 執骨佛事
shikyō 四教
shimon 四問

shin (C. *zhen*) 真
shinbutsu bunri 神仏分離
Shinden 寝殿
shin-ei 真影
shingon 真言
Shinjōin 真乗院
Shinkō ō (king) 秦広王
shinnō 親王
Shinnyoji 眞如寺
Shinran 親鸞
Shinran shōnin e-den 親鸞上人絵伝
Shinrenbō 心蓮房
Shinshōbō Rōken 真証房浪賢
Shirakawa (emperor) 白河天皇
shiraki 白木
shiraki ihai 白木位牌
shiro neriginu 白練絹
shironuno hitatare 白布直垂
shiro tabi 白足袋
shishin 四身
shishōtai 四聖諦
shitennō 四天王
shiu 四有
Shōchiin 正智院
Shōchō (era) 正長
shōgatsu 正月
Shōgeki 少外記
Shōgoin 聖護院
shōgon 荘厳
shōgongū 荘厳具
Shōju 性壽
shōko 鐘鼓
shōkō 焼香
shōkō gohottai 相公御法体
Shōkokuji 相国寺
shōkon 招魂
shokudai 燭台
Shoku Nihongi 続日本紀
Shōmu (emperor) 聖武天皇
shonanoka 初七日
Shonyōhachiji 撞鐃鉢寺
shosan no gi 初参儀
Shōshinbō Tankū 正信房湛空
Shōsōin 正倉院

Shōunbōji/Seiunbōji 聖雲房寺
Shōwa (era) 正和
shōzō (C. *xiaoxiang*) 肖像
shōzoku 装束
Shugyōmon 修行門
shuji 種子
Shukaku Hosshinō 守覚法親王
shukke no gi 出家儀
shumidan 須弥壇
Shunjō/Shunshō 舜昌
Shuryōgon kyō 首楞厳経
Shūshō 宗昭
shutsuri shōji 出離生死
Sōen Hōgen 宗円法眼
sofuku 素服
Sōhōmitsu 葬法密
sōjōden/sōbadono 葬場殿
sōkaren 葱華輦
sokushin jōbutsu 即身成仏
sokutai 束帯
Sōkyoku 曹局
Sōmon 総門
songan 尊顔
songi 尊儀
sosei 蘇生
soshizō 祖師像
Sōsōryō 喪葬令
sotoba 卒塔婆
sōzoku no gi 相續之儀
su 酢
sugi 杉
suigai 透垣
suinichi 衰日
suiren 翠簾
Sukō (emperor) 崇光天皇
sun 寸
suō 素襖
Tadain 多田院
Taiheiki 太平記
Taima mandara 当麻曼荼羅
taimatsu 松明
Taira no Nobunori 平信範
tairyō shōsan 對靈小参
Takakura-dono 高倉殿

Takakura Gosho 高倉御所
take 竹
tamadono 玉殿・魂殿・霊殿
tamafuri 魂振
tamashii 魂
tamashii bukuro 魂袋
tamashizume/chinkon 鎮魂
tamaya 玉屋・魂屋・霊屋
tamayobai 魂呼ばい
tamayobi 魂呼び
tan 端
tan/sumi 炭
Tanba 丹波
tatebumi 立文
tatekan 立棺
tatsugashira 竜頭
tekkō 手甲
tencha 奠茶
tencha butsuji 奠茶佛事
Tendai 天台
tendoku 轉讀
tengai 天蓋
tenjindō 天神道
Tennōji 天王寺
Tennōji zōri 天王寺草履
Tenryūji 天竜寺
tentō 奠湯
tentō butsuji 奠湯佛事
Toba (emperor) 鳥羽天皇
tōchirimen 唐縮緬
tōgaku 等覺
Tōin Kinkata 洞院公賢
Tōji 東寺
Tōjiin 等持院
Tōjiji 等持寺
tokudatsu 得脱
Tokugawa Ieyasu 徳川家康
tonsha 頓写
tora no koku 寅刻
Toribeno 鳥辺野
Tosa Yukihiro 土佐行広
Tōshōdaiji 唐招提寺
tōshoku 燈燭
Tōshōsha engi 東照社縁起

List of Japanese Words

Toyotomi Hideyoshi　豊臣秀吉
tsuifuku　追福
tsuigasane　衝重
tsuiji　築地
tsuitate　衝立
tsuizen　追善
tsuizen kabuse　追善加布施
tsuizen kuyō　追善供養
tsuna　綱
tsune gosho　常御所
tsune no godei　常御出居
tsurukame shokudai　鶴亀燭台
tsuzumi　鼓
uchi gaki　内垣
ujidera　氏寺
Ungoji　雲居寺
unyō sansō　右遶三匝
Uramatsu Shigeko　浦松重子
Urindō　雲林堂
Urin'in　雲林院
usunibi　薄鈍
uwaya　上屋
waka　和歌
wakame　和布
waki tsukue　脇机
wara　藁
waragutsu　藁沓
waraji　草鞋
Weipai　位牌
xing　形
Yakushi　薬師
Yakushi Nyorai　薬師如来
Yamashina Noritoki　山科教信

Yasaka Shrine　八坂神社
Yi li　儀禮
yingxiang　影像
Yōmei Bunko　陽明文庫
yonanoka　四七日
yorikakari　寄懸
yorishiro　依代
Yōrō (era)　養老
Yōrō sōsō ryō　養老葬送令
Yoshihito (prince)　栄仁親王
yuigon　遺言
Yuima kyō　維摩経
yu no ki　湯器
yurong　御容
Yūzūdō　融通堂
Yūzū nenbutsu engi　融通念仏縁起
zakan　座棺
zenchishiki　善知識
zen no tsuna　善の綱
Zenshin shōnin-e　善信聖人絵
Zenshin shōnin Shinran den-e　善信聖人親鸞伝絵
zō (C. *xiang*)　像
zōshi　雑紙
zōsu　臧主
Zuigu darani　随求陀羅尼
Zuigu kyō　随求經
zukin　頭巾
zukō　塗香
zukyō　誦経
zukyōmono　誦經物
zushi　厨子

Bibliography

Primary Sources

Unless otherwise indicated, the city of publication is Tokyo.

Boki ekotoba. Zoku Nihon no emaki, vol. 9. Edited by Komatsu Shigemi. Chūō Kōronsha, 1990.
Chōshūki (Minamoto no Morotoki). *Zōho shiryō taisei*. 2 vols. Edited by Zōho Shiryō Taisei Kankōkai. Kyoto: Rinsen Shoten, 1965.
Denryaku (Fujiwara Tadazane). *Dai Nihon kokiroku*, vol. 12, pt. 1. Tokyo Daigaku Shiryōhensanjo, comp. Iwanami Shoten, 1960–1984.
Eiga monogatari. Nihon koten bungaku taikei, vol. 76. Edited by Matsumura Hiroji and Yamanaka Yutaka. Iwanami Shoten, 1965. Translated into English by William H. McCullough and Helen Craig McCullough as *A Tale of Flowering Fortunes: Annals of Japanese Aristocratic Life in the Heian Period*. Stanford, CA: Stanford University Press, 1980.
Eiga monogatari zenchūshaku. 9 vols. Edited by Matsumura Hiroji. In *Nihon koten hyōshaku zenshūshaku sōsho*. Kadokawa Shoten, 1969–1982.
Entairyaku (Tōin Kinkata). *Shiryō sanshū kokirokuhen*. 8 vols. (7 vols. published). Zoku Gunsho Ruijū Kanseikai, 1967–.
Gososō sahō. Dai Nihon shiryō, vol. 5, pt. 7. Edited by Tōkyō Daigaku Shiryōhensanjo. Tōkyō Daigaku Shuppankai, 1930–1970.
Gukanki (Konoe Michitsugu). Dai Nihon *shiryō*, vol. 6, pt. 21. Edited by Tōkyō Daigaku Shiryōhensanjo. Tōkyō Daigaku Shuppankai, 1930–1970.
Heihanki (Taira no Nobunori). 2 vols. *Zōho shiryō taisei*. Edited by Zōho Shiryō Taisei Kankōkai. Kyoto: Rinsen Shoten, 1980.
Hōnen shōnin e-den. Zoku Nihon no emaki, vol. 3. Edited by Komatsu Shigemi. Chūō Kōronsha, 1990.
Hōnen's Senchakushū: Passages on the Selection of the Nembutsu in the Original Vow.

Translated and edited by Senchakushū English Translation Project. Honolulu: University of Hawai'i Press; and Tokyo: Sōgō Bukkyō Kenkyūjo, Taishō University, 1998.

Ihon eiga monogatari. 5 vols. Edited by Matsumura Hiroji and Yoshida Kōichi. In *Koten bunko*, vols. 51–56. Koten Bunko, 1952.

Inryōken nichiroku (Kikei Shinzui et al.). *Dai Nihon bukkyō zensho*, vols. 133–137. Edited by Bussho Kankōkai. Meicho Fukyūkai, 1978–1983.

Jimon denki horoku 8 [*Tōbōki*]. *Dai Nihon shiryō*, vol. 1, pt. 1. Edited by Tōkyō Daigaku Shiryōhensanjo. Tōkyō Daigaku Shuppankai, 1930–1970.

Jingihaku sōmoki. *Nihon kyōiku bunko*, vol. 10 (*shūkyō*). Edited by Kurokawa Mamichi. Dōbunkan, 1910–1911.

Jishōindono ryōan sōbo. *Dai Nihon shiryō*, vol. 7, pt. 10. Edited by Tōkyō Daigaku Shiryōhensanjo. Tōkyō Daigaku Shuppankai, 1930–1970.

Kanmon gyōki (Sadafusa Shinnō). In *Zoku gunsho ruijū: hoi 2* (suppl. 2). Gunsho Ruijū Kanseikai, 1930–1985.

Kennaiki (Madenokōji Tokifusa). *Dai Nihon kokiroku*, vol. 14. Iwanami Shoten, 1963–1987.

Kichiji ryakki. In *Shinkō gunsho ruijū* (*zatsubu* 77), ed. Hanawa Hokinoichi and Kawamoto Keiichi. Tokyo: Meicho Fukyūkai. 1977–1978.

Kichiji shidai. In *Shinkō gunsho ruijū* (*zatsubu* 77), ed. Hanawa Hokinoichi and Kawamoto Keiichi. Tokyo: Meicho Fukyūkai. 1977–1978.

Kitano tenjin engi. In *Zoku Nihon no emaki*, vol. 15. Edited by Komatsu Shigemi. Chūō Kōronsha, 1991.

Meigetsuki (Fujiwara Teika). In *Kunchū meigetsuki*. 8 vols. Compiled and annotated by Inamura Eiichi. Matsue: Imai Shoten, 2002.

Moromoriki. See *Shiryō sanshū: Moromoriki*.

Nichiren shōnin chūgasan. In *Zokuzoku Nihon emaki taisei: denki, engi hen*, vol. 2. Edited by Komatsu Shigemi. Chūō Kōronsha, 1993.

Nihongi: Chronicles of Japan from the Earliest Times to A.D. 697. Translated by W. G. Aston. Rutland, VT, and Tokyo: Charles E. Tuttle Company, 1975.

Noritoki kyōki (Yamashina Noritoki). *Dai Nihon shiryō*, vol. 7, pt. 10. Edited by Tōkyō Daigaku Shiryōhensanjo. Tōkyō Daigaku Shuppankai, 1930–1970.

Sakeiki (Minamoto no Tsuneyori). *Ruijū zatsurei*. In *Zōho shiryō taisei*, ed. Zōhō Shiryō Taisei Kankōkai. Kyoto: Rinsen Shoten, 1975.

Sanetakakō-ki (Sanjōnishi Sanetaka). 13 vols. Tokyo: Taiyōsha, 1931–1938 (vols. 1–5); Kokusho Shuppan Kabushiki Gaisha, 1944 (vol. 6:1); Zoku Gunsho Ruijū Kanseikai, 1962–1967 (vols. 6:2–13; Takahashi Ryūzō, ed.).

Sankaiki (Nakayama [Fujiwara] Tadachika). 3 vols. (vols. 19–21). In *Shiryō taisei*, 30 vols. Naigai Shoseki Kabushiki gaisha, 1935.

Shingihaku sōmoki. In *Nihon kyōiku bunko*, vol. 10 (*shūkyō*), ed., Kurokawa Mamichi. Dōbunkan, 1910–1911.

Shiryō sanshū Moromoriki (Nakahara Moromori). 11 vols. Compiled and annotated by Fujii Sadafumi and Kobayashi Hanako. Zoku Gunsho Ruijū Kanseikai, 1968.

Sōhōmitsu. In *Nihon kyōiku bunko*, vol. 10 (*shūkyō*), ed., Kurokawa Mamichi. Dōbunkan, 1910–1911.
Sōsōryō. In *Kokushi taikei*, vol. 24 (*Ryōshūkai*). Edited by Kuroita Katsumi. Yoshikawa Kōbunkan, 1964.
Taiheiki. *Nihon koten bungaku taikei*, vol. 36. Edited by Matsumura Hiroji and Yamanaka Yutaka. Iwanami Shoten, 1971.
Taishō shinshū daizōkyō. Edited by Takakusu Junjirō and Watanabe Kaigyoku. Taishō Issaikyō Kankōkai, 1924–1934 (1967 reprint).
Tōshōsha engi. *Zokuzoku Nihon emaki taisei: denki/engihen*, vol. 8. Edited by Komatsu Shigemi. Chūō Kōronsha, 1994.
Yūzū nenbutsu engi. *Zoku Nihon no emaki*, vol. 21. Edited by Komatsu Shigemi. Chūō Kōronsha, 1992.
Zenshin shōnin Shinran den-e. *Zokuzoku Nihon emaki taisei: denki, engi hen*, vol. 1. Edited by Komatsu Shigemi. Chūō Kōronsha, 1994.

Secondary Sources

Abe, Stanley K. "Art and Practice in a Fifth-century Chinese Buddhist Cave Temple." *Ars Orientalis* 20 (1990): 1–31.
———. *The Weaving of the Mantra: Kūkai and the Construction of Esoteric Buddhist Discourse*. New York: Columbia University Press, 1999.
Akamatsu Toshihide. "Ashikaga shi no shōzō ni tsuite." *Bijutsu kenkyū* 152 (January 1949): 24–46.
———. *Kamakura bukkyō no kenkyū*. Kyoto: Heirakuji Shoten, 1957.
———. "Kano Masanobu no Ashikaga Yoshimitsu shutsujin ei ni tsuite." *Gasetsu* 65 (1942): 405–411.
———. "Miedō ni tsuite." In *Kamakura bukkyō no kenkyū*, 337–355. Kyoto: Heirakuji Shoten, 1957.
———. "Moriyakebon den Ashikaga Takauji zō ni tsuite." *Nihon rekishi* 250 (1969): 66–67.
Akata Mitsuo. *Saigi shūzoku no kenkyū*. Kōbundō, 1980.
———. *Sorei shinkō to takai kannen*. Kyoto: Jinbun Shoin, 1986.
Akazawa Eiji. "Jūgo seiki ni okeru kinbyōbu ni tsuite." *Kokka* 849 (December 1962): 567–579.
Amino, Yoshihiko. "Some Problems Concerning the History of Popular Life in Medieval Japan." *Acta Asiatica* 44 (1983): 77–97.
An Zhimin. "Changsha xin faxian de Xi Han bohua shitan." *Kaogu* 1 (1973): 43–53.
Andrews, Allan A. "Myth and History in the Life and Biographies of Hōnen." *Pure Land*, n.s. 2 (December 1985): 21–29.
Appadurai, Arjun, ed. *The Social Life of Things*. Cambridge: Cambridge University Press, 1986.
Asahi Shinbunsha. *Nihon bijutsu ni egakareta joseitachi: Emakimono, byōbue, shōzōga, ukiyoe*. Asahi Shinbunsha, 1985.

Baudrillard, Jean. *Symbolic Exchange and Death.* Translated by Iain Hamilton Grant. London: Sage Publications, 1993.
Bedini, Silvio A. *The Trail of Time: Time Measurement with Incense in East Asia.* Cambridge: Cambridge University Press, 1994.
Bell, Catherine. "Discourse and Dichotomies: The Structure of Ritual Theory." *Religion* 17 (1987): 95–118.
———. *Ritual Perspectives and Dimensions.* New York and Oxford: Oxford University Press, 1997.
———. *Ritual Theory, Ritual Practice.* New York: Oxford University Press, 1992.
Belting, Hans. *Likeness and Presence: A History of the Image before the Era of Art.* Translated by Edmund Jephcott. Chicago: University of Chicago Press, 1994.
Bernstein, Andrew. "Fire and Earth: The Forging of Modern Cremation in Meiji Japan." *Journal of Japanese Religious Studies*, vol. 27, nos. 3–4 (Fall 2000): 297–334.
———. *Modern Passings: Death Rites, Politics, and Social Change in Imperial Japan.* Honolulu: University of Hawaiʻi Press, 2006.
Bialock, David. *Eccentric Spaces, Hidden Histories: Narrative, Ritual, and Royal Authority from The Chronicles of Japan to the Tale of the Heike.* Stanford, CA: Stanford University Press, 2007.
Blacker, Carmen. *The Catalpa Bow: A Study of Shamanistic Practices in Japan.* London: George Allen & Unwin, 1975.
Bock, Felicia G. *Classical Learning and Taoist Practices in Early Japan with a Translation of Books XVI and XX of the Engi Shiki.* Occasional Paper No. 17. Phoenix: Center for Asian Studies, Arizona State University, 1985.
Bodiford, William M. *Sōtō Zen in Medieval Japan.* Honolulu: University of Hawaiʻi Press, 1993.
———. "Zen in the Art of Funerals: Ritual Salvation in Japanese Buddhism." *History of Religion* 32, no. 2 (November 1992): 146–164.
Borgen, Robert. *Sugawara Michizane and the Early Heian Court.* Cambridge, MA: Harvard University Press, 1986.
Bourdieu, Pierre. *Distinction: A Social Critique of the Judgment of Taste.* Translated by Richard Nice. Cambridge, MA: Harvard University Press, 1984.
Braudel, Fernand. *The Structures of Everyday Life: Civilization and Capitalism 15th–18th Century.* Translated by Sian Reynolds. New York: Harper & Row, 1981.
Brilliant, Richard. *Portraiture.* Cambridge, MA: Harvard University Press, 1991.
Brock, Karen L. "E'nichibō Jōnin, the Saint's Companion." In *Artist as Professional*, ed. Melinda Takeuchi. Stanford, CA: Stanford University Press, 2004.
———. "The Shogun's 'Painting Match.'" *Monumenta Nipponica* 50, no. 4 (Winter 1995): 433–484.
Brown, Delmer M., and Ichirō Ishida. *The Future Past: A Translation and Study of the Gukanshō, an Interpretative History of Japan Written in 1219.* Berkeley, Los Angeles, and London: University of California Press, 1979.
Bukkyō girei jiten. Edited by Fujii Masao. Tōkyōdō, 1977.
Bukkyōgo daijiten. Edited by Nakamura Hajime. Tokyo Shoseki Kabushikigaisha, 1975.

… Bibliography …

Carr, Kevin Gray. "The Lives of Shōtoku: Narrative Art and Ritual in Medieval Japan." Ph.D. diss., Princeton University, 2005.
Carruthers, Mary. *The Craft of Thought: Meditation, Rhetoric, and the Making of Images, 400–1200*. Cambridge: Cambridge University Press, 1998.
Cho Summie. "Chōson Ōchō jidai shōzōga no ruikei oyobi shakaiteki kinō." *Bijutsu kenkyū* 374 (February 2002): 233–256.
Cole, Alan. "Upside Down/Right Side Up: A Revisionist History of Buddhist Funerals in China." *History of Religions* 35, no. 4 (May 1996): 307–338.
Collcutt, Martin. *Five Mountains: The Rinzai Zen Monastic Institution in Medieval Japan*. Harvard East Asian Series 85. Cambridge, MA, and London: Council on East Asian Studies, Harvard University, 1981.
———. "Musō Soseki." In *The Origins of Japan's Medieval World: Courtiers, Clerics, Warriors, and Peasants in the Fourteenth Century*, ed. Jeffrey P. Mass. Stanford, CA: Stanford University Press, 1997.
———. "The Zen Monastery in Kamakura Society." In Jeffrey P. Mass, ed., *Court and Bakufu in Japan: Essays in Kamakura History*. New Haven, CT: Yale University Press, 1982.
Conlan, Thomas Donald. *State of War: The Violent Order of Fourteenth-Century Japan*. Ann Arbor, MI: Center for Japanese Studies, University of Michigan, 2003.
Cunninghan, Michael R., et al. *Buddhist Treasures from Nara*. Exh. cat. Cleveland Museum of Art, 1998.
Daihōrin Henshūbu, ed. *Senzō kuyō to sōsō girei (Daihō rinkaku sensho 17)*. Daihō Rinkaku, 1985.
De Certeau, Michel. *The Practice of Everyday Life*. Translated by Steven Rendall. Berkeley: University of California Press, 1982.
Dobbins, James C. "The Biography of Shinran: Apotheosis of a Japanese Buddhist Visionary." *History of Religions* 30, no. 2 (1990): 179–196.
———. "Envisioning Kamakura Buddhism." In *Re-Visioning "Kamakura" Buddhism*, ed. Richard Payne. Honolulu: University of Hawai'i Press, 1998.
———. *Letters of the Nun Eshinni: Images of Pure Land Buddhism in Medieval Japan*. Honolulu: University of Hawai'i Press, 2004.
———. "Portraits of Shiniran in Medieval Pure Land Buddhism." In *Living Images: Japanese Buddhist Icons in Context*, ed. Robert H. Sharf and Elizabeth Horton Sharf. Stanford, CA: Stanford University Press, 2001.
Doi, Takuji, Yoneshi Satō, Shōji Inokuchi, Chōshū Takeda, Takayoshi Mogami, and Hisayoshi Uwai. *Sōsō bosei kenkyū shūsei*. Meichō Shuppankai, 1979.
Durkheim, Emile. *The Elementary Forms of the Religious Life: A Study in Religious Sociology* [1912]. Translated by Joseph Ward Swain. London: Allen & Unwin, 1915.
Ebersole, Gary L. *Ritual Poetry and the Politics of Death in Early Japan*. Princeton, NJ: Princeton University Press, 1989.
Ebrey, Patricia Buckley, trans. *Chu Hsi's Family Rituals: A Twelfth-Century Chinese Manual for the Performance of Cappings, Weddings, Funerals, and Ancestral Rites*. Princeton, NJ: Princeton University Press, 1991.

———. "Portrait Sculptures in Imperial Ancestral Rites in Song China." T'oung Pao 83, nos. 1–3 (1997): 42–92.
Eliade, Mircea. Cosmos and History: The Myth of Eternal Return. Translated by Willard R. Trask. New York: Harper & Row, 1949.
Faure, Bernard. "The Buddhist Icon and the Modern Gaze." Critical Inquiry 24, no. 3 (Spring 1998): 768–813.
———. The Rhetoric of Immediacy: A Cultural Critique of Chan/Zen Buddhism. Princeton, NJ: Princeton University Press, 1991.
———. Visions of Power: Imagining Medieval Japanese Buddhism. Princeton, NJ: Princeton University Press, 1996.
Fister, Patricia. "From Sacred Leaves to Sacred Images: The Buddhist Nun Gen'yō's Practice of Making and Distributing Miniature Kannons." In International Symposium: Figures and Places of the Sacred. Kyoto: International Research Center for Japanese Studies, 2003.
Flanigan, C. Clifford. "The Moving Subject: Medieval Liturgical Processions in Semiotic and Cultural Perspective." In Moving Subjects: Processional Performance in the Middle Ages and Renaissance, ed. Kathleen Ashley and Wim Hüsken. Atlanta, GA: Rodopi, 2001.
Foard, James H. "Ippen Shōnin and Popular Buddhism in Kamakura Japan." Ph.D. diss., Stanford University, 1977.
———. "In Search of a Lost Reformation: A Reconsideration of Kamakura Buddhism." Japanese Journal of Religious Studies 7, no. 4 (1980): 261–291.
Forester, Kurt W. "Metaphors of Rule, Political Ideology and History in the Portraits of Cosimo I de'Medici." Mitteilungen des Kunshistorischen Institutes in Florenz 15 (1971): 65–104.
Foulk, T. Griffith. "Religious Functions of Buddhist Art in China." In Cultural Intersections in Later Chinese Buddhism, ed. Marsha Weidner. Honolulu: University of Hawai'i Press, 2001.
Foulk, T. Griffith, Elizabeth E. Horton, and Robert H. Sharf. "The Meaning and Function of Ch'an and Zen Portraiture." Paper presented at the panel "Likeness and Lineage: Religious Portraiture in Asia." New York City, February 17, 1990.
Foulk, T. Griffith, and Robert H. Sharf. "On the Ritual Use of Ch'an Portraiture in Medieval China." Cahiers d'Extrême-Asie 7 (1993): 149–219.
Fowler, Sherry Dianne. Murōji: Rearranging Art and History at a Japanese Buddhist Temple. Honolulu: University of Hawai'i Press, 2005.
Freedberg, David. The Power of Images: Studies in the History and Theories of Response. Chicago: University of Chicago Press, 1989.
Friedlander, Max J. Landscape, Portrait, Still Life. New York: Schocken Books, 1963.
Fujii Masao, ed. Bukkyō sōsai daijiten. Yūzankaku, 1980.
———. Sosen sairei no girei kōzō to minzoku. Kōbundō, 1993.
Fujii Masao and Yagisawa Sōichi. Nihon sōsō bunka daijiten. Shikisha, 2007.
Fujimoto Masayuki. "Moriyakebon busō kibazō gazō sairon." Shigaku zasshi 53, no. 4 (1984): 25–40.
Fujishima Ganjirō. Chūsonji. Kawade Shobō Shinsha, 1971.

Fujita Meiji. "Shuden no seiritsu katei to sono igi." In *Chūseiteki kūkan to girei*, ed. Suzuki Hiroyuki et al. *Shirizu toshi, kenchiku, rekishi 3*. Tōkyō Daigaku Shuppankai, 2006.

Fujitani Takashi. *Splendid Monarchy: Power and Pageantry in Modern Japan*. Berkeley, Los Angeles, London: University of California Press, 1998.

Fushichō no tera Miidera: Chisho daishi issen hyaku nen go-onki kinen. With editorial assistance from Shinshūsha. Ōtsu City: Sōhonzan Onjōji (Miidera), 1990.

Futaki Ken'ichi. *Chūsei buke girei no kenkyū*. Yoshikawa Kōbunkan, 1985.

Gilday, Edmund T. "Bodies of Evidence: Imperial Funeral Rites and the Meiji Restoration. *Japanese Journal of Religious Studies* 27, nos. 3–4 (2000): 273–296.

———. "Dancing with Spirit(s): Another View of the Other World in Japan." *History of Religion* 23, no. 3 (February 1990): 273–300.

Goble, Andrew. "Vision of an Emperor." In *The Origins of Japan's Medieval World: Courtiers, Clerics, Warriors, and Peasants in the Fourteenth Century*, ed. Jeffrey P. Mass. Stanford, CA: Stanford University Press, 1997.

Gomi Fumihiko. "Emaki no shisen: Jikan, shinkō, kuyō (chūsei no bunka kūkan). *Shisō* 829 (July 1993): 4–27.

Gomi Fumihiko and Saiki Hideo, eds. *Chūsei toshi Kamakura to shi no sekai*. Kōshi Shoin, 2002.

Gomi Fumihiko, Sano Midori, and Matsuoka Shinpei. *Chūsei Nihon no bi to chikara*. Chūō Kōronshinsha, 2002.

Goodwin, Janet R. "Shooing the Dead to Paradise." *Japanese Journal of Religious Studies* 16, no. 1 (1989): 63–76.

Gorai Shigeru. "Sō to kuyō." *Tōhōkai* 112 (1983): 34–42.

———. *Sō to kuyō*. Osaka: Tōhō Shuppan, 1992.

Grapard, Allan. "Flying Mountains and Walkers of Emptiness: Toward a Definition of Sacred Space in Japanese Religions." *History of Religions* 20, no. 3 (1982): 195–221.

———. "Linguistic Cubism: A Singularity of Pluralism in the Sannō Cult." *Japanese Journal of Religious Studies* 14, nos. 2–3 (1987): 211–233.

———. "Lotus in the Mountain, Mountain in the Lotus." *Monumenta Nipponica* 41 (1986): 21–50.

———. *The Protocol of the Gods: A Study of the Kasuga Cult in Japanese History*. Berkeley, Los Angeles, Oxford: University of California Press, 1992.

Graybill, Maribeth. "Kasen-e: An Investigation into the Origins of the Tradition of Poet Pictures in Japan." Ph.D. diss., University of Michigan, 1983.

Grimes, Ronald. *Beginnings in Ritual Studies*. Lanham, MD: University Press of America, 1982.

Groner, Paul. "Icons and Relics in Eisons's Religious Activities." In *Living Images: Japanese Buddhist Icons in Context*, ed. Robert H. Sharf and Elizabeth Horton Sharf. Stanford, CA: Stanford University Press, 2001.

———. *Saichō: The Establishment of the Japanese Tendai School*. Berkeley, CA: Buddhist Studies Series, University of California, 1984.

Guth, Christine M. E. "The Divine Boy in Japanese Art." *Monumenta Nipponica* 42, no. 1 (1987): 1–24.

Habu, Junko. *Ancient Jomon of Japan*. Cambridge: Cambridge University Press, 2004.
Haga Kōshirō. *Higashiyama bunka*. Hanawa Shobō, 1962.
Haga Noburu. *Kaitei zōhō: Sōgi no rekishi*. Yūzankaku, 1970.
Hagiwara Hidesaburō and Sutō Isao. *Sōsō to kuyō (Nihon shūkyō minzoku zuten 2)*. Kyoto: Hōzōkan, 1985.
Hall, John W., Keiji Nagahara, and Kozo Yamamura, eds. *Japan before Tokugawa: Political Consolidation and Economic Growth, 1500–1650*. Princeton, NJ: Princeton University Press, 1981.
Hall, John W., and Jeffrey P. Mass. *Medieval Japan: Essays in Institutional History*. Stanford, CA: Stanford University Press, 1988.
Hall, John W., and Toyoda Takeshi, eds. *Japan in the Muromachi Age*. Berkeley: University of California Press, 1977.
Hanley, Susan B. *Everyday Things in Premodern Japan: The Hidden Legacy of Material Culture*. Berkeley, Los Angeles, London: University of California Press, 1997.
Harris, Victor, ed. *Shintō: The Sacred Art of Ancient Japan*. London: The British Museum Press, 2001.
Hasebe Kōichi. "Zenmon no girei (I)." *Aichi Gakuin Zen kenkyūsho kiyō* 2 (1972): 40–52.
Hashimoto Hatsuko. "Chūsei no kuge shakai to onmyōdō ni tsuite: Moromoriki ni miru." *Onmyōdō sōsho*, vol. 2 (chūsei), Murayama Shūichi et al., eds. Meiyō Shuppan, 1993.
Hayami Akira. *Kinsei nōson no rekishi jinkōgakuteki kenkyū*. Tōyō Keizai Shinpōsha, 1973.
Hayami Tasuku. *Jigoku to gokuraku: Ōjō yōshū to kizoku shakai*. Yoshikawa Kōbunkan, 1998.
———. *Nihon no shakai ni okeru hotoke to kami*. Yoshikawa Kōbunkan, 2006.
Hayashi Masahiko et al. *Sei to shi no zuzōgaku: Ajia ni okeru sei to shi no cosumoroji*. Shibundō, 2003.
Hirose Ryōkō. "Chūkinsei ni okeru Sōtō zensō no katsudō to sōsai ni tsuite." *Shūgaku kenkyū* 27 (1985): 143–150.
———. "Sōtō zensō ni okeru shinjin kedō akurei chin'atsu." *Indogaku bukkyōgaku kenkyū* 21, no. 2 (1983): 233–236.
Hisanaga Toshikazu. "Tennō-ke no sōsō girei to Muromachi-dono: Gyokō gubu o chūshin ni." *Kokugakuin Daigaku daigaku kiyo: Bungaku kenkyūka* 34 (2002): 307–331.
Hooke, S. H., ed. *The Labyrinth: Further Studies in the Relation between Myth and Ritual in the Ancient World*. London: Society for Promoting Christian Knowledge, 1935.
———, ed. *Myth and Ritual*. London: Oxford University Press, 1933.
Hori Hiroshi. "Tennō no shi no rekishiteki ichi: Nyozai no gi o chūshin ni." *Shirin* 81, no. 1 (January 1998): 38–39.
Hori, Ichirō. "Self-mummified Buddhas in Japan: An Aspect of the Shūgendō Sect." *History of Religions* 1, no. 2 (1962): 222–242.
Huntington, Richard, and Peter Metcalf. *Celebration of Death: The Anthropology of Mortuary Ritual*. New York: Cambridge University Press, 1979.

Ichino Chizuko. "Fushimi Gosho shūhen no seikatsu bunka: Kanmon nikki ni miru." *Shoryōbu kiyō* 33 (1981): 20–39.
Idemitsu Bijutsukan, ed. *Egakareta gokuraku to jigoku: Bukkyō kaiga meihin ten*. Benridō, 2002.
Iijima Isamu. "Chinsō ni tsuite." *Museum* 80 (1957): 17–20.
Imae Hiromichi. "Hōke Nakahara shi keizu kōshō." *Shoryōbu kiyō* 27 (1975): 18–38.
Imatani Akira. "Jūyon-jūgo seiki no Nihon—Nanbokuchō to Muromachi bakufu." In *Iwanami kōza Nihon tsūshi*, ed. Asao Naohiro et al. Iwanami Shoten, 1994.
Inada Natsuko. "Nihon kodai sōsō girei no tokushitsu." *Shigaku zasshi* 109, no. 8 (August 2000): 1–34.
Inagaki Hisao (in collaboration with P. G. O'Neill). *A Dictionary of Japanese Buddhist Terms: Based on References in Japanese Literature*. Kyoto: Nagata Bunshodō, 1988.
Inoguchi Shōji. *Nihon no sōshiki*. Hayakawa Shobō, 1965.
———, ed. *Sōsōbosei kenkyūshūsei*. Vol. 2: *Sōsōgirei*. Meicho Shuppan, 1979.
Ishida Ichiryō. *Jōdokyō bijutsu: Bunkashi gakuteki kenkyū joron*. Perikansha, 1991.
Ishikawa Hideo. "Dogū keiyōki to ganmenzuki toki." *Yayoi bunka no kenkyū* 8 (1987): 160–164.
Ishikawa Rikisan. "Chūsei zenshū to sōsō girei." *Indogaku bukkyōgaku kenkyū* 35, no. 2 (1987): 299–304.
———. Zen no sōsō. *Nihongaku* 10 (1987): 139–149.
Itō Toshiko. "Kosode ishō no tenkai: Josei shōzōga o chūshin ni shite." *Yamato Bunka* 56 (1972): 22–23.
Itō Yuishin. "*Moromoriki* ni miru chūsei sōsai bukkyō." In *Sōsō bosei kenkyū shūsei*, vol. 5, ed. Uwai Hisayoshi, 215–237. Meicho Shuppan, 1979.
Jogensen, John. "The 'Imperial' Lineage of Ch'an Buddhism: The Role of Confucian Ritual and Ancestor Worship in Ch'an's Search for Legitimation in the Mid-T'ang Dynasty." *Papers on Far Eastern History* 35 (1987): 89–133.
Kagamishima Genryū, Satō Tatsugen, and Kosaka Kiyū, eds. *Yakuchū Zen'en shingi*. Sōtōshū Shūmuchō, 1972.
Kajima Masaru. "Kondō kanjō ban." *Nihon no kokuhō* 043 (December 14, 1997): 72–73.
Kajitani Ryōji. *Sōryō no shōzō*, vol. 388 of *Nihon no bijutsu*. Shibundō, 1998.
Kanda, Christine Guth. *Shinzō: Hachiman Imagery and Its Development*. Harvard East Asian Monographs, no. 119. Cambridge, MA: Harvard University Press, 1985.
Kanda, Fusae. "Behind the Sensationalism: Images of a Decaying Corpse in Japanese Buddhist Art." *The Art Bulletin* 87, no. 1 (March 2005): 24–49.
———. "Hōnen's *Senchaku* Doctrine and His Artistic Agenda." *Japanese Journal of Religious Studies* 31, no. 1 (2004): 3–27.
Kasuya Makoto. *Bukkyō setsuwaga no kōzō to ginō: Shigan to higan no iconoroji*. Chūō Kōron Bijutsu Shuppan, 2003.
Katō Hideyuki. "Buke shōzōga no shin no zōshu kakutei e no shomondai: Hasegawa Nobuharu hitsu Takeda Shingen, den Nawa Nagatoshi zō narabi ni den Ashikaga Takauji, dō Yoshihisa zō ni tsuite." *Bijutsu kenkyū* 345 (November 1989): 159–173, and 346 (March 1990): 1–15.

Katsuda Itaru. *Nihon chūsei no haka to sōsō*. Yoshikawa Kōbunkan, 2006.
———. *Shishatachi no chūsei*. Yoshikawa Kōbunkan, 2003.
———. "Toribeno kō." In *Nihon shakai no shiteki kōzō: Kodai, chūsei* [Ōyama Takahira kyōju taikan kinenkai hen]. Shibunkaku Shuppan, 1997.
Katsuura Noriko. "Tonsure Forms for Nuns: Classification of Nuns According to Hairstyle." In *Engendering Faith: Women and Buddhism in Premodern Japan*, general ed. Barbara Ruch. Michigan Monograph Series in Japanese Studies 43. Ann Arbor: The University of Michigan Center for Japanese Studies, 2002.
Kawada Sadamu with Anne Nishimura Morse. "Japanese Buddhist Decorative Arts: The Formative Period." In *Object as Insight: Japanese Buddhist Art and Ritual*, exh. cat. Katonah Museum of Art, 1996.
Kenney, Elizabeth. "Shinto Funerals in the Edo Period." *Japanese Journal of Religious Studies* 27, nos. 3–4 (Fall 2000): 239–271.
Kidder, Edward J. *Japan before Buddhism*. London: Thames & Hudson, 1959.
———. *The Lucky Seventh: Early Hōryūji and Its Time*. International Christian University and Hachiro Yuasa Memorial Museum, 1999.
Kieschnick, John. *The Impact of Buddhism on Chinese Material Culture*. Princeton and Oxford: Princeton University Press, 2003.
Kin to gin: Kagayaki no Nihon bijutsu. Tokyo National Museum, 1999.
Kirby, R. J. "Ancestor Worship in Japan." *Transactions of the Asiatic Society of Japan* 38 (1911): 233–267.
Klein, Bettina. "Japanese *Kinbyōbu*: The Gold-leafed Folding Screens of the Muromachi Period (1333–1573)." *Artibus Asiae* 45, no. 1 (1984): 5–33, and nos. 2–3 (1984): 101–173.
Kobayashi Takeshi. "Saidaiji Eisonzō ni tsuite." *Bukkyō geijutsu* 28 (1956): 30–37.
Kobayashi Tatsurō. *Emaki Shinran Shōnin e-den*. Nihon no bijutsu 415. Shibundō, 2000.
Kobayashi Tsuyoshi. *Shōzō chōkoku*. Yoshikawa Kōbunkan, 1995.
Koizumi Kazuko et al., eds., *Emakimono no kenchiku o yomu*. Tōkyō Daigaku Shuppan, 1996.
Kokuhō Daigoji ten: Yama kara orita honzon. Compiled by Tokyo National Museum, Daigoji, Nihon Keizai Shinbun, Inc. Nihon Keizai Shinbun, 2001.
Kuroda Hideo. "Kiba mushazō no zōshu: Shōzōga to *Taiheki*." In Kuroda Hideo et al., *Shōzōga o yomu*. Kadokawa Shoten, 1998.
———. "Moriyabon kiba mushazō no zōshu." In *Tōkyo Daigaku shiryō hensanjo kiyō* 5 (1995).
———. *Ō no shintai, ō no shōzō*. Heibonsha, 1993.
———. "Shinran den-e to inugamijin." In *Shūkan Asahi hyakka Nihon no rekishi: kaiga shiryō no yomikata*. Asahi Shinbunsha, 1988.
Kuroda Hideo et al. *Shōzōga o yomu*. Kadokawa Shoten, 1998.
Kuroda Satoshi. *Chūsei shōzō no bunkashi*. Perikansha, 2007.
Kuroita Katsumi. "Ashikaga Takauji no gazō ni tsuite." *Shigaku zasshi* 31, no. 1 (1920): 82–83.
Kuwada Tadachika, ed. *Ashikaga shogun retsuden*. Akita Shoten, 1975.

Kyoto Kokuritsu Hakubutsukan. *Nihon no shōzō: Tokubetsuten*. Kyoto: Kyoto Kokuritsu Hakubutsukan, 1976.
LaFleur, William R. *The Karma of Words: Buddhism and the Literary Arts in Medieval Japan*. Berkeley, CA: University of California Press, 1983.
Lai, Whalen. "After the Reformation: Post-Kamakura Buddhism." *Japanese Journal of Religious Studies* 5, no. 4 (December 1978): 258–284.
Lay, Hyde Arthur. "Japanese Funeral Rites." *Transactions of the Asiatic Society of Japan* 19 (1891): 507–544.
Levine, Gregory P. A. *Daitokuji: The Visual Cultures of a Zen Monastery*. Seattle: University of Washington Press, 2005.
———. "Switching Sites and Identities: The Founder's Statue at the Zen Buddhist Temple Kōrin'in." *The Art Bulletin* 87, no. 1 (March 2001): 72–104.
Loewe, Michael. "The Imperial Way of Death in Han China." In Joseph P. McDermott, ed., *State and Court Ritual in China*. Cambridge: Cambridge University Press, 1999.
Ma Yong. "Lun Changsha Mawangdui hihao Han mu chutu bohua." *Kaogu* (1973) 2: 118–125.
Macé, François. "Les funérailles des souverains japonais." *Cahiers d'Extrême-Asie* 4 (1988): 157–165.
———. *La mort et les funérailles dans le Japon ancien*. Paris: Publications Orientalistes de France, 1986.
———. "Origine de la mort et voyage dans l'au-delà selon trois sequences mythiques du *Kojiki* et du *Nihonshoki*." *Cahiers d'études et de documents sur les religions du Japan* I (1976): 75–113.
Mainichi Shinbunsha. *Nihon no shōzō: Kyukōzoku kazoku hizō arubamu*. Vols. 1–9. Mainichi Shinbunsha, 1989–1990.
Matsubara Shigeru. *Emaki—Yūzū nenbutsu engi. Nihon no bijutsu* 302. Shibundō, 1991.
———. *Gaka, bunjintachi no shōzō (Nihon no bijutsu 386)*. Shibundō, 1998.
Matsudaira, Narimitsu. "The Concept of Tamashii in Japan." In *Studies in Japanese Folklore*, ed. Richard M. Dorson. Bloomington: University of Indiana Press, 1963.
Matsuura Shūkō. *Sonshuku sōhō no kenkyū*. Sankibō Busshorin, 1985.
———. *Zenke no sōhō to tsuizen kuyō no kenkyū*. Sankibō Busshorin, 1972.
McCallum, Donald F. *Zenkōji and Its Icon*. Princeton, NJ: Princeton University Press, 1994.
McCullough, William H., and Helen Craig McCullough, trans. *A Tale of Flowering Fortunes: Annals of Japanese Aristocratic Life in the Heian Period*. 2 vols. Stanford, CA: Stanford University Press, 1980.
McDannell, Colleen. "Interpreting Things: Material Culture Studies and American Religion." *Religion* 21 (1991): 371–387.
McMullen, David L. "The Death Rites of Tang Daizong." In *State and Court Ritual in China*, ed. Joseph P. McDermott. Cambridge: Cambridge University Press, 1999.
Metcalf, Peter, and Richard Huntington, eds. *Celebrations of Death: The Anthropology of Mortuary Ritual*. New York: Cambridge University Press, 1991.

Minamoto Toyomune. "Jingoji zō Takanobu hitsu no gazō ni tsuite no gi." *Yamato bunka* 13 (1954): 10–19.
Mitsuhashi Tadashi. "Rinshū shukke no seiritsu to sono igi." *Nihon shūkyō bunkashi kenkyū* 1, no. 1 (1997).
Miyajima Shinichi. *Buke no shōzō* (*Nihon no bijutsu* 385). Shibundō, 1998.
———. *Shōzōga*. Yoshikawa Kōbunkan, 1994.
———. "Shōzōga no mukō ni mieru mono." *Hongō* 8 (1996).
———. *Shōzōga no shisen: Minamoto no Yoritomozō kara ukiyoe made*. Yoshikawa Kōbunkan, 1996.
Mizoguchi, Koji. *An Archaeological History of Japan: 30,000 B.C. to A.D. 700*. Philadelphia: University of Pennsylvania Press, 2002.
Mogami Takayoshi. "The Double-grave System." In *Studies in Japanese Folklore*, ed. Richard M. Dorson. Bloomington: University of Indiana Press, 1963.
Mōri, Hisashi. *Japanese Portrait Sculpture*. Translated and adapted by W. Chie Ishibashi. Tokyo, New York, San Francisco: Kodansha International Ltd. and Shibundo, 1977.
Mori Masato. *Fushiminomiya bunkaken no kenkyū: Kakugei no kyōju to sōzō no ba to shite*. Kumamoto: Morimasato, 2000.
Mori Shigeaki. *Chūsei Nihon no seiji to bunka*. Kyoto: Shibunkaku Shuppan, 2006.
Mori Tōru. *Kamakura jidai no shōzōga*. Misuzu Shobō, 1971.
Morita Kyōji. *Ashikaga Yoshimasa no kenkyū*. Osaka: Izumi Shoin, 1993.
Morse, Anne Nishimura, and Samuel Crowell Morse. *Object as Insight: Japanese Buddhist Art and Ritual*. Exh. cat. Katonah Museum of Art, 1996.
Mortuary Rites in Japan. Special issue of the *Japanese Journal of Religious Studies* 27, nos. 3–4 (Fall 2000).
Motoi Makiko. "Jūōkyō to sono kyōju: Gyakushu, tsuizen butsuji ni okeru shōdō o chūshin ni." *Kokugo kokubun* 766 (June 1998): 22–33, and (July 1998): 17–35.
Müller, F. Max. *Lectures on the Science of Languages* [1861]. New York: Scribner, Armstrong and Co., 1967.
Murai, Yasuhiko. "Josei shōzōga to sono jidai." *Yamato bunka* 56 (1972): 1–11.
Murakami, Kōkyō. "Changes in Japanese Urban Funeral Customs during the Twentieth Century." *Japanese Journal of Religious Studies* 27, nos. 3–4 (Fall 2000): 335–352.
Murashige Yasushi. *Tennō, kuge no shōzō* (*Nihon no bijutsu* 387). Shibundō, 1998.
Murata Masashi. *Murata Masashi chosakushū*. Vol. 7. Kyōto: Shibunkaku Shuppan, 1986.
Murayama Shūichi et al., eds. *Onmyōdō sōsho*. 4 vols. Meicho, 1993.
Nakagawa Manabu. "Iseisha no shi o meguru shokue kannen no kinseiteki tenkai: Shōgun no shi to chōtei." *Nihonshi kenkyū* 477 (May 2002): 1–27.
Nakamura Hajime. *Bukkyōgo daijiten*. Tōkyo Shoseki Kabushikigaisha, 1975.
Nakano Masaki et al. *Engi-e to nise-e: Kamakura no kaiga, kōgei*. Kōdansha, 1993.
Nakano Yoshio. *Rekishi no naka no shōzōga*. Chikuma Shobō, 1974.
Nakazato Yoshio. *Nihon no shōzōga*. Iwasaki Bijutsusha, 1990.
Namiki Seishi. "Kano Masanobu no shōzōga seisaku ni tsuite: Jizōinzō kiba mushazō o megutte." *Kyōto Geijutsu Tanki Daigaku kenkyū kiyō*, no. 13 (1991).

Naquin, Susan. "Funerals in North China: Uniformity and Variation." In *Death Ritual in Late Imperial and Modern China*, ed. James L. Watson and Evelyn S. Rawski. Berkeley: University of California Press, 1988.
Naruse Fujio. *Nihon shōzōgashi*. Chūō Kōron Bijutsu Shuppan, 2004.
Naruse Yoshinori. *Bukkyō to girei monoshiri jiten*. Shin Jinbutsu Ōraisha, 1992.
Newel, William, ed. *Ancestors*. The Hague: Mouton, 1976.
Nihon kokugo daijiten [*shukusatsuban*]. Ed. Nihon Daijiten Kankōkai. 10 vols. Shogakkan, 1982.
Nihon no shōzōga: Tokubetsuten. Edited by Yamato Bunkakan. Nara: Yamato Bunkakan, 1991.
Nihonshi daijiten. Edited by Shimononaka Hiroshi. 7 vols. Heibonsha, 1994.
Nishiguchi Junko. "Where the Bones Go: Death and Burial of Women in the Heian High Aristocracy." Translated and adapted by Mimi Yiengpruksawan. In *Engendering Faith: Women and Buddhism in Premodern Japan*, gen. ed. Barbara Ruch. Ann Arbor: The University of Michigan Center for Japanese Studies, 2002.
Nodelman, Sheldon. "How to Read a Roman Portrait." *Art in America* 63, no. 1 (1975): 27–33.
Nōtomi Jōten. "Kamakura jidai no shari shinkō: Kamakura o chūshin to shite." *Indogaku bukkyōgaku kenkyū* 33, no. 2 (1985): 447–451.
Ōbayashi Taryō. *Sōsei no kigen*. Kadokawa Shoten, 1977.
Ōchō no butsuga to girei: Zen o tsukushi, bi o tsukusu. Edited by Kyōto Kokuritsu Hakubutsukan. Kyōto: Kyōto Kokuritsu Hakubutsukan, 1998.
Ōemaki ten. Edited by Kyōto Kokuritsu Hakubutsukan. Yomiuri Shinbunsha, 2006.
Ogino Minahiko. "Moriyakebon den Ashikaga Takaujizō no kenkyū." *Kokka* 906 (September 1969): 7–22, and (October 1969): 7–13.
Ōnishi Hiroshi. *Ikkyū o megutte nani ga okotta ka: Shōzōga ni okeru 'hakaku' no mondai*. Rikiesuta no kai, 2001.
Ooms, Herman. "The Religion of the Household: A Case Study of Ancestor Worship in Japan." *Contemporary Religions in Japan* 8, nos. 3–4 (1967): 201–333.
———. "A Structural Analysis of Japanese Ancestral Rites and Beliefs." In *Ancestors*, ed. William Newel. The Hague: Mouton, 1976.
Osgood, Cornelius. *Ingalik Material Culture*. New Haven, CT: Yale University Press, 1940.
Ozaki Shōzen. "Sōtō-shu sōsō girei no onmyōdō: Taianjizō *ekō narabi shikihō*; Eikyū bunkozō *nenjū gyōji seiki* ni kanshite. *Bukkyōgaku kenkyū* 45, no. 13 (December 1996): 202–205.
Payne, Richard, ed. *Re-Visioning "Kamakura" Buddhism*. Honolulu: University of Hawai'i Press, 1998.
Pearson, Richard. *Ancient Japan*. George Braziller/Sackler Gallery, 1992.
Phillips, Quitman E. "Narrating the Salvation of the Elite: The Jōfukuji Paintings of the Ten Kings." *Ars Orientalis* 33 (2003): 121–145.
———. *The Practices of Painting in Japan 1475–1500*. Stanford, CA: Stanford University Press, 2000.

Plath, David W. "Where the Family of God Is the Family: The Role of the Dead in Japanese Households." *American Anthropologist* 66, no. 2 (1964): 300–317.

Rawson, Jessica. "Ancient Chinese Ritual as Seen in the Material Records." In *State and Court Ritual in China*, ed. Joseph P. McDermott. Cambridge: Cambridge University Press, 1999.

Rosenfield, John M. "Studies in Japanese Portraiture: The Statue of Vimalakirti at Hokkeji." *Ars Orientalis* 6 (1966): 213–222.

Rowe, Mark. "Stickers for Nails: The Ongoing Transformation of Roles, Rites, and Symbols in Japanese Funerals." *Japanese Journal of Religious Studies* 27, nos. 3–4 (2000): 353–378.

Ruch, Barbara. "Coping with Death: Paradigms of Heaven and Hell and the Six Realms in Early Literature and Painting." In *Flowing Traces: Buddhism in the Literary and Visual Arts of Japan*, ed. James H. Sanford, William R. LaFleur, and Masatoshi Nagatomi. Princeton, NJ: Princeton University Press, 1992.

———, gen. ed. *Engendering Faith: Women and Buddhism in Premodern Japan*. Ann Arbor: Center for Japanese Studies, University of Michigan, 2002.

Ruppert, Brian D. *Jewel in the Ashes: Buddha Relics and Power in Early Medieval Japan*. Cambridge, MA: Harvard University Asia Center, 2000.

Saitō Tama. *Shi to mononoke*. Shinjuku Shobō, 1986.

Sakai Tadayoshi and Esaka Teruhisa. "Yamagata-ken Akumi-gun Warabioka-mura Sugisawa hakken no daitō C2-shiki no dogū no shutsudo jōtai ni tsuite." *Kōkogaku zasshi* 39, nos. 3–4 (1954).

Sakakura Atsuyoshi, Honda Giken, and Kawabata Yoshiaki, eds. *Konjaku monogatari-shū, honchōzokubu*. 4 vols. Shinchōsha, 1978–1984.

Sasaki Tokutarō. *Nihonjin no sei to shi*. Iwasaki Bijutsusha, 1968.

Satō Kenji. "Sōsō to tsuizen butsuji ni miru kanpaku-ke gyōji no seiritsu." *Shigaku zasshi* 103, no. 11 (November 1994): 37 (1925)–63 (1951).

Seckel, Dietrich. "The Rise of Portraiture in Chinese Art." *Artibus Asiae* 53, nos. 1–2 (1993): 7–26.

Seidel, Anna. "Dabi." In *Hōbōgirin*, 6: 573–585. Paris: Adrien Maisonneuve, 1983.

Sekine Shun'ichi. *Butsu, bosatsu to dōnai to shōgon*. Nihon no bijutsu 281. Shibundō, 1989.

Senchakushū English Translation Project, trans. and ed. *Hōnen's Senchakushū: Passages on the Selection of the Nembutsu in the Original Vow* (Senchaku hongan nembutsu shū). Honolulu: University of Hawai'i Press, 1998.

Sharf, Elizabeth Horton. "Chinzō and Ōbaku Portraiture." In *Contacts between Cultures*, vol. 3, ed. Bernard Hung-Kay Luk, 422–427. Lewiston, NY: Edwin Mellen Press, 1992.

Sharf, Robert H. "The Idolization of Enlightenment: On the Mummification of Cha'an Masters in Medieval China." *History of Religions* 32, no. 1 (1992): 1–31.

———. "The Scripture on the Production of Buddha Images." In *Religions of China in Practice*, ed. Donald S. Lopez. Princeton, NJ: Princeton University Press, 1996.

Sharf, Robert H., and Elizabeth Horton Sharf, eds. *Living Images: Japanese Buddhist Icons in Context*. Stanford, CA: Stanford University Press, 2001.

Shimosaka Mamoru. *Egakareta Nihon no chūsei: Ezu bunseki ron.* Kyoto: Hōzōkan, 2003.

———. "Moriyakebon kiba mushazō no zōshu ni tsuite." *Gakusō* 4 (1982): 43–59.

Shintani Takanori. *Nihonjin no sōgi.* Kinokuniya Shoten, 1992.

Smith, Robert J. *Ancestor Worship in Contemporary Japan.* Stanford, CA: Stanford University Press, 1974.

———. "Ihai: Mortuary Tablets, the Household and Kin in Japanese Worship." *The Transactions of the Asiatic Society of Japan,* ser. 3, vol. 9 (1966): 171–188.

Snodgrass, Adrian. *The Symbol of the Stupa.* Ithaca, NY: Cornell University Press, 1985.

Sommer, Deborah A. "Images into Words: Ming Confucian Iconoclasm." *National Palace Museum Bulletin* 29, nos. 1–2 (1994): 1–24.

Spiro, Audrey. *Contemplating the Ancients: Aesthetic and Social Issues in Early Chinese Portraiture.* Berkeley and Los Angeles: University of California Press, 1990.

Stevenson, Daniel B., intro. and trans. "Death-Bed Testimonials of the Pure Land Faithful." In *Buddhism in Practice,* ed. Donald S. Lopez, Jr. Princeton, NJ: Princeton University Press, 1995.

Stone, Jacqueline I. *The Buddhist Dead: Practices, Discourses, Representation.* Kuroda Institute Studies in East Asian Buddhism 20. Honolulu: University of Hawai'i Press, 2007.

———. "By the Power of One's Last Nenbutsu: Deathbed Practices in Early Medieval Japan." In *Approaching the Land of Bliss: Religious Praxis in the Cult of Amitābha,* ed. Richard K. Payne and Kenneth K. Tanaka. Kuroda Institute Studies in East Asian Buddhism 17. Honolulu: University of Hawai'i Press, 2004.

———. "Rebuking the Enemies of the Lotus: Nichirenist Exclusivism in Historical Perspective." *Japanese Journal of Religious Studies* 21, nos. 2–3 (1994): 231–259.

Stone, Jacqueline I., and Mariko Namba Walter, eds. *Death and the Afterlife in Japanese Buddhism.* Honolulu: University of Hawai'i Press, 2008.

Stuart, Jan. "Calling Back the Ancestor's Shadow: Chinese Ritual and Commemorative Portraits." *Oriental Art* 43, no. 3 (Autumn 1997): 8–17.

Stuart, Jan, and Evelyn S. Rawski. *Worshiping the Ancestors: Chinese Commemorative Portraits.* Stanford, CA: Stanford University Press, 2001.

Suitō Makoto. *Chūsei no sōsō, bosei: Sekitō o zōryū suru koto.* Yoshikawa Kōbunkan, 1991.

Suzuki, Hikaru. "Japanese Death Ritual in Transit: From Household Ancestors to Beloved Antecedents." *Journal of Contemporary Religions* 13, no. 2 (1998): 171–188.

———. *The Price of Death: The Funeral Industry in Contemporary Japan.* Stanford, CA: Stanford University Press, 2000.

Suzuki Hisashi. *Hone wa monogataru Tokugawa shogun, daimyōke no hitobito.* Tōkyō Daigaku Shuppan, 1985.

Suzuki Norio. *Kuyōgu to sōgu* (*Nihon no bijutsu* 283). Shibundō, 1989.

Takagi Yutaka. *Nichiren: Sono kōdō to shisō. Nihonjin no kōdō to shisō* 4. Hyōronsha, 1970.

Takagishi Akira. *Muromachi ōken to kaiga: Shoki Tosa-ha kenkyū.* Kyoto: Kyōto Daigaku Gakujitsu Shuppankai, 2004.

———. "Seiryōjibon 'Yūzū nenbutsu engi' to Ashikaga Yoshimitsu shichikaiki tsuizen." *Bukkyō bijutsu* 264 (September 2000): 50–70.

Takahashi Hatsuko. "Chūsei no kuge shakai to onmyōdō nit suite: *Moromoriki* ni miru." In *Onmyōdō sōsho: 2 chūsei*, comp. Murayama Shūichi et al. Meicho Shuppan, 1993.

Takahashi Osamu. "Hino (Uramatsu) Shigeko ni kansuru ikkōsatsu." *Kokushigaku* 137 (1989): 1–20.

Takahashi Shigeyuki. *Sōsai no nihonshi*. Kōdansha, 2004.

Takeda Chōshū. *Sōsōbosei kenkyū shūsei 3: Senzokuyō*. Meicho Shuppan, 1979.

Takeda Tsuneo. "Kinpeki shōhekiga ni tsuite." *Bukkyō geijutsu* 59 (December 1965): 105–122.

Takemura Toshinori. *Shinsen Kyōto meisho zue*. 7 vols. Kyoto: Shirakawa Shoin, 1975.

Takeuchi Rizō. *Nara ibun*. 2 vols. Tōkyōdō, 1943–1944.

Tamamuro Taijō. *Sōshiki bukkyō*. Daihōrinkaku, 1971.

Tambiah, S. J. "A Performative Approach to Ritual." In *Proceedings of the British Academy* 65:113–169. New York/London: Oxford University Press, 1981.

Tamura Hanae. "Chūsei shōzōga ni okeru 'za' no mondai." In Kuroda Hideo et al., *Shōzōga o yomu*. Kadokawa Shoten, 1998.

Tanabe, George Joji, and Willa Tanabe, eds. *The Lotus Sutra in Japanese Culture*. Honolulu: University of Hawai'i Press, 1989.

Tanaka Hisao. *Sosen saishi no kenkyū*. Kōbundō, 1978.

Tani Nobukazu. "Muromachi jidai ni okeru shōzōga no seisaku katei." *Kokka* 475 (May 1937): 129–133, and 476 (June 1937): 159–162.

———. "Shutsujin ei no kenkyū: Jizōinbon wa Ashikaga Yoshihisa zō naru koto." *Bijutsu kenkyū* 67 (July 1937): 269–279, and 69 (August 1937): 352–361.

Tazawa Hiroyoshi. *Josei no shōzō*. Nihon no bijutsu 384. Shibundō, 1998.

Teiser, Stephen F. *The Ghost Festival in Medieval China*. Princeton, NJ: Princeton University Press, 1988.

———. *The Scripture on the Ten Kings and the Making of Purgatory in Medieval Chinese Buddhism*. Honolulu: University of Hawai'i Press, 1994.

Tōji to Kōbō daishi shinkō: Tōji mieidō, chikai to inori no fūkei. Edited and compiled by Tōji (Kyōōgokuji) Hōmotsukan. Benridō, 2001.

Tokubetsu tenrankai: Ōchō no butsuga to girei: Zen o tsukushi, bi o tsukusu. Kyoto National Museum, 1998.

Tōkyō Kokuritsu Hakubutsukan. *Tokubetsu chinretsu: Nihon no shōzōga*. Tōkyō Kokuritsu Hakubutsukan, 1991.

Toynbee, J. M. C. *Death and Burial in the Roman World*. Ithaca, NY: Cornell University Press, 1971.

Turner, Victor. "Frame, Flow and Reflection: Ritual and Drama as Public Liminality." *Japanese Journal of Religious Studies* 6, no. 4 (December 1979): 465–498.

———. *The Ritual Process Structure and Anti-Structure*. Ithaca, NY: Cornell University Press, 1969.

Tylor, Edward B. *Primitive Culture: Researches into the Development of Mythology, Philosophy, Religion, Language, Art, and Custom* [1871]. London: John Murray, 1919.

Ueno Teruo. *Nihon shōzōga*. Kōbundō Shobō, 1940.
Umezu Jirō. "Fujiwara Kanetsune zō." *Kokka* 88 (1965): 10–20.
———. "Kamakura jidai yamatoe shōzōga no keifu: Zokunin zō to sōryo zō." *Bukkyō geijutsu* 23 (1954).
van Gennep, Arnold. *The Rites of Passage* [1909]. Translated by Monika B. Vizedom and Gabrielle I. Caffee. Chicago: University of Chicago Press, 1960.
Varley, H. Paul. "Ashikaga Yoshimitsu and the World of Kitayama: Social Change and Shogunal Patronage in Early Muromachi Japan." In *Japan in the Muromachi Age*, ed. John Whitney Hall and Toyoda Takeshi. Berkeley, Los Angeles, London: University of California Press, 1977.
Vinograd, Richard. *Boundaries of the Self: Chinese Portraits, 1600–1900*. Cambridge: Cambridge University Press, 1992.
Wakasugi Junji. *Nise-e*. Nihon no bijutsu 469. Shibundō, 2005.
Wakita Haruko. "Muromachiki no keizai hatten." In *Iwanami kōza Nihon rekishi*, vol. 7. Iwanami Shoten, 1976.
Wakita Osamu. *Kinsei hōkensei seiritsu shiron*. Tōkyō Daigaku Shuppankai, 1977.
Watsky, Andrew M. *Chukubushima: Deploying the Sacred Arts in Momoyama Japan*. Seattle and London: University of Washington Press, 2004.
Watson, James L., and Evelyn Rawski, eds. *Death Rituals in Late Imperial and Modern China*. Berkeley and Los Angeles: University of California Press, 1988.
Williams, Duncan Ryūken. *The Other Side of Zen: A Social History of Sōtō Zen Buddhism in Tokugawa Japan*. Princeton and Oxford: Princeton University Press, 2005.
Winfield, Pamela D. "Curing with *Kaji*: Healing and Esoteric Empowerment in Japan." *Japanese Journal of Religious Studies* 32, no. 1 (2005): 107–130.
Wolf, Arthur P. "Chinese Kinship and Mourning Dress." In *Family and Kinship in Chinese Society*, ed. Maurice Freedman. Stanford, CA: Stanford University Press, 1970.
Wu Hung. *Monumentality in Early Chinese Art and Architecture*. Stanford, CA: Stanford University Press, 1995.
Yamamoto Gyōshun. "Sōshiki o kangaeru: Indō o chūshin ni." *Tendai* 12 (1987): 46–51; 13 (1988): 36–43; 14 (1989): 74–82.
Yamamoto Kōji. *Kegare to ōharae*. Heibonsha, 1992.
Yamamoto Nobuyoshi. "Hakke hakkō to Michinaga no sanjū kō." *Bukkyō geijutsu* 77 (1970): 71–84, and 78 (October 1970): 81–95.
Yampolsky, Philip B., ed. *Selected Writings of Nichiren*. Translated by Burton Watson et al. New York: Columbia University Press, 1990.
Yanagita Kunio. "Sōsei no enkaku ni tsuite." In *Yanagita Kunio shū*, 14:289–306. Chikuma Shobō, 1975.
———. *Sōsō shūzoku goi*. Minkan Denshō no Kai, 1937.
Yiengpruksawa, Mimi. *Hiraizumi: Buddhist Art and Regional Politics in Twelfth-Century Japan*. Cambridge, MA: Harvard University Press, 1998.
———. "The House of Gold: Fujiwara Kiyohira's Konjikidō." *Monumenta Nipponica* 48, no. 1 (Spring 1993): 33–52.
———. "In My Image: The Ichiji Kinrin Statue at Chūsonji." *Monumenta Nipponica* 46, no. 3 (Autumn 1991): 329–347.

Yifa. *The Origins of Buddhist Monastic Codes in China: An Annotated Translation and Study of the Chanyuan qinggui*. A Kuroda Institute Book. Honolulu: University of Hawai'i Press, 2002.

Yokoi Kiyoshi. "'Nikki' to 'gyoki' no aida." *Bungaku* 52, no. 7 (1984): 69.

Yonekura Michio. *Minamoto no Yoritomo zō: Chinmoku no shōzōga*. Heibonsha, 1995.

———. *Nihon ni okeru bijutsu shigaku no seiritsu to tenkai*. Tōkyō Kokuritsu Bunkazai Kenkyūjo, 2001.

Zheng Yan. "Muzhu huaxiang yanjiu." In *Liu Dunyuan xiansheng jinian wenji*. Jizhou: Shangdong Daxue Chubanshe, 1997.

INDEX

Page numbers in **boldface** refer to figures.

abbots, Zen funerals, 17, 48, 76, 161, 164
Akamatsu Masanori, 159
altars: burials in, 94, 105–107; at cremation sites, 139–140, 174; memorial tablets on, 94; portraits displayed on, 162, 173, 174; ritual objects on, 143–145
Amida: images of, 25, 35, 40, 60, 133, 142, 143, 144; Pure Land of, 93, 142
Amida Sutra (*Amida kyō*), 26, 32, 36, 39, 40, 46, 190n127
Amida Triad images, 36, 40, 42, 144, **144,** 169
ancestors: memorial services for, 48; portraits, 147, 150, 157; transition of deceased to, 37–38; veneration, 44, 48, 150, 165
aristocracy. *See* elites
Ashikaga family temple. *See* Tōjiin
Ashikaga Mochiuji, 62, 195n57
Ashikaga shoguns: clothing of mourners, 129–130; cremation sites, 98; memorial tablets, 63, 94–95, 165; portraits, 39, 48, 58, 177; Zen-style funerals, 70
Ashikaga Takauji: funeral, 48–49, 65; at imperial memorial services, 190n115; portrait, 65, 170, 177; temple established by, 62
Ashikaga Yoshiharu, 92
Ashikaga Yoshihisa, 92, 159
Ashikaga Yoshikatsu, 67
Ashikaga Yoshikazu, 62
Ashikaga Yoshimasa: funeral, 71, 162, 171; memorial services, 171; at mother's funeral, 68–70; portrait, 155, 158, 159, 162, 171; as shogun, 67–68

Ashikaga Yoshimitsu: funeral, 50, 71–74, 76, 77–78, 127, 172; Golden Pavilion (Kinkakuji), 94; memorial services, 171; memorial tablet, 165; portraits, **160,** 161, 171–172, 177; wife, 67, 181n24
Ashikaga Yoshimochi: clothing of mourners, 129; coffin, 63, 126; cremation, 65, 101, 164; cremation site, 58, 103, 164; death, 62, 163; funeral, 7, 50, 62–67, 75–76, 78, 124, 163–164; at funeral of predecessor, 72; lying-in-state period, 63, 64, 76; memorial services, 67; memorial tablet, 63, 165; portrait, 63, 66, 78, 158, 163–164, 174; Yoshimitsu's portrait and, 161, 171
Ashikaga Yoshinori: dedication of Yoshimitsu's portrait, 171; marriage, 67; portrait, 177; selection as shogun, 62–63; at Yoshimochi's funeral and memorial services, 65, 66, 67, 126, 129. *See also* Hino Shigeko

banners (*ban*), 119–122, **122, Plate 6**
beggars, 36
Bell, Catherine, 1–2
black, as color of death, 84
black clothing, 29–30, 129
bodies. *See* corpses
Bodiford, William M., 51, 58, 71
Boki ekotoba, 140–141, **140**
Bonmō no jūjū, 26, 28, 32, 33, 35, 38, 39, 40, 46
bronze ritual objects, 113, 132, **132**
Buddhist death rituals: adoption in Japan, 57; codification, 50; contemporary Japanese

practices, 78–79; eclecticism, 93; liminal, 16; postliminal, 16; preliminal, 15–16; purpose, 15, 38; structure, 15–16; temple income, 24–25, 38. *See also* cremation; funerals; memorial services; ritual implements, Buddhist; Zen funeral rituals
burial codes, 6, 116–117. *See also* Yōrō code
burials: popularity in Japan, 183n23; processions to gravesite, 85; temporary, 105; of women, 104–106. *See also* graves

candleholders, 123–124, 164
canopies, 127–128, **Plate 9**
cardinal directions: arrangement of corpses, 54, 78, 84, 91, 101, 111; gates of cremation enclosures, 99–101; in ritual performance, 52, 66–67, 69; yin-yang theory and, 39
carriages, 84, 93, 95, 125. *See also* palanquins
cemeteries, 26, 47. *See also* Ryōzen
censers (*egōro*), 123, 164, **Plate 7**
censers (*kōro*), 123–124
Chan Buddhism: funerals, 164, 165, 166; memorial tablets, 165; monastic codes, 16–17, 145. *See also* Zen funerals
charity, 36
chime (*kei*), 136–137, 141–142
China: Buddhist images, 149–150; funeral processions, 116; monastic codes, 6; portraits, 153–157, 175–176. *See also* Chan Buddhism
Chion'in, 130, 132, 139, 166
chopsticks, positioning of, 29
chūin (or *chūu*), 58–59. *See also* mourning periods
clothes-changing ceremony (*chakufuku no gi*), 28–30, 129
clothing: black, 29–30, 129; colors, 128–130, 207nn67, 68; for corpses, 53, 85, 91; monks' robes, 128; mourning, 29–30, 40, 69, 128–130; white, 29, 69, 84, 96, 129–130
coffins, 86–89; closing ritual (*sagan butsuji*), 17, 63, 64, 69, 77, 173; cloth cords attached to, 63, 65, 69, 79, 126, 196n61, 198n96; at cremation site, 73–74; handscrolls depicting, **87**, 88, **88;** lacquered, 86, 199n15; placement in temples, 72; placing corpse in, 84, 86; preparation, 86–88; ritual for moving to cremation site (*kigan butsuji*), 17, 63, 65, 69, 77, 164; ritual for placing corpse in (*nyūgan butsuji*), 17, 56, 77, 78, 92; round, 126; screens placed near, 70, 92; sizes, 86; stones used to nail lid, 64, 79; timing of encoffining, 56, 68
Cole, Alan, 17
colors: associated with death, 84; of mourning clothes, 29–30, 69, 128–130, 207nn67, 68. *See also* white
commoners, funerals of, 9
condolence calls, 55, 72, 76
Confucianism: ancestor veneration, 150, 165; funerals, 165; influences on Chinese monastic funerals, 16; mourning clothes, 207n64; mourning periods, 53; ritual use of portraits, 176; social structure, 159; view of death, 182n9
containers, functions of, 83, 111–112. *See also* carriages; coffins; palanquins
corpses: avoiding contact with, 21, 41, 84; bathing, 53, 75, 78, 84; danger of moving, 65; head placement to north, 54, 78, 84, 91, 101, 111; lying-in-state periods, 63, 64, 76, 92; moving in secret and at night, 41, 55–56, 118–119; mummified, 94, 106, 150; observation of, 75; odor of, 123; paper covers, 86; pollution associated with, 21, 41, 52, 65; preparation of, 53–54, 86, 111; removal from residences, 41, 55–56, 62, 64, 68–69, 75–76; ritual for moving to temple (*igan butsuji*), 17, 64, 77; robes, 53, 85, 91; separation from living, 84, 111; shrouds, 84, 85–86, **87;** treated as if still alive, 37, 56, 194n36. *See also* burials; cremation
courtiers. *See* elites
cremation: in ancient Japan, 57; Buddhist practices, 19, 57–58; departure of spirit, 57, 173; of imperial family members, 51, 57–58; objects burned, 125, 206n46; purpose, 21; of shoguns, 65; timing, 76
cremation ceremonies (*dabi no gi*), 57, 66; lighting of fire (*ako butsuji*; also *hinko butsuji*), 17, 49, 66, 69, 70, 77, 164, 197n88; retrieving remains (*kikotsu butsuji*), 66, 67, 69, 70, 77, 78; ritual offerings, 66, 69, 77, 78
cremation sites: circumambulations, 65, 100–101, **100;** enclosures, 56, 58, 65, 84–85, 97–103; fences, 97–99; gates, 98, 99–101, **100;** hearths, 102; huts, 84–85, 102; pollution associated with, 66–67; processions to, 57, 63, 65, 69, 72–73, 77, 162, 164; rough, unfinished materials,

84–85, 97; temporary structures, 56, 65, 84–85, 101–103, 164
Cunningham, Michael, 4

dabi no gi. See cremation ceremonies
Daikōmyōji, 51, 53, 54, 56, 60, 192n7
Daily Buddha Offering Ceremony (*nichibutsu kuyō*), 22–24, 30
Dainichi, 27, 38
Daizōkyō (Great collection of sutras), 6
Daoism: ancestor veneration, 150; influences on Chinese monastic funerals, 16
darani. See incantations
death: ancient views of, 15; Chan beliefs, 17; intermediate state following, 58–59; preparation for, 155; right mindfulness at last moment, 91–92; scholarship on, 2–3. *See also* corpses; spirit of deceased
death pollution. *See* pollution, death, protection of living from
death talismans (*monoimi fuda*), 26–27, **27**
deities: of fire, 19–20, 21; hearth-fire, 19–21, 41–42; kitchen, 20
Denpō-e, 115
Diamond World Mandala, 139, 142, 143
diaries, 6–7, 17–18, 152–153
division-of-possessions ceremony (*sōzoku no gi*), 41
donations, 33–34, 35–37, 45–46
dragon heads (*ryūzu sao, tatsugashira*), 119, **120,** 121, **Plate 6**
dragons, association with death, 119–121

Eiga monogatari, 52, 91, 152
Eison, 155–156
elites: memorial services, 167–170; ordinations just before or after death, 19, 53, 68
elites, funerals of: burials in altars, 106; canopies, 127; cremations, 65; in fourteenth century, 48; of Hino Shigeko, 7, 50, 67–71, 76, 92; portraits of deceased, 64–65, 153; preferences, 55; preparations, 75; removal of corpse from residence, 55–56; structure, 16; textual sources, 7–8, 9, 17–18; timing, 162–163; of women, 70–71; Zen-style, 17, 64–65, 78, 161. *See also* funeral processions; imperial funerals; shoguns, funerals of
Enchin, 151–152, **151**
enclosures: as barrier between living and dead, 98; cremation huts, 84–85, 102; of cremation sites, 56, 58, 65, 84–85, 97–103; fences, 85, 97–99, 104, 107–111; functions, 83, 98, 99, 111–112; of gravesites, 104–107; layers, 85. *See also* containers, function of; screens
Engi code, 6
Enmyōin Nitchō, 114, 115, 118, 203n3. *See also Nichiren shōnin chūgasan*
Enshōbō, 28, 33, 35, 37, 39, 40
Entairyaku, 19
Esoteric funeral rituals, 6, 16–17
Esoteric mandala, 100
Etruscan tomb goods, 15

families: clothes-changing ceremony, 28–30, 129; hierarchical organization, 159; offerings by nuclear, 37; portraits commissioned by, 159. *See also* ancestors
fences: at cremation sites, 97–99; enclosing graves, 85, 104, 107–111
Festival of the Dead (*bon*), 79
Flanigan, C. Clifford, 116
flowers: lotus, 93, 119; motifs on screens, 92–93; offerings of, 132, 141; paper, 119, **Plate 6**
flower vases (*kebyō*), 123–124, 164
folding screens (*byōbu*), 53, 54, 89–94. *See also* screens
Foulk, T. Griffith, 156
Freedberg, David, 175
Fudō Myōō, images of, 25, 26, 60, 132, 133, 142, 143
Fugen Bosatsu, images of, 25, 26, 143
Fujiwara no Kishi, 54, 56
Fujiwara no Kiyohira, 94, 106
Fujiwara no Nagaie, 105
Fujiwara no Shōshi, 105
Fujiwara no Shunzei, 64, 86, 104
Fujiwara no Sōshi, 20, 105–106
Fujiwara no Tadahira, 153
Fujiwara no Tadamichi, 20, 105
Fujiwara no Teika, 64
Fujiwara no Teishi, 95, 104–105
Fujiwara no Yoshimichi, 56
funeral manuals, 6, 172
funeral practices, scholarship on, 2–3
funeral processions: banners, 119–122; canopies, 127–128, **Plate 9;** Chinese, 116; communal participation, 117; contemporary Japanese practices, 79; to cremation sites, 57, 63, 65, 69, 72–73, 77, 162, 164; as displays of power, 116; of Hino Shigeko, 68–69; in Meiji period, 204n11; of Nichiren, 115–116, 117–128,

174, **Plates 6–10;** nighttime, 118–119; palanquins, 56, 62, 68, 194n33; purposes, 116, 117; sections, 117–118; size related to status of deceased, 116; timing, 75–76; of Yoshihito, 56–57; of Yoshimitsu, 72–73
funerals: of commoners, 9; contemporary Japanese practices, 121; preparations, 75, 162; regulations, 6, 116–117, 172; timing dependent on season, 76, 162, 163; traditions followed, 37, 39–40, 41, 56, 58, 64, 70. See also Buddhist death rituals; elites, funerals of; imperial funerals; monastic funerals; shoguns, funerals of
Fushiminomiya Sadafusa, Prince, 7, 51, 56, 57, 60. See also *Kanmon gyoki*

Gaki zōshi, 107, **107**
Ganjin (C. Jianzhen), 150–151
Genchū, 66
gender: differences in funeral ceremonies, 71; physical separation at memorial services, 39, 40; status differences, 71, 159; yin-yang theory, 39. See also men; women
Genji monogatari, 52
Genryū Shūkō, 71. See also *Jishōindono ryōan sōbo*
Go-Daigo, Emperor, memorial services, 43, 190n115
Go-Fushimi, Emperor, 51, 130
Go-Ichijō, Emperor: burning of personal items, 93; cremation site, 98, 101–102, 103; funeral, 96, 101–102, 152, 182n4, 204n9; funeral procession, 122, 123; memorial services, 152–153; portrait, 152–153
gold: on buildings, 94; symbolism, 93, 200n38; use for objects connected to death, 94–95
golden carriages, 95
Golden Pavilion (Kinkakuji), 94
golden screens, 70, 92, 93–94
Gorai Shigeru, 2, 99, 119–121
Go-Shirakawa, Emperor, 104
Go-Tsuchimikado, Retired Emperor, 155
Gozen Onkata. See Nakahara Kenshin
grave enclosures (*kuginuki*), 31, 32, 44, 107–111
grave markers: costs, 32, 44; stone, 110; stone pagodas, 31–32, 107; timing of placement, 44–45; use of, 107; wooden, 31
graves: enclosures, 104–107, 107–111, **109, 110;** family visits, 26, 27, 34, 35, 39, 43, 44, 107–108; fences, 85, 104, 107–111; pagodas, 105–106; social status of dead and, 108; Spirit Halls, 104–105; structures built over, 38–39; sutras placed on, 32–33. See also cemeteries
gravestone offering ceremony (*sekitō kuyō*), 33
grave tablets, wooden (*sotoba*), 33, **33,** 38, 107

Haga Noboru, 2
hair-cutting ceremony, 27–28
Hakusōrei (Order for simple burials), 6, 116
handscrolls, documentation of funeral rituals, 8–9, 97. See also scrolls
hanging scrolls, **23,** 59. See also portraits of deceased
Haruhito, Prince, 56, 57, 59, 60
headbands (*hokaku*), 119
healing incantations (*kaji*), 51
hearth-fire god (*kamadogami*), 19–21, 41–42
Heart Sutra (*Hannya shingyō*), 39, 40, 46
Heihanki (*Hyōhanki*), 20
Hell. See Ten Kings of Hell
Higuchidera, 47, 48, 191n131
hinin (beggars), 36
Hino family, 67, 181n24
Hino Shigeko: clothing of mourners, 129–130; cremation, 69–70, 76, 101, 103; death, 68; funeral, 7, 50, 67–71, 76, 92; funeral procession, 68–69, 124; marriage, 67; portrait, 68, 78; screens used at funeral, 93; sons, 67–68
Hino Tomiko, 159
Hōjiji, 41
Hokke mandala offering ceremony (*Hokke mandara kuyō*), 34–35
Hōkyōin darani, 26, 32, 35, 38, 40, 43, 46, 187n76
Hōnen: career, 130; death, 130; *Denpō-e*, 115; memorial services, 131–139, 166; portraits, 166, **167, 168**
Hōnen shōnin e-den (Illustrated biography of priest Hōnen), 8; banners illustrated, 121, **122;** coffin of Hōnen, 88, **89,** 127; creation of, 130; cremation of Hōnen, 97, 98–99, **Plate 4;** funeral procession, 129; Hōnen on deathbed, 89, **90,** 91; memorial processions, 114; memorial services illustrated, 130–139, **131, 134, 135, 136, 137, 138,** 166, **Plate 11;** portrait of Hōnen, 166, **167**
Horikawa, Emperor, 106
Horikawadono, 159
Hōryūji, 121

Huineng, 150

ihai. See memorial tablets
Ikkō sect, 41, 43, 44, 47
imperial family: memorial services, 43, 152–153, 190n115; portraits, 152–153, 157. *See also* Yoshihito, Prince; *individual emperors by name*
imperial funerals: Buddhist ceremonies, 57; burials, 104–105; corpses kept in residences, 64, 76; cremations, 51, 57–58; cremation sites, 98, 101–102; Esoteric, 6; of Go-Ichijō, 96, 101–102, 122, 123, 152, 182n4, 204n9; manuals, 6, 172; mourning halls, 101–102; processions, 84, 95–96; of Shirakawa, 85–86; of Shōmu, 57; shrouds, 85–86; of Toba, 86, 91; of women, 104–105; of Yoshihito, 7, 50, 51–61, 76, 78
Imperial Palace Archives Office (Fudono; also Kyōshoden), 30, 47
impermanence, 112
incantations (*darani*), 26, 32, 46, 54, 55
incense: odor of corpse concealed by, 123; offerings, 55, 59, 60, 66, 123; *shikimi* bark and leaves in, 141
incense burners, 132, **132,** 140–141
Indian Buddhism: canopies, 127; cremation, 57; memorial services, 185n40
Inryōken nichiroku (Daily record of the Inryōken), 7, 50, 67–71, 78, 92, 158, 171
Ippen, 41
Itō Yuishin, 3, 41, 45

Japanese star anise. See *shikimi*
Jibutsudō, 36, 37, 39, 40, 48, 60, 195n48
Jien, 138–139
Jikuun, 69, 70
Jimon denki horoku, 151–152
Jingihaku sōmoki, 121
Ji sect, 41, 163
Jishōindono ryōan sōbo (Complete record of national mourning for Lord Jishōin), 7, 50, 71–74, 77–78, 127, 165, 172
Jitō, Empress, 57
Jizō: devotion to, 170; images of, 25, 26, 33, 142, 143
Jizōdō, 41, 42, 43, 44, 47
Jodō sanbukyō, 33, 93
Juryō-bon, 35, 60, 188n84

Kagutsuchi (fire god), 19–20, 21
Kaiketsu no nikyō, 46

Kakunyo, 140
Kanmon gyoki (Record of things seen and heard), 7, 50, 51–61, 65, 66, 78, 103
Kannon, images of, 25, 30–31, 40, 143
Kannon repentance ceremony (*Kannon senbō*), 60
Kano Masanobu, 94–95, 162, 171
Katsuda Itaru, 3, 126
Kennaiki (or *Kendaiki*; Record of Kenshōin Naifu Madenokōji Tokifusa), 7, 50, 62–67, 78, 103, 158, 163–164, 165, 172, 173, 174
Kichiji ryakki (An outline of auspicious affairs), 6, 86, 91, 98, 99, 102, 103, 172
Kichiji shidai (Order of auspicious affairs), 6, 53, 55, 86, 172
Kikei Shinzui, 7, 67, 68, 69. See also *Inryōken nichiroku*
Kisen Shūshō, 7, 67, 95. See also *Inryōken nichiroku*
Kōdaiji, 94
Kōgimonin, Empress, 51
komorisō (priests in seclusion during mourning period), 28, 31–32, 33–34, 54
Kōmyō shingon: performance at memorial services, 28; recitations, 32, 33, 35, 36, 38, 39, 40, 43, 46, 53; sand ritual, 26, 53, 86; in Shingon funerals, 182n3
Kongō Dainichi Nyorai, 38
Konjikidō, 94
Kōtoku, Emperor, 6
Ku-amidabutsu, 166
Kubota Muneyasu, 114. See also *Nichiren shōnin chūgasan*
Kūichibō, 24, 28, 31–32, 33, 35, 37, 38, 39, 47, 185n45
Kūkai, 52, 152

lacquer: on coffins, 86, 199n15; on memorial tablets, 125, 174; on wooden implements, 113–114
lanterns (*chōchin*), 122–123, 124
leaving-the-house ceremony (*shukke no gi*), 27–28
letters: at memorial services, 133; pledging donations, 33, 35–36, 188n81; requesting sutra recitations, 133
Li ji (Book of rites), 116
lineage portraits (*soshizō*), 152, 177
lotus flowers, 93, 119
Lotus Sutra (*Hoke kyō*): copying, 24, 33, 35, 39, 40, 60; Nichiren's devotion to, 8, 125; phrases written on grave tablets,

38, 40, 43, 46; recitations, 24, 28, 35, 37, 38, 40, 43, 46, 71; scrolls carried in Nichiren's procession, 125

Madenokōji Tokifusa, 65. See also *Kennaiki*
mandala: Diamond World, 139, 142, 143; Esoteric, 100; *Hokke*, 34–35; *Taima*, 92–93
mantras, 26
material culture: definition, 2; scholarship on, 2
Meigetsuki (Fujiwara Teika), 64
memorial services: altars, 139–140; for ancestors, 48; annual, 39–40, 165, 185n40; contemporary Japanese practices, 79; costs, 24; for elites, 167–170; in first forty-nine days, 16, 58–61, 79, 165, 167–170; of Hōnen, 130–139; images used in, 22–24, 142–143; imperial, 43, 152–153, 190n115; in Indian Buddhism, 185n40; locations, 37, 48; monthly, 37–38, 79, 165; offerings, 175; one-hundredth day, 38–39, 45–46; one-month anniversary, 31–32, 37; physical arrangement in temples, 60, **61;** portraits of deceased, 48, 65, 152–153, 156, 165–173, 174–175; proper conduct of, 133; purposes, 16, 133, 175; ritual implements, 124, 130–139; schedules, 16, 22, 34, 35, 38, 40, 42–43, 47, 165; seventh-day ceremonies, 24–26, 27–31, 33–34, 35–37, 42–44, 59, 131–139, 165
memorial tablets (*ihai*): in China, 165; at cremation site, 165; functions, 95, 164, 170–171; at funerals, 161, 165; golden letters, 92, 94–95, 125, **Plate 2;** on graves, 174; lacquered, 125, 174; names written on, 165; of Nichiren, 125, **Plate 8;** in processions, 57, 63, 72; of shoguns, 63, 94–95, 165; as substitute for deceased's body, 164, 165, 170–171; wooden, 125, 165, 174; of Yoshihito, 57, 60; at Zen-style funerals, 161
men: memorial services, 44; mourning clothes, 129; offerings by, 46; portraits of deceased, 159; segregation from women at memorial services, 39, 40. See also gender
menstrual pollution, 34
merit: generated before death, 108, 155; transference, 36–37, 38–39, 44, 46, 70, 125, 155. See also donations; offerings
Miroku, images of, 26
monastic funerals: Chinese traditions, 16–17, 165, 166; illustrations, 8; manuals, 6; Pure Land Buddhism, 8; for Zen abbots, 17, 48, 76, 161, 164; for Zen priests, 8, 48, 63, 64
Monju, 26
monks: lineage portraits, 152; mummified bodies, 150–151; portraits, 149, 150–151, 154, 155–156, 164; robes, 128; wandering (*hijiri*), 52. See also priests
Moromoriki (Record of Moromori), 7, 18–40, 41–48, 65, 129, 143, 157–158, 163, 167–170
Morse, Anne Nishimura, 4
Morse, Samuel Crowell, 4
mortuary rituals: pictorial sources, 8–9, 97, 172–173; rules, 6, 116–117; similarities across societies, 15; textual sources, 6–8, 17–18, 50. See also Buddhist death rituals; funerals; Zen funeral rituals
mourning periods: Buddhist, 16; clothes-changing ceremony, 28–30, 129; clothing, 29–30, 40, 69, 128–130; Confucian, 53; contemporary Japanese practices, 79; Daily Buddha Offering Ceremony, 22–24, 30; first forty-nine days, 16, 22–37, 58–61, 165; images used in, 21–22; status of soul, 58–59, 169, 174–175. See also memorial services
musical instruments, 63, 123, **Plate 7**
Myōhō renge kyō, 46, 190n122

Nakahara family, 183n16; donations by, 33–34, 35–36, 45–46; hereditary office, 30, 47; memorial services for ancestors, 48; visits to graves, 26, 27, 34, 35, 39, 43, 44
Nakahara Gakumyō, 42, 158, 169
Nakahara Goryō, 29, 34, 35, 36, 43
Nakahara Kenshin (Gozen Onkata): burial, 41–42, 46–47, 104, 163; clothes-changing ceremony, 29; death, 40, 41; donations by, 36; family visits to grave, 43, 44; funeral, 41, 163; funeral compared to husband's funeral, 44, 45–48, 71; grave marker, 44–45, 47; illness, 41, 42; memorial services, 42–44, 45–46, 169; portrait, 40, 42, 157–158, 163, 167–170; portrait of husband dedicated by, 39, 167; tonsure taken by, 27–28, 41; visits to husband's grave, 26, 34, 35
Nakahara Morokō, 30
Nakahara Moromori: clothes-changing ceremony, 29, 129; mourning clothes, 129; offerings to portraits, 42, 169–170; re-

Index

turn to work, 36; visits to father's grave, 26, 27, 35, 40; visits to mother's grave, 43, 44. See also *Moromoriki*
Nakahara Moroshige: clothes-changing ceremony, 29, 129; illness, 43; mourning clothes, 129; placement of father's grave marker, 31–32; visits to father's grave, 26, 27, 35, 40; visits to mother's grave, 44
Nakahara Morosuke: burial, 19; death, 18–19; family visits to grave, 26, 27, 34, 35, 39; funeral, 19–21, 37, 163; funeral compared to wife's funeral, 44, 45–48, 71; grave, 32–33, 46–47, 107–109, 191n133; grave marker, 31–32, 44; hall over grave, 38–39, 40; *Hokke* mandala offering ceremony, 34–35; memorial services, 24–26, 28–31, 33–36, 37–40, 44, 45–46, 143, 167; memorial services schedule, 22, 35, 38, 40; office, 30, 47; portrait, 39, 40, 42, 157–158, 159, 167–170; tonsure taken by, 19
Nakahara Yūa, 33, 188n80
names, Buddhist (*kaimyō*), 94–95, 165, 200n35
Nanbu Toshiyasu, 94
Nenbutsu: concentrated recitation, 143; performance by nuns, 33, 34, 35, 40; recitations, 26, 32, 41, 43, 131; special, 33, 38
Nenbutsu services, 144–145, **145**
nenju, 29, 54, 55, 69, 193n28
Nichibutsu, 21, 22–24
Nichiren: attacks on, 204n13; followers, 116, 117–118, 128, **Plate 10;** memorial tablet, 125, **Plate 8;** portrait, 174
Nichiren sect, 114, 115
Nichiren shōnin chūgasan (Annotated illustrations of priest Nichiren), 8; creation of, 114–115; cremation of Nichiren, 97, 98–99, 101, 102, **Plate 3;** funeral procession, 115–116, 117–128, 174, **Plates 6–10;** grave of Nichiren, 110–111, **110;** palanquin, 116, 117, 125–127, **Plate 9;** ritual implements illustrated, 116, 117, **Plates 6–9**
Nihongi (also *Nihon shoki*), 19–20, 21, 121
Nison'in, 166
Nissei, 114, 115
Noritoki kyōki (Record of Lord Noritoki), 72

offerings: on behalf of deceased, 24, 37, 38, 55, 132, 175; to deities, 43, 124; during forty-nine-day mourning period, 22, 25, 33, 37; incense, 55, 59, 60, 66, 123; on one-hundredth-day memorial, 45–46; of plants and flowers, 132, 141; to portraits of deceased, 42, 169–170, 173, 174; purposes, 24, 25, 44, 185n44; to spirit of dead relative, 37, 44, 125; of tea and water, 66, 69, 77, 78, 125, 164
offering trays, 125, **Plate 8**
offering vessels (*mitsu gusoku*), 123–124, 132, **132,** 140, **Plate 7**
Okanoya kanpakuki, 153
Okitsuhiko no kami, 20
Okitsuhime no mikoto, 20
onion-flower palanquins (*sōkaren*), 126
onmyōdō. *See* yin-yang practices
Ooms, Herman, 169
ordinations: just before or after death, 19, 53, 68; tonsure types, 28; of widows, 27–28, 41, 54–55
oxcart, golden, 95

pagodas (*sekitō*), 31–32, 105–106, 107, 187n73
paintings: Chinese Buddhist images, 149–150; images of buddhas (*honzon*), 21–22, 26, 60, 133. *See also* handscrolls, documentation of funeral rituals; portraits
palanquins: as container of deceased, 84; *gan*, 126; of Nichiren, 116, 117, 125–127, **Plate 9;** onion-flower, 126; processions with, 56, 62, 68, 194n33; screens held around, 84, 95–96; white ropes attached to top, 126
paradise imagery, 92–93
Phillips, Quitman E., 155, 157, 158, 176
plants: motifs on screens, 92–93; offerings of, 132, 141. *See also* flowers; *shikimi*
pollution, death: associated with spirit of dead, 38, 65; of corpse, 21, 41, 52, 65; at cremation sites, 66–67, 96, 99, 103; in graveyards, 26; of women dead in childbirth, 95
pollution, death, protection of living from: avoiding contact with corpses, 21, 41; at cremation sites, 96, 99, 103; with enclosures and containers, 83, 98, 111–112; with gold, 92, 93; during movement of corpses, 41, 65, 84; by priests, 52, 54; removal rituals, 66–67; with screens, 84, 92, 96, 99; with talismans, 26–27, **27;** warning messages on houses, 79; with white cloth or paper, 84, 96, 205n35
pollution, menstrual, 34

portraits: accuracy, 175–176; Chinese, 153–157, 175–176; of imperial family members, 152–153, 157; lineage (*soshizō*), 152, 177; of living individuals, 153–156, 161–162, 212n34; of living monks, 149, 150, 154, 155–156; of priests (*chinsō*), 149; taboos associated with, 153

portraits of deceased: accurate depictions, 175–176; as artworks, 148–149, 177; in China, 149–150, 153–154, 155, 157, 165, 166; contemporary Japanese practices, 79, 148; costs, 40; creation of, 154–155, 156, 161–162, 177; at cremation site, 58, 66, 78, 162, 174; differences from other ritual objects, 147–148, 177; displayed at funerals, 39, 58, 63, 64–65, 78, 156, 161–165, 173–174; in funeral processions, 124–125, 172, 174, **Plate 7;** hanging ritual (*kashin butsuji*), 17, 63, 64, 77, 158, 163, 171, 173; of Hino Shigeko, 68, 78; lack of documentation, 172–173; materials, 148; meaning and functions, 147, 152, 164, 170–171, 176–177; at memorial services, 48, 65, 152–153, 156, 165–173, 174–175; of monks, 150–151, 164; multiple, 160, 171–172; of Nakahara Kenshin, 40, 42, 157–158, 163, 167–170; of Nakahara Morosuke, 39, 40, 42, 157–158, 159, 167–170; offerings to, 42, 68, 169–170, 173, 174; patrons, 158–161; photographs, 148; in pre-Buddhist Japan, 150, 211n19; in processions, 72, 77; rituals, 173–174; scholarship on, 148–149, 154; sculptures, 148, 150–152, 155–156; of shoguns, 39, 48, 58, 63, 177; spirit of deceased transferred to, 170–171, 173, 174; stored in family temples, 148, 177; as substitute for deceased's body, 42, 164, 165, 170–171, 173; surviving examples, 148–149, 156; of Yoshihito, 58; of Yoshimochi, 63, 66, 78; in Zen-style funerals, 64–65, 161, 162, 163–164, 170–171, 173

portrait terminology, 153–158; Chinese, 153–157; *eizō* (reflected image; C. *yingxiang*), 39, 40, 151–152, 157, 158; *goei/gyoei* (revered reflection), 156, 157; *izō/yixiang* (made after subject's death), 153–154, 155–156; *juzō/shouxiang* (made during subject's lifetime), 153, 154, 155–156; *katashiro* (proxy forms), 42, 156, 157–158; *miei* (revered shadow), 58, 63, 156, 157, 158; *shin* (true form; C. *zhen*), 58, 68, 156, 158; *shōzō* (image that resembles; C. *xiaoxiang*), 157; *zō* (C. *xiang*), 156–157

priests: control of funerals, 116–117; cremation sites, 97, 98–99; donations to, 33–34, 35–37, 45–46; graves tended by, 40; of Ikkō sect, 43, 44, 47; illustrated biographies, 114, 115; of imperial family, 103; *komorisō* (in seclusion during mourning period), 28, 31–32, 33–34, 54; management of death pollution, 52, 54; mummified bodies, 150; payments for memorial services, 24; portraits, 149; preparation of corpses, 52, 53–54, 55. *See also* monks

processions. *See* funeral processions

Pure Land Buddhism: funerals, 8, 16–17, 170–171, 182n3; Ikkō sect, 41; paradise imagery, 92–93; sutras, 26, 46, 93

Rawson, Jessica, 2
rebirth: effects of actions of living, 16, 25, 38, 39, 59; paths of existence, 25, 175; timing, 174–175; of women, 71, 106
relics, 94, 106, 152
religious guides (*chishiki*), 41, 189n109
reliquaries, 94
Ritsu sect lineage portraits, 152
ritual implements, Buddhist: arrangements, 71, **73, 74;** as art objects, 3, 4; bronze, 113, 132, **132;** censers, 123–124, 164, **Plate 7;** at cremation sites, 66, 73–74, **74,** 164; at deathbeds, 143–145; lanterns, 122–123, 124; for memorial services, 124, 130–139; museum displays, 3, 4, 113; offering trays, 125, **Plate 8;** offering vessels, 123–124, 132, **132,** 140, **Plate 7;** in processions, 69, 72–73, **73,** 77, 114–130, **Plates 6–9;** production, 146; scholarship on, 3–5, 113; surviving examples, 113, 146; torches, 118–119, 124, **Plate 6;** use in general rituals, 5, 36, 123, 130, 140–141; in Zen-style funerals, 145–146
ritual objects: Chinese, 113–114; materials, 113–114; relationship to ritual structure and performance, 2; scholarship on, 3–5
rituals, use of term, 2
ritual studies, 1–2, 15
Rōken, 42, 43, 44, 47
Rokujō Jishū, 47
Rokuonji, 94
Ryōchi, 21, 22, 189n104
Ryōnin, 86, **87,** 88–89, 142, 143, 144
Ryōshinbō, 28, 31–32, 33, 35, 37, 38, 39, 40

Ryōzen, 19, 26, 38–39, 40, 46–47
Ryūōmaru, 128

Sakeiki (Minamoto no Tsuneyori), 97, 99, 101–102, 103
Sanada Nobuyuki, 94
sand, ritual sprinkling on corpse, 26, 53, 86
Sankaiki (Nakayama Fujiwara), 104
screens: around coffins, 70, 92; as boundaries between living and dead, 54, 84, 96; contemporary Japanese practices, 78–79; flower and plant motifs, 92–93; folding, 53, 54, 89–94; functions, 96; at funerals, 92; golden, 70, 92, 93–94; hanging fabric (*kichō*), 89; held around palanquin during procession, 84, 95–96; inner (*gyōshō/kōshō*), 95–96, **95;** at memorial services, 60, 132; moving, 95–96, **95;** outer (*hoshō*), 95–96; painted sides reversed, 91, 92; placement around corpses, 53, 54, 78–79; placement around dying person, 84, 89–91; protection from death pollution, 92; repeated use, 93–94; subjects of paintings, 92; white, 84, 95–96
scrolls: carried in procession, 124–125, 174, **Plate 7;** documentation of funeral rituals, 8–9, 97, 172–173; hanging, 59; at memorial services, 132, 133. *See also* portraits of deceased
sculptures, portrait: ashes and bones placed in, 152; of Buddhist masters, 150–152; of elites, 148; or monks, 155–156. *See also* portraits of deceased
seclusion, ritual, 28, 186n62
Seikaku, 138, 208n85
Seishi, Empress, 105, 202n78
Shaka, images of, 25, 26, 30–31, 60, 142
Sharf, Elizabeth Horton, 4–5
Sharf, Robert H., 4–5, 156
shelters at cremation sites (*kishoya/uwaya/hiya*), 102
shikimi (Japanese star anise), 53, 132, 133, 134, 141, 193n24
Shingon Buddhism: funeral rituals, 6, 16, 119, 172, 182n3; lineage portraits of founders, 152
Shinran: coffin, 88, **88,** 127; cremation, 97, **Plate 5;** death, 203n89; on deathbed, **88,** 89, 91; grave enclosure, **109,** 110. *See also Zenshin shōnin Shinran den-e*
Shinshōbō Rōken, 41
Shinto shrines, 121
Shirakawa, Retired Emperor, 85–86

shoguns, funerals of: portraits displayed, 39; textual sources, 7; of Tokugawa shoguns, 207n60; Zen-style, 48–49, 70. *See also* Ashikaga shoguns
Shōmu, Emperor, 57, 122
shrouds, 84, 85–86, **87**
Shukaku Hosshinō, 6, 86. *See also Kichiji shidai*
Shuryōgongyō, 36
social status: commoners, 9; cremation enclosure sizes related to, 97; funeral differences, 75, 162; funeral procession sizes and, 116; gender and, 71, 159; grave types and, 108; hierarchy, 159. *See also* elites
Sōen Hōgen, 40
Sōhōmitsu (Esoteric funeral practices), 6, 119, 172
songi (exalted form), 55, 58
Sōsōryō (Laws governing funerals and mourning), 172
sotoba. *See* grave tablets, wooden
Sōtō Zen funerals, for lay women, 71
souls. *See* spirits
soul-shaking (*tamafuri*) or soul-quieting (*tamashizume*) rituals, 52
soul-summoning ritual (*tamayobi/shōkon*), 52–53, 78, 84, 198n2
Spirit Halls (*tamadono/tamaya*), 104–105
spirit of deceased: as ancestral spirit, 37–38; association with dragons, 119–121; calling back to body, 52–53, 84; death pollution and, 38, 65; departure from body during cremation, 57, 173; hovering near corpse, 65, 169; judgment of, 16, 22–25, 133, 169, 174–175; offerings to, 37, 44, 125; protection of living from, 21; soul-shaking or soul-quieting rituals, 52; soul-summoning ritual, 52–53, 78, 84, 198n2; transference from corpse to portrait, 170–171, 173, 174; transitional state, 38, 58–59, 169; veneration of male and female at different sites, 48; views of, 37–38, 52–53. *See also* rebirth
spirits: harmful, 21, 52, 53, 118, 124; protection of corpse from malevolent, 41, 52, 118, 124; protection of living from, 21, 185n44; wandering, 41, 192n11
star anise. *See shikimi*
status. *See* social status
stupas: enclosures, 99; five-tiered (*gorintō*), **31,** 32, 107, 187n75; pagoda-like (*hōkyōintō*), **31,** 32, 187n76

Suitō Makoto, 3, 21
sutras: copying, 33; gender-specific, 190n129; offerings of, 125; placed on grave, 32–33; recitations, 46, 56, 66, 133. See also *Lotus Sutra*
sutra tables (*kyōzukue*), 125
Suzuki, Hikaru, 64, 79

Taiheiki, 48–49
Taika Reforms (646), 6
Taima mandara, 92–93
Taira no Nobunori, 20
Takamatsu Chūnagon, 104
talismans, death, 26–27, **27**
Tambiah, S. J., 1–2
Tanaka Hisao, 21
temples: gates, 197n82; income from funerals, 24–25, 38
Ten Buddhas, 22
Tendai Buddhist funerals, 16, 182n3
Ten Kings of Hell: buddhas associated with, 22, 25–26, 133; Chinese beliefs, 22–24, 155; examination of soul of deceased, 25, 133; images of, 22–24, 143, **Plate 1**
Tenryūji, 43, 190n115
Thirteen Buddhas and bodhisattvas, 22
Thirteen Buddhas hanging scroll, **23**
Toba, Retired Emperor, 86, 91, 104, 105
Tōin Kinkata, 19
Tōjiin, 195n51; Ashikaga portraits, 177; Buddha Hall, 163, 177; funerals held at, 62, 68, 92, 103, 163, 171; memorial services, 67; memorial tablet, **Plate 2**
Tokugawa shoguns, burials, 207n60
tonsure. See ordinations
torches (*taimatsu*), 118–119, 124, **Plate 6**
Tosa Yukihiro, 63, 163, 215n68
Toyotomi Hideyoshi, 94

van Gennep, Arnold, 15
Vimalakirti Sutra (*Yuima kyō*), 121

Wakasugi Junji, 115
white: protection of living from death pollution, 84, 205n35; symbolism, 198n4
white banners, 119, 122
white fabric: clothing, 29, 69, 84, 96, 129–130; cords attached to coffins, 63, 65, 69, 79, 126, 196n61, 198n96; headbands, 119; silk screens, 84, 95–96; wrapped around cremation site, 84–85, 99
women: burials, 104–106; deaths during childbirth, 95, 105; destruction of hearth-fire god image, 20; funerals of elite, 70–71; menstrual pollution, 34; mourning clothes, 129; obstacles to salvation, 71, 106; offerings by, 46; portraits commissioned by, 159; segregation from men at memorial services, 39, 40; sutras for, 190n129; tonsure taken by widows, 27–28, 41, 54–55; Zen-style funerals, 71

Xunzi, 15

Yakushi, images of, 25, 26, 28, 43, 143
Yamashina Noritoki, 72, 74
Yiengpruksawan, Mimi, 106
Yi li (Ceremonies and rites), 116
Yin-Yang Masters (*onmyōji/onyōji*): auspicious dates determined by, 31, 38, 44, 47; divinations, 34; influence, 47, 59, 75; memorial service schedules determined by, 22, 34, 35, 38, 40, 42–43, 47; purification ceremonies, 42, 158
yin-yang practices (*onmyōdō*), 8, 39, 47, 184n39
Yōrō code, 6, 116, 128, 194n33
Yoshihito, Prince: condolence calls, 55; cremation, 51, 54, 57–58, 66, 78, 173; cremation site, 56, 57, 103; death, 51, 192n6; funeral, 7, 50, 51–61, 76, 78; funeral procession, 56–57, 78; heir, 56; memorial services, 54, 58–61, 124; memorial tablet, 57, 60; movement of corpse to temple, 55–56, 64, 76, 78; portrait, 58, 65; testament, 54
Yūzū nenbutsu engi (Origins of the Yūzū sect), 86, **87,** 88–89, 142, **142,** 143–145, **144, 145**

Zen funeral rituals, 17, 63–64, 76–78; closing coffin lid (*sagan butsuji*), 17, 63, 64, 69, 77, 173; hanging portrait (*kashin butsuji*), 17, 63, 64, 77, 158, 163, 171, 173; lighting of fire (*ako butsuji*; also *hinko butsuji*), 17, 49, 66, 69, 70, 77, 164, 197n88; moving coffin to cremation site (*kigan butsuji*), 17, 63, 65, 69, 77, 164; moving coffin to temple (*igan butsuji*), 17, 64, 77; offerings of tea (*tencha butsuji*), 17, 66, 69, 77, 78, 125, 164; offerings of water (*tentō butsuji*), 17, 66, 69, 77, 78, 125, 164; placing corpse in coffin (*nyūgan butsuji*), 17, 56, 77, 78, 92; priest's consultation (*tairyō shōsan*), 17;

retrieving remains (*kikotsu butsuji*; also *shikkotsu/shūkotsu butsuji*), 66, 67, 69, 70, 77, 78

Zen funerals: for abbots, 17, 48, 76, 161, 164; Chinese influences, 16–17, 145, 164; circumambulations of cremation site, 100–101; for elites, 17, 64–65, 78, 161; encoffinings, 56; in fourteenth century, 48–49; increase in, 161; influence of priests, 75; for lay individuals, 71, 76–78, 161; movement of corpse to temple, 64; portraits of deceased, 64–65, 161, 162, 163–164, 170–171, 173; for priests, 8, 48, 63, 64; ritual implements, 145–146; sequence, 17; for shoguns, 48–49, 70; for women, 71

Zen priests: funerals, 8, 48, 63, 64; lineage portraits, 152

Zenshin shōnin Shinran den-e, 8; coffin of Shinran, 88, **88,** 127; creation of, 115; cremation of Shinran, 97, **Plate 5;** grave of Shinran, **109,** 110; Shinran on deathbed, **88,** 89

Zuigu darani, 40, 189n102

About the Author

Karen M. Gerhart is professor of Japanese art history at the University of Pittsburgh. She is the author of *The Eyes of Power: Art and Early Tokugawa Authority* (1999).